REVEALING INDIA'S PAST

(Based on Archaeological Investigations: 2002-2018)

REVEALING INDIA'S PAST

(Based on Archaeological Investigations: 2002-2018)

G. K. LAMA

PATHAK PUBLISHER AND DISTRIBUTORS
New Delhi (INDIA)

Revealing India's Past (Based on Archaeological Investigations: 2002-2018)

Author : G. K. Lama

ISBN : 978-81-948916-4-2

Price : 5500/-

First Edition: 2021

Published by :
PATHAK PUBLISHER AND DISTRIBUTORS
E-6/33c & 34, Ground Floor, Sangam Vihar
New Delhi-110080
E-mail: pathakppd@gmail.com

Type Setting by
G. R. Sharma

Printed by
R. K. Offset, Delhi

Contents

Preface

In the field of archaeology attention was not made properly in the region of North-East India, especially in the state of Sikkim which became a part of India in 1975. Although a number of archaeological expeditions were done in eastern and western UP to reveal the shrouded mysteries of the region and fill up the cultural gaps, but still more work is needed to understand the archaeology of Ganga plain and the extension of Harappan culture. A lot of archaeological investigations were done in the state of Bihar, the ancient Magadha, which has a glorious past but still not only some areas are untouched but a cultural gap is noticed in those areas where archaeological investigations were carried out. For example, attention was made to the world famous Buddhist centre Nalanda and its peripheral area and the findings of recent excavations are pushing back the antiquity of the area. But still a village to village survey is needed for the documentation of the sites having archaeological importance and excavations on a broad level which will reveal not only the shrouded mysteries of the area but also help to fulfill the cultural gaps. A deep study is also needed on the artistic features of the region which will be helpful to establish Nalanda as a centre of art. A long gap is noticed after excavation of Chirand and Senuwar in the field of pre-history. Some more Neolithic sites should be discovered in the Vindhyan region. Varanasi is famous as a religious, historical and trade centre since time immemorial. Excavations at Sarnath, Rajghat, Aktha and Ramnagar were carried out by the ASI and Banaras Hindu University from time to time but documentation of archaeological sites in Varanasi region is still left.

So to solve the aforesaid problems the author has done explorations and excavations with his team from 2002-2018 and tried his best to fulfill all the gaps. Hence, this book is compiled which may answer a number of unsolved questions and add some new chapters in the archaeology of aforesaid regions. Although the author has actively participated as a team-member in a number of explorations and excavations conducted by his department, such as explorations along the River *Gomati* in district-Jaunpur, Eastern UP: 2005-06 and in the same area including Nindaur, Bhabhua, Bihar:2008-09 and excavations at Agiabir, district-Mirzapur, Eastern UP: 2006-07 and 2007-08; Sarepur, Eastern UP: 2008-09, but he had felt that he is not the authorized person to write on those expeditions. Brief report of these archaeological investigations had been already published in various volumes of the departmental journal *Bharati*.

—G.K. Lama

Introduction

After 16 years of rigorous archaeological field work in the states of Sikkim, eastern and western UP and Bihar the author has decided to compile them in a single book which not only throws light on the archaeologicxal findings of those regions but also added some new information in the Indian archaeology. During 2002-04 an exploration work was carried out in the state of Sikkim and a number of Neolithic sites were discovered. Special mention may be made of those Neolithic tools which are not reported from any other Neolithic site of India. These tools are similar to those tools which were recovered from Yunnan, a province of west China. An exploration work was done by the author and his team along the rivers *Yamuna* and *Hindon* in western UP. A village to village survey was done in District-Meerut, Baghpat, Muzaffarnagar and Saharanpur and a number of sites were discovered having archaeological importance. Findings of this region suggest that the spread of Harappan culture may not be limited up to Meerut but it may extend and cover more areas. There is a great desideratum to compare Black Painted Red Ware, which occurs in profusion in the explored sites, with already reported Harappan sites in neighboring area. During 2010-11author has explored a number of sites in eastern UP along the River *Chhoti Saryu* (Tons) in the districts of Azamgarh, Ballia, Ghazipur and Mau. Findings of this region enable to the archaeologists to understand the various cultures of this region. In 2010-11 exploration work was done at Pakkakot, Ballia, UP by the author and his team to understand the cultural sequence of the site because previously archaeologists have suggested that it is a NBPW or Chalcolithic site but having seen the findings of the site the team has observed that first settlers of the site were Nerolithic people.

After a number of explorations the author and his team has decided to excavate the site of Pakkakot which was carried out in two seasons *i.e* 2010-11 and 2011-12 and the findings has proved the site as a Neolithis settlement. A five fold cultural sequence was noticed at the site without any break in between them: Neolithic, Chalcolithic, NBPW, Sunga-Kushan and Gupta and Post Gupta. Pakkakot lies on the ancient trade route from Pataliputra to Lumbini via Masarh>Buxur>Tika Deori>Khairadih>Sohgaura>Kopia>Kapilvastu and Lumbini. A careful analysis of the ceramic assemblage and other artifactual data of Pakkakot show the transition from rural to urban settlement at the site. The cultural relics obtained from the site are ascribable from Neolithic culture to Gupta and post-Gupta period (5000 BCE-700 CE). We have recovered one sealing of baked clay of Period-V having the legends "Chetak Vihare" and "Matibharadhikaranasya" from Mound-4. To find out Buddhist site in surrounding area the team has explored neighbouring area and found a site named "Matahi" which is located about 2 kms west from the site. The name Matahi is well comparable with Matibhar. This site has a profile of a religious monument. A female figurine made of silver is a rare discovery of this site which was recovered from the pre-Mauryan level. This type of figurine is not reported from any site of Ganga plain. Although Ghosh has reported about a golden figure recovered from Laurianandangarh (Bihar) in his book *An Encyclopaedia of Indian Archaeology* but its photograph is not published and its present status is not known. About half dozen sealings found from the site have more than five impressions which are also not reported from any site of Ganga plain. Some of them show the antiquity of the name Ram and Gopal in 2nd century BCE. Any archaeological evidence is not yet available to prove the antiquity of both gods in Sunga period. Special mention may be made of two pendants, one is tortoise made of banded agate and other is a parrot made of crystal found from the NBPW level.

Nalanda was certainly one of such glorious spots from which the light emitted and not only India but the neighbouring countries were also illuminated. The history of the place remained shrouded with mystery for long and despite untiring efforts made during a century and half, several layers remain concealed. There has been still a need for a comprehensive work on various aspects of Nalanda. Keeping in mind of these facts I have done archaeological exploration in the district during 2012- 2013, 2013-14 and 2015-16 along with my Research Scholar Mr. Pankaj Kumar. Archaeological Survey of India, New Delhi has permitted me for the exploration work and given license for the purpose. During exploration 68 sites were found having archaeological importance. Findings of these sites proved that the antiquity of the region may go back up to Chalcolithic period. It was proved by the excavations carried out at Ghorakatora and Juafardih where from remains of Chalcolithic culture was recovered. A few Palaeolithic tools were also recovered during exploration from Banganga valley. Excavations on broad label will be able to reveal the shrouded mystry of the region and may be able to fulfill the cultural gap.

During exploration done by the author during 2012-15, he found hundreds of sculptures scattered on various sites unprotected and unpreserved. He had seen more than 50 inscribed Brahmanic and Buddhist Sculptures. The author had taken help from Prof. Arvind Kumar Singh, Jiwaji University, Gwalior and Prof. Suman Jain of his own department to decipher these inscriptions. Most of the Buddhist sculptures are inscribed with famous Buddhist creed-"Ye Dhamma Hetuppabhava…." It is noted that the number of Brahmanic sculptures is not less than Buddhist sculptures. It is also observed that these Brahmanic sculptures belong to Shaiva, Vaishnava and Saur (Sun) cult. Hence, the purpose of the author is to attract attention of the Art Historians and Archaeologists to find out the possibility of establishing Nalanda School of Art. On the basis of the iconographical study if we analyze the possibility of Nalanda School of art then we come at a conclusion that it was a continuous process of centuries which was developed in a broad area including other local art styles. Art objects since

Gupta to Pala-Sena period were recovered from Nalanda. Sculptors made Buddhist images in stucco, stone and bronze and also expressed their art skills in paintings since 6th century to 12th century CE. Although Nalanda School imbibed inspiration from Sarnath School of Art, but it could not maintain the classical grace and beauty for years. If the sculptures of Nalanda dated 6th-8th century CE are carefully examined, it is easily noticed that the classical grace evaporated and a meaningless and drowsy heaviness characterize the sculptures produced in this time bracket. The quantity of images recovered from the region till date proves that there must be a centre of art in this place. Now the question arises that is the manufacturing of images in the region was only the contribution of Pala emperors? Because the art developed at Nalanda and its vicinity is named as Pala School of Art but making of sculptures was prevalent in the region before Palas. Although the number of Gupta images at Nalanda is less in comparison to Pala period. In this way we can say that Nalanda was developed as a centre of Art since Gupta period. Sankalia also supported this theory and told that during Gupta period Nalanda became a centre of sculpture making. Local sculptors of Nalanda adopted the special characteristics of the art schools of pre-Mauryan, Greeko-Bactrian, Persian, Mathura, Amaravati and other art schools and produced a number of Buddhist images under a new art style which was different from the earlier art styles. It was done during Gupta period because without a regular centre of art it is impossible to recover such a huge number of images from the region. Making of sculptures was done here at local level because it is impossible to impoprt images in such a huge quantity. Local sculptors have given a new dimension to the Nalanda art under the skillfull direction of Dhiman and Bitapal. The facts analyzed above shows that a centre of art was already developed and images were made without any interruption at Nalanda long before the Palas so it is useless to connect it with Pala School of Art. So it is a narrow minded thought to link up it with a dynasty. As Sarnath, Mathura, Gandhara art schools were named after their birthplace so that the art form which was developed at Nalanda and was given a different form must be known as "Nalanda School of Art".

It is a sad thought to note that iconoclasts invaded Nalanda and carried destructive activities, arson and loot. Nalanda is now in ruins. It is however, strange to note that in spite of such wanton damages inflicted upon Nalanda; quite a good number of sculptures survived the onslaughts of invading iconoclasts. These images are mostly installed in different museums in India and abroad. Some of these are in personal collections while a few are still in situ. The site during the span of last hundred years yielded not only the ruins of stupas and viharas in course of explorations and excavations but has also laid bare innumerable number of stone and bronze sculptures and stucco figurines. The number of artifacts discovered so far from Nalanda, has led certain scholars to infer that, perhaps, the carving of stones and the moulding of metal images were included in the regular curriculam of the Mahavihara otherwise it could not be possible either by Dhiman or Bitpala alone or even by a dozen of their disciples to produce such a large number of icons at Nalanda.The available writings do not give an overall view about the nature and content of Nalanda's sculptures. Impact of Nalanda Art may be noticed not only on the art objects of other regions of India but it's fusion may also be seen on the art of neighbouring countries like Bangladesh, Nepal, Tibet, Indonesia etc. In fact, a systematic and comprehensive survey of Nalanda Art as a whole has been long over due.

During the exploration work carried out during 2012-2015 by the author in district-Nalanda it was decided to explore its vicinity, so was done in the year 2015-16 and a number of sites having archaeological importance were reported. Our exploration indicates that Jethian and Tapovan are the larger settlements might have some connectivity to each other. Tapovan is also connected with the epic king Jarasandha. Buddha used this path while traveling from Bodh Gaya to Kushinagar. The images found in this region are almost made of basalt and belong to the Pala period. On the basis of above investigations it can be said that the region is full of archaeological potential and need to explore other remaining area of the region. Recent excavations done at Rajgir and its vicinity indicates its Chalcolithic feature and approximately datable to 1200 BCE. Without proper investigation and excavation in the hilly areas of the region the settlement pattern and its connection with Rajgir could not be traced.

Since 1999 up to 2014 a few excavations were conducted by the Archaeological Survey of India and successfully revealed some architectural remains in district-Nalanda like- Stupas and Votive Stupas, Temple-complex and Monasteries. During exploration of the district a number of sites were found having archaeological importance by the author and finally it was decided by his team to excavate one of them named Rukhaegarh which lies on the route from Rajgir to Patna, the present capital city of Bihar. The site is surrounded by three rivers *i.e. Nonai, Chiraiya and Mohane.* The river *Nonai* flows about 2 km west while the other two rivers flow 1 and 2 km east to the village respectively showing uniqueness of the site. The limited excavation brought to light four-fold cultural sequence *i.e.* from NBPW Culture to Early Medieval period without any break in between all of them.The site might be destroyed by flood activity during pre-NBPW period because more than 2 mts sand-deposit was found after NBPW level up to the natural soil in trench nos. A1 and XA1. Recovery of a good number of bowls and flanged bowls of deluxe variety of NBPW show that these ceramics might be used by Buddhist monks for alms. The distance between Nalanda to Pataliputra is near about 90 kms; Rukhae is about 30 kms from the ruins of Nalanda, so it seems natural that the site was a halting-place for the Buddhist pilgrims.

Noticing the archaeological importance of Varanasi and its Vicinity the author has decided to do a village to village survey and document the remaining sites having archaeological importance with the kind permission of the Archaeological Survey of India. The exploration work was done during 2016-17 and a number of sites were discovered having archaeological importance. Prime objectives of the exploration in the region were documentation of archaeological sites in the area, comparative study of the ceramics and antiquities collected during exploration with other sites of the middle Ganga plain and find out the ancient trade-route. Apart from Varanasi the team had explored few another sites on Varanasi-Chandauli border. A comparative study of pot-sherds and antiquities recovered from these sites shows that they may be ascribable from Chalcolithic to early medieval period. Sites of Mahavan and Koilon are very rich in the sense of archaeological potential. Horizontal excavations of both the sites may be able to throw light on various aspects and give a new dimension to the archaeology of mid Ganga plain.

After the discovery of the Neolithic site Chirand in Bihar, it was desired to obtain details regarding the nature of the settlement and distribution pattern of sites particularly of the Neolithic-Chalcolithic phases in Bihar. The fieldwork done by Birendra Pratap Singh in the region revealed a number of Neolithic sites, like Senuwar, Sakas, Malaon, Badalgarh, Daindih Akorhi etc. Among these sites Senuwar was excavated horizontally by Birendra Pratap Singh.To understand the nature of settlement, social systems and relationship between the inhabitants and the environment in the hinterland of Senuwar during Neolithic, Chalcolithic and NBPW periods and also evaluate the processes that occurred in the rise of urbanization in the region a reconnaissance survey was done by the author and his team in the month of April, 2017. During exploration a good variety of pot-sherds along with a few antiquities were collected from the surface. Location of the ancient settlement of Sakas was advantageous in many ways, viz., availability of vast alluvial plains facilitating agriculture, pastures for animals, stone for manufacturing tools and artifact, hunting, fishing etc. The Kaimur hills, overgrown with shrubs and trees, are an ideal home for games, variety of edible roots and fruits. R.S.Pappu in his study "Catchment Analysis" in relation to Senuwar suggested that settlement like Sakas was not only related to the parent settlement of Senuwar but was completely depended on that. He is of the view that "this was temporary seasonal settlement set up in such favourable place where it could carry out number of activities such as collection of wild plants, pastoral activity, hunting, artifact manufacturing etc., in the vicinity of raw material." Our knowledge about the Neolithic pottery of mid Ganga plain is insufficient. The evidence obtained from Chirand, Taradih, Maner and Chechar-Kutubpur showed close resemblance and suggests widespread and long lived cultural facies. The ceramic assemblage and other cultural traits from Sakas as compared with the excavated materials of Senuwar, it showed the repetition of the same cultural sequence and close identity with the material remains of Neolithic, Chalcolithic and NBPW Culture. However, probability of Mesolithic deposit may be postulated because of recovery of a few microliths along with, cores and raw materials.

So the book comprises all the archaeological findings mentioned above in detail. This is an original work done by the author and his team within a time span of about 16 years. The comparative study of the findings of aforesaid archaeological investigations not only throw light on the archaeology of those region but also help in the plannings of future activities. The author has left scope for the young archaeologists to rethink about what next steps should be taken. Hope the book will be helpful to the new generation who has keen interest in the archaeology of aforesaid region.

Acknowledgement

An archaeological journey of 16 years completed succecessfully by the author was well supported by various institutions, scholars and archaeologists. First of all the author is thankful to the Archaeological Survey of India, New Delhi for permitting him a number of times for archaeological investigations in various parts of Indian subcontinent. Special thanks are due to Dr. Gautam Sen Gupta, Dr. B.R.Mani and Dr. Rakesh Tewari who were associated with ASI during author's journey. Secondly the author is grateful to the University Grants Commission, New Delhi for the financial help by accepting the Major Research Project of archaeological investigations in district-Nalanda and its peripheral area. The author would like to pay his gratitude to the Co-ordinators of the Centre of Advanced Study, Department of AIHC & Archaeology, Banaras Hindu University Prof. Md. Naseem and Prof. S.R.Dubey for giving financial help to do excavation work at Rukhaegarh, Nalanda and also for the exploration work in Varanasi. The author has a great respect for all the Deans and Heads who have permitted him for the field work.

The author would like to give special thanks to Prof. S.R.Dubey who made him Co-director in the excavations of Pakkakot for two seasons *i.e.* 2010-11 and 2011-12. Without a strong support of the team-members the author will never be successful in achieving his ultimate goal, so the author is grateful to his team-members Prof. S.R.Dubey, Prof R.N.Singh, Dr. A.K.Singh, Dr. S.K.Singh, Mr. B.K.Sinha, Mr. A.K.Pandey, Mr. Rambadan Ram, Mr. Shiv Kumar, Dr. Dhirendra Pratap Singh, Mr. Shiv Shankar Prajapati, Dr. Sanjay Kumar Kushwaha, Dr. Pankaj Kumar, Mr. Bipin Kumar Singh and Dr. Amit Ranjan. The author is also thankful to the villagers of Pakkakot and Rukhaegarh by whom he had got full co-operation. Thanks to the media persons and administration of Sikkim, Eastern and Western UP and Bihar for their kind co-operation and full support.

Finally the author is thankful to the publisher who has published the book in time and given it a catchy look.

—G. K. Lama

List of Figures

List of Plates

List of Tables

1

Archaeological Exploration in Sikkim: 2002-2004

The Land

The name "Sikkim" is said to be a variation of the Limbu word *Su Khumm* meaning "New Place". The Tibetans call it *Be-mul-Denjong* or the Hidden Valley of Rice, and the Lepchas call it *Nye-Mae-el* or *Mayel Nyang* which means Paradise (Coelho.1970:2-3). Sikkim, the 22nd state of the Indian Union represents a unique ethnological amalgamation combined with a distinctive natural and cultural heritage. The state is situated in Eastern Himalayas (Latitude: 27-28^0 N, Longitude 88-89^0 E). It is bounded to the West by Nepal, to the North by Tibet, to the East by Tibet and Bhutan and to the South by the state of West Bengal. It is spread over an area of 7,896 sq km. *Tista* is the life-line of the state and its tributaries are *Lhachen, Lhachung, Rungeet* and *Rungnu-chhu*. Gangtok, the capital of the state lies at its heart and is the nucleus of all activities in the state. At present Sikkim is divided into four zones-North, South, East and West for administrative purposes. From Gangtok, the nearest rail-heads are Siliguri and New Jalpaiguri, at a distance of 114 and 125 kms respectively. It is also connected by road with Siliguri, New Jalpaiguri, Darjeeling and Kalimpong.

The People

The people of the state now consist of three different ethnic groups, namely, the Lepchas, the Bhutias, and the Nepalese. The earliest settlers of Sikkim or *Denjong*, the land of rice, were the Lepchas, who called themselves *Rongpa* or dwellers of the valley. They were believed to have come from the east, along the foot-hills from the direction of Assam and Myanmar. Distinct from the Lepchas are the Bhutias, people of Tibetan origin, of good physique having Mangolian features. It is indeed curious that the largest group of people in the state is Nepali who was migrated from Nepal. There is an addition, a fourth group, small but distinct known as *Tsongs*, originally settlers of the *Tsang-po* valley of Tibet. The term "Sikkimese" has thus no single or common linguistic or ethnological interpretation. Despite these factors, a widespread feeling of national consciousness has arisen and developed a strong degree of historic and cultural unity (Risley.2010:i)

Geographical Scenario

Located in the north of India and to the south of Tibet there lie 18 tracts of land sloping southwards. In the midst of these there is a tract with its hill tops in the north and the bases of the hills extending southwards. The peaks of *Kanchanjunga* appear like a king seated on his throne, his four corners appearing as if hung round with a white silk scarf. At the top of the valley the five perpetual snow-clad peaks look like a crown. Seven crystal lakes lie in the front looking like a set of water offerings and white cliffs on the right and left look like lions romping up towards the sky adorned with vulture's nests. The middle of the country looks like a bowl containing gems set down with the lid raised; the valleys look like a hand with the fingers stretched out, the arms of the ridges and spurs of hills resemble the third stomach of a yak. The foot of the hills look like a big granting tree fallen down with the mountain adorning the upper part of the valleys and rivers issuing from the base of the hills. These waters have medicinal virtues like nectar with the left banks always extending in grassy slopes. The entire region is richly wooded and the caves, ravines and gorges are covered with dense forest and lead onto immense plains. The larger and longer mountain ranges run out like a tigress rushing forward with spurs like leopard cubs jumping forward. The currents of the rivers look like swords sliding downwards; the smaller brooks and rivulets appear like string of pearls with cascades and falls resembling white silk curtains spread out. The sound of the falls mixing with the sounds of the forests produce a rhythmic sound like those produced by the repetitions of the mantras. The whole resembles like a vast heart shaped stupa (Mishra. 2008: 3-4).

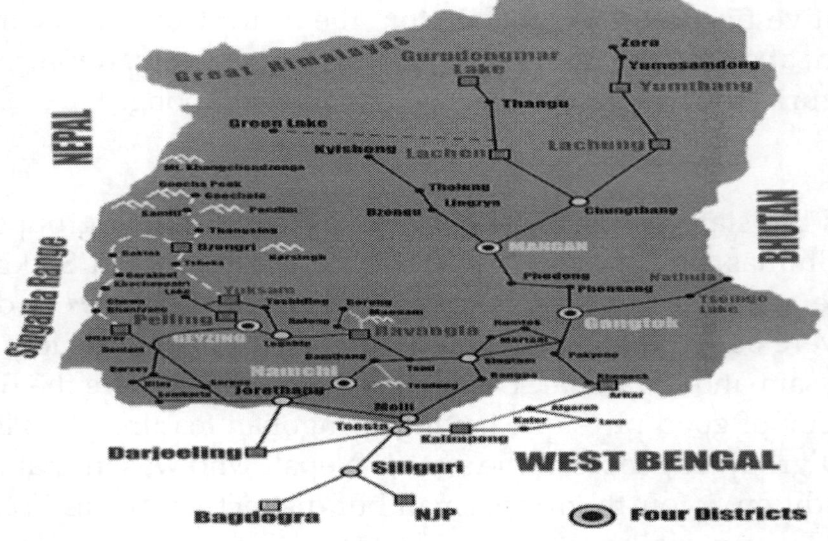

Figure 1: Map of Sikkim

The climatic conditions tend to change within short distances. The summer temperature of the state reaches a maximum of 20^0 C and a minimum of 13.1^0 C. The pre-monsoon begins towards the end of March whereas the proper monsoon begins from May and continues till the end of September. Winter rains are a regular feature and June and July are the wettest months of the year. Annual rainfall of the state recorded as 3,894 mm. The soil is usually sandy and progressively clayey in the lower reaches of the valleys. Soil in the foothills is alluvial in nature being either loams or sandy loams mixed from highest attitudes. Soils in the valley are clayey alluvium and rich in organic content. The landscapes of the state are generally green. The forest types range from tropical evergreen in the foothills through temperate green in the middle ranges to coniferous on the higher elevations.

Historicity

Of the early history of Sikkim a few doubtful glimpses reach us through the thick mist of Lepcha tradition. In the absence of authentic and authoritative records we must give credence to the introduction in the book of law ascribed to the foremost king of the region whose account is also supported by the oral narratives. In the guide book of *Ster-Ston-Ratna-Lingpa* it is said that Sikkim is the best of all sacred places of pilgrimage as it will be resorted to in the evil times. Firstly Avalokiteshvara blessed it followed by Tara and Indra and then Tibetan king Srong-bstan-gampo and lastly by Guru Padmasambhava during his travels in Tibet and its western region. They all took possession of the land, tilled it, blessed it and sowed all kinds of seeds in it.

As far as the monarchy of Sikkim is concerned, it is said that Gyalwa Lhatsun Chhempo was a native of Kongbu, in the lower valley of the Tsangpo born in 1595 CE. He concentrated his attention in preaching the Dhamma amongst the simple and gentle Lepcha people. Having won their confidence, he with the help of two other Lamas named Sempah Chhempo and Rigdzin Chchempo consecrated a Bhutia Chief, Phuntsong Namgyal as the first king of the region with the title of *Chhogyal* (Dharma Raja). This happened at Yoksam (The three superior ones) in west Sikkim. At that time Chhogyal was 38 years old. This was believed to have taken place in 1642 CE. The king ushered Sikkim into a new era of vigorous political, religious, social and cultural activities under a settled government and ruled up to 1670 CE. Other kings were Tensung Namgyal (1670-1700 CE), Chakdor Namgyal (1700-1717 CE), Gyurme Namgyal (1717-1733 CE), Phuntsong Namgyal (1733-1780 CE), Tenzing Namgyal (1780-1793 CE), Tsugphud Namgyal (1793-1863 CE), Sidkeong Namgyal (1863-1874 CE), Thotob Namgyal (1874-1914 CE), Sidkeong Tulku (1914 CE), Tashi Namgyal 1914-1963 CE) and Palden Thondup Namgyal (1965-1975 CE). In 1976 Sikkim became the 22nd state of India.

Previous Archaeological Investigations

The puzzles of the past have always managed to wrest human attention into founding a suitable answer to them. Even the archaeologists have applied themselves to untangle the riddles of yore with the available evidences unearthed from the womb of the earth.

As far as the state of Sikkim is concerned, extensive investigations were made by K.D. Banerjee and A.K.Sharma, as a result of which a large number of Neolithic sites were brought to light. Despite all these discoveries are we in a position to answer the question-Have we been able to give a continuous picture of development of human cultures in North-East India? There are still many yawning gaps in this study and it should be our endeavor to fill up these gaps to give a coherent picture. If we see the published accounts, it is clear that some discoveries from North-East India are reported which pertain to the Stone Age, Neolithic times, historical period followed by medieval and late medieval periods. Finds from Sikkim is suggestive of a fruitful line of further studies through well planned future excavations of potential sites in the region to give a comprehensive picture. In this chapter I have tried to pay attention on the present archaeological scenario of Sikkim from Neolithic to late medieval period.

Neolithic findings

The word Neolithic has been derived from two Latin words i.e. Neo (New) and lithic (stone). These polished Celts of Neolithic culture continued to occupy the attention of archaeologists for a long time. Recent studies on Neolithic culture both in western Asia and east and south-east Asian countries have brought to light much information which drastically changes our traditional concept about Neolithic culture. In view of the recent discoveries made in Western Asia and South-east Asian countries, it is now felt that instead of typo-technological evolution, the Neolithic culture should be defined in terms of subsistence economy. The Neolithic period was cultural or economical stage, which is characterized by the occurrence of polished stone axes, domestication of animals like sheep, goat, pig, dog etc., permanent sedentary settlements and the introduction of pottery. During this period man discarded his predatory hunting and food-gathering level of subsistence and passed on to the food producing stage.

Sikkim and the adjoining regions witnessed the development of a unique Neolithic culture, characterized by the use of harvester. There are certain distinctive traits by which this region can claim itself a composite culture; this might have derived its origin from the south China specially the Yunnan province. A similar view was also expressed by Banerjee (Banarjee.1987:41-46) on the basis of an extensive exploration undertaken by him in Sikkim region. It is interesting to note in this connection that the Neolithic complex of Sikkim region also uses harvesters like those of the Neolithic population in the Kashmir valley. However, the tool is quite unique in India, but apart from that, the material assemblages of both the region display enough differences between the two.

In 1904 E.H.G. Walsh (Walsh.1904:20-24)explored the Sikkim region and collected a large number of Neolithic implements from the hill slopes, then the archaeologists have been reported of the discovery of the Neolithic tools from different parts of the plateau fringe area and the foot hills of Himalayas from time to time. This has indeed opened up a new horizon of prehistoric research in this region. But serious scientific study of Neolithic culture in this region was started from 1940. Banerjee explored the eastern and the northern part of Sikkim and collected a large number of Neolithic tools.

But nevertheless, except the tool types, the other associated problems of Neolithic culture of this region remain still unknown. Despite serious research undertaken by archaeologists and scholars no comprehensive account of the Neolithic culture pattern of the region has been available. There is no doubt that the works of Dani (1981), Thapar (1985) and T.C. Sharma (Sharma.1980) should be considered as pioneering work on Neolithic culture of the eastern India. The researchers working in Pre-history of eastern India are indeed indebted to aforesaid scholars for their path finding works. The works of this trio have given correct guidelines to the scholars working in the line.

Explored Neolithic Sites in Sikkim

As far as Neolithic specialty of the state is concern, some scholars consider that the region served as a corridor through which the Neolithic Celt making techniques entered into India from South-east Asia. The tools in this region are made on dolerite, shale, slate and fossil wood. The typological analysis of the tools suggests:

- An early phase with tools being wholly chipped and the edge ground,
- A late phase with pecked and edge ground and fully ground tools.

The early phase shows common feature with the Hoabinhian culture of South-east Asia dated to 10,000 BC and the late phase shows a close affinity with that of south China and South-east Asia. The Neolithic tools were mainly manufactured in four stages called flaking, pecking, grinding and polishing. After polishing the final outcome is a well polished Neolithic tool. The main types of Neolithic tools are Celts, Axes, Mace heads, Harvesters, Picks, Hoes, Chisels, Ring stones and Adzes.

Except a few finds of Neolithic culture from the southern part of Sikkim, nothing was known about the Pre-history of the state till 1980, when exploration work was undertaken by the Pre-history Branch of ASI under the guidance of the then Superintending Archaeologist K.D.Banrjee in the North and South zones of Sikkim. Banerjee (1980-81) has identified following Neolithic sites in the state of Sikkim:

North Sikkim

Table 1
Neolithic sites in North Sikkim

S.No.	*Name of the site*	*Latitude*	*Longitude*
1.	Barpak	27^0 31′ 30″N	88^0 28′ 15″ E
2.	Gnon	27^0 26′ 40″N	88^0 29′ E
3.	Gor-Terang	27^0 25′ 30″N	88^0 30′ 10″ E
4.	Gytong	27^0 29′ 10″N	88^0 31′ 10″ E
5.	Lingden	27^0 29′ 10″N	88^0 27′ 50″ E
6.	Lingdong	27^0 30′ 35″N	88^0 33′ 10″ E
7.	Lingthen	27^0 31′ 20″N	88^0 28′ 30″ E
8.	Linkyong	27^0 24′N	88^0 29″ E
9.	Manshitong	27^0 40′N	88^0 35′30″ E
10.	Samdong	27^0 27′ 30″N	88^0 30′ E
11.	Sangkalang	27^0 30′ 20″N	88^0 32′ 50″ E
12.	Terang	27^0 26′ 10″N	88^0 30′ 30″ E

East Sikkim

Table 2
Neolithic sites in East Sikkim

S.No.	*Name of the site*	*Latitude*	*Longitude*
1.	Pakyong	27^0 14′ 30″N	88^0 36′ E
2.	Samsung	27^0 15′ 10″N	88^0 36′20″ E

The major tool types of the region are Adzes. Celts, Chisels, Perforated Celts, Splayed Axes, Knives, Harvesters etc. Among these, Adzes and Celts are predominant tool types of the industry. Shouldered Celts, Bar Celts and Ring stones typical of south-western region, are completely absent. Moreover, no ceramic industry has been found in association with this Neolithic culture.

The most interesting feature of the Neolithic tools, collected from Sikkim, isthe local belief of a common magical concept about the tools. These tools are considered as medicine for any kind of treatment. The analysis of these materials show that only tools made on silt stones are having rubbing marks. This may be due to the chemical properties of silt stone which are susceptible to certain diseases. These tools are locally called as *Vajra Dunga* meaning the lightening stones which are generally found after torrential rains. These practices are however prevalent in China. J. Coggin Brown (Brown.1909:299-305) has referred such practices in south Chinese Neolithic culture where Neolithic implements have been found as mortuary finds from graves of the Chau dynasty (1122-249 BCE). He further suggested that the burial of Jadeite implements was much practiced during the historical period of Chau dynasty and continued down to the epoch of the two Han dynasties during 206-221 BCE. He further referred that "In some districts I have noticed that stone implements are occasionally placed before the image of the God Thunder in the temple devoted to his worship by sick people."Finally he concluded that "Even at the present day the Yunnanese/ Chinese attribute a celestial origin to such Neolithic stone implements which they plough up in their fields and there are few villages in which several specimens are not kept, either in the local temple or in the ancestral shrines of some of the inhabitants. The implements are believed to have occult medicinal properties and to be efficacious in the treatment of disease."

Exploration: 2002-2004

During exploration work carried out in the year 2002-04 in the surrounding area of 25 kms of Gangtok, the capital city of Sikkim, 29 Neolithic sites were found where from 10 Axes, 7 Adzes, 14 Celts, 2 Perforated Celts, 1 unfinished Harvester and 1 unfinished Sling Ball were recovered. A brief description of those sites along with their findings is given below:

Figure 2: Explored Area of Sikkim (2002-2003)

1. *Adampool*

This site is located 18 km. away from Gangtok in west direction. This site yielded a Neolithic Celt of 8.9x5.5x1.9 cm. size. The material is Schist. The tool is polished all over.

2. *Adampool Basti*

The site is located 7 km away from Gangtok towards west. The tool collected from here is an unfinished Harvester. It is measuring 7.3x4.8x1.4 cm. This is made of basalt and polished all over(Pl.I).

3. *Aho*

Situated 9 km away from Gangtok towards south and 11 km away from AhoBasti, this site yielded a Neolithic Celt which measures 6.0x4.3x1.6 cm. It is made of Dolerite having polished on both sides. The edge is very sharp (Pl. II).

4. *Aho Basti*

This site is located 9 km away from Gangtok towards south. The area is known as Pakhyong. A Neolithic Axe has been collected from here. The size is 6.2x4.6x1.3 cm. and is made of Schist. The colour is brownish and tagging mark is shown in central portion of the tool. The half of the edge side is broken.

5. *Assam Lingzey*

This site is situated 9 km away south- east of Gangtok. A Neolithic Celt has been collected from this site. The size is 5.6x4.1x1.1 cm. This is made of Basalt. The tool is polished all over and one side of the edge is sharp.

6. *Bojoghari*

This site is located 5 km away from Gangtok towards north. A Neolithic Axe has been discovered during exploration from this site. The measurement is 6.7x4.2x1.6 cm. It is made of Dolerite and having sharp edge. Apart form edge the remaining portion is slightly rough.

7. *Burtuk*

The site is located 6 km west of Gangtok. A Neolithic Adze is discovered from here. The tool is small and measuring 5.3x3.3x1.4 cm. It is made of Dolerite and is brown in colour. It is polished all over and the edge is sharp.

8. *Jalipool*

This site is situated 7 km south of Gangtok. This area is also known as ChhotaSingtam. A Neolithic Axe has been discovered from this site in the cultivated field. The size of Celt is 5.9x3.7x1.7 cm. The colour of the tool is brown and made of Dolerite. The upper portion of the tool has been broken from left side. Both sides of the tool are polished. The edge from one side is repolished and get it straight.

9. *Lingtham Sajong*

This site is situated 21 km eastward from Gangtok. The tool from this site is a Neolithic Celt of 8x5x1.7 cm. size. It is made of Schist and the colour is light brown. The Celt is polished all over. The edge is sharp but some portion is broken.

10. *Lower Sichey Basti*

This site is located 16 km away, towards west from Gangtok. A Neolithic Axe has been collected from this site. The size is 6.4x4.2x1.6 cm. This tool is made of Dolerite. The edge of the tool is sharp. The remaining portion of the axe is flaked just like early Stone Age hand axes.

11. *Martam (Dokandara)*

This site is located 23 km away from Gangtok towards west. A Neolithic Celt has been collected from this place. It is made of black Basalt and the size is 9.5x5.4x2.2 cm. The tool is completely polished and the edge is very sharp. The upper portion is broken.

12. *Namcheybong*

This site is located 10 km away from Gangtok towards south. The area is known as Pakhyong. The Neolithic Adze found from this site is made of Schist and the size is

10.8x4.6x1.1 cm. The Adze is flat on both sides. The edge of tool is broken from one side. Another tool from this site is a Neolithic perforated Celt (Pl.III), which is made of Schist and squares in shape. It bears two holes (5mm) on upper side. Its size is 5.6x4.1x0.7 cm.

13. Nandok

This site is situated 9 km away from Gangtok towards south. A Neolithic Adze has been found from this site which measuring 8.6x4.1x1.9 cm in size. It is conical in shape and polished. The edge of the tool is sharp.

14. Penglong La

This site is situated in North Sikkim, 5 km away from Gangtok towards north. The site has yielded a Neolithic unfinished Sling ball which is unfinished (Pl. IV). It is made of Basalt.

15. Phaungma

This site is located 4 km. south-west of Gangtok (Pl. V-VI). A Neolithic Axe made of Basalt has been collected from this site during exploration. The measurement is 10.7x5.3x2.3 cm. The upper portion is slanting. The tool is polished and the edge is very sharp (Pl. VII).

16. Phongla

This site is located towards north about 9 km away from Gangtok. This site has yielded a Neolithic Adze which is measuring 7.2x4.2x1.6 cm. It is made of Basalt and the colour is brown. The edge of the tool is sharp and polished all over.

17. Radang Basti

Situated at 16 km away from Gangtok towards south- west has been yielded a small Celt. It is made of Jasper of light grey colour. Both sides of the Celt are polished. The edge is very sharp and middle portion is broken. The size of the tool is 6.9x4.7x1.5 cm.

18. Ranipool

This site is situated 7 km away from Gangtok in southern direction. A Neolithic Celt has been found here. The material is Basalt and the size is 9.5x4.1x2.1 cm. The edge of tool is smoothly polished and sharp and the shape of the tool is conical.

19. Ranka Burdang

This site is located at a distance of 24 km south- west of Gangtok. The tool, collected from this site during exploration is a Neolithic Celt. The size is 5.8x4.2x1.6 cm. This is made of Dolerite.

20. *Ranka Rai Basti*

This site is situated 19 km from Gangtok towards west. This site has yielded a Neolithic perforated Celt. The measurement is 6.2x3.2x0.8 cm. The Celt is rectangular in shape. It is made of schist.

21. *Ranka Raigaon*

(i) This site is located 20 km away from Gangtok towards west. This site has yielded three tools they are:

(ii) Neolithic Celt made of Dolerite and the size of the tool is 7.4x4.3x2.0 cm. It is conical in shape and polished all over. The edge is very sharp and colour is brownish.

(iii) It is a small Neolithic Axe. The size is 4.5x3.7x1.6 cm. It is made of black Basalt and small in size. The tool is polished on both sides. The shape is conical and the edge is very sharp.

The third tool yielded from this site is a Neolithic Adze. The size is 10.9x5.1x2.8 cm. and made of Basalt. The shape is conical (Pl.VIII).

22. *Ranka Santag*

This site is located 20 km. west of Gangtok. This site has yielded a Neolithic Celt which is measuring 10.5x5.3x2.3cm. It is made of black Basalt. The tool is polished all over and the edge is very sharp. The upper portion of the Celt is flaked.

23. *Samdur*

This site is 4 km away from Gangtok in the west direction. A Neolithic Celt has been collected from this site of 7.1x4.3x1.5 cm. in size. It is made of Dolerite. The tool is rectangular in shape and well polished all over. The edge is very sharp and straight (Pl. IX).

24. *Sangkhola*

This site is located 17 km towards south western direction from Gangtok. This site yielded an Adze made of black Basalt (Pl. X). The size is 5.6 x 3.6x1.6 cm. The tool is conical- shaped. The edge is very sharp. Only edge portion of the tool is polished and the remaining portion is comparatively rough.

25. *Saureni*

This site is located in North Sikkim 10 km north-east of Gangtok. A Neolithic Adze has been collected from here. It is measuring 6.7x4.1x1.7 cm. It is made of Basalt. The tool is polished and edge is very sharp.

26. *Tambutar*

This site is located 9 km away from Gangtok towards south. This site yielded a Neolithic Axe which is made of Basalt. The size is 4.0x4.6x1.6 cm. It is a small size tool having trapezoid shape. Its edge is sharp and one side is polished.

27. Tingda

This site is located 9 km north of Gangtok in North Sikkim. A Neolithic Celt has been collected from here. It is measuring 8.1x5.4x1.5 cm. It is made of Basalt. The tool is polished all over and the edge is very sharp.

28. Tingla

This site is located 10 km away from Gangtok towards south. The site yielded a Neolithic Axe, measuring 5.8 x 4.6 x 2.2 cm.It is made of Dolerite. The tool is well polished and the edge is very sharp.

29. UpperSamdur

This site is situated 8 km away from Gangtok towards west. A small Neolithic Celt has been found here. The size is 5.2x4.0x1.2 cm. The shape of the tool is almost squares. It is made of black Basalt and well polished on both sides. The edge is sharp and is damaged from one side (Pl. XI).

Classification of tools

The present analysis of material assemblages of Sikkim is based on tools collected from this region by K.D. Banerjee (1980-81) and Pre-history branch, ASI (2002-04). The major tool types of this region are Adzes, Celts, Chisels, and perforated Axes etc.

AXES-North Sikkim

Table 3
Axes recovered from North Sikkim

S.No.	*Year*	*Site*	*Location*	*Length*	*Width*	*Maximum thickness*	*Material*	*Description*
1.	1980-81	Barpak	(Lat. 27⁰ 31′ 30″N, Long. 88⁰ 28′ 15″ E)	8.3 cm	6.3 cm	2.2 cm	Basalt fine grained	Rectangular cross-section
2.	1980-81	Gorterang	(Lat. 27⁰ 25′ 30″N, Long. 88⁰ 30′ 10″ E)	9.8 cm	5.0 cm	2.4 cm	Basalt fine grained	
3.	1980-81	Lingdong	(Lat. 27⁰ 30′ 35″N, Long. 88⁰ 33′ 10″ E)	9.7 cm	6.8 cm	2.0 cm	Basalt	
4.	1980-81	Linkyong	(Lat. 27⁰ 24′N, Long. 88⁰ 29″ E)	5.7 cm	4.5 cm	1.8 cm		
5.	1980-81	Gnon	(Lat. 27⁰ 26′ 40″N, Long. 88⁰ 29′ E)	4.7 cm	3.5 cm	1.9 cm	Chlorite schist	
6.	2002-04	Tingla	(Lat. 27⁰ 16′N, Long. 88⁰ 36′ E)	5.8 cm 5.6 cm	4.6 cm 5.2 cm	2.2 cm 1.5 cm	Basalt Basalt	Sharp edge Polished

East Sikkim

Table 4
Axes recovered from East Sikkim

S. No.	*Year*	*Site*	*Location*	*Length*	*Width*	*Maximum thickness*	*Material*	*Description*
1.	1980-81	Samsing	(Lat. 27^0 15′ 10″N, Long. 88^0 36′20″ E)	5.3 cm	4.5 cm	1.2 cm		
2.	1980-81	Pakyong	(Lat. 27^0 14′ 30″N, Long. 88^0 36′ E)	6.3 cm	2.8 cm	2.0 cm		
3.	2002-04	Tambutar	(Lat. 27^0 16′N, Long. 88^0 35′ E)	4.0 cm	4.6 cm	1.5 cm	Basalt	Trapezoid shaped
4.	2002-04	Jalipool	(Lat. 27^0 16′N, Long. 88′ 35′ E)	5.9 cm	3.7 cm	1.7 cm	Dolerite	Sharp edge, well polished
5.	2002-04	RankaRaiga-on	(Lat. 27^0 16′N, Long. 88′ 30′ E)	4.5 cm 5.9 cm	3.7 cm 5.1 cm	1.6 cm 1.2 cm	Basalt Basalt	Conical shaped All over pol-ished
6.	2002-04	AhoBasti	(Lat. 27^0 15′N, Long. 88^0 35′ E)	6.2 cm	4.6 cm	1.3 cm	Schist	Co-lour-Brown-ish, tagging mark
7.	2002-04	Lower Sichey-Basti	(Lat. 27^0 18′N, Long. 88^0 29′ E)	6.4 cm	4.2 cm	1.6 cm	Dolerite	Planked axe
8.	2002-04	Bojoghari	Lat. 27^0 15′N, Long. 88^0 35′ E)	6.7 cm	4.2 cm	1.6 cm	Dolerite	Sharp edge
9.	2002-04	Phaungma	Lat. 27^0 18′N, Long. 88^0 35′ E)	10.7 cm	5.3 cm	2.3 cm	Basalt	Polished

ADZES-North Sikkim

Table 5
Adzes recovered from North Sikkim

S. No.	*Year*	*Site*	*Location*	*Length*	*Width*	*Maximum thickness*	*Material*	*Description*
1.	1980-81	Lingdong	(Lat. 27^0 30′ 35″N, Long. 88^0 33′ 10″ E)	8.4 cm 7.3 cm 6.8 cm 5.0 cm	5.2 cm 5.0 cm 4.8 cm 3.5 cm	1.25 cm 2.0 cm 1.7 cm 1.1 cm	Basalt	Broken vertical-ly into half
2.	1980-81	Samdong	(Lat. 27^0 27′ 30″N, Long. 88^0 30′ E)	5.7 cm 8.2 cm 6.9 cm	5.9 cm 5.2 cm 5.0 cm	2.0 cm 1.8 cm 2.0 cm		

S. No.	*Year*	*Site*	*Location*	*Length*	*Width*	*Maximum thickness*	*Material*	*Description*
3.	1980-81	Terang	(Lat. 27^0 26′ 10″N, Long. 88^0 30′ 30″ E)	5.9 cm 5.5 cm	4.6 cm 5.15 cm	1.3 cm 1.5 cm	Jesper	
4.	1980-81	Gytong	(Lat. 27^0 29′ 10″N, Long. 88^0 31′ 10″ E)	8.5 cm 4.6 cm	5.4 cm 5.5 cm	1.5 cm 1.3 cm		Broken
5.	1980-81	Linkyong	(Lat. 27^0 24′N, Long. 88^0 29″ E)	5.4 cm 5.6 cm	3.4 cm 5.1 cm	1.5 cm 1.6 cm		
6.	1980-81	Lingthen	(Lat. 27^0 31′ 20″N, Long. 88^0 28′ 30″ E)	5.1 cm	4.9 cm	1.5 cm	Schist	Rectangular in section, oblisides, concave flat butt
7.	1980-81	Sang-kalang	(Lat. 27^0 30′ 20″N, Long. 88^0 32′ 50″ E)	5.8 cm	5.0 cm	1.7 cm		
8.	2002-04	Pengla	(Lat. 27^0 24′N, Long. 88^0 36′ E)	7.2 cm	4.2 cm	1.6 cm	Basalt	Dolerite
9.	2002-04	Swarani	(Lat. 27^0 25′N., Long. 88^0 37′ E.)	6.7 cm	4.1 cm	1.7 cm	Basalt	Polished

East Sikkim

Table 6
Adzes recovered from East Sikkim

S. No.	*Year*	*Site*	*Location*	*Length*	*Width*	*Maximum thickness*	*Material*	*Description*
1.	1980-81	Samsing	(Lat. 27^0 15' 10"N, Long. 88^0 36'20" E)	6.6 cm 4.7 cm	4.9 cm 3.9 cm	1.7 cm 1.4 cm		
2.	1980-81	Pakyong	(Lat. 27^0 14' 30"N, Long. 88^0 36' E)	5.5 cm 5.0 cm	4.4 cm 4.4 cm	1.7 cm 1.5 cm		
3.	2002-04	Namcheybong	(Lat. 27^0 14' N, Long. 88^0 35' E)	10.8 cm	4.6 cm	1.1 cm	Schist	Flat edge
4.	2002-04	Sangkhola	(Lat. 27^0 15'N, Long. 88^0 30' E)	5.6 cm	3.6 cm	1.6 cm	Black Basalt	Conical shaped

S. No.	*Year*	*Site*	*Location*	*Length*	*Width*	*Maximum thickness*	*Material*	*Description*
5.	2002-04	RankaRaigaon	(Lat. 27^0 16'N, Long. 88^0 30' E)	7.4 cm	4.3 cm	2.0 cm	Dolerite	Conical shaped
6.	2002-04	Nandok	(Lat. 27^0 16'N, Long. 88^0 35' E)	8.6 cm	4.1 cm	1.9 cm	Basalt	Conical shaped
7.	2002-04	Burtuk	(Lat. 27^0 20'N, Long. 88^0 34' E)	5.3 cm	3.3 cm	1.4 cm	Dolerite	Dolerite

POLISHER-North Sikkim

Table 7
Polisher recovered from North Sikkim

S.No.	*Year*	*Site*	*Location*	*Length*	*Width*	*Maximum thickness*	*Material*	*Description*
1.	1980-81	Manshi-tong	(Lat. 27^0 40'N, Long. 88^0 35'30" E).	9.0 CM	2.9 CM	1.3 CM	Schist	A hole on the top

East Sikkim

Table 8
Polisher recovered from East Sikkim

S.No.	*Year*	*Site*	*Location*	*Length*	*Width*	*Maximum thickness*	*Material*	*Description*
1.	1980-81	Samsing	(Lat. 27^0 15' 10"N, Long. 88^0 36'20" E)	5.5 cm	3.2 cm	2.7 cm	Schist	

HARVESTER-North Sikkim

Table 9
Harvester recovered from North Sikkim

S.No.	*Year*	*Site*	*Location*	*Length*	*Width*	*Maximum thickness*	*Material*	*Description*
1.	1980-81	Lingden	(Lat. 27^0 29′ 10″N, Long. 88^0 27′ 50″ E).	14.0 cm	4.5 cm	0.7 cm	Greenish schist	Single eyed with double convex cross-section
				5.4 cm	3.0 cm	0.7 cm	Basalt slaty black	Single eyed
2.		Barpak	(Lat. 27^0 31′ 30″N, Long. 88^0 28′ 15″ E.).	15.5 cm	6.2 cm	2.0 cm	Shale	

East Sikkim

Table 10
Harvester recovered from East Sikkim

S.No	Year	Site	Location	Length	Width	Maximum thickness	Material	Description
1.	2002-04	Adampool-Basti	(Lat. 27^0 16′N, Long. 88^0 35′ E).	7.3 cm	4.8 cm	1.4 cm	Basalt	Polished all

PERFORATED AXE-North Sikkim

Table 11
Perforated Axe recovered from North Sikkim

S.No.	Year	Site	Location	Length	Width	Maximum thickness	Material	Description
1.	1980-81	Barpak	(Lat. 27^0 31′ 30″N, Long. 88^0 28′ 15″ E).	10.3 cm	5.6 cm	1.4 cm	Dolerite	With double perforation of the butt end, strait sides, rectangular cross-section
2.		Gnon	(Lat. 27^0 26′ 40″N, Long. 88^0 29′ E)	6.8 cm	5.1 cm	1.6 cm		With double hole

CELTS-North Sikkim

Table 12
Celts recovered from North Sikkim

S.No	Year	Site	Location	Length	Width	Maximum thickness	Material	Description
1.	2002-04	Tingda	(Lat. 27^0 23′N, Long. 88^0 36′ E)	8.1 cm	5.4 cm	1.5 cm	Basalt	Polished over

East Sikkim

Table 13
Celts recovered from East Sikkim

S.No	Year	Site	Location	Length	Width	Maximum thickness	Material	Description
1.	2002-04	Adampool	(Lat. 27^0 16′N, Long. 88^0 33′ E)	8.9 cm	5.5 cm	1.9 cm	Schist	Sharp edge uniform thickness
2.		Aho	(Lat. 27^0 15′N, Long. 88^0 35′ E)	6.00 cm	4.3 cm	1.6 cm	Dolerite	Sharp edge,polished

S.No	Year	Site	Location	Length	Width	Maximum thickness	Material	Description
3.		Assam Lingzey	(Lat. 27^0 16′N, Long. 88^0 37′ E)	5.6 cm	4.1 cm	1.1 cm	Basalt	Well polished, sharp edge
4.		LingthamSajong	(Lat. 27^0 16′N, Long. 88^0 33′ E)	8.00 cm	5.00 cm	1.7 cm	Schist	Well polished
5.		Martam (Dokandara)	(Lat. 27^0 16′N, Long. 88^0 33′ E)	9.5 cm	5.4 cm	2.2 cm	Basalt	Well polished, sharp edge
6.		RadangBasti	(Lat. 27^0 15′N, Long. 88^0 31′ E)	6.9 cm	4.7 cm	1.5 cm	Jasper	Sharp edge
7.		RankaBurdang	(Lat. 27^0 13′N, Long. 88^0 37′ E)	5.8 cm	4.2 cm	1.6 cm	Dolerite	Sharp edge
8.		RankaRaigaon	(Lat. 27^0 16′N, Long. 88^0 35′ E)	7.4 cm 8.0 cm	4.3 cm 4.9 cm	2.0 cm 1.6 cm	Dolerite Basalt	Sharp edge Rectangular shaped
9.		RankaSantag	(Lat. 27^0 16′N, Long. 88^0 30′ E)	10.5 cm	5.3 cm	1.6 cm	Black Basalt	Sharp edge 8 mm hole
10.		Retipool	(Lat. 27^0 18′N, Long. 88^0 35′ E)	9.5 cm	4.1 cm	2.1 cm	Basalt	Sharp and smooth edge
11.		Samdur	(Lat. 27^0 16′N, Long. 88^0 35′ E)	7.1 cm	4.3 cm	1.5 cm	Dolerite	Rectangular shaped,Well polished
12.		Upper Samdur	(Lat. 27^0 14′N, Long. 88^0 34′ E)	5.2 cm	4.00 cm	1.2 cm	Dolerite	Rectangular shaped, Well polished

PERFORATED CELTS-North Sikkim

Table 14
Perforated Celts recovered from North Sikkim

S.No	Year	Site	Location	Length	Width	Maximum thickness	Material	Description
1.	2002-04	RankaRaiBasti	(Lat. 27^0 24′N, Long. 88^0 31′ E)	2 cm	3.2 cm	0.8 cm	Schist	Rectangular Shaped

East Sikkim

Table 15
Perforated Celts recovered from East Sikkim

S.No	*Year*	*Site*	*Location*	*Length*	*Width*	*Maximum thickness*	*Material*	*Description*
1.	2002-04	Namchey-bong	(Lat. 27^0 14′N, Long. 88^0 35′ E)	5.6 cm	4.1 cm	0.7 cm	Schist	Square shaped

SLING BALL

Table 16
Sling Ball recovered from Penglong La

S.No	*Year*	*Site*	*Location*	*Length*	*Width*	*Maximum Diameter*	*Material*	*Description*
1.	2002-04	Penglong La	Lat. 27^0 14′N, Long. 88^0 35′ E)	------------	------------	3.2 cm	Basalt	Unfinished

The distribution of tool types and their respective percentages is shown in the Table below:

Table 17
Distribution of tool types and their respective percentages from Sikkim

Tool Type	*No.*	*%*
Adze	17	51.51
Celt	09	27.27
Faceted tools		
Chisel		
Pestle		
Splayed axe		
Polisher	01	03.03
Perforated Celt	03	09.09
Socket Celt		
Elongated pick		
Flat Celt		
Wedge Blade		
Harvester	02	06.06
Knife	01	03.03
Total	33	99.99

The Table shows that the diagnostic Neolithic tool types of this region are Adzes and Celts while other types occur in variable proportions. Adzes and Celts comprise 51.51% and 27.27% respectively showing a good deal of similarity in the distribution pattern. They constitute together 78.78% in the total collection. This shows the predominant character of Adzes and Celts in the tool population of the region while other types remain insignificant. Faceted tools, Chisels, splayed edged Axes and flat Celt are conspicuously absent in Sikkim. The presence and absence of few tool types may be due to optimum condition for explorations. However the minor types in Sikkim constitute 21.22%.

Raw Materials

The selection of raw materials was strictly guided by two factors viz, the availability of local rocks and the associated technology. Naturally, we cannot strictly say that there was a complete switch over from metamorphic to igneous group of rocks as suggested by Sankalia. But the total withdrawal from the previous quartz and quartzite was mainly due to the introduction of altogether a new technology, which is otherwise known as chipping, grinding and polishing. Although a fourth stage of packing has been suggested by many scholars but the relevance of such a separate stage is doubtful since packing or smoothing of the rough or uneven chipped surface could have also been done during chipping or flaking of tools. But nevertheless, this change in raw material during Neolithic period may be due to basic changes in technology and altogether a different subsistence economy.

Technology

Technology is an important device without which man could hardly do anything. The concept of technology actually led to the emergence of culture. There was a close relationship between the emergence of culture and the development of technology. As a matter of fact, we do not exactly know when, where and how the concept of technology was developed, but we can assume that in response to selective pressure man developed the concept of technology through the application of his intuitive power for securing elements of his survival. Man's persistent struggle against nature to secure his survival was made possible through the development of technology. If there was no technology, there would have been no culture and hence no man. Therefore we can conclude that man is the product of interaction between biology and culture and technology played the most crucial role for the development of culture.

Basic changes in the structures of economy and culture would also be reflected through changes in technology. A well-developed Neolithic Technology could support a large number of people through changes in economic structure and cultural complexity. The Neolithic technology basically comprises chipping, grinding and polishing. Although a fourth stage commonly known as pecking has often been suggested by a number of scholars, but even so the actual relevance of such a separate stage is doubtful.

It appears that the practice, customs and local tradition in respect of the Neolithic tools found from Sikkim and South China specially Yunnan province are same suggesting the transmigrations of such practices from either of the places and in this regard, the possibility of such migration from south China is very high. Naturally, the traditions, myths and legends associated with these Neolithic tools are also supposed to have been travelled along with the culture.

What is remaining?

As we have seen that the human settlement in Sikkim begins from Neolithic period which is evidenced by only explored materials. The question arises that what was the scenario during Palaeolithic and Mesolithic periods? After Neolithic the cultural sequence is missing from Chalcolithic to historical age which shows a long cultural gap. So it is the need of the time that archaeologist must try to fill up this gap and reveal the shrouded mysteries of this state which is only possible by doing extensive archaeological exploration and excavation in the region.

References

Banerjee, K.D. 1987. "Stone Age Migrations in India. *Archaeology and History.*"Edited by D.P. Chattopadhyay.New Delhi.

Brown, Coggin J. 1909. *Journal of Asiatic Society of Bengal,* New Series V.

Coelho, V.H. 1970. *Sikkim and Bhutan.* New Delhi: Vikas Publications. New Delhi.

Mishra, P.K. 2008. *Archaeological Exploration in Sikkim.* New Delhi: Sundeep Prakashan.

Risley, H.H. 2010. Rep.*The Gazetteer of Sikkim.* New Delhi: B.R. Publishing Corporation.

Sharma, T.C. 1980. ": The Neolithic Pattern of India." Paper presented at IAS and ISPQS at Allahabad.

Walsh, E.H.G. 1904. "A Note on stone implements in the Darjeeling district." *Journal of Asiatic Society of Bengal* 3.

2

Archaeological Exploration in Western UP along the Rivers *Yamuna* and *Hindon* (Meerut, Baghpat, Muzaffarnagar and Saharanpur): 2006-07

The present exploration work was conducted by the author and his team including Prof. R.N.Singh and Dr. A.K.Singh during the summer of 2007 to asses the archaeological potentials of the sites along the rivers *Yamuna* and *Hindon* in western U P. This preliminary survey was focused on revisiting archaeological sites identified in previous surveys and recording their precise geographical location to review their antiquity. These areas were specifically chosen because of their geographical relationship to the present courses of the perennial *Yamuna* and *Hindan* rivers (Districts-Meerut, Baghpat, Ghaziabad and Gautam Buddha Nagar, Western UP). The prime objective of the present survey is to asses the current stage of knowledge of the Harappan presence in Western UP and to examine the distribution of regional and non-Harappan sites in the light of recent researches conducted by the ASI particularly at Sanauli (Baghpat) and Mandi (Muzaffarnagar), UP. It may be noted that the credit must goes to K.A.A.Ansari of ASI for the discovery of Harappan presence in Doab (1935-36). However, his discovery remains unnoticed until the discovery of Alamgirpur in 1958 and subsequent excavations done by Y.D. Sharma of ASI. We have visited more than two dozen sites, amongst them following are of considerable importance:

Alamgirpur (Long. 29^0 0′ N, Lat. 77^0 29′ E)

This Harappan site, situated in district Meerut is totally disturbed (Pl. XII). It is extended in more than 3 acres. Red Ware, Painted Red Ware and Grey Ware were scattered on the mound. A portion of about 50 meter is available for trial trench just opposite of the excavated trenches (1958). Alamgirpur was excavated by Y.D. Sharma of ASI in 1958- 59 who revealed cultural sequence of four periods with a break in all of them. Mr.Sharma (1958-59:55) has divided these periods as Harappan, PGW, Early Historical and very late medieval periods and concluded that, "Any greater chronological precision will be unwarranted." Considering the problem raised by earlier work and new findings in the archaeology of Western UP, new excavations focused on dating the cultural sequence of the site were carried out in May-June, 2008 by the team of archaeologists of Banaras Hindu University. The primary aim of this test investigation was to reassess the stratigraphic chronology of the site and to obtain new samples for radiometric dating. These excavations have also provided an opportunity to sample for plant remains and phytoliths, and also to investigate the micro-morphology of the occupation deposits and the underling old land surface.

During the course of excavation, trenches ZA1 and ZA2 were found disturbed having filled materials of earlier excavation. However, in trench ZB1, the remains of a wall made up of medieval bricks have been recovered in the highest portion of the surviving mound. In trench ZB2, 12 layers were identified in a cultural deposit of 4.10m and trench YD2, located in the south-western slope of the mound, recorded a cultural deposit of 3.10 m divisible into 9 layers. Finding of these excavations may be compared favourably with the earlier cultural materials. This excavation revealed that there is no gap between PGW and the Harappans. It has been observed that there was an overlap phase of PGW and Harappans. It appears that there were two phases in period I representing pit-dwelling activity just over the natural soil followed by mud walls and rammed circular floors with post holes. A series of ritualistic miniature pots, other interesting feature of the mature Harappan phase, were reported in situ. Amongst the other noteworthy findings mention can be made of the occurrence of iron artifacts from the lower level of PGW. Other significant discovery of the PGW period is the cluster of furnaces, perhaps for ceramics production and treatment. It was observed that the inhabitants of this period were familiar with the use of lime. It has been attested by the recovery of lime in huge quantity in the vicinity of floors and the pits adjacent to the furnaces. Further, a number of completed pots (dishes and bowls) were kept found in arranged fashion lying upside down just near the furnaces. Most of the pots were having peculiar painting of mature PGW phase. The study of the samples collected from the excavations of Alamgirpur is being conducted in collaboration with the University of Cambridge, Deccan College, Pune and the Birbal Sahni Institute of Palaeobotany, Lucknow and the result will be published shortly.

Barnawa (Long. 29^0 6´ N, Lat. 77^0 25´ E)

This mound is located on the conference of the River *Krishni* and *Hindon* in district-Baghpat, locally known as *Lakshagriha.* It is 35 km from Meerut-Barout Road and 5km from Binauli. The mound extends in an area of more than 15 acres with a height of 30 m. Amongst the cultural deposit mention can be made of Red Ware, Grey Ware, burnt bricks with finger impression and a medieval structure (Watch tower/ minar) found on the western portion of the mound.

Buland Khera (Long. 28^0 30´ N, Lat. 77^0 33 ´E)

Fully intact mound of Buland Khera is situated on a Nala probably a tributary of *Hindon*, west from Sakipur village, 10 km from Dadri in the district of Gautam Buddha Nagar (Pl. XIII). The site rises about 8 m from the surrounding plain and covers an area of 10 acres. Potsherds of PGW, Black and Red Ware, Grey Ware, Black painted Red potsherds, a piece of pendent, stone chips and a Terracotta Dabber were collected from the mound.

Gulistanpur (Long. 28^0 31´ N, Lat. 77^0 30´ E)

It is situated 6 km from Dadri on Dadri-Noeda road in Surajpur industrial area 'C' in Gautam Buddha Nagar. The site is extended in 6 acres having 5 m height. Black-painted red potsherds were collected from the surface of the mound. The site is totally destroyed and presently occupied by the builders.

Hastinapur (Long. 29^0 9 ´N, Lat. 77^0 0´ E)

Having historical importance the site of Hastinapur lies close to the west bank of the Ganges. The main mound was excavated by B.B. Lal in 1954-1955. Most of the mounds are currently covered by a dense growth of trees, but there are a number of modern shrines atop the largest mound.

Isopur Til (Long. 29^0 18´ N, Lat. 77^0 9´ E)

This site is situated on the left bank of the *Yamuna* River in Muzaffarnagar district. It is 15 km west from Kandhela via Gangera. It is at least 30 to 40 acres in area and stands to a height of 30 m above the surrounding plain. There are clear signs of PGW with Painted Red Ware, Black and Red Ware, Black Slipped Ware and plenty of burnt bricks. A probable opening of gate towards east side is also noticed. The site is totally intact and located on the border of Meerut, Baghpat and Muzaffarnagar. A modern temple of Krishna is constructed on the mound.

Kot Gaon

This ancient settlement is situated on the left corner of Dadri- Bulandsahar Road, about 10 km from Dadri town. The mound covers more than 5 acres of area with extent height of 10m. Brick bats, Red Ware and Grey ware are scattered all over the mound. A modern school is constructed on the top of the mound.

Kurdi (Long. 29^0 14´ N, Lat. 77^0 9´ E)

Kurdi is situated on the left flood plain of the River *Yamuna*, about 9km south-east of Isopur Til. It stands to a height of 30m above the surrounding plain and extends in more than 20 acres. It is located between Tanda and Chaprauli. Potsherds of PGW, Red Ware and Painted Red Ware are scattered on this intact mound but painted ceramics are less than Isopur Til. A new temple is constructed on the mound.

Mandola (Long. 28^0 48 ´N, Lat. 77^0 16´ E)

The ancient site of Mandola is situated inside the modern village of same name of the Delhi-Loni-Baghpat Road in district- Ghaziabad. A small portion of the mound is surviving which is extended in 4 acres with a height of 15m. Potsherds of PGW and Grey Ware are present in the lower profile of the section.

Parshuram Khera (Long. 28^0 59´ N, Lat. 77^0 27 ´E)

This ancient site is situated between Pura Mahadev I and II on the right bank of River *Hindon* in Baghpat district. It is about 3 km from Alamgirpur on Baleni-Pura Mahadev Road. The mound is extended in 4 to 5 acres with a height of 10m. A good number of Painted Grey Ware, Grey Ware, Black and Red Ware and Red Ware have been recovered.

Pura Mahadev I (Long. 29^0 0´N, Lat. 77^0 27 E)

Situated in district Baghpat, the site is totally covered by the modern village of same name. It extended in 5 acres and extent height of the mound is more than 5 mt.

Pura Mahadev II (Long. 29^0 0´N, Lat. 77^0 27 E)

This mound is situated in district Baghpat on the right bank of *Hindon* River, about 3.5 km north from Baleni Bazar on Baleni-Pura Mahadev Road. The site is fully occupied by agriculturists, extended in 3 acres with 5mt cultural deposit. Red Ware Vases are scattered all over the mound.

Saini (Long. 29^0 2´ N, Lat. 77^0 47´ E)

The ancient settlement of Saini is situated on the left bank of River *Kali* on Meerut-Mawana Road, 11km north from Meerut City. The site is fully occupied by the villagers of Saini. It is extended in 5 acres with a height of 15m; the presence of PGW, Grey Ware, Red Ware and Kushan bricks are noted in a south facing section along with a medieval Minar on the top of the mound.

Sanauli (Long. 29^0 8´ N, Lat. 77^0 12´ E)

The cemetery site of Sanauli is situated in the doab region of western UP. It was discovered in 2004 and excavated by ASI over two seasons. Major importance of the site is due to unique mixture of Copper Hoard, OCP and Harappan cultural material found from the graves.

Sirsalgarh (Long.29^0 03 ´N, Lat. 77^0 23^0 E)

This site is situated on Baleni Road, 8 km from Aminagar Sarai on the old bed of *Krishni* in Baghpat district (Pl. XIV). It extends in an area of 10 acres with an average height of about 15m. Burnt bricks of different sizes and painted Black and Red Ware were scattered on the surface of the mound. No PGW recovered from this site.

Tussiana (Long. 28^0 32′ N, Lat. 77^0 28′ E)

This site is situated near a lake, 15 km from Dadri in Noeda industrial area, District-Gautam Buddha Nagar. It extends in an area of 4 acres and the height of the mound is 3m. The mound is mostly destroyed by modern constructional activities. Amongst the cultural assemblages, mention can be made of Red Ware and Painted Red Ware. Presently a new temple is constructed on the mound.

Apart from above mentioned sites the team has visited a few less important sites like Valmiki Mandir, Katha, Loni, Garhi Kalanjari and Habibpur Khera. Valmiki Mandir is situated in district Baghpat on the right bank of the River *Hindon* about 25 km west from Meerut on Meerut-Baghpat Road and one km west from the village Baleni. The mound is totally occupied by the temple in which medieval bricks (Lakhauri) are used. The ancient site of Katha is totally occupied by villagers and is 6 km far from Delhi-Loni Road on the flood plain of *Yamuna* in Baghpat district. Garhi-Kalanjari is also an ancient site, situated on the right bank of River *Hindon* in Baghpat district totally covered by a major construction. More than 30 m high mound of Loni in Ghaziabad district is also fully destroyed and occupied by the villagers. A new industry is constructed on the mound of Habibpur Khera which has completely destroyed the mound. Red ware has recovered from this site, situated in Gautam Buddha Nagar.

Apart from visiting excavated sites like Alamgirpur (Meerut) and Sanauli (Baghpat), the sites which have archaeological potentials, are Buland Khera, Sirsal Garh and Isopur Til. There is a great desideratum to compare Black Painted Red Ware, which occurs in profusion in the above mentioned recently explored sites, with already reported Harappan sites in neighboring area. Considering the chronological problem, the spread of Harappans and existence of regional cultures prior or contemporary to Harappans in this part of the land the archaeologists of Banaras Hindu University has conducted excavations in Alamgirpur and Buland Khera in order to reaffirm the chronological sequence and to collect sample for environmental studies and for radiometric dating. Report of the excavation will be published shortly.

References

Chakrabarti, D.K., R.N.Singh, D.K.Lahiri and R.Tewari. 2006. "Further Thoughts on the Harappan Issue in Western UP: Sites in Saharanpur-Muzaffarnagar-Hartidwar Area." *South Asian Studies* 22.

Indian Archaeology 1958-59-A Review. Delhi: Archaeological Survey of India.

Joshi, J.P., M.Bala and J.Ram.1984. "The Indian Civilization: A Reconsideration on the basis of distribution maps." *Frontiers of the Indus Civilization* (Eds.) B.B.Lal and S.P.Gupta. Delhi: Books & Books.

Shinde, V., Toshiki Osada, M.M.Sharma, Akinori Uesugi, T. Uno, H.Maemokui, P.Shivalkar, S.Deshpandey. 2008. "Exploration in the Ghaggar Basin and Excavations at Giradwad, Farmana (Rohtak) and Mitathal (Bhiwani district), Haryana." *Linguistics, Archaeology and the Human Past* 3. Kyoto: RIHN.

3

Archaeological Exploration in Eastern UP along the River *Chhoti Saryu* (Tons), UP (Azamgarh, Ballia, Ghazipur and Mau): 2010-11

The River *Chhoti Saryu* is a tributary of the *Ghaghara* and discharges itself in the *Ganga,* about 3 km south-east of the ancient site of Waina in district-Ballia. Dilip Chakrabarty had explored many sites along the river *Chhoti Saryu* (Chakrabarty.2001:233-239). P.Singh and his team has also done a pioneer work in the region and explored and excavated so many sites (Singh *et al.*1994-95:24-27; 1996-97:33-38). During 2010-11 an exploration work was done by the author along the *Chhoti Saryu* River. Four districts lie along the *Chhoti Saryu*. The exact geographical position of each settlement and the nature of the cultural deposit on them are briefly enumerated below:

District-Azamgarh

Bhairosthan

An extensive but low structural mound of the post-Gupta period having a modern temple on the top.

Chiraiakot

A low mound near Karhi where brickbats and pottery of the early centuries of Christian era are clearly visible. Fuhrer (1891:187) had reported Punch-marked coins from this place.

Deokali/Deolas

This mound is located to the east of Azamgarh and between Muhammadabad and Ghosi. Presently it covers about 5 acres of area. The site yields BRW and later sherds and structural remains are noticed in its upper levels.

Gopalpur

The mound covers 3 acres of area having 2 m height, showing structural debris of early centuries of Christian era; one can also locate BRW. Presently the mound is cut by the road from Azamgarh to Muhammadabad via Chiraiakot.

Kauria

It is located to the north-west of Azamgarh, extended in 15 acres having height of 5 m. An extensive spread of pottery of early centuries of Christian era and later are noticed in the fields.

Madhuban

A small structural mound of post-Gupta period located between Ghosi and Azamgarh. Fuhrer (1891:189) found an inscription of 7th century CE at this site.

Nahush –ka-tila

This fortified mound covering 500 m east-west and 700 m north-south lies near Ghosi bazar. A mud rampart having a brick wall on the top still rises 6 m from the surrounding area and yields BRW and NBPW from its core. One can see the towers at the south-west and north-west corners. Apart from this there was one entrance on each of the four sides. Fuhrer (1891:188) reported an inscription of 12th -13th century CE at Ghosi.

Raja-Bhar-ka-kotwa

This structural mound covering an area of 15 acres is located near a modern village named Bhatri. The site yields BRW, NBPW and BSW and human settlement continues here up to the post-Gupta period. When Carlleyle (1885:106-7) visited the site it was extended into 2400 ft north-south and 1500 ft east-west. He also reported the ruins of a stupa nearby.

District -Ballia

Alam Ka Tola

About 28 km north of the Ballia town and 3 km west of Janwan on Ballia-Sikandarpur road this medieval settlement is in Bansdih Tehsil. Extended in 5 acres having height of 2 mts, the mound yields potteries of medieval period.

Atrauli

The site is in Dist. Ballia located about 8 km north-east of Ratanpur Railway Station. The mound represents post-Gupta period extended in about one acre and the extant height from the surrounding plain is 5 m. It may represent a temple or stupa site.

Barhmain

It is 6 km to the north of Ballia. H.B.W.Garrick visited the site in 1881-82 and traced a Buddhist monastery with cells where the modern temple of Kalpa Mai has been constructed over its ruins (Garrick.1885:49-59). Still the mound is 3 m high and overlooks an off-shoot of the most famous watery depression of the district *i.e. Suraha Tal*. The site is full of brickbats extended in about 3 acres having 2 m height. It seems to date from the early centuries of Christian era with a possible Black-and-Red ware antecedent.

Bakwa

It is located in the north-west of Sahodih in Dist.-Ballia. The mound is 4-5 m high and circular in shape. It may represent a stupa but a small habitation section yielding Black-and-Red ware was also noticed.

Bansdih

It is a small dilapidated mound full of brickbats and potteries of early centuries of Christian era near the old Bazar of this small town.

Bansdih Road

It is located near the Railway Station of the same name and shows a scatter of sherds including Black-and-Red ware in the fields.

Basantpur

It is located about 8 km north of Ballia on the bank of a watery depression. It measures less than one acre but suggests an extensive former spread. Along with brickbats, Black-and-Red ware and Black Slipped ware were noticed on the mound.

Bharatpura

It is located near Barhmain. The extant height of the mound is 3 m and extended in about 5 acres. Garrick (1885:56) refers it as a large mound of only clay. Basically it is an earthen mound without apparent traces of brickbats datable to early historic and later.

Bhimpura

Located about 14 km west of Nagara this mound is 5 m high and extended in 2 acres. It may be dated to the early centuries of Christian era and later. It is interesting to note that no brickbats are visible in the exposed sections.

Bhunadih

The site lies about one km east of Janwan (Tehsil-Bansdih) on the right bank of the *Bahera Nala*. Extended in about 4 acres with extant height of 1m, the site yielded Black-and-Red ware, Black Slipped ware and Corded ware. The site was excavated by Dept. of AIHC & Archaeology, Banaras Hindu University. Due to encroachment of local people the stratigraphic position of archaeological relics is highly disturbed. Ceramics of the site may be well compared with the ceramics of Chirand and Khairadih.

Bidahara

This mound is extended in about 2 acres having 2 m of height. Basically it is a structural mound of the post-Gupta period, with a modern Hanuman temple on the top.

Bijalipur

It is located 6 km west of Maniar on the Maniar-Sikandarpur road and covers an area of 12-15 acres. River *Ghaghra* flows 1 km west to the mound. It may be datable to the early centuries of Christian era and later.

Chandayar

It is 5 km west of Maniyar and 1 km north-west of Bahadura village in Bansdih Tehsil. Covering an area of 8 acres the site yields BSW, Grey ware, Red ware and terracotta beads.

Chhatarsand

Near Zimichack this ancient settlement extends in 10 acres. Red ware and burnt bricks recovered from the mound may be datable to Kushana-Gupta times.

Chhatha

It is located near Gharauli and extended in about 2 acres. The site may be dated to the early centuries of Christian era. Fuhrer (1891:192) found an umbrella type ruined stupa here.

Deokali

About 12 km west of Sikandarpur the site is located on the Ballia-Belthara road. Datable to early centuries of Christian era and later there is an image of Durga on her chariot lion and another of Surya in two small modern temples on its top.

Deorhi

It is located in Bansdih Tehsil near *Puni Tal*, an offshoot of *Dah Tal*. Black-and- Red ware and brickbats of the early centuries of Christian era were noticed. Fuhrer (1891:191) has reported both Bansdih and Deorhi.

Ekail

Extended over a ground of 2 acres the site is located about 11 km west of Sikandarpur on the Sikandarpur-Nagara Road. The mound is 7 m high yielding NBP, BSW and later wares.

Forsatar

This mound is located about 3 km south of the Belthara Road. It is 2 m high and extended in 3 acres. It belongs to post-Gupta period.

Gharauli

Datable to the early centuries of Christian era the site is near Ballia and occupies one acre of area.

Hajauli

About 5 km north of Chikahar it is a medieval settlement. Covering an area of about 5 acres there is a temple made of *Lakhauri* bricks dedicated to Lord Shiva on the top of the mound.

Halpur

About 19 km from Ballia town it is located in Bansdih tehsil on Ballia-Maniyar road. Extended in 10 acres on the edge of *Dah Tal*, the site yields Red ware and fragments of spouted jars.

Isar Pithapatti

About 3 km west of Lakhanapar village on Sikandarpur-Nagra road this site is located in Bansdih Tehsil. Extended in about 3 acres, two ring wells are found on the mound which is still functional.

Jagdishpur

It is located 18 km west of Ballia on Ballia-Rasara road. Covering an area of 8 acres the site yields Red ware and brickbats of Kushana-Gupta times.

Janwan

It lies on the bank of the *Bahera Nala* about 20 km north-west of Ballia on the Ballia-Sikandarpur Road. It is 2 m high compact mound full of brickbats and covers an area of about 15-20 acres. The mound is cut by the Ballia-Sikandarpur Road and gives the general impression of being a Buddhist monastery site of the post-Gupta period.

Karnai

This is a small but 6 m high mound with a modern temple locally known as Brahmasthan. About 8 km north-west of Ballia on the Ballia-Sikandarpur Road the whole complex overlooks a watery depression and might be datable to early centuries of Christian era.

Karsanar

It is located under the jurisdiction of Pakri Police Station in Bansdih Tehsil. The *Bahera Nala* flows about one km south of this site. Red ware and burnt bricks of Gupta and medieval times were recovered from the site.

Kandasar

It is about 2.5 m south of Barawa on Pandaha-Rajbaha Road and about 1 km north of *Bahera Nala*. The mound is completely occupied by modern settlers.

Kurmipur

Extended in 5 acres this site is situated 16 km west of Ballia, 3 km south of Sihachaur and 1/2 km east of Pakkakot in Phephana Police Station , Tehsil-Ballia on the right bank of *Lakra Nala*, a tributary of *Chhoti Saryu*.

Khairadih

The mound lies on the southern bank of the Ghaghra, at a river crossing. It was excavated by the Dept. of AIHC & Archaeology, Banaras Hindu University. The present extent of the mound is 30-40 acres and near the river side it is about 20 m high, with a modern Matha on the top. The mound has yielded a sequence beginning with BRW. It has been partly cut by the river, and brick walls are clearly visible in the gullies. A.C.L.Carlleyle (1885:107) had mentioned it as a very ancient fortified city, measuring 1600 ft north-south and 1500 ft east-west.

Lakhaneshwardih

Extended in 15 acres having 8 m height this mound is located 8 km south-west of Rasara on the northern bank of *Chhoti Saryu*. The mound has yielded BRW and NBP. Fuhrer (1891:193) refers to its immense piles of debris in which pieces of sculptures have occasionally been found.

Loria-ka-Tila/Bhiradih

It is located to the north-west of Barhmain and covers an area of 20 acres strewn with BRW and brickbats of Gupta period. Garrick (1885:56) mentioned it as Myra Dih while Fuhrer reported it as Mira Dih (1891:192).

Majhol

This site is located near Deorhi. Extended into 5 acres having 2 m height the site is datable to the early centuries of Christian era.

Muryari

The site belongs to medieval period. Covering one acre of area it is situated 5 km west of Maniyar in Bansdih Tehsil.

Nichuadih

Situated about 6 km north of Nagara this site is extended into about 20 acres. Structural activities were noticed which is datable to early centuries of Christian era and later.

Pakkakot

Extended into about 30 acres having 10 m height and four bastions, this fortified site lies between the *Chhoti Saryu* and the *Budhi Nala*. The modern village of Pakkakot lies within the fortified area and covers the south-east area. Fuhrer (1891:192) noticed the site but did not provide any details. Dilip Chakrabarty and R.N.Singh has reported it as NBPW site. Further, they also mentioned a small BRW settlement to the east of

Pakkakot situated on the *Budhi Nala* (Chakrabarti and Singh.1998:108). Actually it was the extension of the same site. The author with his team has visited the site in the month of July, 2010 and observed that the site belongs to Neolithic to medieval period (Dubey, *et al*.2010:203), which was well supported by the result of excavations done in the months of Feb.-May, 2011-12(Dubey, *et al*.2012:200-204). The details of the excavations are given in another chapter in this book.

Panchmukhi Temple

This large mound extended into about 25 acres is located near Reoti Railway Station. The Railway line has cut across this extensive mound of the early centuries of Christian era. Three m high section is exposed with the modern Panchmukhi temple on the top.

Sahodih

About 10 km towards Bansdih from Ballia, the entire mound has been covered by modern remains. It may be datable to the early centuries of Christian era.

Sanwaradih

This ancient settlement is situated 23 km west of Ballia on Ballia-Mau road under Rasara Police Station on the left bank of *Budhi Nala*. The mound spreads over an area of 5 acres and yielded BSW, Red ware and Grey ware.

Sihpur

About 16 km north of Ballia town it is situated in Phephana Police Station in Ballia Tehsil. Extended in about 6 acres the site yields BSW, Red ware and Grey ware. A few ring wells and burnt bricks of Kushana-Gupta periods were also recovered from the mound.

Sikandarpur

About 28 km north-west of Ballia, this low but extensive mound looks basically earthen but shows some brickbats as well. According to Fuhrer (1891:194) it dates to 15th century CE and later.

Ser/Barki Seria

Located near Reoti this mound is extended into 3 acres having 8 m height. It may be datable to the early centuries of Christian era.

Sidhauli/Kaithauli

Located on the bank of *Suraha Tal* potteries of early centuries of Christian era are scattered on the site.

Tika Deori

About 9 km south of Rasara the site is located on the northern bank of the *Chhoti Saryu*. About one km along the river bank remains of BRW, BSW, NBPW and later are spread.

Waina

It is located about 8 km to the west of Ballia on Ballia-Mau road. Extended into 15 acres having 8 m height the mound was excavated by P.Singh and his team. It has yielded Corded Ware to NBPW and later (Singh & Singh.1995:6).

Zimichack

To the north of village Pur in Bansdih Tehsil on Ballia-Nagra road this ancient settlement may be dated to Kushan-Gupta periods. Important finds are Red ware, terracotta pestles, terracotta figurines and beads.

Zirabasti

About 6 km from Ballia on the Ballia-Sikandarpur road, this mound is highly destroyed. A roughly circular 3 m high portion survives which seems to represent a stupa with traces of a settlement in the vicinity. Fuhrer (1891:195) describes it as a large mound.

Unai

About 10 km south-west of Rasara on Ballia-Mau road the site covers an area of 6 acres and yielded Red ware along with terracotta animal figurines.

District-Ghazipur

Amhat Kot

Located in Muhammadabad tehsil the site yields BSW, Grey Ware and Red Ware. Important shapes are dishes, bowls sprinklers and handled *karahis* along with terracotta pestles and pottery discs.

Asawar

This ancient settlement flourished during Kushan, Gupta and Medieval periods. It is located 6 km south from Rasara Railway Station in district-Ghazipur. The site yields BSW, NBPW and Grey Ware. Important shapes are vases, dishes and ink-pot lid along with terracotta human figurines.

Bahutara

About 7 km west of Bahadurganj in the Sadar Tehsil of Ghazipur district this site is on the right bank of *Bhainsahi River*, extended in area of 10 acres. Lids and vases of Red ware along with terracotta animal figurines, dabbers and pestles were found on the site.

Banka

About one km west of Bahadurganj town in Ghazipur district the site is located on the right bank of the *Chhoti Saryu*. Red ware pottery of Kushana and Gupta periods along with terracotta human and animal figurines are the important finds of the site.

Banki Khurd

The site belongs to Gupta and post-Gupta periods. Situated 5 km west of Karimuddinpur in Muhammadabad Tehsil the site yields Red ware.

Baswari Kot

Extended in 5 acres the mound is located 5 km west of Bahadurganj town on the left bank of River *Bhainsahi*. The site yields Red ware along with burnt brick structures of Kushan and Gupta periods.

Bhainsara

About 4 km south-west of Bahadurganj town the site is situated in Muhammadabad Tehsil. It may be dated to Kushan and Gupta periods. Besides sprinklers and lids of Red ware, terracotta beads, human figurines and pestles were reported from the site.

Bhaisradih

This medieval settlement is located 0.5 km west of Salamatpur.

Chandidih

The west portion of Siuri Amhat village is locally known as Chandidih. Its cultural deposit belongs to medieval period.

Durgathan

About one km east from Mehraur Chatti in Muhammadabad Tehsil this site is on the right bank of *Chhoti Saryu*. Burnt brick structures and *Lakhauri* bricks indicate that the site belongs to medieval period.

Gopalpur

Extended in about 5 acres this ancient site is located 5 km south-west of Bahadurganj town in Muhammadabad Tehsil of Ghazipur district. The site yields Red ware pottery along with terracotta figurines and balls of Kushana and Gupta periods.

Kalyani

About 6 km from Bahadurganj market in district Ghazipur this site is situated on the right bank of *Bhainsahi* River. Extended in 5 acres the site yields Red ware pottery along with animal and human terracotta figurines, terracotta pestles, iron slags and burnt brick structures of Kushan and Gupta times.

Kandhara

About 9 km south of Rasara in Muhammadabad Tehsil the site yields Red ware and brick fragments of Kushan, Gupta and medieval times.

Karmadih

This early historic site yielding Red ware and burnt brick structures is located on the right bank of *Bhainsahi* River, about 4 km south of Bahadurganj town.

Kot/Deoli

Having cultural deposit of Kushana-Gupta and medieval times this mound is situated 2 km south of Bahadurganj town in Muhammadabad Tehsil.

Mahdewa

It is situated in Muhammadabad tehsil having cultural deposits of BSW, NBPW and Kushana-Gupta and medieval times including terracotta pestles and animal figurines.

Matehun

About 3 km south-west of Barhua Godam this ancient site yields vases and sprinklers of Red ware and burnt bricks of Kushana-Gupta periods.

Pali/Pawaria Ka Dih

This site is situated 6 km west of Mehraur Chatti in Muhammadabad Tehsil on the right bank of *Chhoti Saryu*. There are two mounds; the earliest one is Pawaria Ka Dih having cultural deposit of Chalcolithic to Gupta periods. Extended in about 5 acres the mound yields Black-and Red ware, BSW, NBPW, Grey ware and Red ware. The next mound belongs to medieval times and presently occupied by the villagers of Pali.

Pattigarh

This mound of medieval period is located 12 km south-west of Mau on the Mau-Yusufpur road.

Pindari

This medieval settlement is situated one km west of Lakhneswardih on the right bank of *Chhoti Saryu* in Muhammadabad Tehsil.

Rajapur

It is located 3 km west of Siuri Amhat on the Muhammadabad-Rasara road in Muhammadabad Tehsil. Bricks of medieval period are visible on the surface.

Sagapali

Located 3 km west of Amhat in Muhammadabad Tehsil it is a medieval settlement.

Shahbajpur

About 4 km east of Mehraur Chatti in Muhammadabad Tehsil the site yields fragments of burnt bricks of medieval times.

Sihoradih

This mound is situated on the right bank of *Bhainsahi* River 4 km south of Bahadurganj town. Extended in about 10 acres the site yields Black-and Red ware, BSW, NBPW, Grey ware and Red ware. Important shapes are bowls, flanged bowls, dishes, lipped basins along with miniature vessels. Other finds are beads of terracotta, carnelian and agate; copper bangles, terracotta animal figurines and pottery discs.

Sikraurdih

This ancient settlement belongs to Kushan-Gupta periods and situated 2 km west of Siuri-Amhat in Muhammadabad Tehsil. Lids and vases of Red ware along with terracotta animal figurines and pestles are the important finds of the site.

Tandwa

This medieval settlement is located 1 km south of Pali.

Urenv

Extended in an area of about 20 acres this site is located 6 km east of Mehraur Chatti in Muhammadabad Tehsil. Having cultural deposit of Kushan, Gupta and post-Gupta periods the site yields only Red ware. Important shapes are lids, sprinklers, and vases. Other important finds are terracotta figurines, balls and pestles. A few fragments of stone sculptures of post-Gupta times were also collected from the surface.

Dhaka Kop

This ancient settlement of Kushan-Gupta times, extended in 10 acres is located 8 km west of Rasara in district-Ballia. The site yields BSW and Red ware of Kushan-Gupta periods. Brickbats of Kushan, Gupta and medieval periods are scattered on the surface. Special mention may be made of 5 copper coins of Kushan period collected by P.Singh and his team.

District-Mau

Adadih

Extended in an area of about 10 acres this mound is located on the Mau-Yusufpur road about 4 km east of Mau. Yielding Red Ware having the shapes of handled *karahis*, lids and sprinklers of Kushana-Gupta period the other small finds include terracotta gamesman, dabber, pestles, discs and human figurines.

Ardauna

This site is located on the northern bank of *Ishakpur Lake* about 10 km west of Ratanpura in Mau district. The site yields Red Ware, BSW, and NBPW.

Aurangabad

It is situated on the right bank of the *Chhoti Saryu*, 2 km north-west of Mau. The mound covers an area of about 5 acres yielding Red Ware, Grey Ware and BSW having the shapes of dishes, bowls, basins, vases and handled *karahi*. Apart from ceramics, terracotta human figurines of Kushana period were also found on the mound.

Bhadesara

About 4 km north of Mau on the right bank of *Chhoti Saryu* this site is extended in an area of about 15 acres. One- third portion of the mound is occupied by the present villagers. Red Ware of Kushana and Gupta periods and burnt bricks of the same period are scattered on the mound. Other finds are terracotta human figurines, balls and pestles.

Bilauwadih

It is located 3 km north-east to Bilauwa and represents relics of medieval period. Red ware along with burnt brick structures have been noticed here.

Chhedapura

About 1 km north-west to Mau Railway Station it is located on the right bank of *Chhoti Saryu*. The mound covers an area of about 5 acres yielding mainly Red Ware. Probably the mound was inhabited during early historic period. Burnt brick structures of early medieval period were noticed in the sections of the mound.

Chorpa Khurd

Extended in an area of about 10 acres this settlement of medieval period is located about 9 km east of Mau on the left bank of *Chhoti Saryu*.

Garha

It is located on the eastern bank of *Garha Tal* about 2 km west from Ratanpura in Mau district. The site yields Red ware, Black-and Red ware, BSW and NBPW. Principal shapes are bowls, dishes, vases and lipped basins. Other finds include terracotta beads, balls and pottery discs.

Garthauli

About 4 km west of Mau extended in an area of 10 acres it is located on the ancient bed of *Chhoti Saryu*. The site yields Black-and-Red ware, BSW, Red ware and Cord-impressed Red ware. Important shapes are pedestalled bowls, vases and beakers. Major part of the mound was occupied by the modern settlers.

Hathini

About 9 km east of Mau the site is located in Maunath Bhanjan Tehsil. Remains of Kushana and Gupta periods were found on the site.

Imlidih

It is located on the left bank of *Bhainsahi* River and covers an area of 10 acres. The site yields Red ware, Grey ware, BSW and NBPW. Important shapes are bowls, dishes and basins. Other finds include terracotta beads.

Intaura

This site is located 8 km north-east to Bahadurganj market in Maunath Bhanjan Tehsil of district-Mau on a small lake near *Kharia Nala*. It is extended in an area of about 5 acres yielding Red ware pottery, terracotta balls and brickbats of medieval period.

Kandhairi

It is located 9 km north-east of Mau. The site yields Red ware pottery, terracotta beads, animal figurines, balls, glass bangles, agate beads and brickbats of Kushan and Gupta periods.

Kunwaridih/Dataura

About 3 km south-west of Ratanpura in Tehsil Maunath Bhanjan, District-Mau this intact mound is extended in an area of about 5 acres. The site yields Red ware, Grey ware, BSW and NBPW along with terracotta beads, gamesman, pestles, iron slags and furnaces.

Maraili

This medieval settlement is located 4 km south-west of Ratanpura.

Mubarakpur

This medieval settlement is located 1 km north to Ratanpura market on Pakwa Inar road in Mau district. The mound covers an area of 5 acres.

Musaldah

About 2 km east of Mau on the Mau-Yusufpur road this mound is on the right bank of *Chhoti Saryu*. Extended in an area of about 10 acres the site yields Red ware, Grey ware, Black Slipped ware and Black-and-Red ware. Important shapes are pedestalled bowls and lipped basins along with terracotta beads and pottery discs.

Nasopur

This medieval site is located 3 km east of Mau on the Mau-Yusufpur road and extends in about 10 acres.

Pilkhi Chaunri

Extended in about 4 acres this medieval settlement is located 5 km west of Ratanpura market in Maunath Bhanjan tehsil of Mau district. The site yields Red ware along with terracotta objects of medieval period.

Piparsath

Located on the right bank of the old bed of *Sarangi Nala*, a tributary of *Chhoti Saryu* this medieval settlement is 1 km east of Thaicha Chatti in Tehsil-Maunath Bhanjan. One can notice here Red ware and *Lakhauri* bricks.

Ratanpur Mathia

This early medieval settlement yielding Red ware pottery is located 4 km south-west of Kopaganj railway station, on the right bank of *Chhoti Saryu*.

Sahroj

It is located 3 km north-west from Kopaganj on the right bank of the *Chhoti Saryu*. The site is extended in about 10 acres yielding burnt brick structures of Kushan-Gupta and medieval times.

Samogar/Ardauna

This site is located 6 km south of Parsa-Mohaddinpur Chatti in Mau tehsil. Extended in an area of 8 acres, the site yields Red ware pottery along with terracotta human figurines and glass bangles. Burnt bricks of Kushan and Gupta periods are visible on the surface. Temple of goddess Samogar and an intermediate school is situated on the mound.

Sarayan Kot

The settlement of medieval period is located 3 km west of Barhua Godam on Mau-Ghazipur road and extends in about 2 acres.

Sarwan

Located on the Mau-Yusufpur road, 6 km east of Mau it is a settlement of medieval period.

Umanpur

About 7 km east of Mau on the Mau-Yusufpur road it is a site of medieval times yielding pottery and structures of medieval period.

Archaeological investigations done along the River *Chhoti Saryu* made it clear that the region was inhabited during Neolithic period. Archaeological sites of the succeeding Chalcolithic culture are noticed at various places in the region. On analogy of the chronological sequence proposed for pre NBPW culture, one may conclude that these sites were inhabited in about 13th century BC. Remains of NBPW culture have also been noticed at many places and found just double in number comparing to the pre-NBPW culture. It indicates an increase in population which forced the people to inhabit new sites. The associated ceramic industries of NBPW like BSW and Grey ware are present on all these sites. During Kushana-Gupta times the number of settlements further increased. It is noticed that while pre-NBPW culture sites are generally confined to the banks of the *Chhoti Saryu,* settlements of Kushana-Gupta times are found in the hinterlands as well. Remains of post-Gupta and medieval times indicate that there is a decrease in the number of sites comparing to Kushana-Gupta periods. Actually the deposits of the medieval period naturally being on the top of the mounds have been badly robbed for burnt bricks by the present inhabitants. They have been eroded by rain water also. For agricultural purposes these sites have also been razed to the ground.

References

Chakrabarti, 2001. *Archaeological Geography of the Ganga Plain: The Lower and the Middle Ganga,* Delhi.

Dubey, S.R., A.K. Singh & G.K. Lama. 2010. "Archaeological Investigation in Ballia District with special reference to Pakkakot." *Puratattva.* 40.

Dubey, S.R., A.K. Singh & G.K. Lama. 2012. *Pakkakot: Some New Archaeological Dimensions of Mid-Ganga Plain.* New Delhi: Rishi Publications.

Singh, P., A.K. Singh and Brahmanand Singh.1994-95. "Protohistoric Investigations in Ballia District." *Pragdhara,* No. 5. Lucknow

Singh, P., A.K. Singh and R.N.Singh.1996-1997. "Explorations along the *Chhoti Saryu* River." *Pragdhara,* No. 7. Lucknow

4

Excavations at Pakkakot, Ballia, UP: 2010-12

The ancient settlement of Pakkakot (Lat. 25^0 45′ 10″ N, Long. 84^0 0′ 30″ E) is located on the ancient bed of the River *Chhoti Saryu* (Tons) in District-Ballia (UP) (Pl.XV). The district is the eastern most part of the state, lies between 25^0 33′and 26^0 11′North Latitude and 83^0 38′ and 84^0 39′ East Longitudes. The district covers an area of 2981 sq km. Ballia got the status of a district on November 1st, 1879. There are 6 Tehsils in the district namely Ballia Sadar, Bansdih, Rasara, Belthara, Bairia and Sikanderpur. Blocks in the district are 17 in number. The district comes under the North-Eastern Railway Zone. It lies on the Main Line of the Chhapra-Varanasi section passing through Aurihar, Ghazipur, Phephana and Ballia. A Branch Line runs from Phephana to Shahganj. The North-Western part of the district is served by the Bhatni-Aurihar-Prayagraj section passing through Indara, Mau, Aurihar, Varanasi and Madho Singh. Metalled roads connect the district with Ghosi, Mau and Ghazipur (Fig.3).

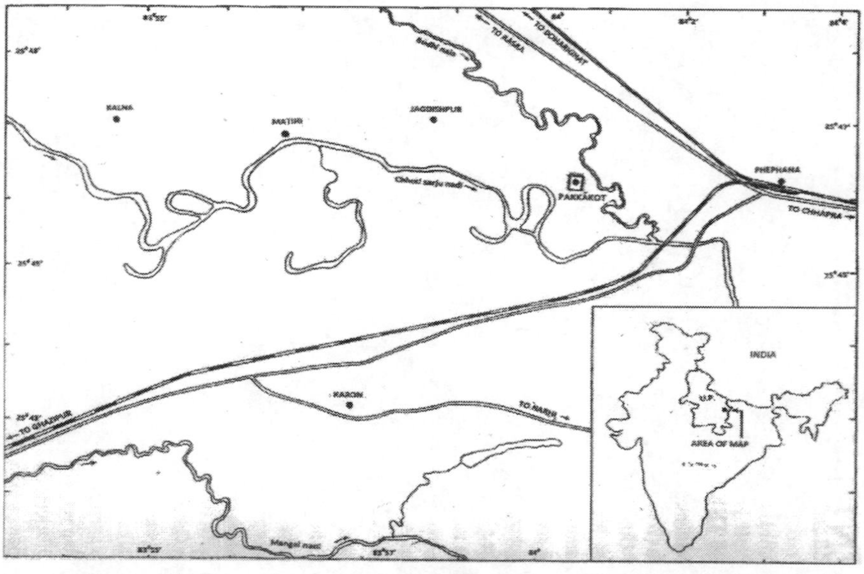

Figure 3: Location map of Pakkakot and adjoining sites

Ballia comprises an irregular shaped tract extending westward from the confluence of the Rivers *Ganga* and the *Ghaghara;* the former separating it from the state of Bihar in the south and the latter from Deoria and Bihar in the north and east respectively (Singh.1973: 20). The boundary between Ballia and Bihar is determined by the deep streams of these two rivers. Ballia is bounded on the west by Azamgarh, on the north by Deoria, on the north-east and south-east by Bihar and on the south-west by Ghazipur (Singh.1973: 24). Physiographically, the area may be divided into two units' *i.e.* central uplands region and lower land tract along the Rivers *Ganga* and the *Ghaghara* (Singh.1965: 165). The uplands comprise the eastern half of the district comprising almost the whole of Rasara Tehsil and a small strip of country extending eastwards into Bansdih and Ballia Tehsils. They extend in the south-west up to the River *Saryu*. In the interior the level is only broken by scattered depressions. The low land tract comprises the rest of the district. The surface of the low land is often very uneven being scored in every direction by irregular depressions. Main source of irrigation is through ground water and canal. For drinking water supply pipe line schemes and hand pumps exist in the district. The main rivers of the district are the *Ganga*, the *Ghaghara* and the *Saryu*. The *Ganga* and the *Ghaghara* cause extensive floods in the district and badly affect the life of the people, property and standing crops (Singh.1973: 27). The tributaries of the *Ghaghara* are small and of an insignificant character. The chief tributary of the *Ganga* is the *Saryu* which separate Ballia from Ghazipur for several miles (Singh.1986: 345). Lakes and tanks are fairly common, the most important being the *Suraha Tal* because of its size (8, 500 Acres). Among other lakes of considerable importance are *Taleji Tal, Goka Tal, Dah Mundiari, Dah Reoti* etc.

Importance of the site

Pakkakot lies on the ancient trade route from Pataliputra to Lumbini via Masarh>Buxur>Tika Deori>Khairadih>Sohgaura>Kopia>Kapilvastu and Lumbini (Chakrabarti.2001: 21). A little beyond Buxur was a major ferry point across Ganga and the modern Railway Bridge to the Ballia side follows broadly this ferry alignment. If this was a ferry point in the ancient context, there should be an ancient site on the other side of the Ganga in this direction. Pakkakot clearly fits the bill of such an ancient settlement. Beyond Pakkakot the other city sites like Jagdishpur, Matahi, Tika Deori and Lakhaneshwaradih on the *Chhoti Saryu* deserve notice. These are early historical sites and are taken together with the general significance of this sector in early historic context. The next fixed point, before one crosses the *Ghaghara* at Turtipar, is Khairadih, a major early historical settlement. Having crossed the *Ghaghara* at Khairadih, the route possibly followed for some time the alignment of what is locally known as 'Ram-Janaki Road' along the *Ghaghara* towards the west. At some point it branched off the Ram-Janaki Road and moves towards Kopia which is a fortified early historic city site passing Sohgaura, an undisputably Mauryan administrative centre on the way. The fixed point in the direction of Lumbini beyond Kopia is Bansi which yielded a fragment of an Asokan pillar capital (Gupta.1980: 27). The place where this fragment was discovered lies a little outside the modern Bansi Bazar, which still remains the most convenient stopping place before proceeding to modern Birdpur, Kapilvastu and Lumbini. Thus, every stage of suggested Pataliputra-Lumbini route there are clear archaeological sign-posts, and we are in a position to claim that this was the most direct route that Asoka could have adopted for visiting Lumbini. There were two major river-crossings on the way, one over the Ganga a liitle to the east of Buxur, and other over the Ghaghara at Turtipar/Khairadih. The geographical situation of Pakkakot made it possible for its inhabitants to have commercial links with other contemporary towns and cities like Rajghat, Pataliputra and Vaishali. The archaeological evidences show that by the Sunga-Kushan period Pakkakot developed into a full-fledged urban centre.

The site of Pakkakot is extended in a wide area and is not comparable to any other sites in Mid-Ganga plain in extension and catchment area. The site is not only extended in about 4x1 km but its catchment area extends in about 8 kms having other sites like Matahi, Jagdishpur, Akauni, Chitbaragaon, Waina, Karo etc. At present the River *Chhoti Saryu* (Tons) flows about 1.5 km south from the site whiles the *Budhi* River (Lakda Nala) flows just north of the site which mingles in *Tons* near Chitbaragaon. The team has observed the unique geographical feature of the site. Contour plan of the site shows that the present mettled road from Sihachaur to Simhapur (Sronipur) was constructed on the same ancient road which was used probably by traders during Sunga-Kushan period and it was continued upto medieval period (Fig.4).

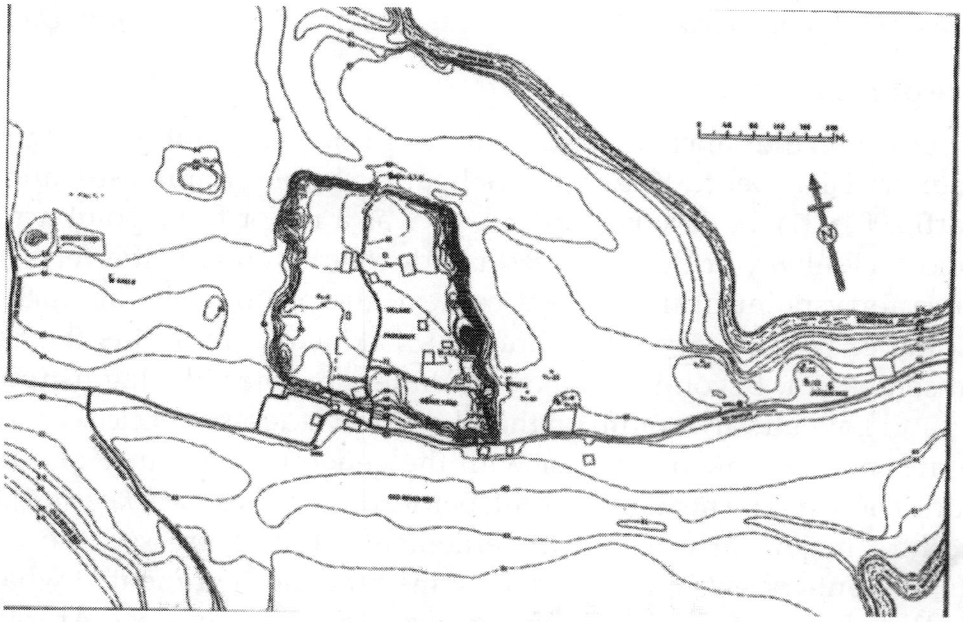

Figure 4: Contour-plan of Pakkakot mounds

It is proved by the ponds and wells which lie on both sides of the present road. The mound of Pakkakot is found covered with fortification walls and four watch-towers which are almost intact. Several walls of burnt brick structures are still visible in the section. A careful anslysis of the pottery and other artefacts recovered during exploration done in 2010 by the author and his team (Prof. S.R.Dubey and Dr. A.K.Singh) show the transition from rural to urban settlement at the ancient site of Pakkakot. The site has got the status of a full-fledged urban centre during Sunga-Kushan periods.

Historicity

In ancient times the region covered by the present district of Ballia lay in the kingdom of Kosala. It is probable that thr River *Ganga* in its sweep towards the north-east of present town formed the boundary of Kosala which included the whole of the present district as far as the junction of the *Sadanira* and the *Gandak* (Pathak.1963:19). The back-strewn mounds and fragmentary remains of structures which evoke memories not only of mythology but also of history are found at a number of places in the district. The ruins in the neighbourhood of Brahmain and Hanumanganj, consisting of a large mound called Mira Dih, covered with broken bricks and pottery of a dark hue, are probably the remains of an ancient city. Khairadih, near Turtipar in Tehsil Rasara, which is also a ruined site of a very ancient city named Bhargavapur, is presumed to have been the place where Rishi Jamadagni used to live. The explorations carried out by the archaeologists of Banaras Hindu University, Varanasi have brought to light relicks of the Black and Red Ware culture (1450-1200 BC) at various sites such as Bhumapar Dih, Bijulipur, Godabirgarh, Lovika ka Topa, Mira Dih, Pakkakot and Wainagarh, indicating that the tract enjoyed settled life and civilization from this early time.

Popular legends also witness to the antiquity of these sites. One such famous legend is related to the village of Karon in Ballia Tehsil; its name being considered to be a corrupted form of the word *Kam-anaunya*. The legend is that Lord Shiva being enraged at the attempts of Kamadeo (the god of love) to beguile him from his meditation, burnt him to ashes at this spot (Mishra.1988:19). Ballia itself is supposed to have derived its name by the eruption of the name Valmiki, the great sage who is said to have had his hermitage or to have dwelt here for some time. It is also associated with Bhrigu, another renowned sage who, according to a local legend, came and dwelt here because of the sacredness of the place. Other Rishis like Garga, Parashar, Vashishtha and Atri are traditionally believed to have visited the neighbourhood of Ballia attesting to the sacredness of its environs extending to a circuit of about 16 km. according to tradition, Hansnagar (town of swans), a village 9.6 km east of Ballia, is said to taken its name from the legend that a swan turned into a man and a crow into a swan by drinking the water of the holy river Ganga at this place. At a distance of about 137 km from Ballia there is an ancient tank named *Dharmaranava Pokhara* where an excavation is said to have revealed that thousands of Rishis practiced austerities there and that to the north and east of it there were traces of the previous existence of an ancient forest, probably a remnant of the ancient *Aranya*. Some other places of the district are also associated with the Vedic sages. Bhalsand in Tehsil Ballia is said to have derived its name from Bhardwaja who resided here for some time and Dhuband, also in Tehsil Ballia, to be a corrupt name of Durvasa, signifying the abode of Durvasa, a celebrated Rishi.

The early political history of this region is complex. Accortding to the Puranic tradition the Solar dynasty of Kshatriyas, founded by one Manu, was the earliest known dynasty which give Kosala a systematic form of government and of which Ikshvaku, the eldest son of Manu, famed in Vedic tradition, was the first ruler. The line that descended from Ikshvaku produced a number of illustrious kings till the accession of Rama who was the greatest ruler of this dynasty. Lakhaneshwardih in Tehsil Rasara is named after Lakshman, the brother of Rama, who is said to have visited this place and built a temple in honour of Lord Shiva. The remains of an ancient town are still to be seen on the high band of the river in the form of immense piles of ruins, from which numerous pieces of sculptures have been obtained from time to time which bear testimony to the fact that even in those early times it was a settled abode with a flourishing population. The site was excavated in 1956-57 by K.M.Nagar, the then Director, State Museum, Lucknow, which yielded NBPW, terracotta figurines, stone pestles etc. (*IAR* 1956-57: 29). Lakshman's son Chandraketu, entitled Malla (valiant) in the *Ramayana*, established a kingdom known as the Malla state, of which some portion of Ballia district formed a part. It is probable that the territories of the Mallas touched those of Kashi in the south, Magadha in the south-east and Kosala in the south-west, of which an area of the present day Ballia district then formed a part. It came to be the largest and the most important of the autonomous states of Kosala in respect of territorial extent and political influence.

In 6th century BC, Kosala came to be known as one of the 16 Mahajanapadas. At that time it was ruled by king Mahakosala. His son Prasenjit, the last great monarch of the solar dynasty of Kosala, was an important figure of his time. During his reign the kingdom attained great glory and prosperity. The Malla kingdom also figured as one of the 16 Mahajanapadas with an independent entity and status equal to that of Kosala itself. Its chief Bandhula was a close ally of Prasenjit as well as of Mahali, the Lichchavi prince of Vaishali. They were deeply influenced by the teachings of two great religious exponents-Mahavira and Buddha and Jainism and Buddhism found many followers among the Mallas. The period gave rise to a different culture that of the NBPW, as has been revealed by explorations conducted at Ajaneraghar, Bhimapurdih, Bijulipur, Godabirgarh and Masumpur. After Prasenjit the kingdom of Kosala began to decline rapidly and the history of this area is shrouded in obscurity.

The existence of numerous ruined forts and other remains in the district connected with Bhars and the Cherus in legend and folklore point to the fact that they might have held domination over the major part of the district at that time. The Bhars were the occupants of the western part of the district. According to the local legend the heaps of the broken earthen bricks in the parganas of Lakhneshwar, Bhadaon and Sikandarpur belong to the time of Bhars. The Cherus probably ruled over the eastern half of the district. Kopachit in Tehsil Rasara is believed to have been the western limit of the Cheru dominion. Tradition states that Bansdih lay in the heart of the Cheru country. Though no remains attributable to the group are found in Bansdih itself, the remnants of a fort are in the neighbouring area and now almost deserted village of Deorhi. A number of places in Ballia Tehsil are also associated with this group. Karnai is believed to have been originally owned by the Cherus. Garwar is alleged to have been founded by them and a small mound near the village and a large brick mound at Zirabasti are presumed to be the debris of Cheru strongholds. Extensive ruins at Pakkakot are also said to be the debris of a fort and other buildings dating back to the time when the Cherus ruled the district. According to tradition the large inland lake, the *Suraha Tal* at Basantpur, was constructed by the Cherus but no traces are found of any artificial construction. The significance of the tradition implies how completely the power of the Cherus has been impressed upon the imagination of the people.

About the middle of the 4th century BC the realm of Kosala was brought to an end by Mahapadma Nanda, who has been described in the Puranas as the exterminator of the Kshatriya race and who, by uprooting the Kosalans, extended his empire over the major part of the region. He was the first great historical emperor of northern India. But a part of the district under the Mallas did not come under the domination of this emperor as they saved their authority and existence by merely accepting the supremacy of the Nandas. The Nandas were supplanted by the Mauryas under Chandragupta (324-300 BC) who ruled over a vast empire and the district became a part of the Mautya dominion except the portion under the Mallas, which remained independent. Kautilya, who took a leading part in this revolution, mentions in his *Arthashastra* that this republic was Sangha or a state in a federation. He enjoins upon Chandragupta Maurya to cultivate friendship with the Mallas: "It was better to have a Sangha on your side than to acquire an army or to secure an ally." The most illustrious king of this dynasty was Asoka (273-236 BC), Chandragupta's grandson, who became a Buddhist and combined in himself the zeal of a monk with the wisdom of a king. The explorations show the possibility of remains of a stupa at Matahi, Ballia, and the ruins of Buddhist monasdteries here and at Brahmain. The latter has remains of old walls and very large bricks measuring about 45x23x11 cm and many carved and ornamental specimens.

After the decline of the Mauryas a new dynasty that of the Sungas came to power under Pushyamitra (187-151 BC) whose dominion covered only the central portion of the Maurya Empire. The fact is confirmed by an inscription found at Ayodhya, describing him as the lord of Kosala. As he uprooted the Malla republic, the whole of the area covered by the district came under his sway. During his reign, the Greeks of Bactria invaded India and it is likely that the district also suffered the effects of the invasion of Menander, who carried his arms for Madhyamika, Saketa and Pataliputra. The history of the district in the era immediately following the fall of the Sungas is shrouded in obscurity till the advent of the Kushanas. That Ballia became a part of the Kushan dominion is undoubted as evinced by the finding of a large number of coins, mostly of this period, in the ruins of Khairadih. The large bricks, measuring

60x45.13 cm, found in the ruins are a witness to the antiquity and the prosperity of the place.

After the dismemberment of the Kushan empire the history of Ballia is mostly enveloped in darkness but a glimpse of the history of the district is provided by a number of inscribed coins found at the ancient city of Ayodhya of certain rulers such as Satyamitra, Ayumitra (Aryamitra), Sanghamitra, Vijayamitra, Devamitra, Ajavarman and Kumudasen, who had flourished after the end of the Kushan rule in present eastern UP including the area then covered by district Ballia. Among aforesaid rulers, only Kumudasena was called a Raja. It is surmised that the Guptas, probably Samudragupta, conquered this region and annexed it to the empire in the 4th century CE. During the reign of his son, Chandragupta II (380-413 CE), the celebrated Chinese pilgrim Fa-hian (400-411 CE) came to India to pay homage to the holy places related to Buddhism. He mentions that on his way from Kashi to Pataliputra, he came across a Buddhist monastery and a Buddhist temple which bore the name of 'the vast solitude.' The Indian name is not given but the literal translation of the term used is 'Vrihadaranya' or 'Bidaran.' The decline of the Gupta Empire was precipitated by the assumption of independence by its feudatories. About the beginning of the 2nd quarter of the 6th century CE Yashodharman of Malwa overran the whole of northern India and Ballia seemd to have come under his meteoric sovereignty after which it passed under the rule of the Maukharis of Kannauj. They established an empire comprising the whole of modern UP in addition to a large part of Magadha. Thus the glory of Magadha was eclipsed with the rising power of Kannauj. The Maukharis were succeeded by Harshavardhan (606-647 CE) who established an extensive empire, and Ballia formed a part of the Vardhan Empire. During his reign another famous Chinese pilgrim Hiuen-tsang (629-644 CE) visited India and passed through this district on his way from Varanasi to Nepal. He describes the Buddhist monastery of 'Aviddhakarba' which he calls 'A-pi-te-ka-la-na Sangharama' (the monastery of the brethren with unpierced ears) situated close to the town of Ballia. According to him this monastery had been built for the use of Buddhist pilgrims. From there he went to the temple of Narayana, which he describes as being of two stories with halls and terraces beautifully adorned with the most marvelous sculptures in stone in the most beautiful style of art. Carlleyle identified the ruins of an ancient temple at Narainpur in Tehsil Ballia with the remains of the temple mentioned by the pilgrim.

After the death of Harsha his empire broke up and anarchy prevailed for about half a century. The history of Ballia between Harsh's death and the rise of Yashovarman, nearly three quarters of a century, is again obscure. Yashovarman must have reigned in the latter part of the 7th and 1st part of the 8th century CE and the district Ballia is likely to have formed an integral part of his dominion. After Yashovarman the kingdom of Kannauj (which included modern UP) was a dependency of the empire of Dharmapala of Bengal, who nominated Chakrayudha as the ruler of Kannauj but who was to be directly subordinate to him. In the 1st part of the 9th century, probably soon after the capture of Kannauj by Nagabhatta II, it came under the sway of the rising power of the Gurjar Pratiharas of whom Bhoja was the strongest ruler in northern India. He maintained peace in his kingdom and defended it against external dangers but the power of the Gurjar Pratiharas began to decline in the latter half of the 10th century and was brought to an end by Mahmud Ghazani's invasion in 1018 CE. The downfall of the Gurjar Pratiharas was followed by a period of chaos which came to an end in the last decade of the 11th century by the establishment of the Gahadwala dynasty at Kannauj under Chandradeva. The only reference of this suzerainty is that he was the protector of the holy places of Kashi, Kusika (Kannauj), Uttarakosala (Ayodhya) and the city of Indra (Indraprastha). It will thus be sen that Chandradeva'a jurisdiction comprised almost the whole of present UP. Therefore, it may be presumed that the district of Ballia was also under his control. Reference to a Rajput Raja Ramdeo of Haldi, who ruled in the 11th and 12th centuries CE, shows that some parts of the district were subjugated by local chiefs.

Previous Archaeological Investigations

Inspite of rich archaeological wealth and hoary past, Ballia has not received adequate attention of archaeologists. Archaeological remains recovered from District-Ballia push back the permanent settlements of human habitation from Neolithic to Medieval period. For the first time archaeological investigations in this region was done by A.C.L.Carlleyle who explored a few sites of archaeological importance in 1874-75 under the guidance of Alexander Cunningham. After that exploration work was carried out byA.Fuhrer in 1891 and subsequently by the Department of Ancient Indian History, Culture and Archaeology, Banaras Hindu University in early sixties and after that in 1994-95 (*IAR*.1963-64:43; Singh and Singh.1994-95:21-36). In this connection Black-and-Red wares were reported from Bhimapurdih, Bijalipur, Godabirgarh, Lovika-ka-Tapa, Khairadih, Pakkakot and Waina. The same university has conducted archaeological excavations at Khairadih during 1980-86 and in 1996-97 (Singh.1987-88:28-34; 1990-91:78-86; Tripathi *et al*.2004:1-70). The excavations revealed the deposits of Chalcolithic period to Kushan period (Fig. 5).

The ancient site of Lakhaneshwaradih was excavated in 1956-57 by a team of State Museum, Lucknow which yielded NBPW, stone pestles, terracotta figurines etc, (*IAR*.1956-57:24). An extensive village to village survey was conducted by Banaras Hindu University in 1993-94 (Singh *et al*.1994-95:21-36); the sites reported were: Janwan, Bhunadih, Alam ka Tola, Zimichak, Chhatarsand, Karsanar, Isar, Pithapatti, Halpur, Deorhi, Muryari, Chandayar (all located in Tehsil-Bansdih), Waina situated on Ballia-Ghazipur Road, Sihpur and Kurmipur located in Tehsil-Ballia, Pakkakot, Jagdishpur and Hajauli located on Ballia-Rasara Road and Tika Deori, Unai, Lakhneshwaradih and Surwaradih on Ballia-Mau Road. All these sites were reported to be Chalcolithic, NBPW and of historical periods. Among aforesaid sites Waina (1995) and Bhunadih (1996) were excavated. The protohistoric settlement of Waina is situated on the ancient bed of *Chhoti Saryu*. Here the excavation revealed deposits of Neolithic to Post Gupta period ranging in date from pre 2nd millennium BC to CE

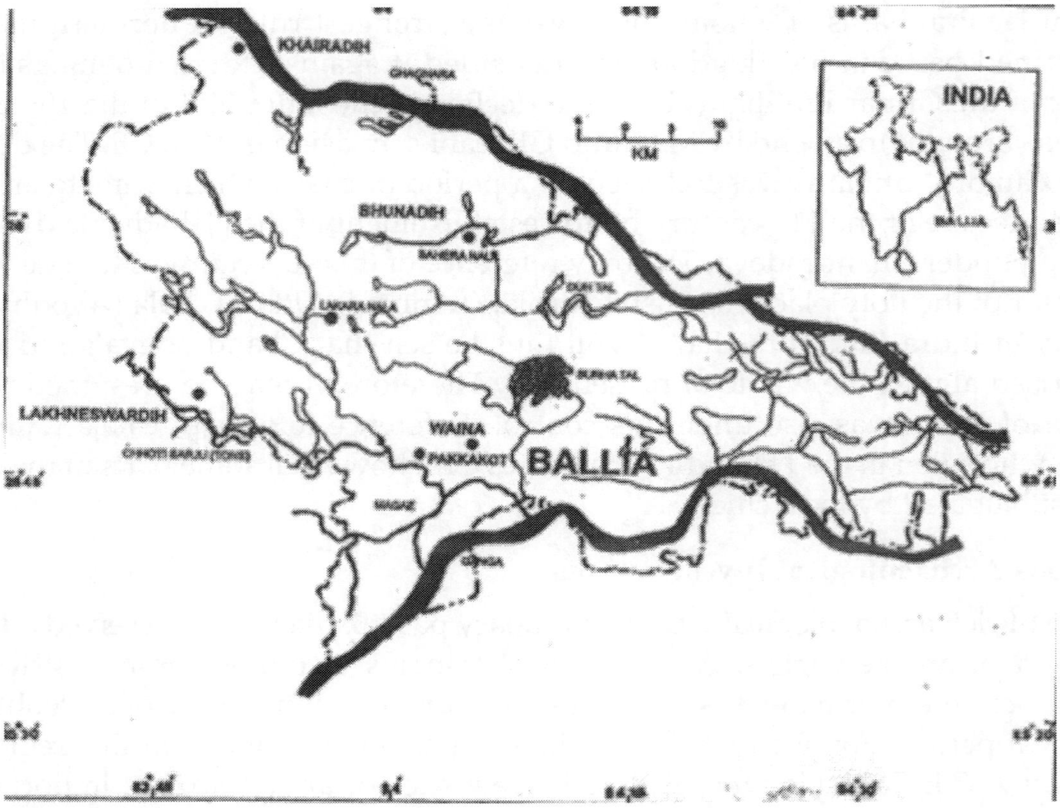

Figure 5: Excavated sites of Ballia District

700 (Singh *et al.*1995-96:41-61). Bhunadih, located 2 km east of Janwan on the right bank of Bahera Nala, about 28 km north of Ballia town on Ballia-Sikanderpur Road was excavated in 1996 which revealed two fold cultural sequence from Neolithic to Chalcolithic culture ranging in date from pre 2nd millennium BC to 1st millennium BC (Singh *et al.*1997-98:11-29).

Exploration: 2010-11

An exploration work conducted by the author and his team (Prof. S.R.Dubey, Prof R.N.Singh, Dr. A.K.Singh, Dr. S.K.Singh, Mr. B.K.Sinha, Mr. A.K.Pandey and Mr. Rambadan Ram, Mr. Shiv Kumar and Shiv Shankar Prajapati) at Pakkakot and its peripheral area in the month of July, 2010 resulted in some new dimensions (Dubey *et al.*2010:200-204). The location of the site is very important as it lies on the ancient route of Pataliputra to Kapilavastu. The cultural relics obtained during exploration are ascribable from Neolithic to Kushan period. The pottery of Cord-impressed Red Ware, Black-and-Red Ware, Black Slipped Ware, Grey Ware and Red Ware has been recovered from the site. The principal types in these wares are bowls, vases, dishes and basins. Several antiquities of terracotta like human and animal figurines, beads, balls and discs were also recovered from the mound. A furnace, probably of iron, alongwith iron slags is intact in the eroded western section of the mound. The pottery repertoire recovered during exploration suggests the Neolithic presence with some sherds of Cord-impressed pottery. This cultural sequence is known at Bhunadih which is situated 30 km north-east from the site. We may compare the resemblance of pottery with similar type of sites such as Chirand, Senuwar etc. The present village of Pakkakot occupies western as well as southern portion of the mound. Many modern houses were constructed with the help of ancient bricks of the mound. The people are rapidly destroying the cultural remains of the site. Before the site looses its archaeological importance, the present team has decided to excavate the site. Archaeological Survey of India, Govt. of India, New Delhi has permitted our team to do so. Excavation of the site in two seasons' *i.e.*2010-11 and 2011-12 has answered many unknown facets of history. It supplemented our knowledge of the archaeology of this region as well as the cultural history of the site. The excavation also provided informations regarding its link with other Neolithic sites such as Bhunadih and Chirand located about 30 and 40 km north-east and east from the site.

Excavations: 2010-2012

Aims and Objectives

The site was excavated in two seasons' *i.e.*2010-11 and 2011-12 under the joint direction of the author and Prof S.R.Dubey and Dr.A.K.Singh alongwith other team members namely Dr. S.K.Singh, Mr. B.K.Sinha, Mr. A.K.Pandey, Mr. Rambadan Ram, Mr. Shiv Kumar and Shiv Shankar Prajapati. The mound is extended in a wide area, about 2 km square and located on at least four different mounds at the site. Following are the aims and objectives of the excavation:

- To know the cultural sequence of the site.
- To locate the fortification-wall and the moat.
- Trace out the main entrance of the fortified area.
- To know the purpose of the watch-towers.
- Horizontal excavation to find out structural remains.
- Find out other sites in the surrounding area.
- Similarities and dissimilarities with other sites of Mid-Ganga plain.
- Find out the possibility about trade linkage from other contemporary sites of the region.

The main challenge of the first year excavation was to know the cultural sequence of all the four mounds. We opened 16 trenches on different mounds. During excavation the behaviour of the River *Tons* was noticed and found that it has played a vital role in the settlement of the inhabitant of the site in different periods. On account of menace of the river, the inhabitants were forced to settle at the safer places in different periods. It is well proved from the flood deposits in the section of the trenches. In the later period the inhabitants made fortification and watch-towers for the security reasons.

The Cutting and Stratigraphy

There are four mounds at the site extended in area of more than 2 km. Sixteen trenches were excavated at different places of the mounds. Trench nos.1-8 was taken on mound-2 which is main fortified mound. Of these, trench nos 1-4 are located in the eastern portion of the main mound while trenches 5, 7 and 8 are situated on the northern outer fringe outside the main entrance (Pl.XVI-XVII). A number of seals and sealings were recovered from these trenches. A burnt brick wall of 14 courses of Mauryan period was noticed in trench no. 7 (Pl. XVIII). After cutting the section in the eastern portion of the mound, a furnace and a burnt brick wall were visible. To know the cultural context of both the furnace and the wall four trenches (1, 2, 3 and 4) were taken in this area. The burnt brick structure was running in north-south direction and it was made by Sunga bricks (Pl.XIX). Due to some geological disturbances this wall was twisted on one side. The furnace with three holes for fitting the pipe was noticed. A chamber with full of ash was noticed nearby this furnace. Seven post-holes presumably for a circular hut alongwith rammed floor were noticed nearby the furnace (Pl. XX; Fig. 6). The furnace and the structure belong to NBPW period. The purpose and use of the furnace are still uncertain. Trench no.6 is located almost in the centre of the mound which was excavated up to natural soil (Pl. XXI; Fig.7) which provided the cultural sequence of Mound-2, while the other trenches were partly excavated. A burnt brick wall of nine courses of Kushan period was noticed in this trench (Pl. XXII). This wall was further used in Period V as well with its 11 courses (Fig. 8). Two ovens of Period IV were noticed in Trench 6 (Pl. XXIII). The burnt brick structures had been heavily robbed and damaged by the local people. Traces of destruction were noticed in Trench nos. 5, 6, 7 and 8. Trench nos. 9, 10, 13 and 14 were exposed on Mound-1 which located about 400 m south-east of the main mound. Trench nos. 10 and 13 were found badly disturbed although they have been excavated up to natural soil. Trench nos. 9 and 14 were dug up to natural soil which provided the first three periods (Pl. XXIV-XXV). Mound-3 is situated about 500 m east from Mound-1. Trench nos. 11, 12 and 15 were opened on this mound. Trenches 11 and 12 were excavated up to natural soil (Figs. 9-10). Trench 15 was found disturbed and was partly excavated. A ring-well (Pl. XXVI) was noticed in Trench-11 which was exposed up to a depth of 2.20 m. Mound-4 is situated 500 m west from Mound-2. Trench-16, situated on the northern fringe of the mound, was excavated up to the natural soil. All the trenches were measuring 5x5 m except Trench-8 which measures 3x5 m.

Cultural Sequence

The limited excavations carried out on Mound nos. 1-4 had brought to light a five fold cultural sequence ranging in date from 5000 BCE to 7th century CE without ant break in between all of them. All the five periods were characterized by their typical ceramic industry and other objects. The features of these periods are described below:

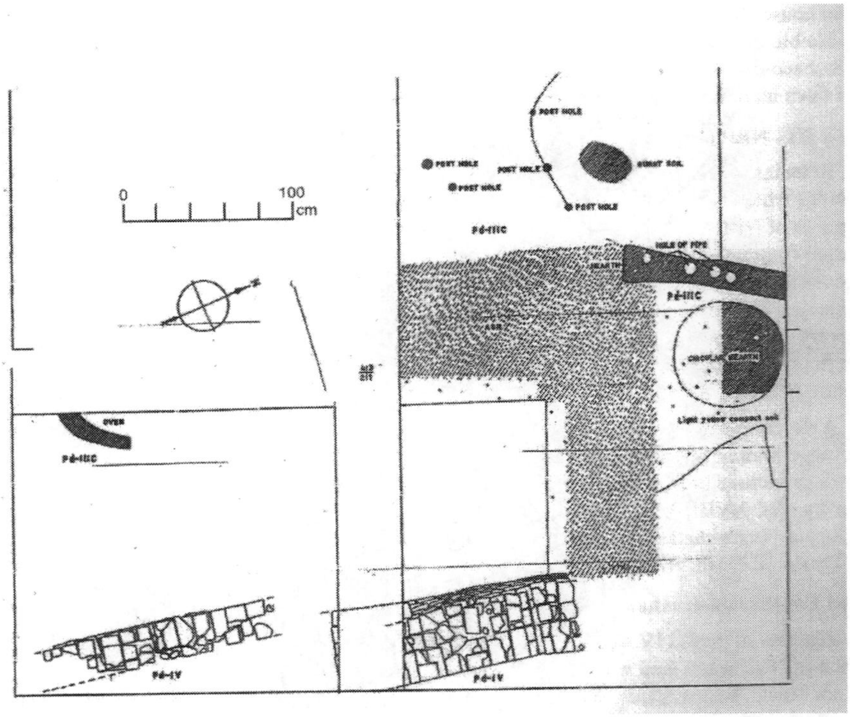

Figure 6: Plan of structures of Period III and IV (Trenches 1, 2, 3)

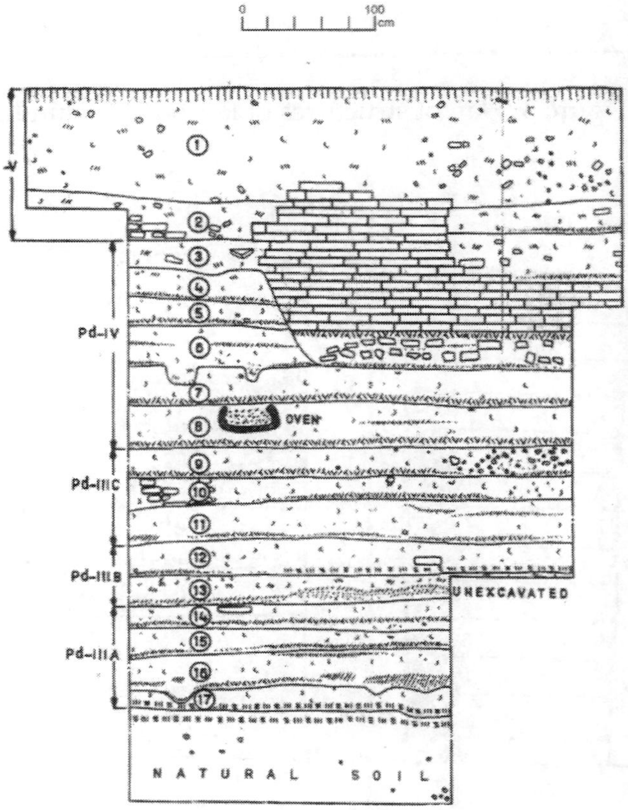

Figure 7: Section of Trench 6, Mound-2

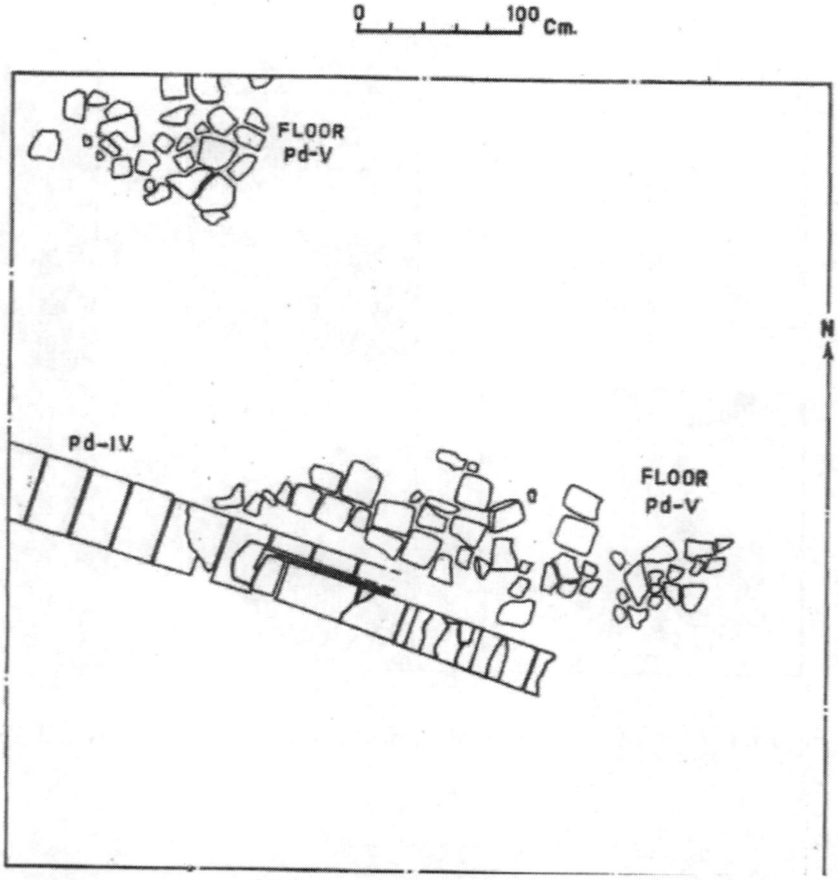

Figure 8: Plan of structures of Period V, Mound-2

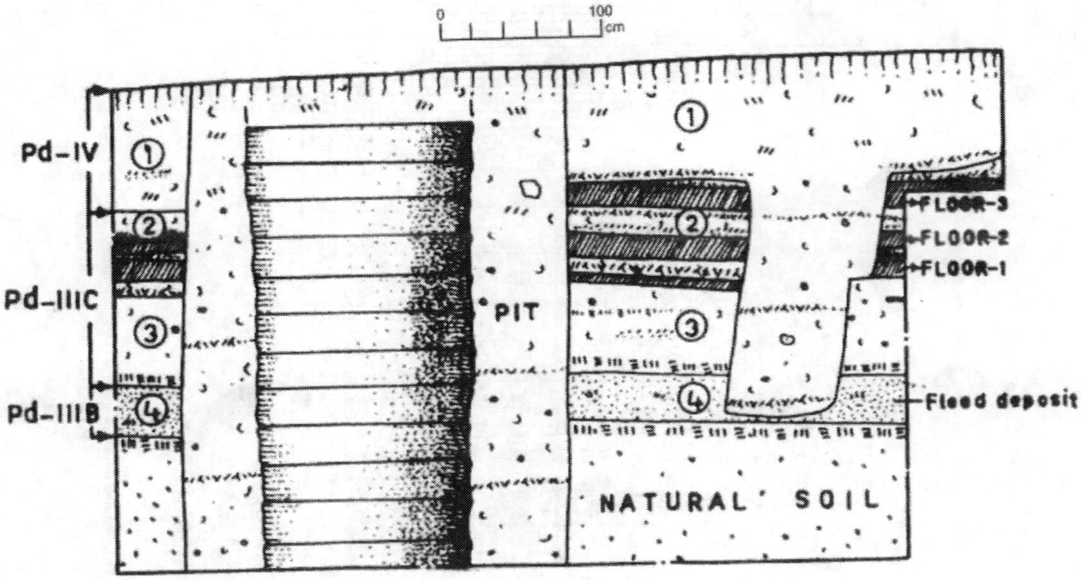

Figure 9: Section of Trench 11, Mound-3

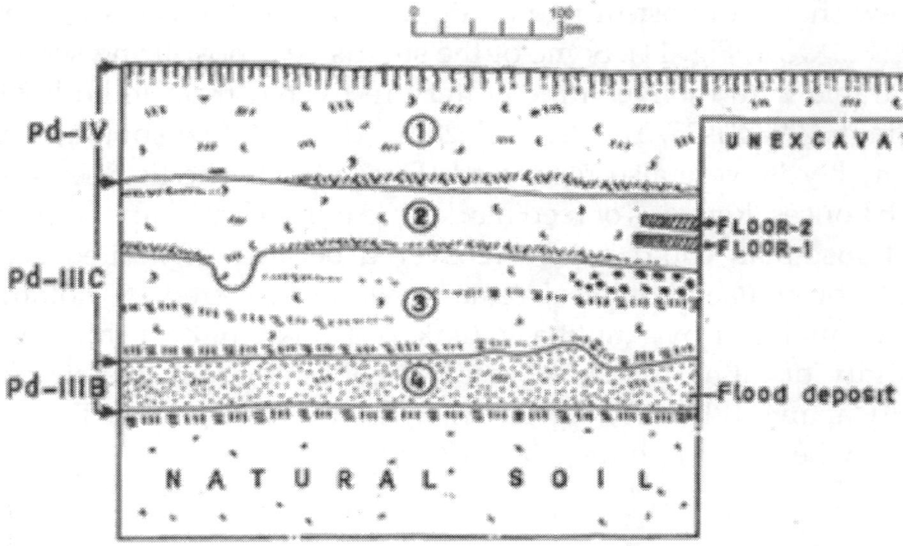

Figure 10: Section of Trench 12, Mound-3

Period I: Neolithic

The deposit of early habitation was found on Mound-1 only represented by about 45 cm of cultural deposit. It is marked by the pottery of Cord-impressed Red Ware and Plain Red Ware (Pls. XXVII-XXVIII; Figs. 11-15). The principal shapes are vases

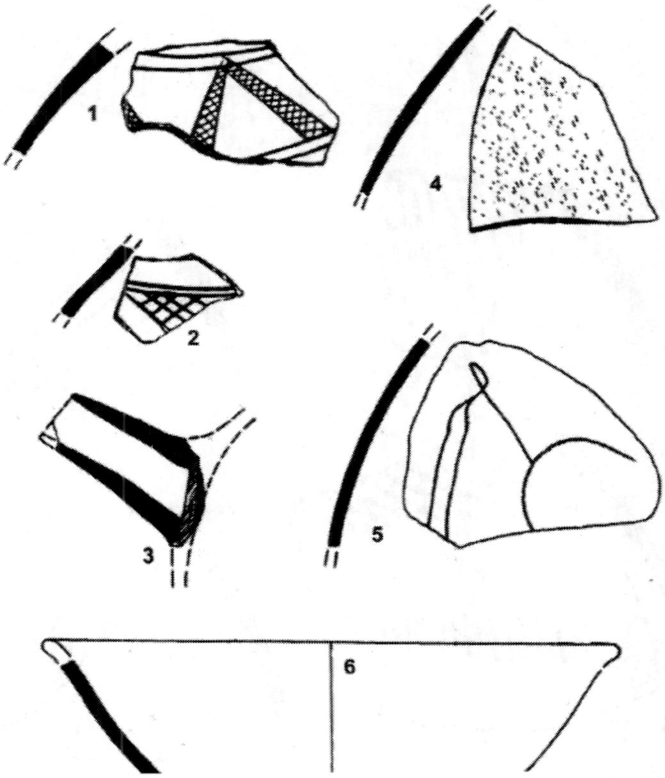

Figure 11: Vessels of Red Ware with post-firing designs, Period-I

and bowls. A few sherds of post-firing painting, mostly on the vases were recovered from this level (Pl. XXIX; Fig. 11). Some of the sherds bear post-firing scratching and are well comparable with the Neolithic pottery recovered from Imlidih Khurd and Lahuradeva (Singh.1993:21-35; Tewari *et al*. 2002: 54-62). A few spouted vessels and appliqué design sherds were also recovered (Figs. 14-15). The first settlers lived in wattle and daub houses. Remains of reed marks and burnt clay lumps were recovered. The complete house-plan could not be recovered because of limited excavations. A good quantity of archaeo-botanical remains were recovered by flotation which was scientifically analysed by Anubha Pathak and R.N.Singh in the departmental lab. Good quantity of faunal remains was also collected from this stratum which was scientifically analysed by P.P.Joglekar of Deccan College, Pune. The small finds include bone arrowheads and pottery discs (Pl. XXX- XXXI).

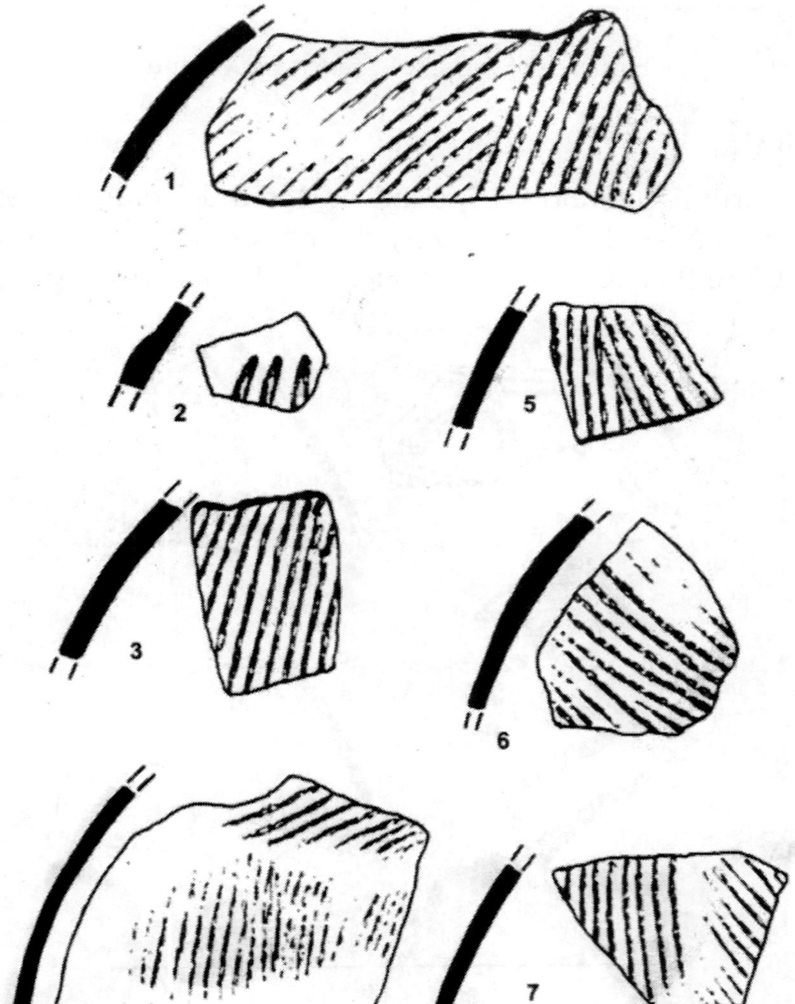

Figure 12: Vessels of Cord-impressed Red Ware, Period-I

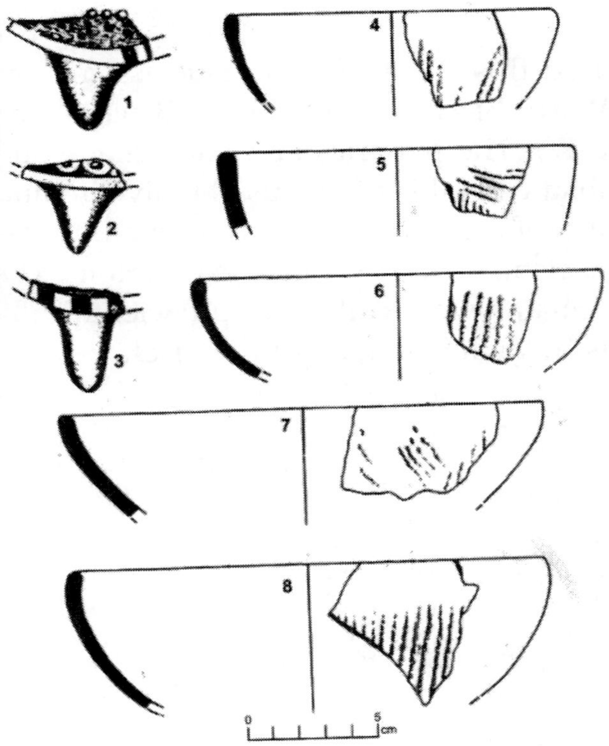

Figure 13: Bowls and footed vessels of Red Ware, Period-I

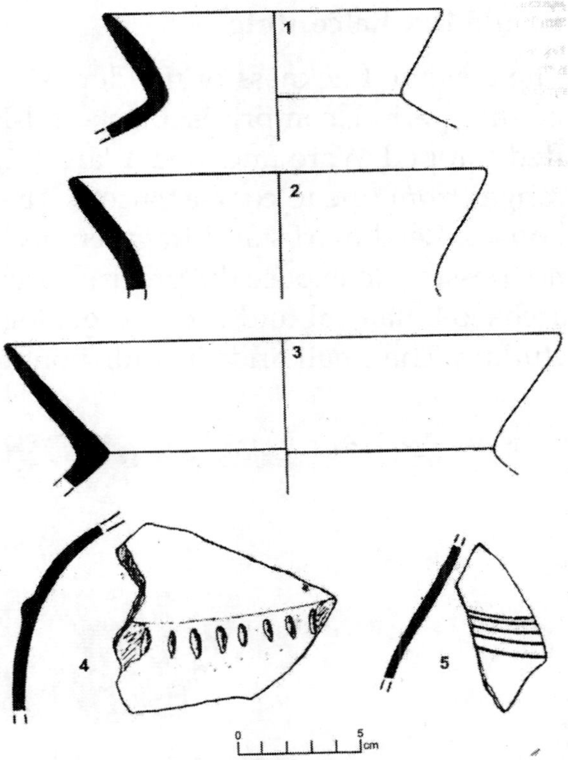

Figure 14: Vases of Red Ware, Period-I

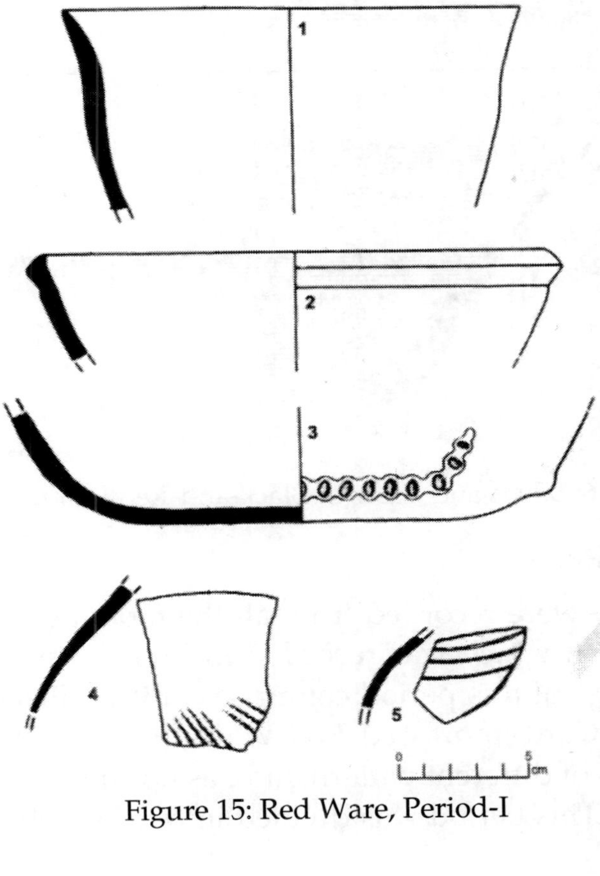

Figure 15: Red Ware, Period-I

Period II: Chalcolithic

The average thickness of the deposit of Period-II is 60 cm. The ceramic assemblage of this period comprises Black-and-Red Ware, Black Slipped Ware, Black Ware, Red Slipped Ware and Red Ware (Figs. 16-17). The potteries are wheel-made and ranges from fine to coarse variety. The inhabitants of this period used to live in mud houses. Reed marks and fragmentary remains of burnt mud were recovered. It was not possible to expose the precise nature of structures due to limited excavations. The archaeo-botanical and archaeo-geological remains were collected and scientifically studied. The small finds include bone-points, arrowheads and pottery discs.

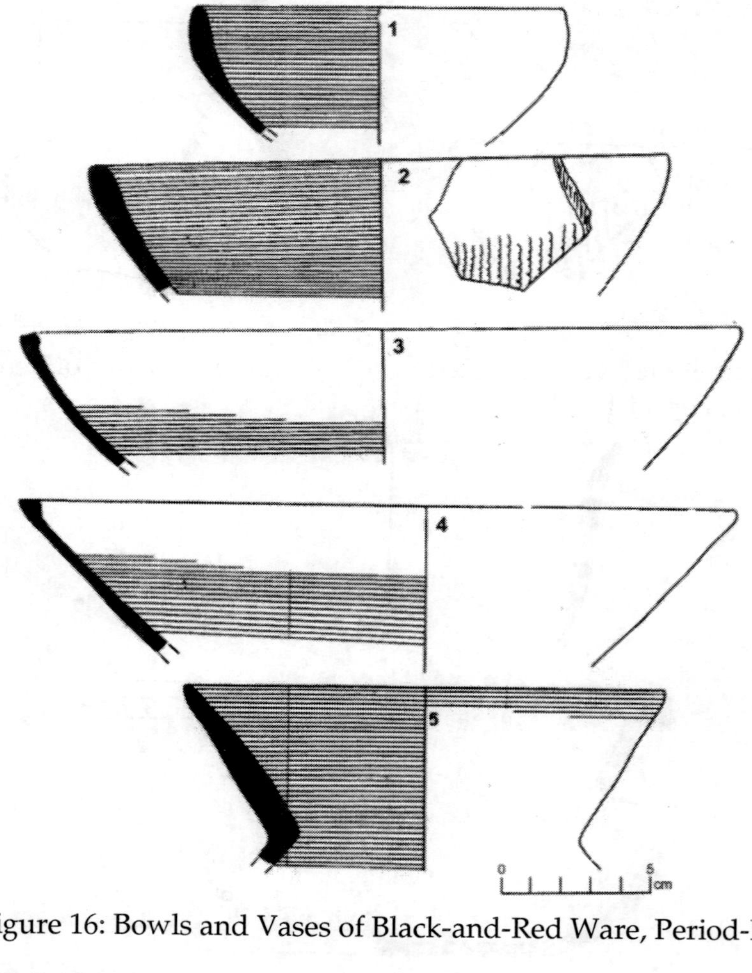

Figure 16: Bowls and Vases of Black-and-Red Ware, Period-II

Period III: NBPW Period

Remains of this period were recorded from all the mounds. The cultural deposit of this period is about 3 m which was recorded in Trench no. 6 of the main mound. The ceramic assemblage of this period comprises NBPW, Black Slipped Ware, Grey Ware, Red Ware and Cord-impressed Red Ware (Fig. 18-28). The Cord-impressed design of this period is of different pattern and has no similarities with Neolithic and Chalcolithic potteries. This period was divided into three sub-periods *i.e.* III A, III B

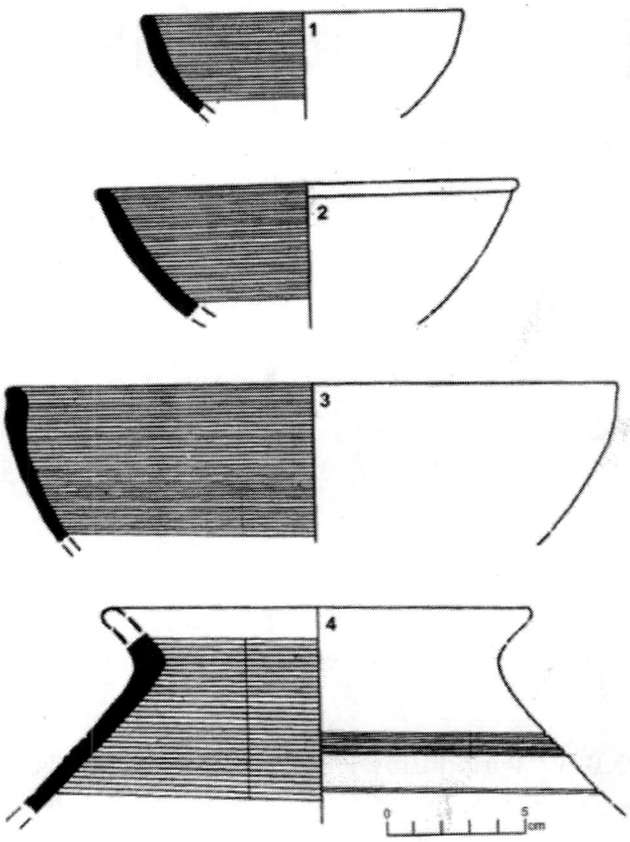

Figure 17: Bowls and Vases of Black-and-Red Ware, Period-II

and III C on the basis of ceramics. The structures of this period comprised of post-holes and wattle-and-daub also. A noteworthy discovery of this period is a circular structure. Remains of post-hole of this structure alongwith rammed burnt floor was recorded in Trench-4. A furnace, possibly for pottery making, was noticed nearby this structure (Pl. XX).

A silver female figurine is a rare discovery from pre- Mauryan level (Pl. XXXII). This is a unique finding because such a silver figurine has not been reported from any other site in India. There are no silver ores in India. Most of the silver is obtained as a by-product of the smelting of lead ores. The major source of silver has been the argentiferous lead-zinc ores of the Dawdwin mines in Myanmar and the Zewar mine, Dist. Udaipur, Rajasthan. It is quite likely that silver ores were also obtained from Baluchistan, Afghanistan, Iran etc. A small amount of silver could have come from the gold mines of south India where this metal is found naturally alloyed with gold and is believed to have been used since the Harappan period (Ghosh. 1989 : 326-327). A silver bangle and a few silver fragments are reported from Lothal. One hundred two silver plates were recovered in association with the Copper Hoards from Gangaeria. A hoard of silver punch-marked coins was discovered from Narhan (Singh. 1994. Pls. LVI-LVII).The regular use of silver is marked by the introduction of silver punch-marked coins by 600 BC. Silver is reputed to have been worked in antiquity.

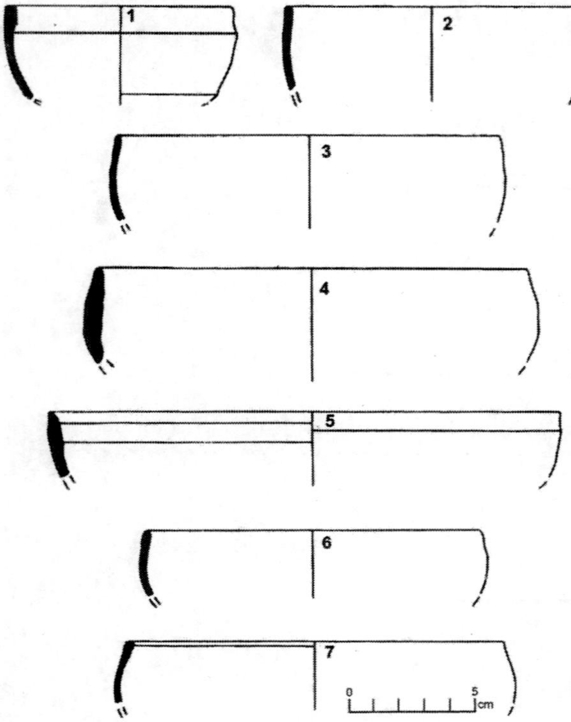

Figure 18: Bowls of NBPW, Period III A

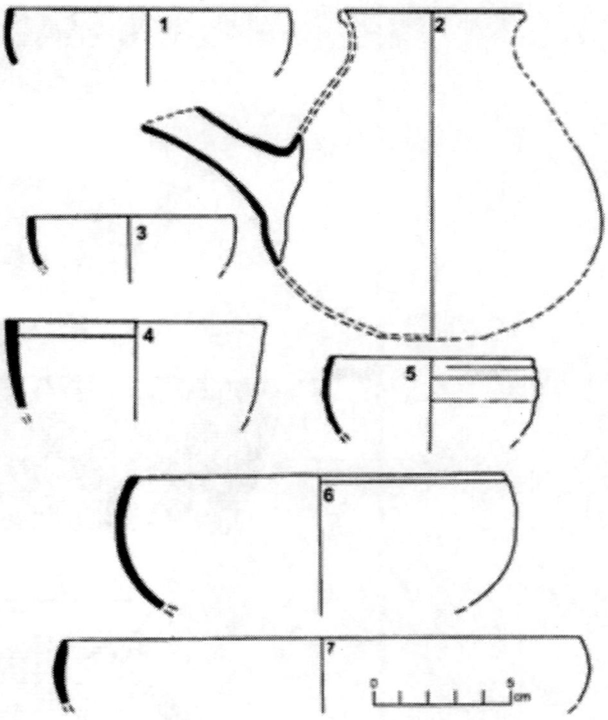

Figure 19: Bowls of Black slipped Ware and NBPW, Period III A

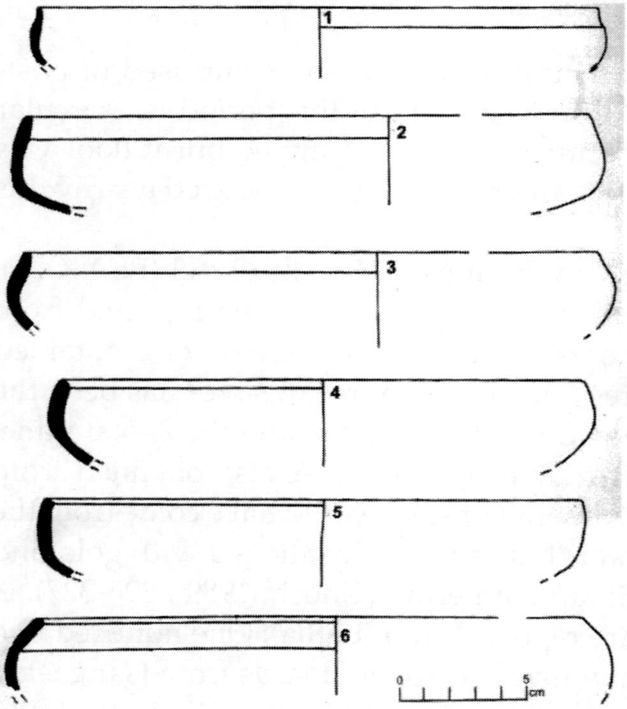

Figure 20: Dishes of NBPW, Period III A

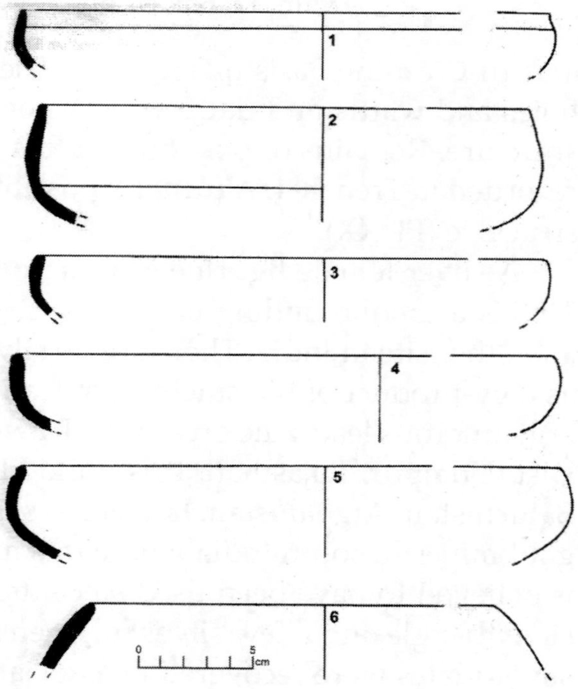

Figure 21: Dishes of Black slipped Ware and NBPW, Period III A

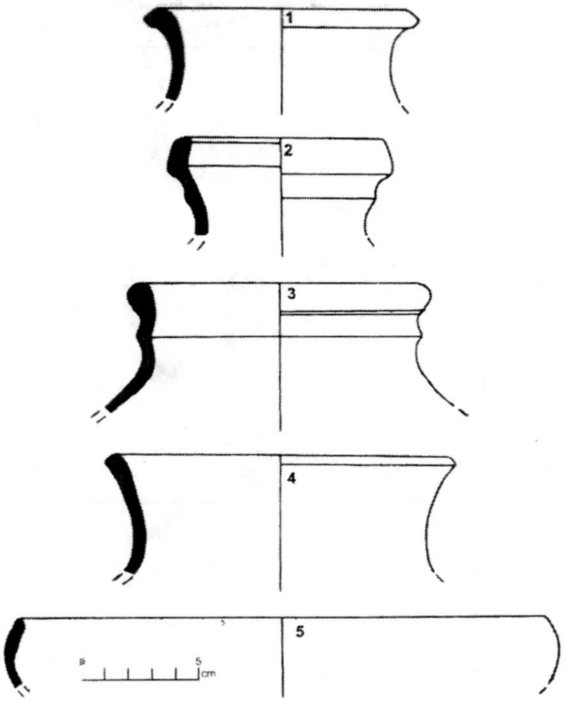

Figure 22: Vases and dishes of Red Ware, Period III A

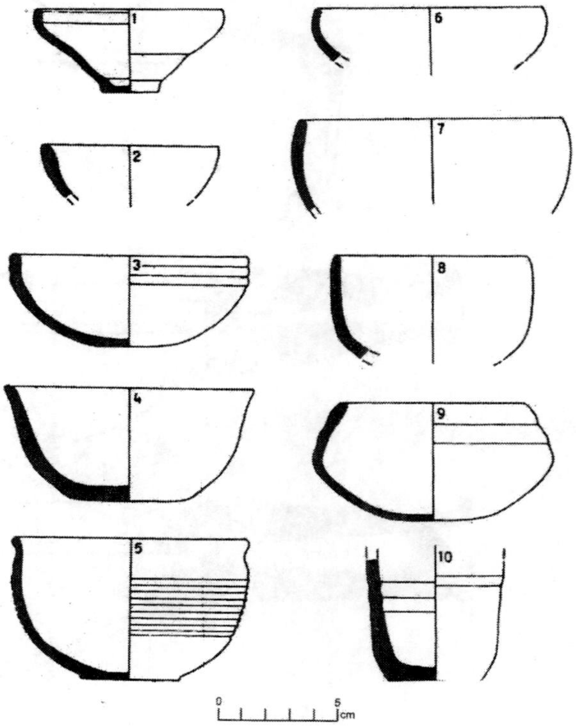

Figure 23: Bowls of Red Ware, Period III B

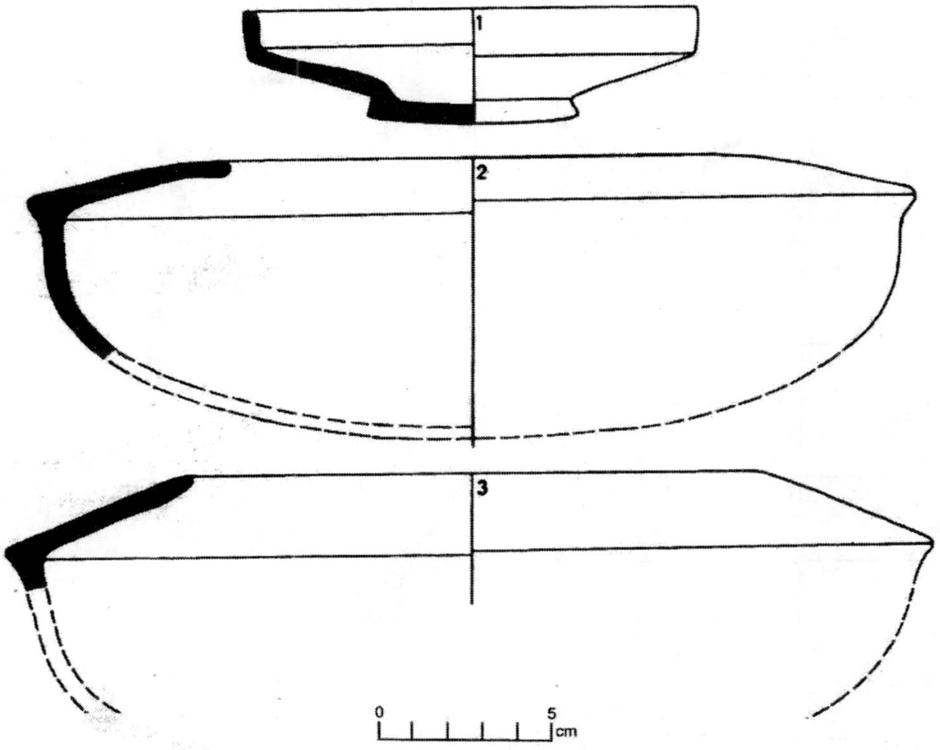

Figure 24: Platter and carinated Handi of Grey Ware, Period III B

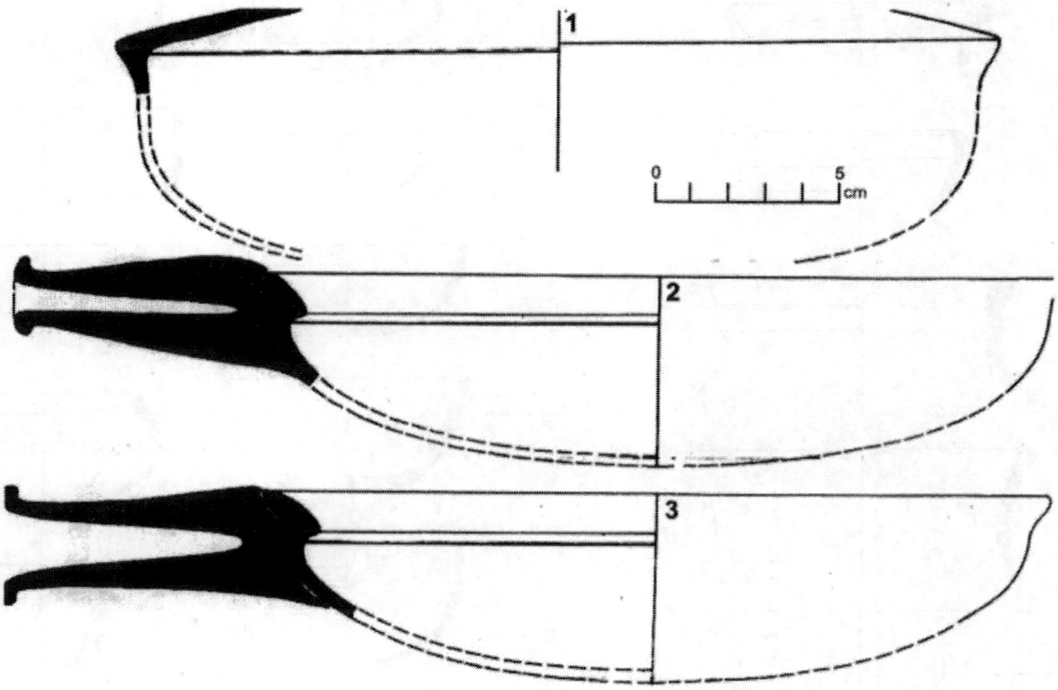

Figure 25: Frying pans of Grey Ware, Period III B

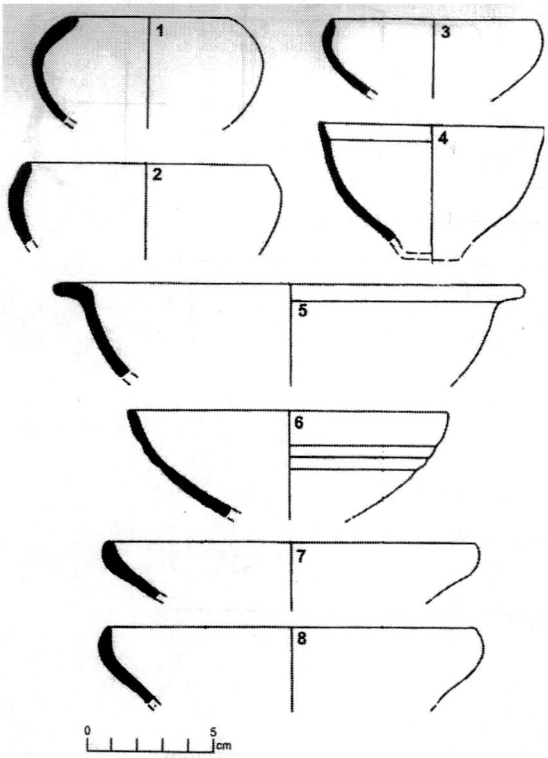

Figure 26: Bowls of Red Slipped Ware, Period III C

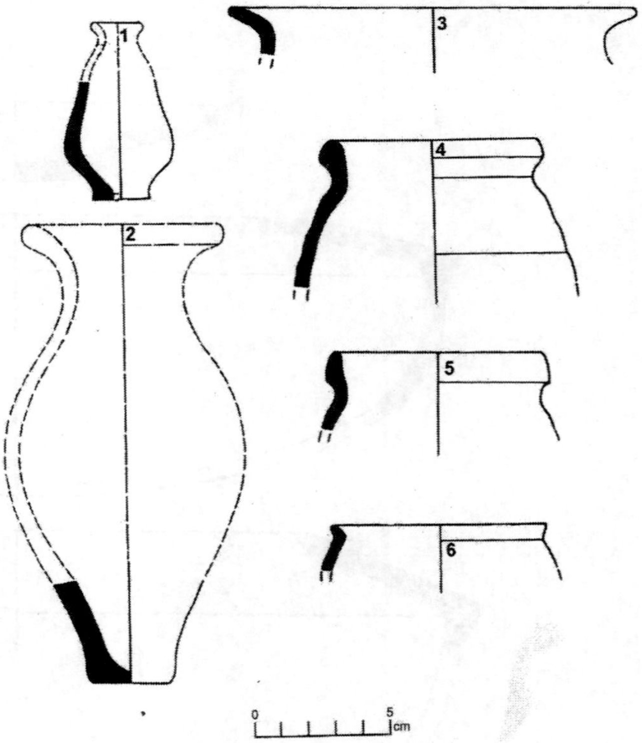

Figure 27: Vessels of Red Ware, Period III C

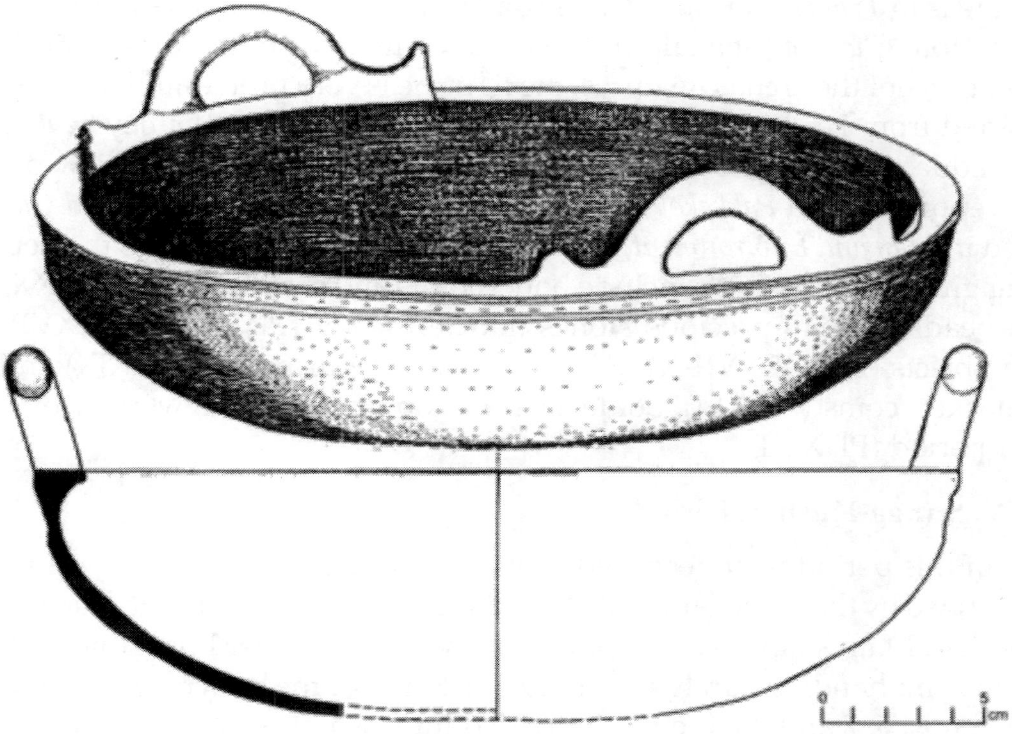

Figure 28: Handled Karahi of Red Ware, Period III C

Silver female figurine recovered from the present site from the pre-Mauryan level with a punch-marked coin is a rare discovery of the site. This silver female figurine measuring 10.75 cm long is a masterpiece of art. This type of silver figurine is not reported from any site at this context. It was made by cutting the silver sheet. Headdress is shown by incised lines. Design of dots is shown below the headdress. Hairs are well combed and parted in the middle. Locks of hair are shown on both sides of the cheeks. High eyebrows and flat nose represent the archaic feature. Right ear is broken while an ear ring is worn in the left ear. A necklace is shown by wide strips. Head of the figurine is found broken and seems to be attached separately. Incised lines are shown from neck to the waist on both obverse and reverse sides. Rounded breasts seem to be uncovered. Incised lines are also shown on both hands and on both sides from shoulder to below the elbow which may have been made to show bangles. There are four bangles in both wrists. Fingers of both hands are found slightly broken. Left hand has been found broken from the elbow. The upper portion of the body is conical-shaped and the waist is very thin while the hips are very large and heavy. This type of hip is named *Prithusroni* in *Abhijñānashakuntalam*. The term *Vrihada Sroni* is used by V.S. Agrawal for this type of hip. He has opined that large hips of females are helpful for easy delivery. A button type design within a circle is shown in the middle of the hip. Two parallel lines with dots are also shown on both sides of the hip. A large genital organ is beautifully carved. An anklet is shown in the right leg by four incised lines. Fingers of the right leg are slightly raised upwards. It seems that the figurine is in *Tribhanga mudra*. C.Margabandhu observed that a terracotta figurine recovered from *Champa* (Bhagalpur, Bihar) has same type of features while B.R.Mani opines that except the archaic features, the figurine is very much similar to the dancing girl reported from Harappa. Left leg of the figurine is broken (Dubey *et al.* 2012:200-204). K. Paddayya of Deccan College, Pune, also suggested in his review of our first season's report entitled *Pakkakot-some new archaeological dimensions of mid-Ganga Plain* published in *Man and Environment*, Vol. XXXVII (1)-2012 that it shows the depiction of a dancing girl. The other finds include bone-points and arrow-heads (Pl. XXX; XXXIII-XXXIV), beads of semi-precious stones and terracotta (Pls. XXXV-XXXVI), copper and iron objects (Pls. XXXVII-XXXVIII), terracotta figurines (Pl. XXXIX) and copper punch-marked coins (XL-XLI). Some seals of copper and bone were also recovered from this period (Pl. XLII).

Period IV: Sunga-Kushan Period

Remains of this period were recorded from Mound nos. 2, 3 and 4. This period is characterized by the absence of NBPW; Red Ware is the dominant ceramic assemblage of this period. Main shapes are bowls, basins, vases, sprinkler lids (Ahichhatra 10 A), frying pans and handled karahis (Figs. 29-31). Some of the structures were noticed in the Trench nos. 5, 7 and 8 which was divided into two phases' *i.e.*Sunga and Kushan periods (Fig.32). Small finds of this period comprised bone-points and arrowheads (Pl. XLIII), copper and iron objects (Pls. XXXVII, XLIV), beads of semi-precious stones and terracotta (Pls. XLV- XLVIII), copper cast coins (Pl. XLIX-L), seals and sealings (Pls. LI-LIII), terracotta figurines (Pls. LIV-LV) and terracotta and pottery discs.

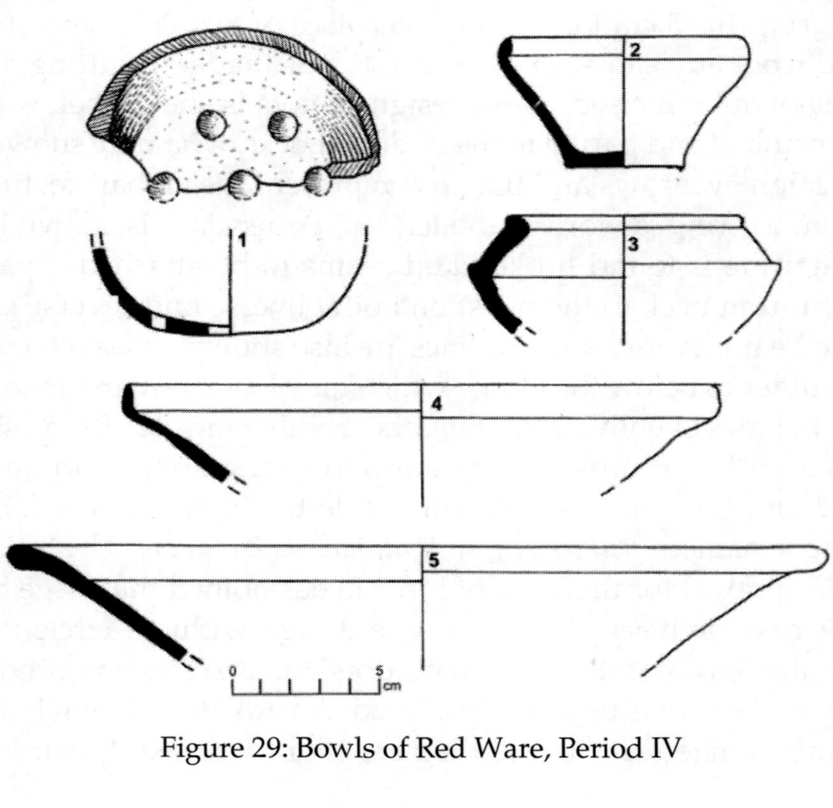

Figure 29: Bowls of Red Ware, Period IV

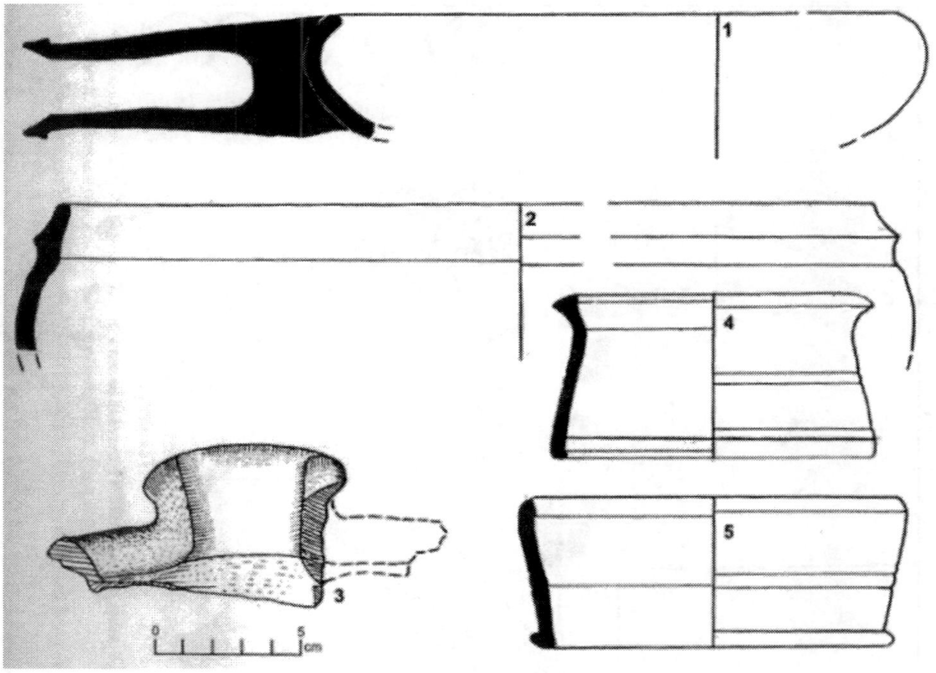

Figure 30: Frying pan, Basins and stands of Red Ware, Period IV

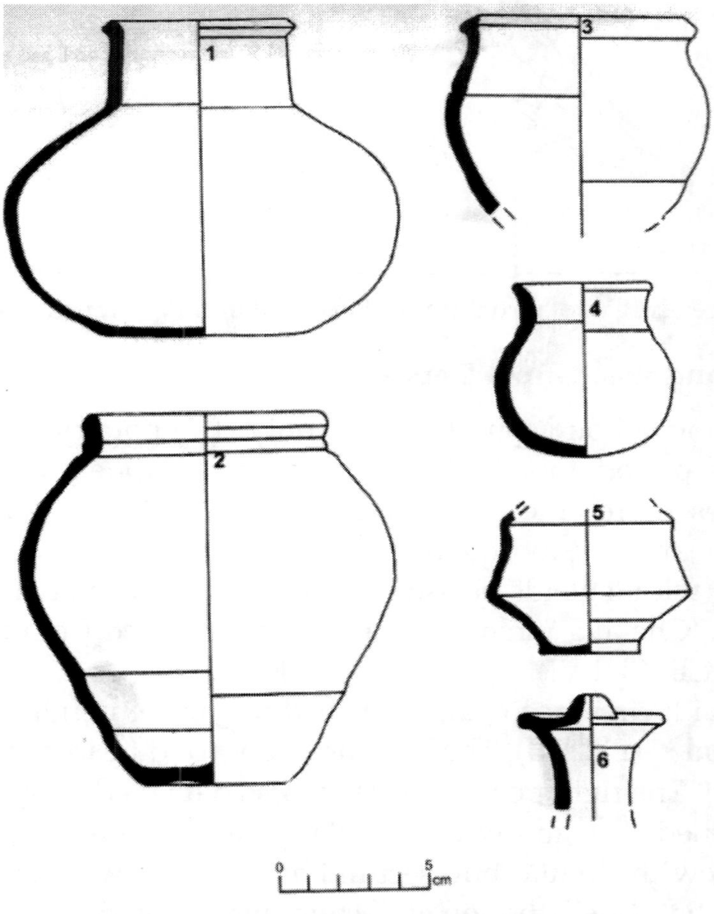

Figure 31: Vessels of Red Ware, Period IV

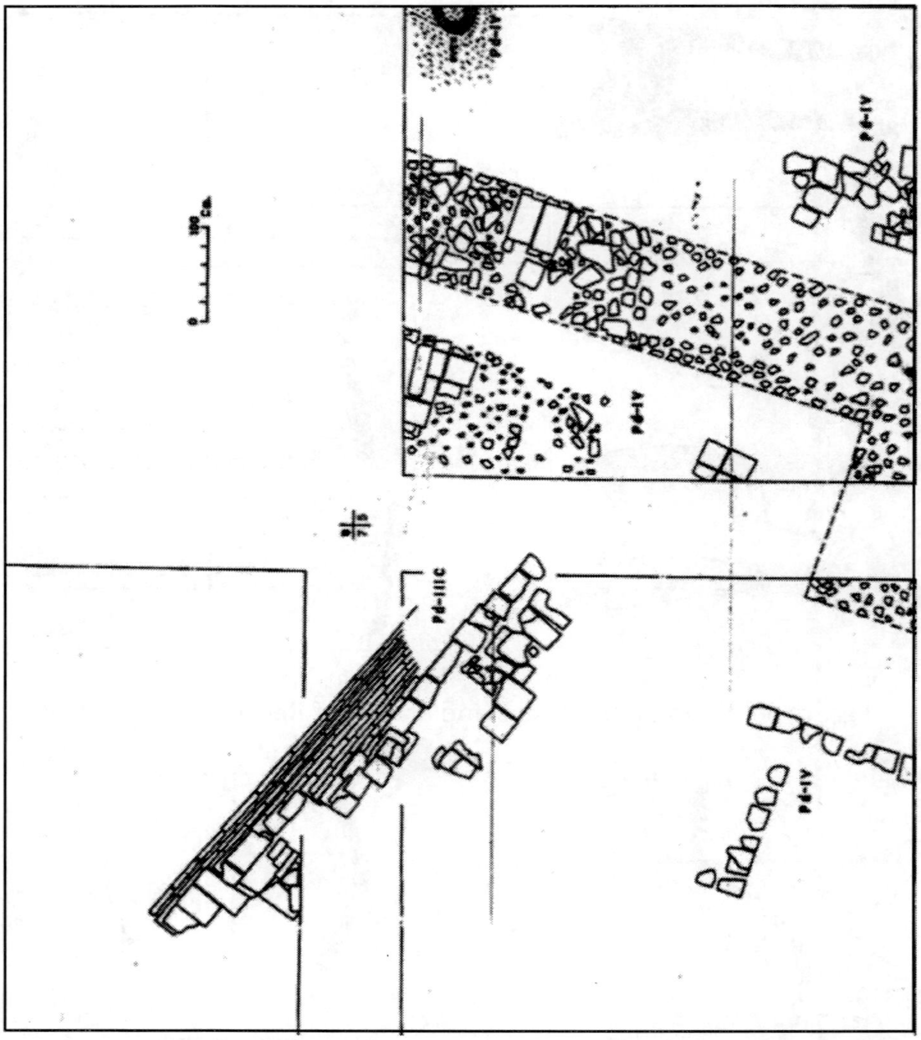

Figure 32: Plan of structures of Period III and IV (Trenches 5, 7, 8)

Period V: Gupta and Post Gupta Deposits

This period was noticed on Mound 2 and 3 only. The pottery of proceeding period continued in this period too. Both slipped and unslipped variety of Red Ware was found; shapes represented by bowls with everted rims (parai), knobbed lid, vases and storage jars. A good quantity of terracotta figurines was also recovered. Terracotta sealing with legends bearing two separate impressions "Matibharadhi.... (Karanasya)" and "Chetaka Vihare" respectively recovered from this period belongs to late 6th century CE (Pl. LVI).

A stone slab with circular top and the head of Shiva emerging from it was found from a pit of Period V (Pl.LVII). The left portion beyond head and the portion below chin are broken off. The right portion of slab is also damaged. The back portion of slab is flat and unadorned. The god wears circular pearl rings in elongated ear lobes and an elegant *Jatajuta* with circular bun secured by a fillet of which the string bifurcates the hair into two halves on the lower section and ends in a circular amulet in the middle on the forehead. The face of god shows an expression of bliss and repose with closed lips; the drooping eyes have narrow eyelids with marked pupils; the nose is sharply out; and the third eye is incised with pupil.

Chronology

The chronology of various periods of the site was decided on the basis of cultural relics of each period, their stratigraphic position and comparative study of recovered findings with other excavated sites of this region. The problem of the antiquity of the Neolithic culture of the Vindhyan range is still not finally settled but now we have some relevant C^{14} dates from the excavated Neolithic sites of the Vindhyas and the Ganga plain. Considering three of C^{14} dates reading 4530 ± 185 BCE (PRL 101), 5440±240 BCE (PRL 100) and 6570±210 BCE (PRL 224) obtained from Koldihwa as dependable, the culture was dated to the 7th -6th millennium BCE (Sharma *et al.* 1980: 81). But doubts were raised about such an early antiquity. The C^{14} date belonging to the transitional phase of the Neolithic to Chalcolithic is 1440±120 BCE (PRL 223). The absolute dates obtained from Mahagara also indicated a late date to the culture, though these dates have the possibility opf contamination of samples. Two TL dates, 2265 BCE and 1616 BCE and four C^{14} dates 1440±150 BCE (PRL 409), 1330±120 BCE (PRL 408), 1440±100 BCE (PRL 407) and 1480±110 BCE (BSI) have been obtained from the samples recovered from Mahagara. These dates are not consistent with the stratigraphy possibly due to contamination of samples. In the light of C^{14} dates obtained from Kunjhun, reading 4600±80 BCE, the revised chronology of the Vindhyan Neolithic culture was proposed to 4th millennium BC (Clark and Khanna.1989: 81). C^{14} dates which have come to light from recent excavations at Lahuradeva in the mid-Ganga plain read as 5320±90 BP (BS 1951; Cal BCE 4220, 4196, 4161) and 6290±160 BP (BS 1966; Cal BCE 5298) (Tewari *et al.*2001-02: 37-68, 2002-03:38-67).Three relevant C^{14} dates have been obtained from Tokwa. When calibrated these dates read 6591 BCE (BS-2417), 5976 BCE (BS-2369) and 4797 BCE (BS-2464). An AMS C^{14} date for carbonized domesticated rice would push the antiquity of the Neolithic culture at Lahuradeva to 7th millennium BCE (Tewari *et al.* 2005:40). From the Neolithic horizon of Jhusi on the confluence of the Ganga-Yamuna in Prayagraj three C^{14} dates have been obtained. These dates when calibrated, read 7477 BCE (BS-2526), 5837 BCE (BS-2524) and 6196 BCE (BS-2525). The earliest date obtained from the site would put the beginning of the Neolithic culture of the site in 8th millennium BCE. The combined testimony of the available C^{14} dates obtained from Koldihwa and Tokwa in the North-Central India and Jhusi and Lahuradeva in the mid-Ganga plain would push the antiquity of the Neolithic culture in the Northern Vindhyas and the mid-Ganga plainto a hoary past.

Taking all these questions in the mind the team had selected the fortified site of Pakkakot to be excavated. The excavation work was done during February to May, 2011. It supplemented our knowledge of the archaeology of this area as well as the cultural history of the site. While comparing the ceramics of the site with other sites of the region, it has been noticed that it is similar to the sites like Waina, Bhunadih, Jhusi,

Sohgaura, Lahuradeva, Tokwa and Hetapatti in UP and Senuwar, Chirand, Chechar Kutubpur and Taradih in Bihar. The pottery and other finds of the aforesaid sites are intimately related to each other for the origin and development of Neolithic culture. The C^{14} dates of Jhusi and Lahuradeva suggest that the region was one of the early centres of agriculture in the Ganga plain. The available evidence indicates that in the early stage of the culture of aforesaid sites including Pakkakot, people were using handmade pottery but subsequently the slow wheel appears to have been used for the purpose. The pottery assemblage of Pakkakot and nearby sites includes Red Ware, Lustrous Red Ware, Burnished Ware (Red, Black and Grey), Rusticated Ware, Black-and-Red Ware and Corded Ware. The clay used for manufacturing the pots is not well levigated. Pots are generally ill-fired and have blackish grey core. Painted sherds of the site are similar to the potteries recovered from Imlidih Khurd, Lahuradeva, Chirand and Senuwar. Pots with appliqué bands are also a special feature of this site. On the basis of ceramic assemblage of the site as compared with nearby sites its cultural sequence may be dated between 5000 BCE to 7th century CE.

As far as urbanization is concerned, Pakkakot got the status of a full-fledged urban centre during Sunga-Kushan period. The beginning of urbanization at the site is witnessed in Period III B which is marked by the use of NBPW. The geographical situation of the site made it possible for its inhabitants to have commercial links with other contemporary cities like Rajghat, Pataliputra and Vaishali. Pakkakot lies on the ancient trade route from Pataliputra to Lumbini. The site is extended in about 4x1 km of area with fortification walls and four watch-towers. A good number of terracotta seals and sealings were also recovered from the site from NBPW to Gupta and post-Gupta periods. Twentyfour sealings were recovered from the site from which six have more than five impressions which is a unique feature. Special mention may be made of two pendants, one is tortoise, made of banded agate and the other is a parrot made of crystal and a miniature lota recovered from NBPW period. The silver female figurine is also a rare discovery of the site recovered from the pre-Mauryan level. Antiquities recovered from the site are enough to prove the site as an urban centre. The catchmernt area of the site is extended in about 8 kms having other archaeological sites like Matahi, Jagdishpur, Akauni, Chitabaragaon, Waina, Karo etc.

The findings of Pakkakot highlight the fact that the site had been a cradle of human civilization right from the Neolithic age down to the blossoming of urban phase. The concept of cultivating two crops in a year had already come in practice during Neolithic-Chalcolithic period at the site and is datable to 5000 BCE. Cultivation of rice, wheat, barley, various types of pulses and oil seeds was done in the Neolithic age. The Neolithic people were not dependent on agriculture alone for their subsistence. They domiscated animals and exploited wild plants and animals in the nearby areas. The rivers and nalas not only provided suitable land for agriculture but also provided food in the form of aquatic animals like fish, tortoise, snail etc.

FINDINGS OF THE EXCAVATION

Pottery

Pottery is one of the most important components of ancient cultures owing to its socio-economic and religious values. It is an important asset for archaeologists to bridge the gaps in human cultural past. It is the key constituent of material unearthed during an excavation. It helps us to define, distinguish, demarcate and delineate a culture. It may also be mentioned that the pottery making tradition provided a base for the ceramic crafts of the succeeding periods. The most striking feature of the potteries of early period at Pakkakot is the general tendency of being coarse, modelled on the slow wheel and ill-fired, though the major bulk was wheel-turned, handmade pots which also formed an important part of each of the pottery categories. The wheel in the modelling of utensils and various methods of baking were the new dimensions added to the ceramics. The ceramic assemblage of Pakkakot has been studied periodwise. The first three periodsdemonstrate some changes in pottery types either in the form of technological improvement or degeneration or appearance and disappearance of new and old shapes respectively. Stratigraphically Period-I is the earliest and is confined to layer 4 of Trench no. 9 and 10 at Mound-1 only. In general it includes Cord-impressed Red Ware and Plain Red Ware. The characteristic features of these wares are infrequent post-firing scratching, appliqué designs and painted tradition. The Red Slipped Ware does possess rustications on the outer surface but has no incised decorations. In Period-II Black-and Red Ware, Black Slipped Ware, Red Slipped Ware and Red Ware are the principal wares. During Period-III, improvement in manufacturing technology and introduction of number of new shapes in NBPW and Black Slipped Ware has been attested alongwith enhancement in the grace of vessels. The vessels of Period-IV and V deteriorate and the percentage changes with an increase in the coarse wares. Periodwise details of the pottery are given below:

Period I

The ceramic assemblage of Period-I is essentially crude Red Ware and occasionally decorated with Cord-impressed, post-firing scratching and appliqué designs. A few sherds are burnished in the interior portion. The clay contains good amount of degraissant which got burning during firing and resulted into a porus surface. Most of the pots are made with turnette method on slow wheel; some of the pots are handmade also. The ceramic assemblage of Period-I may be categorized mainly in the following groups:

- **Corded Ware**

  Designs on the Cord-impressed pottery of the site have been executed on the exterior of the pots (Figs.12-13). The design of cord impression include rope pattern and excised notches. After making these patterns, a thick paste has been applied in the pre-firing stage. The principal shapes are bowls and vases. Bowls are spherical, ovaloid with incurved rim. The rim portion of the bowls is made separately and attached to the body of the bowls. Some of the bowls have a bright burnishing in the interior portion. Typologically, this type is comparable with the bowls of Period-I of Imlidih Kurd (Singh.1993: 21-23; Fig.1, Nos. 1-17) and Lahuradeva (Tewari *et al.*2002-03:37-68; Fig.3, Nos 1-5). The second type of vessel is the vase with short neck and globular body. It has the cording pattern all over the body. The thick coating of clay on the exterior is similar to that of the bowl. The section of the vases is very thin and the pots are generally ill-fired.

- **Rusticated Ware**

This type of pots are recovered in a good number from Period-I. The rustication was applied on the base of the vases only and are found ill-fired and of coarse variety. The shapeless sherds of Rusticated Ware were also recovered in a good number. The vessels are bigger in size and bear light red colour.

- **Red Ware**

The important shapes of Red Ware of Period-I are bowls, basins and different type of vases. A few perforated legged bowls were also recovered from this period. The fabric of perforated legged bowls is thick and sturdy and in some cases it has bright red slip on the interior. Besides them, several spouts have also been found from Period-I ranging in length from 6 cm to 7 cm. they commonly bear a red slip on the interior. These spouts have been luted to which type of vessels is not clear. A close similarity of these spouts with the spouts of Imlidih Khurd (Singh.1993:21-23; Fig.4, Nos 2-5) and Bhunadih (Singh and Singh.1998:141-149; Fig. 5, Nos. 1-5) suggests that it has been luted to the carinated *Handi* or *Martban*.

- **Decoration on the Pottery**

To decorate the pottery of Period-I at Pakkakot several methods were used. The first method comprises post-firing painting in red ochre. It was done on the rim portion of the vases only and is recorded from Period-I A at Senuwar (Singh.2000-2001:111). This post-firing painting is a characteristic ceramic trait of south Indian Neoliths. The second method of decorating a vessel was post-firing scratching by a sharp instrument which includes geometrical patterns (Fig. 16, Nos. 1, 2 and 5). Such type of decoration have been reported from Period-I at Imlidih Khurd (Singh.1993: 21-23; Fig. 3, Nos. 1-9), Waina (Singh and Singh. 1995-96: 41-61; Fig.5, Nos.13-17) and Lahuradeva (Tewari *et al*. 2001-02:54-62). The third method of decorating the pottery was the appliqué method. This method is confined on the vases and large basins (Fig.16, No. 3). For making the appliqué design, a strip of clay was generally affixed on the exterior of the vessel. Various types of rope and chain patterns were executed on the added strip of clay on the external portion of the pottery. The principal shapes of this period are illustrated below:

Fig. 11

1. Fragment of a vessel of Red Ware having incised designs on the exterior executed by a sharp instrument in post-firing stage. The hatched designs have been executed in two rectangles on the exterior of the pot, bright red slip on the exterior, Period-I. Similar type of potteries has been reported from Period-I at Imlidih Khurd (Singh.1993: 21-23; Fig. 3, Nos. 4, 7 and 8).
2. Fragment of a vessel of Red Ware with square lines scratched on the exterior in post-firing stage, Period-I.
3. Spout of Red Ware, length 6 cm, bright red slip has been applied on the exterior which is peeled-off at places, medium fabric, Period-I.
4. Fragment of a vase of Rusticated Ware, external surface is gritty and rough, devoid of any slip or wash, Period-I.
5. Fragment of a vessel of dull Red Ware having a post-firing design, possibly a flower and its leaf, devoid of any slip or wash, Period-I.
6. Bowl of burnished Grey Ware with externally thickened rim, diam. 21.40 cm, uniform convex sides, burnished external sureface, medium fabric, Period-I.

Fig. 12

1. Fragment of a vase of Cord-impressed Red Ware with heavy cord impression on the exterior, gritty core, coarse fabric, Period-I.
2. Fragment of a vase of Red Ware having micaceous red slip on the exterior and appliqué band with typical rope impressions, Period-I.
3. Fragment of a vessel of Red Ware with vertical cord-impression on the exterior. The interior bears a bright red slip, Period-I.
4. Same as above with irregular cord-impressed design on the exterior, handmade, ill-fired, gritty core, coarse fabric, Period-I.
5. Fragment of a vessel of Red Ware with cord-impression on the exterior, made on slow wheel, gritty core, coarse fabric, Period-I.
6. Same as above, Period-I.
7. Same as above, ill-fired, smokey grey in colour, coarse fabric, Period-I.

Fig.13

1. Lower portion of a footed vessel of Red Ware with perforated bottom. It is a thick sturdy pot. It has one leg and eight perforations in the bottom, Period-I. Similar vessels occur at Narhan Period-I (Singh.1994:84-89; Fig.34, Nos. 20-26; Hastinapur III (Lal.1954-55: 5-151; Fig.19, type-L), Atranjikhera III (Gaur.1983: 39; Fig.51, Nos.1-7) and Sravasti I (Sinha.1967: 59; Fig.11, No. XLIX).
2. A variant of the above. It has one leg and two perforations at the bottom, Period-I.
3. Same as above, Period-I.
4. Fragment of a bowl of Red Ware with incurved thickened rim, diam. 14.80 cm, vertical cord-impressed pattern on the exterior, convex sides, coarse fabric, Period-I.

5. Bowl of Red Ware with thickened featureless rim, diam. 16 cm having cord impression on the exterior, almost vertical sides. The core of the pot is gritty having smoky grey colour. The interior has bright red slip, medium fabric, Period-I.
6. Fragment of a bowl of Red Ware with incurved thickened rim having cord-impressions on the exterior, diam. 18.2 cm, convex sides, smooth interior surface, gritty core, Period-I.
7. Bowl of Red Ware with incurved thickened rim, diam. 21.70 cm, convex sides, and the exterior has impressions of irregular strokes going to various directions. The interior has bright red slip, Period-I.
8. Fragment of a bowl of Red Ware with incurved thickened rim, diam. 21.20 cm, cord-impressios on the exterior, convex sides. It has a gritty core having rice husk and vegetal material used as degressaint, ill-fired and has a smoky grey colour, coarse fabric, Period-I.

Fig.14

1. Vase of Red Ware with splayed out rim, diam. 14.70 cm, expanding sides, constricted neck, medium fabric, Period-I.
2. Fragment of a vase of Red Slipped Ware with flaring rim, diam. 14.40 cm, progressively thickened at the neck, bright red slip on both the sides, medium fabric, Period-I.
3. Vase of Red Ware with sharpened flaring rim, progressively thickened at the base, diam. 24.30 cm, expanding sides, post-firing red painting at the neck, medium fabric, Period-I.
4. Fragment of a vessel of Red Ware having appliqué band on the exterior with rope pattern incised on it, coarse fabric, Period-I.
5. Fragment of a vase with five horizontal lines scratched on the exterior in the post-firing stage, bright red slip on both the exterior, gritty core, medium fabric, Period-I.

Fig.15

1. Deep bowl of Red Slipped Ware with out turned sharpened rim and gently expanding sides, diam. 19.80 cm, medium fabric, Period-I.
2. Bowl of Red Ware with out turned sharpened rim and uniform convex sides, diam. 22.10 cm, medium fabric, Period-I.
3. Fragment of a vessel of Red Slipped Ware with appliqué design on the exterior at the point of base. A chain pattern has been carved on the added strip of clay by indentation. A bright red slip has been applied above the chain pattern. The exterior below the chain pattern and the interior of the vessel are devoid of any slip. The core is gritty and of coarse fabric. Similar type of vessels occurs in Period-I at Imlidih Khurd (Singh.1993: 21-23; Fig.2, Nos. 1-5).

4. Fragment of a vase of Red Ware with cord-impressed design on the exterior, medium fabric, Period-I.
5. Fragment of a vase of Red Slipped Ware with three horizontal lines on the exterior, bright red slip on the exterior which is peeled-off at places, medium fabric, Period-I.

Period II

The ceramic assemblage of this period comprises four main wares, i.e. Black-and Red Ware, Black Slipped Ware Red Ware and Red Slipped Ware. Most of these wares formed an integral part of the culture. However, there are also sites in UP where lithic tools, which are essentially Chalcolithic application, are absent. Particular mention in this regard may be made of Khairadih, Sohgaura, Narhan, Imlidih Khurd, Bhunadih etc. Three main techniques of firing were adopted for their manufacture, viz. firing under oxidizing and reducing conditions and inverted firing. Majority of the pots are wheel made. A few vessels are found handmade also. Important features of each ware are described below:

Black-and Red Ware

It is an important pottery of Period-II. Painted specimens are absent at this site and shapes are mostly bowls and vases of different sizes. The ware ranged in fabric from thin to medium and thick. Bowls are either fine or of medium fabric and have internally bevelled, flaring or featureless rim. Some of them have collared or clubbed rim also. Bowls with splayed out rim with tapering sides have also been recovered (Figs. 16, 17). Pedestalled bowls are the principal type. The vases are made medium to coarse variety. The clay of vases is micaceous and mica particles are visible in large numbers. The vases with splayed out/flaring rim and carinated neck are recovered in good quantity (Figs. 15-16). The diam. of its mouth ranges from 11 cm to 25 cm. Most of the vases were used for storing cereal grains and other agricultural produce.

Black Slipped Ware

This type of pot sherds are less in number as compared to other sites. The important shapes are straight sided bowls with their variants, convex sided bowls, beakers with external grooves at the waist and *lota* shaped vessels. The dishes are absent in this ware. The ware ranged in fabric from thin to medium. The latter are prominent in frequency. The slip applied on the vessels is treated with light black slip or is dull in appearance.

Red Ware

The vessels of Red Ware recovered from the site are mostly devoid of any surface treatment and range in fabric from medium to thick. The clay is not well levigated and contains stone gravels and other organic materials. The firing of the pots is not perfect resulting the core as gritty and porus. The main shapes are bowls, basins and vases.

Red Slipped Ware

This type of pottery is recovered in three fabrics: thin, medium and thick. All the pots are wheel made. The vessels of thin fabric are mostly treated with fine red slip showing smoothened surface. The clay used is devoid of any admixture. The core is compact and impervious. The shapes represented are bowls, spouted vessels, basins and vases. Spouts range from 7.50 to 9.30 cm. Three pieces of perforated bowls were also recovered from this period (Fig.33, No1). Perforated bowls have been reported from the Neolithic levels at Chirand and Chalcolithic levels at Narhan, Khairadih, Imlidih Khurd, Waina and Bhunadih.

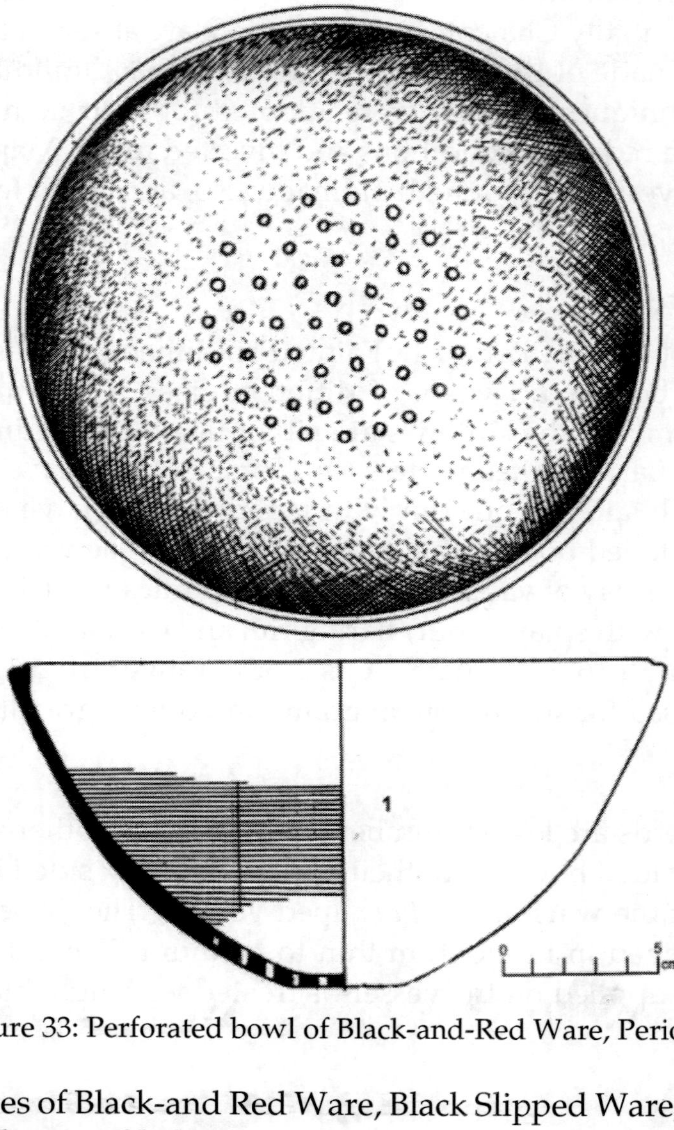

Figure 33: Perforated bowl of Black-and-Red Ware, Period II

Important shapes of Black-and Red Ware, Black Slipped Ware, Red Ware and Red Slipped Ware are illustrated below:

Fig.16

1. Bowl of Black-and Red Ware with incurved thickened rim and progressively thinner at the base, diam. 14.10 cm, devoid of any slip, medium fabric, Period-II.

2. Fragment of a bowl of Black-and Red Ware with externally thickened rim, diam. 22 cm. It has vertical strokes of cord-impressed design on the exterior, devoid of any slip, medium fabric, Period-II.
3. Fragment of a bowl of Black-and Red Ware with internally collared rim, diam. 27.10 cm, and tapering sides. It has a lustrous surface on the interior as well as exterior, fine fabric, Period-II.
4. Same as above, diam. 30.20 cm, Period-II.
5. Vase of Black-and Red Ware with flaring sharpened rim, diam. 18.20 cm, carinated neck and expanding body. It has a bright red slip on the exterior, medium fabric, Period-II. Similar shape has occurred in Period-I B at Waina (Singh and Singh.1995-96: 41-61; Fig8, No.11).

Fig. 17

1. Bowl of Black-and Red Ware with externally thickened featureless rim, diam. 11.80 cm, medium fabric, Period-II.
2. Fragment of a bowl of Black-and Red Ware with externally beveled rim, convex sides, diam. 15.60 cm, medium fabric, Period-II.
3. Deep bowl of Black-and Red Ware with straight sides and out-turned thickened rim, convex sides, diam. 22.50 cm, medium fabric, Period-II.
4. Fragment of a vase of Black-and Red Ware with short flaring rim, diam. 15.70 cm, expanding sides, and four horizontal lines on the exterior. A bright red slip on the exterior, medium fabric, Period-II.

Fig.33

1. A complete perforated bowl of Black-and Red Ware with internally flat ribbed rim, sides progressively thickened to a flat base, diam. 22.50 cm. it has 45 perforations on the base. The perforated bowls with footed leg have occurred from Period-II at Imlidih Khurd (Singh.1996: 91; Fig. 3, No.4) and in Period-I at Narhan (Singh.1994:89; Fig.34, Nos.20-27).

Period III A (Early Phase)

All the wares also continued in this period except Black-and Red Ware, whereas Grey Ware is included in this period. A large no of NBPW having two varities-monochrome and biochrome, has been recovered in this sub-period. The different colours of NBPW like black, steel blue, silvery, golden and pink have been recovered from this phase. The core portion of this ware is normally grey in majority. This type of pottery is reported from a number of sites in the Mid-Ganga plain. Bowls and dishes are the main types of this ware and have a close similarity with other sites like Rajghat, Prahladpur, Agiabir, Kausambi etc. the important shapes noted in this ware are hemispherical bowls, convex sided bowls and dishes, corrugated flaged bowls and dishes of varying sizes (Figs. 18, 20, 34, 35).

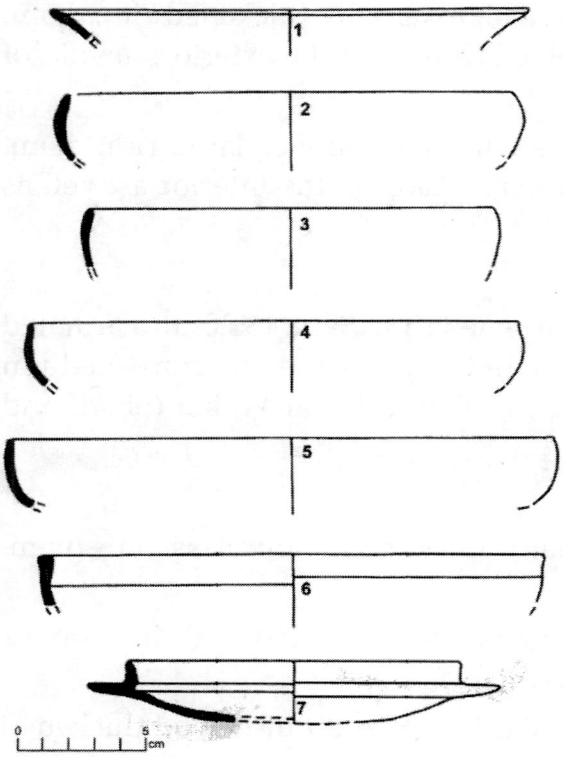

Figure 34: Bowls and dishes of NBPW, Period III A

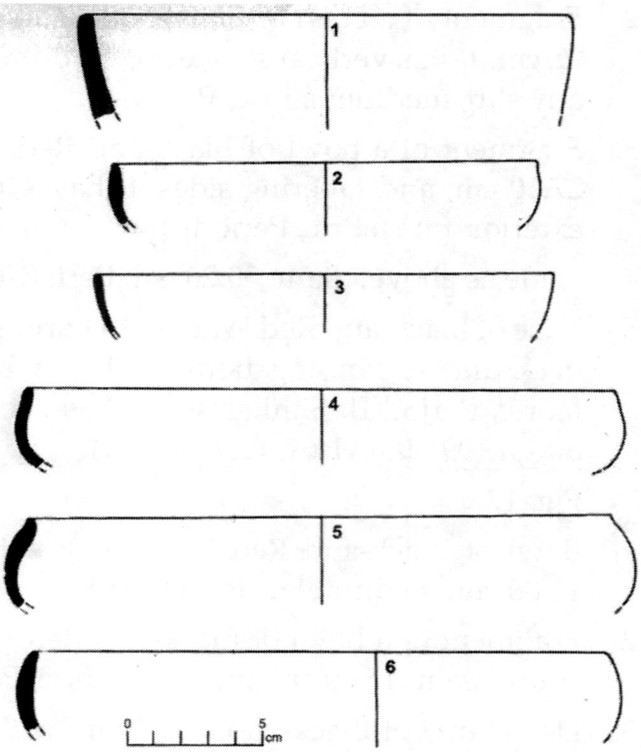

Figure 35: Bowls of NBPW, Period III B

In Black Slipped Ware dishes are the principal type followed by knife edged bowls. The fabric and core of these vessels are very thin and light. Red Ware is principal ceramic assemblage of this period. The fine and medium fabric bowls, dishes, basins and vases have been recovered from this phase. The common types are bowls, with straight sides and inverted rim, knife edged bowls, dishes with incurved rim and sagger base and vases of varying sizes. Basin with incurved collared rim is the other type of Red Ware. Vases with splayed out rim have been recovered in a good number from this sub-phase. In Grey Ware, the pottery types of NBPW and Black Slipped Ware continues. The important shapes of Period-III A are illustrated below:

Fig. 18

1. Fragment of a flanged bowl of NBPW with vertical featureless rim, steel blue in colour, diam. 9.20 cm, fine fabric, Period-III A.
2. Bowl of NBPW with featureless rim, almost straight sides, diam. 13.10 cm, fine fabric, Period-III A.
3. Corrugated bowl of NBPW with everted rim, convex sides, steel blue in colour, diam. 17.10 cm, fine fabric, Period-III A.
4. Fragment of a corrugated bowl of NBPW with inverted thickened rim, thicker towards base, medium fabric, diam. 19.30 cm, Period-III A.

5. Bowl of NBPW with internally sharpened rim, convex sides, medium fabric, diam. 22.60 cm, Period-III A.
6. Fragment of a bowl of NBPW with inverted featureless rim, thin fabric, steel blue in colour, diam. 14.40 cm, Period-III A.
7. Covex sided bowl of NBPW with thickened flat rim, diam. 16.30 cm, fine fabric, Period-III A.

Fig. 19

1. Fragment of a bowl of Black Slipped Ware with inverted featureless rim, diam. 12.60 cm, fine fabric, Period-III A.
2. Spout of a vase of NBPW, length 7 cm. smooth shining surface, Period-III A. This is a new shape of NBPW reported so far in the mid-Ganga plain.
3. Bowl of NBPW with inverted featureless rim, diam. 9.20 cm, black in shade, Period-III A.
4. Fragment of a bowl of of NBPW with vertical featureless rim, ledge at the shoulder and tapering sides to a rounded base, diam. 11.60 cm, thin black coating, black in shade, Period-III A.
5. Corrugated bowl of Black Slipped Ware with inverted featureless rim, corrugation all over the exterior body, diam. 9.2 cm, fine fabric, Period-III A.
6. Fragment of a bowl of Black Slipped Ware with featureless rim, diam. 17 cm, globular body, smooth shining surface, Period-III A.
7. Deep bowl of NBPW with inverted sharpened rim, diam. 23.20 cm, convex sides, black in shade, Period-III A.

Fig.20

1. Dish of NBPW, diam. 25.06 cm, incurved featureless rim, medium fabric, Period-III A.
2. Fragment of a dish of NBPW with inverted thickened rim, convex sides, sagger base, diam. 33.02 cm, Period-III A.
3. Same as above, convex sides, diam. 32 cm, medium fabric, Period-III A.
4. Dish of NBPW with internally thickened rim, convex sides, diam. 23.07 cm, Period-III A.
5. Fragment of a dish of NBPW with featureless rim, diam. 24.50 cm, almost straight sides, Period-III A.
6. Dish of NBPW with incurved featureless rim, convex sides, shining surface, diam. 27.02 cm, Period-III A.

Fig.21

1. Dish of Black Slipped Ware with incurved externally chamfered rim, convex sides, diam. 29.04 cm, Period-III A.

2. Dish of Black Slipped Ware with externally thickened rim, convex sides, diam. 28 cm, Period-III A.
3. Fragment of a dish of NBPW with slightly incurved rim, flattened from the top, convex sides, medium fabric, diam. 28 cm, Period-III A.
4. Dish of NBPW with incurved thickened rim, convex sides, diam. 35.4 cm, medium fabric, Period-III A.
5. Fragment of a dish of NBPW with incurved thickened rim, convex sides, medium fabric, Period-III A.
6. Bowl of Black Slipped Ware with internally sharpened rim, closing mouth, thickened convex sides, medium fabric, diam. 23 cm, Period-III A. similar type is reported from Period-I at Sarai Mohana (Singh and Singh.2004: 42; Fig. 9, No. 7B).

Fig. 22

1. Fragment of a vase of Red Ware with everted rim, diam. 11.70 cm, flattened from the top, long vertical neck, coarse fabric, Period-III A.
2. Vase of Red Ware with externally thickened clubbed rim, diam. 9.70 cm, vertical neck, ridge on the rim, coarse fabric, Period-III A.
3. Vase of Red Ware with featureless thickened rim, diam. 13.30 cm, prominent ridge on the neck, coarse fabric, Period-III A.
4. High necked jar/vase of Red Ware with splayed out externally thickened rim, diam. 15.50 cm, coarse fabric, Period-III A.
5. Dish of Red Ware with incurved thickened rim, diam. 24.10 cm, medium fabric, Period-III A.

Period III B (Middle Phase)

The frequency of NBPW diminishes in this sub-phase. Although some sherds of this ware continue with its fineness; some new shapes in Red Ware are included in this sub-phase. The carinated cooking *handis* with featureless rim and almost rounded base is a noteworthy addition in this sub-phase. Pear-shaped vases (Ahichhatra 10 A) with collared rim and its several variants appear in this sub-phase. In Black Slipped Ware, there is no change in the types of preceding sub-phase. The pottery types of this sub-phase have close similarity, both in form and fabric, with contemporary sites of mid-Ganga plain. Important shapes of this phase are illustrated below:

Fig. 23

1. Fragment of a miniature bowl of Red Ware with incurved rim, tapering sides and flat base, diam. 8.50 cm, medium fabric, Period-III B.

2. Bowl of dull Red Ware with incurved thickened rim, diam. 8.00 cm, convex sides, medium fabric, Period-III B.
3. A complete bowl of Red Ware with incipient featureless rim, diam. 10.80 cm, three corrugated lines on the exterior, medium fabric, Period-III B.
4. Fragment of a bowl of Red Ware with externally thickened rim, diam. 11.30 cm, convex sides and thickened flat base, medium fabric. It has a very clear thread mark at the base, Period-III B.
5. A complete flanged, corrugated bowl of Red Ware, diam. 10.70 cm, convex sides and flat base, medium fabric, Period-III B.
6. Miniature bowl of Red Ware with incurved featureless rim, diam. 10.50 cm, convex sides, thin fabric, Period-III B.
7. Bowl of Red Slipped Ware with incurved sharpened rim, diam. 12.10 cm, convex sides, medium fabric, Period-III B.
8. Same as above but having vertical sides and flat base, diam. 8.90 cm, medium fabric, Period-III B.
9. A complete rimless miniature vessel of Red Ware with corrugated profile, carinated neck and flat base, diam. 8.50 cm, medium fabric, Period-III B.
10. Lower portion of a tumbler of Red Ware with vertical corrugated sides and flat base, medium fabric, Period-III B.

Fig.24

1. Shallow plater of Grey Ware with short vertical rim, diam. 14.80 cm, convex sides and carinated towards a flate base, medium fabric, Period-III B.
2. Fragment of a carinated rimless *handi* of Grey Ware with almost rounded base, diam. 20.00 cm, prominent carination at the meeting point of the base, medium fabric, Period-III B. similar vessels have been reported from Period-I C at Rajghat (Narain and Roy.1977: 79; Fig. 10, No. 10) and Narhan (Singh.1994: 84; Fig. 47, Nos. 15-17).
3. Carinated *handi* of Grey Ware with closing featureless rim and rounded base, diam. 18.50 cm, coarse fabric, Period-III B.

Fig.25

1. Carinated rimless *handi* of Grey Ware with closing featureless rim and rounded base, diam. 20.30 cm, medium fabric, Period-III B.
2. A complete frying pan of Grey Ware with a hollow handle which is luted in the body of pan, diam. 32.00 cm, medium fabric, Period-III B. It is a new shape recovered from the mid-Ganga plain so far. One shape of this category is reported from Period-III at Narhan (Singh.1994:89; Fig.46, No. 1), two specimens come from Tilaura Kot (Mitra.1972. Fig. 15, Pls. CXVII- CXVII A).

3. Same as above with a wide hollow handle, diam. 31.70 cm, medium fabric, Period-III B.

Period III C (Late Phase)

The pottery of this sub-phase showed a change from the preceding sub-phase. In this phase deterioration was noticed in the pottery making while some new types were added. The NBPW showed a marked decline both in frequency as well as in quality. It was observed that the finer variety of NBPW has not been found; a coarse with thicker variety has been recovered in a less number. The emergence of the coarse and thick Grey Ware devoid of any surface treatment is another noteworthy development. Some dishes and bowls of Grey Ware and Black Slipped Ware have concentric circles and raised knob at the centre of the pottery. The fine Grey Ware of the preceding phases is almost absent. Some new shapes in Grey Ware and Red Ware are found. Mention may be made of good quantity of lugged handle *karahis* of Grey Ware and Red Ware recovered from Trench no. 7. A number of carinated *handis* with featureless rim in Grey Ware and Red Ware have also been recovered from this sub-phase. These vessels are made very hardened and possibly used for community cooking. Important shapes of this phase are illustrated below:

Fig.26

1. Bowl of Red Slipped Ware with incurved thickened rim, diam. 7.70 cm, globular sides, medium fabric, Period-III C.
2. Fragment of Red Ware with incurved sharpened rim, diam. 11.40 cm, convex sides, medium fabric, Period-III C.
3. Bowl of Red Ware with incurved featureless rim, diam. 9.70 cm, convex sides, fine fabric, Period-III C.
4. Fragment of a bowl of Red Slipped Ware with featureless rim, almost vertical sides and a flat base, diam. 10.50 cm, fine fabric, Period-III C.
5. Bowl of Red Slipped Ware with flaring rim, diam. 21.90 cm, convex sides, medium fabric, Period-III C.
6. Fragment of a bowl of Red Ware with featureless rim, corrugated profile, diam. 15.00 cm, medium fabric, Period-III C.
7. Bowl of Red Ware with incurved thickened rim, diam. 17.30 cm, convex sides, medium fabric, Period-III C.
8. Same as above, diam. 17.40 cm, medium fabric, Period-III C.

Fig.27

1. Miniature vessel of Red Ware with broken rim, flat base, medium fabric, Period-III C.

2. Fragment of a lower portion of a vessel, flat base, medium fabric, Period-III C.
3. Fragment of a vase of Red Slipped Ware with flaring rim, diam. 16.30 cm, constricted neck, medium fabric, Period-III C.
4. Vase of Red Ware with short thickened rim, corrugated profile, diam. 8.40 cm, coarse fabric, Period-III C.
5. Fragment of a vase with pear-shaped body, diam. 8.50 cm, coarse fabric, Period-III C.
6. Fragment of a vase with incipient rim, diam. 8.70 cm, globular profile, fine fabric, Period-III C.

Fig. 28

An almost complete handled *karahi* of Red Ware, featureless rim, and elongated loop handle with two raised dots, diam. 37.00 cm, convex sides and sagger base, medium fabric, Period-III C. Similar *karahis* are reported from Period-III at Rajghat (Narain and Roy.1977. Fig. 17, Nos. 35-36).

Period IV

The pottery of this period is essentially Red Ware except a few coarse variety of Grey Ware. In comparison to the pottery of the preceding period, the ceramic quality has declined in the clay, surface treatment and firing. The majority of the shape is utilitarian. The important types of Red Ware are large sized vases with splayed out rims and concave neck, ink-pot and knobbed lids, sprinklers, bottle necked jars, *karahis* and pans with elongated loop handle and bowls with inverted rims. Some spouts bearing decorative design have also been recovered. Principal shapes of this period are illustrated below:

Fig. 29

1. Fragment of a bowl of Red Ware with five perforations at the base, broken rim, medium fabric, Period-IV.
2. A complete bowl of Red Ware with incurved sharpened rim, diam. 8.20 cm, sides progressively thickened towards a flat base, medium fabric, Period-IV. Similar vessels have been reported from Period-II at Rajghat (Narain and Roy.1977. Fig. 14, Nos. 1-3).
3. Fragment of a miniature vessel of Red Ware with everted pointed rim, vertical sides, carinated to a thick side, diam. 8.20 cm, medium fabric, Period-IV.
4. Same as No. 2 but bigger in size, diam. 20.50 cm, medium fabric, Period-IV.
5. Fragment of a bowl of Red Ware with thickened flaring rim, diam. 28.30 cm, medium fabric, Period-IV.

Fig. 30

1. Frying pan of Red Ware with hollow handle luted to the body of the pot, diam. 29.90 cm, medium fabric, Period-IV.
2. Fragment of a basin of Red Slipped Ware with externally corrugated flanged rim, diam. 36.00 cm, sides' almost uniformally thickened, medium fabric, Period-IV.
3. Fragment of a lipped basin of Red Ware, sturdy fabric, Period-IV.
4. A complete stand of Red Slipped Ware, diam. 11.50 cm, externally thickened and obliquely cut rim and uniform thickened sides. It has four concentric grooves on the exterior, medium fabric, Period-IV. Similar stands are reported from Period-III at Rajghat (Narain and Roy.1977. Fig. 20, Nos. 77-79).
5. Same as above, diam. 14.30 cm, medium fabric, Period-IV.

Fig.31

1. A complete vessel of Grey Ware with vertical featureless rim, diam. 6.80 cm, an expanding neck, globular body with a flat base, medium fabric, Period-IV.
2. A complete pot of Red Ware with short vertical featureless rim, constricted neck, diam. 8.30 cm, globular body with tapering sides and flat base, coarse fabric, Period-IV.
3. Fragment of a vessel of Red Slipped Ware with everted externally obliquely cut rim, diam. 7.70 cm, globular profile, medium fabric, Period-IV.
4. A complete miniature vessel of Red Ware with everted featureless rim, constricted neck, diam. 5.00 cm, globular body and flat base, medium fabric, Period-IV.
5. An almost complete miniature vessel of Red Ware, broken rim, body carinated to a thick flat base, medium fabric, Period-IV.
6. Sprinkler of Red Ware, obliquely cut, less flanged rim and a centrally placed conical knob with a hole, medium fabric, Period-IV.

Period V

Period-V is characterized by the occurrence of Red Ware only, suggesting open kiln method of firing. The application of lustrous red slip was also appliedin the pottery of this period. Big sized vases, knobbed lids, large sized basins, carinated cooking vessels with shoot marks are recovered from this period. The frequency of miniature pots which are more than the preceding period has been noticed. Vases with out-turned long featureless rim and short concave neck and splayed out rim with expanding body are the other important types (Figs. 36-38).

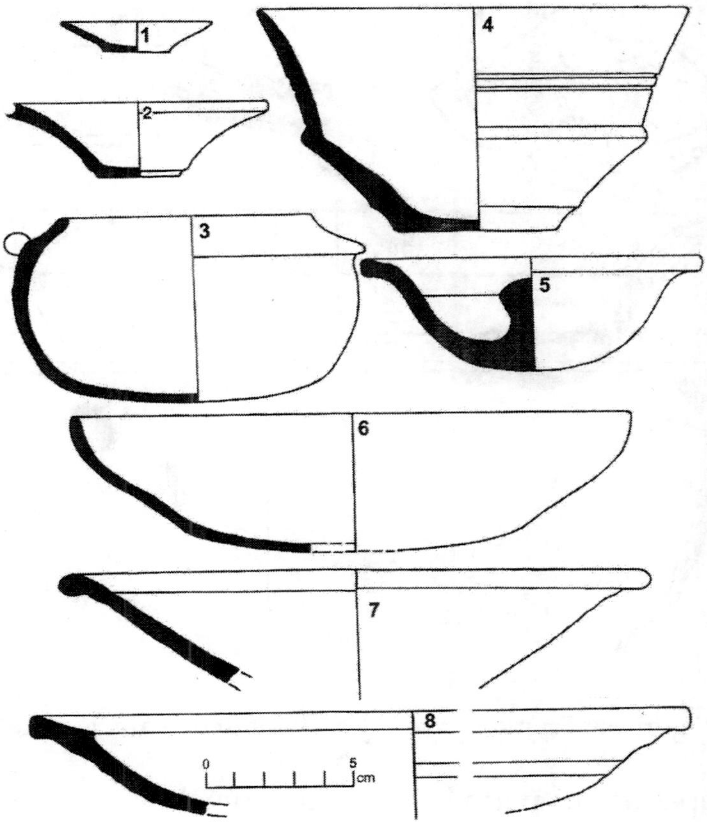

Figure 36: Vessels of Red Ware, Period V

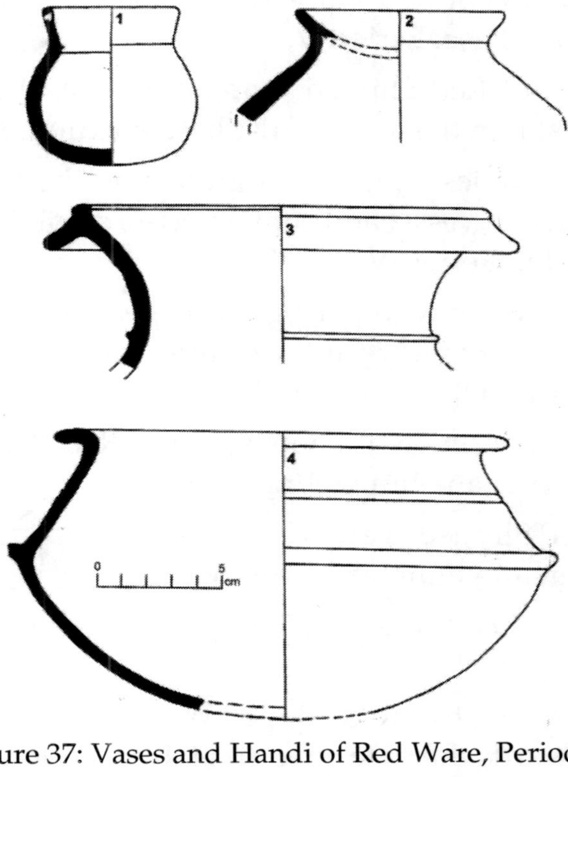

Figure 37: Vases and Handi of Red Ware, Period V

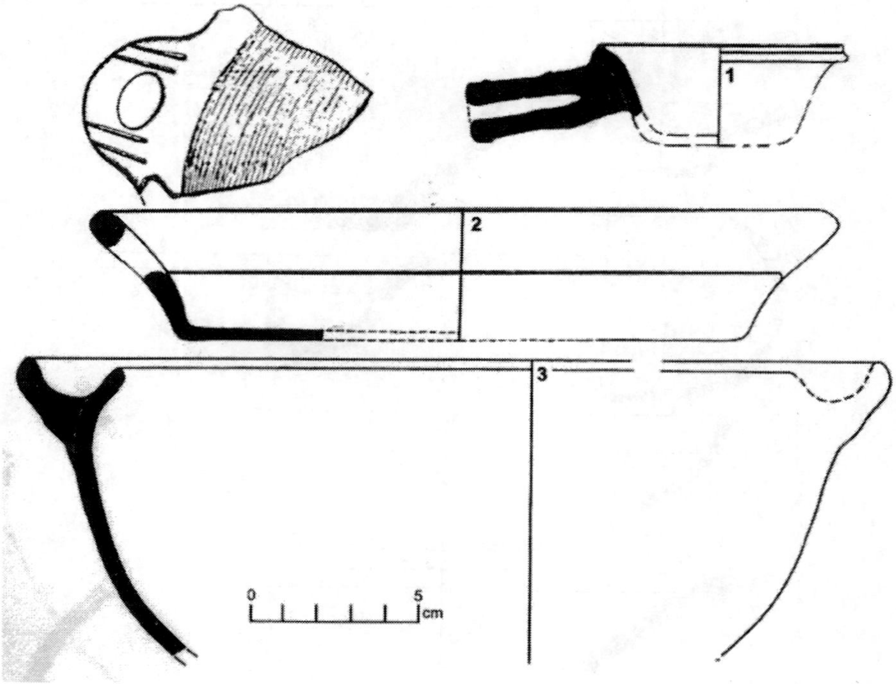

Figure 38: Frying pan and Karahi of Red Ware, Period V

Diagnostic shapes of this period are illustrated below:

Fig. 36

1. Miniature shallow bowl of Red Ware, diam. 6.00 cm, flaring featureless rim and sides tapering to a flat base, Period-V.
2. Fragment of a bowl of Red Slipped Ware, diam. 10.30 cm, featureless rim and tapering sides, red slip in the interior, flat base, medium fabric, Period-V.
3. Lid with closing featureless rim with a groove on the top presumably for close fitting on the mouth of a vessel and convex sides, diam. 10.00 cm, medium fabric, it is devoid of any slip, Period-V.
4. Bowl of Red Slipped Ware with flaring sharpened rim, convex sides, diam. 17.50 cm, flat base, a prominent flange at the centre, bright red slip on the exterior and interior as well, medium fabric, Period-V.
5. An almost complete specimen of knobbed lid of Red Ware with splayed out rim and with a central knob, medium fabric, Period-V.
6. Shallow bowl of Red Slipped Ware with everted sharpened rim, convex sides, flat base, diam. 22.50 cm, medium fabric, Period-V.
7. Fragment of a bowl of Red Ware with flaring clubbed rim, diam. 23.50 cm, medium fabric, Period-V.
8. Fragment of a shallow dish of Red Slipped Ware, flared rim, diam. 26.50 cm, sides bulge internally towards the base, medium fabric, Period-V.

Fig. 37

1. Handmade miniature vessel of dull Red Ware with short featureless rim, diam. 5.50 cm, roughly made, coarse fabric, Period-V.
2. Vase of Red Slipped Ware with short incipient rim, diam. 8.50 cm, expanding sides, medium fabric, Period-V.
3. Fragment of a vase of Red Slipped Ware with externally collared and grooved rim and a concave neck, diam. 17.00 cm, expanding sides, bright red slip on both the sides, medium fabric, Period-V.
4. Fragment of a cooking vessel, flared, featureless rim, multi-grooved concave neck carinated to a sagger base, diam. 18.00 cm. the body below the shoulder is rusticated for the application of soot before cooking, Period-V.

Fig.38

1. Frying pan of Red Ware with a handle, diam. of pan is 13.00 cm, roughly made, coarse fabric, Period-V.
2. Fragment of a cooking *karahi* of Red Ware with a loop handle, diam. 38.00 cm, medium fabric, Period-V. It has rusticated base for the application of soot before cooking.
3. Basin of Red Slipped Ware with short outcurved rim, prominent flanged waist, convex sides, diam. 45.00 cm, medium fabric, Period-V.

Bone Objects and Arrowheads

In Gangetic plains arrowheads are mainly found from 800-200 BC. At Hastinapur they occur mainly in Period-II *i.e.* PGW level (Lal. 1954-55:151). At Kausambi they occur in Period-III *i.e.* NBPW level (Sharma. 1960: 59); socketed arrowheads have been recovered from Sravasti (Sinha. 1967:51). In Bihar the main concentration of the bone points and arrowheads is in the NBP Wperiod (Kumar.1978:47-48). Tanged arrowheads of Senuwar were studied under high magnification and prominent use marks were noticed on them (Thakur and Jayaswal. 1991: 163-170). On the basis of functional edge, arrowheads can be classified under the following categories:

- Tanged arrowheads
- Socketed arrowheads
- Socketed and tanged arrowheads
- Points with sigle ended
- Points with double ended
- Fragmentary specimens
- Roughly worked point

The excavation at Pakkakot yielded large number of bone and ivory points and arrowheads from all the periods. Of these, points are by far the largest in number and account for as many as 330 specimens. Their largest concentration is in Sunga-Kushan period where they account for 257 specimens. The second in order of frequency is tanged arrowheads which account for 26 specimens. Socketed arrowheads account for 7 specimens and socketed with tanged specimen accounts for 1 specimen only. The points have been divided in several categories like single ended, double ended, socketed and tanged etc. The manufacturing technique of these bone points was very simple where a bone was shaped with flaking of bones and tips were retouched for sharpening. The body of the bone points and arrowheads was smoothened and polished with the help of wetstones.

Table 18
Period wise distribution of bone points and arrowheads, Pakkakot

Type	*I*	*II*	*III A*	*III B*	*III C*	*IV*	*V*	*Total*
Points			03	09	59	257	02	330
Arrowheads								
Tanged	01	01	08	03	11	02		26
Socketed			03		02	02		07
Socketed and tanged			01					01
Total	01	01	15	12	72	261	02	364

Metal Objects

Excavations at Pakkakot have yielded antiquities of silver, copper and iron from different periods. Silver female figurine recovered from the pre-Mauryan level is a rarte discovery of the site. Among copper objects recovered from the site mention may be made of antimony rod, needle, nail-parer, ear-ring, crucible, solder, ring-shaped seal, punch-marked and cast coins. Iron antiquities were represented by chisel, nail, sickle, spearhead, *khurpi* etc.

Silver

The major source of silver has been the argentiferous lead-zinc ores of the Dawdwin mines in Myanmar and the Zewar mine, Udaipur, Rajasthan. Silver ores were also obtained from Baluchistan, Afghanistan, Iran etc. a small amount of silver could have come from the gold mines of South India where this metal is found naturally alloyed with gold and is believed to have been used since the Harappan period (Ghosh.1989:326-327). A silver bangle and a few silver fragments are reported from Lothal; 102 silver plates were recovered in association with the Copper Hoards from Gangeria. A hoard of silver punch-marked coins was discovered from Narhan (Singh.1994. Pls. LVI-LVII). The impurity pattern of Mohenjo-daro silver and punch-marked coins in general shows that their source was argentiferous galena rather than electrum. The chemical analysis of Lothal silver is not available. However, silver plates reported from Gangeria show 3.70 % gold and a punch-marked coin well protected in Lucknow museum has been reported with 10.53 % gold. This could imply that a method of separation of silver from gold was worked out during the Copper Hoard period. The regular use of silver is marked by the introduction of silver punch-marked coins by 6th century BCE. Metallurgical studies of silver punch-marked coins reveal that despite primitive techniques by 6th century BCE, Indians could obtain silver of high purity; 0.1 to 0.5 % lead was the main impurity. It indicates that cupellation was carried out with great perfection. Alloying of silver with copper was deliberate and in correct proportion, giving eases in casting, providing optimum strength and wear resistance. It also economized the metal.

The silver female figurine recovered from the site from the pre-Mauryan level measuring 10.75 cm long is a masterpiece of art (Pl.XXXII) and is not reported from any other side at this context. Its brief description is given below:

This silver figurine was found from the pre-Mauryan level alongwith a copper punch-marked coin. It was made by cutting the silver sheet with archaic features. Headdress is shown by incised lines. Design of dots is shown below the headdress. Hairs are well combed and parted in the middle. Locks of hair are shown on both sides of the cheeks. High eyebrows and flat nose represent the archaic feature. Right ear is broken while an ear-ring is worn in the left ear. A necklace is shown by wide strips. Head of the figurine is found broken and seems to be attached separately. Incised lines are shown from neck to the waist on both obverse and reverse sides. Rounded breasts seen to be uncovered. Incised lines are also shown on both hands and on both sides from shoulder to below the elbow which may have been made to show bangles. There are four bangles in both wrists. Fingers of both hands are found slightly broken. Left hand has been found broken from the elbow. The upper portion of the body is conical-shaped and the waist is very thin while the hips are very large and heavy. This type of hip is named *Prithusroni* in *Abhijñānashakuntalam*. The term *Vrihad sroni* is used by V.S.Agrawal for this type of hip. He has opined that large hip of females are helpful for easy delivery. A button type design within a circle is shown in the middle of the hip. Two parallel lines with dots are also shown on both sides of the hip. A large genital organ is beautifully carved. An anklet is shown in the right leg by four incised lines. Fingers of the right leg are slightly raised upwards. It seems that the figurine is in *Tribhanga mudra*. C. Margabandhu has suggested that this pose is very peculiar at that time and same type of terracotta figurine was discovered from Champa (Bhagalpur, Bihar). Left leg is broken. The antiquity and artistic features of the figurine prove its great importance. This unique finding is helpful to prove the site as a city site.

Cultural Context of the silver figurine

The silver figurine was found in Trench no. 11at the depth of 70-75 cm in layer 2 of Mound-3. This layer yielded coarse variety of NBPW, Black Slipped Ware and Grey Ware. The important shapes recovered from this layer are flanged bowls and Ahichhatra 10 A. one copper punch-marked coin was also recovered. These pottery types were recorded from Period-I C at Rajghat and Period-III at Narhan. All these pottery shapes occur in pre-Mauryan phase.

Copper

The excavation yielded 40 objects of copper distributed in Period-III to V. they comprise antimony rods, needles, nails, rings, crucibles and solders (Pl. XXXVII). Some of the specimens are not identifiable due to heavy erosion. Hence these specimens are placed under the indeterminate category. Periodwise distribution of these objects is presented below:

Table 19
Period wise distribution of Copper objects, Pakkakot

Shapes	*I*	*II*	*III A*	*III B*	*III C*	*IV*	*V*	*Total*
Antimony Rod				1	2	5	2	10
Needle				2	1			03
Nail-Parer						1		01
Ear-ring					2			02
Crucible				1				01
Solder (Joining agent)				1				01
Indeterminate			1	7	6	2	5	21
Ring-shaped Seal						1		01
Total			1	12	11	9	7	40

Iron

Total 45 iron objects were recovered from Period-III to V (Pls. XXXVIII, XLIV). a considerable number of these objects are so fragmentary and corroded that their form is difficult to recognize. After cleaning and preservation they are divisible into following categories:

- Agricultural equipments
- Craftsman tools
- Weapons/Hunting tools
- Indeterminate objects
- Objects of miscellaneous use

Periodwise distribution of these objects is presented below:

Table 20
Period wise distribution of Iron objects, Pakkakot

Shapes	*I*	*II*	*III A*	*III B*	*III C*	*IV*	*V*	*Total*
Chisel					1	1		02
Nail			1	2	7	9		19
Sickle							1	01
Spearhead					1	1		02
Indeterminate				3	6	3		12
Khurpi					2			02
Lumps (Slag)					7			07
Total			1	5	24	14	1	45

A glance at the above table reveals that Period-III yielded 30 objects of iron while the subsequent two periods yielded only 14 and 1 objects. This is because of the fact that cultural deposits of Period-V were exposed in a very limited area in comparison to other periods.

Beads, Pendants and Amulets

Beads as an artifact have not received much attention, but it holds considerable potential. Why beads have been long ignored is a matter of speculation. Every serious bead investigator has remarked on the shortcoming and the loss to archaeology due to improper study of beads. Bead making is often an important industry. Many materials such as gold, silver, lead, iron, copper, bronze, brass, faience, glass and more recently aluminum and plastic were employed for beads. Bead making has been often been in the forefront of ceramic and metallurgical developments. A study of bead is useful in providing data. Economic affairs are revealed in their intrinsic worth and their role as currency. Their use as magical chasrms reflects religious beliefs. Beads are employed as social diacritical marks, denoting status. There is considerable information which might be obtained from a detailed study of beads. For such a study a proper methodology and an appreciation is necessary. Especially, beads from burials were usually treated as valuable, while those found elsewhere were often taken to be less regarded. The variety of beads used at any one time makes it impossible to study single assemblage in isolation. For authentication this requires parallel examples from other sites. Ethnographic studies reveal that such beads are the predominant type among primitive peoples. This was true in prehistoric times as well. Thus we are necessarily losing considerable evidence from the earlier periods. A certain amount of specialized bead expertise is highly desirable because bead research is in its infancy. It requires more care than the study of better known artifacts. This may be done by any individual with an interest in them. Beads are properly accessioned in a format reserved for them. Along with their excavation number, location and date of recovery, the following entries are minimum requirements: material, form, colour, size, manufacturing technique and appropriate decoration and perforation. Though beads are small, each requires individual attention and notation.

In the Indian context beads of various raw materials are the important constituents of the assemblage of the antiquities recovered from any excavation, at least the Chalcolithic Period onwards. Some of the important product centres belonging to the different cultural phases are Mohenjo-daro (Kenoyer. 1986: 18-23; Tosi *et al.*1984: 9-37), Chanhu-daro (Mackay.1943: 35-36), Lothal (Rao. 1973: 79), Arikamedu (Wheeler *et al.* 1946: 17-124), Ujjain (Banerjee. 1959: 179-198), Kodumanal (Rajan. 1990: 93-102) and Agiabir (Singh and Singh. 1998: 141-149). The excavation at Pakkakot yielded 155 beads including 91 beads of terracotta. Due to limited excavation of the lower levels, no beads were recovered from the first two periods.

Stone Beads

Among the stone beads recovered from the site, carnelian and agate are more prolific, as they account for 15 and 9 specimens respectively. Crystal comes next in order of frequency of 5 specimens. Glass accounts for 16 specimens and were distributed in Period-III and IV (Pls. XXXV, XLV). Thr glass is either translucent or opaque and the range of colour is limited. The more common colours are green and blue. Ivory is the other popular material accounting for 15 specimens. Jasper and quartz were the other semi-precious stones used for making beads, with 2 and 1 specimen respectively. The above beads are diverse in the shapes. The beads are hexagonal, spherical, elliptical and square in shapes. Some beads have etched bands and some have natural colour. Periodwise distribution of stone beads is shown in the table below:

Table 21
Period wise distribution of stone beads, Pakkakot

Material	*I*	*II*	*III A*	*III B*	*III C*	*IV*	*V*	*Total*
Agate				1	3	5		09
Amythyst			1					01
Carnelian				1	6	8		15
Crystal					1	3	1	05
Glass			2	1	7	6		16
Ivory			3	1	6	4	1	15
Jasper			1		1			02
Quartz						1		01
Total			7	4	24	27	2	64

Terracotta Beads and Pendants

Excavations at` the site yielded 91 beads and pendants of terracotta forming approximately more than 50 % of the total collection of beads. *Ghat* shape is the most common shape which accounted for 55 beads. Most of the beads of this category have been treated with bright red slip. They were fired under oxidizing conditions resulting in a red colour. This type of beads is either standard or short categories. Both varities are present in Period-III to V (Pls. XXXVI, XLVII). Arecanut shaped beads came next in the order of frequency accounting for 28 specimens. This type of beads are made of fine clay on a fast wheel and baked very hard at a high temperature. Probably these beads were fired in closed kilns under reducing condition, resulting in a black or smokygrey surface. Majority of the beads are devoid of any surface treatment but a few have been treated with red or black slip. Disc-shaped and Cylindrical shaped beads are represented by 3 and 2 specimens respectively. Three terracotta pendants were recovered from Periods III A, IIIC and V respectively. Periodwise distribution of terracotta beads and pendants is shown in the table below:

Table 22
Period wise distribution of Terracotta Beads and Pendants, Pakkakot

Shapes	*I*	*II*	*III A*	*III B*	*III C*	*IV*	*V*	*Total*
Arecanut-shaped				3	11	10	4	28
Cylindrical-shaped					1	1		02
Disc-shaped						3		03
Ghat-shaped				8	23	24		55
Pendant			1		1		1	03
Total			1	11	36	38	5	91

Pendants and Amulets

The excavation yielded 21 pendants including one amulet, one each of crystal and agate and 18 of terracotta (Pl. LVIII). The amulet of terracotta was recovered from Period-V. The stone pendants are the best examples recovered from the site. One of the pendants is parrot and another is tortoise shaped. Tortoise shaped pendant have been reported from Rajghat (Narain and Singh. 1977, Pl.VIII, Nos. 9-11). Some terracotta pendants show exquisite craftsmanship. Periodwise distribution of pendants and amulets is shown in the table below:

Table 23
Period wise distribution of pendants and amulets, Pakkakot

Material	*I*	*II*	*III A*	*III B*	*III C*	*IV*	*V*	*Total*
Stone								
Crystal					1			01
Agate					1			01
Terracotta			1		4	12	1	18
Amulet							1	01
Total			1		6	12	2	21

The Pakkakot beads demonstrate that stone beads were imported from other places and terracotta beads were locally produced. As has been postulated for other prehistoric settlements of inland alluvial plains of UP (Sharma *et al.* 1980:89), it may be held that the stones utilized for bead making at Pakkakot were brought by the migrating groups of the Vindhyas.

Coins

Coin is one of the most valuable sources to throw light on ancient history. It not only confirms the data known from other sources but sometimes also throws light on those aspects of history for which no other evidence is avaible. The antiquity of the use of coins in India has been a subject of controversy among historians and Numismatists since a long time. It is beyond doubt that coins existed in India in the age of Buddha (483 BCE) and Panini (5th -4th century BCE). The terstimony of the early Buddhist literature, the *Ashtadhyayi* of Panini and other textx and also the archaeological evidence for the Punch-marked coins prove it conclusively (Goyal. 1995: 59). Excavations at the site yielded 10 copper coins from stratified context. Of these, 2 coins came from Mound-1, 7 coins recovered from Mound-2 and 1 from Mound-3 (Pls. XL-XLI, XLIX-L). Six coins belong to Punch-marked category and four belong to cast-coin. The stratigraphic details of these coins are given below:

Seals and Sealings

Seals and sealings have a great historical value and they are the most reliable source for early Indian history. The legends on seals and sealings are brief, compact and matter of fact. These seals and sealings throw valuable light on the past of political and administrative scenario and the socio-economic and religious conditions of the time.

Table 24
Details of Copper Punch-marked coins, Pakkakot

Sl. No.	Accession No.	Trench	Locus	Depth	Stratum	Period
1.	697	11	------------------------	0.65-0.70 m	2	III B
2.	646	6	NE 2.90 m x NW 5.15 m	5.15 m	3	III A
3.	740	14	------------------------	1.50-1.60 m	Pit-I SB-1	III B
4.	132	2	NE 4.75 m x NW 4.80 m	2.06 m	3	III B
5.	733	13	------------------------	1.20-1.25 m	Pit-I SB-1	III C
6.	554	8	NE 3.00 m x NW 4.00 m	60-65 m	2	III C

Table 25
Details of Copper Cast coins, Pakkakot

Sl. No.	Accession No.	Trench	Locus	Depth	Stratum	Period
1.	623	6	NE 3.00 m x NW 3.00 m	4.35 m	10	III C
2.	924	2	----------------------------	0.75-0.80 m	2	III C
3.	439	7	------------------------------	2.35-2.40 m	3	III C
4.	566	8	NE 3.00 m x NW 3.50 m	0.85-0.90 m	2	IV

A seal is that which is stamped with a device or legend and attached as a means of authentication or attestation. A sealing has the positive impression and the back of the sealing is usually possessed of the string-mark which witnesses that it was normally attached to some letter or other literary document. String markless sealings would most probably indicate the objects to be tokens rather than sealings. The token was not attached to any letter or document; it was probably presented to some person as a symbol or remembrance or given to some messenger with a view to authenticating him to be the actual person sent by the owner of the seal the impression of which the token bore. Most probably the sealings suggest that at a time they were attached to letters or literary documents they held together the stringtied, most probably, round the wooden boards which served as a letter-pad; in the latter case letters were written on the birch-barks or palm-leaves.

Excavations at Pakkakot yielded 10 seals and 24 sealings (Pls. XLII, LI-LIII, LVI). Seals are made of copper, bone and terracotta while sealings are made of terracotta only. Of these, 33 were recovered from different trenches and 1 was found from the surface. Some of them are oval and some are circular shaped. Most of them bear legend while some bear legend and device both and very few bear symbols only. These seals and sealings belong to Period-III to V. Some of the sealings have five impressions on it. A seal has been correctly defined as an engraved stamp bearing singly or collectively device, mark or letters related to the owner. This clearly testifies to the religious and socio-economic conditions especially as a centre of trade of this site. On the basis of stratigraphy and palaeography these finds belong to Maurya, Sunga-Kushan, Gupta and Post-Gupta periods. The largest number of these finds belongs to Sunga-Kushan period. Periodwise and stratigraphic details of seals and sealings are given in table nos. 26-29:

Table 26
Period wise and material wise distribution of seals, Pakkakot

Material	*I*	*II*	*III A*	*III B*	*III C*	*IV*	*V*	*Total*
Copper						1		1
Bone						1		1
Terracotta					5	3		8
Total					5	5		10

Table 27
Period wise and material wise distribution of sealings, Pakkakot

Material	*I*	*II*	*III A*	*III B*	*III C*	*IV*	*V*	*Total*
Terracotta				3	8	11	2	24
Total				3	8	11	2	24

Table 28
Stratigraphic details of seals, Pakkakot

Sl.No.	Material	Accession No.	Trench	Locus	Depth	Stratum	Period
1.	Copper	271	7	-----------	1.10-1.15 m	2	---------
2.	Bone	415	7	----------	2.20-2.25 m	3	---------
3.	Terracotta	543	6	----------	3.80 m	10	III C
4.	Terracotta	507	6	-----------	3.65 m	9	III C
5.	Terracotta	567	8	-----------	80-85 cm	2	III C
6.	Terracotta	371	7	-----------	1.90-195 m	3	III C
7.	Terracotta	344	7	NW 2.40 m x NE 3.20 m	1.90-195 m	3	III C
8.	Terracotta	383	6	NE 1.16 m x NW 3.75 m	2.45 m	7	III C
9.	Terracotta	399	6	NE 1.80 m x NW 4.15 m	2.06 m	7	III C
10.	Terracotta	24	Surface	------------	-----------	Humus	Unstratified

Table 29
Stratigraphic details of Terracotta sealings, Pakkakot

Sl. No.	*Accession No.*	*Trench*	*Locus*	*Depth*	*Stratum*	*Period*
1.	738	14	----------------	1.50-1.55 m	Pit-I SB-1	III B
2.		7	----------------	2.75-2.80 m	5	IIIB
3.	440	7	---------------	2.55-2.60 m	4	IIIC
4.	496	6	NW 3.50 m x NE 2.70 m	3.75 m	10	IIIC
5.	346	7	NW 3.10 m x NE 2.90 m	1.90 m	Pit-I SB-2	IIIC
6.	466 A	6	NE 2.40 m x NW 4.30 m	3.35 m	8	IIIC
7.	497	6	NW 3.80 m x NE 2.60 m	3.75 m	10	IIIC
8.	468 A	6	NE 3.70 m x NW 1.80 m	3.55 m	9	IIIC
9.	165 B	5	NW 1.96 m x NE 3.07 m	0.46 m	1	IV
10.	247 A	7	SW 2.70 M x SE 2.85 m	0.90 m	2	IV
11.	247 A	7	SW 2.70 M x SE 2.85 m	0.90 m	2	IV
12.	887	7-8 (Baulk)	---------------------	0.75-0.80 m	2	IV
13.	711	15	--------------------	1.70-1.75 m	4	IV

Sl. No.	Accession No.	Trench	Locus	Depth	Stratum	Period
14.	183	5	------------------	0.55-0.60 m	2	IV
15.	162	5	SW 3.30 M x NW 4.40 m	0.30 m	1	IV
16.	165 A	5	NW 4.70 m x NE 0.90 m	0.75 m	2	IV
17.	235	6	NE 2.75 m x NW 3.15 m	1.45 m	2	IV
18.	128 B	5	-------------------	0.55-0.60 m	2	IV
19.	380	7	-------------------	1.80-185 m	2	IV
20.	128 A	5	-------------------	0.50-0.55 m	2	IV
21.	172	6	NE 3.12 m x NW 4.87 m	1.08 m	1	V
22.	763	15	------------------	0.55-0.60 m	2	V
23.	776	15	------------------	0.75-0.80 m	Pit-I SB-1	V
24.	595	6	NE 3.20 m x NW 2.30 m	4.18 m	11	III C

Seals and sealings of Pakkakot belong to Period-III A to V dated from 4th century BCE to 7th century CE. It is clear that they had been used for sending materials for trade. It is noteworthy that Pkkakot lies on an important trade route between Pataliputra to Kapilvastu via Buxar. The traders used to cross the Ganges near Buxar and proceeded towards Kapilvastu through Pakkakot. The discovery of a number of seals and sealings from the limited excavation proves that the traders of Pakkakot had taken active part in the riverine and land trade.

Legends engraved on the seals are: "Dara" and "Tri" in Mauryan Brahmi and "Ga-Sena" in Kushanan Brahmi. Apart of these symbols like Sun, leaves, tree etc. are also engraved on various seals recovered from different periods. Now coming on the legends engraved on the sealings, special mention may be made of those having several impressions. The sealing bearing the legend "Revatimitasa" and "Negadisa" in Maurya-Sunga Brahmi script, explains the name of a person and a place respectively. The sealing of "Revatimitasa" was also recovered from Rajghat. The "Negadisa" is a place name of "Nigata." The name is well comparable with a site "Nigatapur" about 30 km west from Rajghat on the left bank of the River Ganga. These sealings show close relationship between Rajghat and neighbouring areas like Pakkakot. The sealings bearing the legend "Ramdasasa" and "Sri Gopalasayasa" have the earliest example of legendary Ram and Gopal in early 2nd century BCE. It was believed that before 5th century CE Vaishnavism was not prevalent in this region due to dominant power of Buddhism but these sealings is able to discard this theory and proves that people were well aware of Ram and Gopal (Krishna), the two famous incarnations of Vishnu. The sealing bearing the legend "Matibharadhikaranasya" in Guptan Brahmi has a close similarity with the place Matahi, situated about 3 km south from Pakkakot on the left bank of River *Chhoti Saryu*. One impression on the sealing is *Gajabhisheka* which is actually Mahamaya Devi standing in the centre and Upasakas are depicted on the right and left sides while another impression is of *Purnaghata*.The legend "Chetakvihare" shows existence of a monastery which is not comparable to any site at the meantime (Dubey *et al*.2012: 241-259). Other legends found on the sealings are: "[Ha] risenaputasa", "Shivadatasa", "Arimitasa", "Savvamasu" and "Savvamitasa" which indicate individual names. Other sealings of the collection which possesses symbols only, like *Swastika*, Crescent on hill, *Nandipada*, and flower are probably used for tokens, passports or identity cards. Another possibility of these sealings may be their use as votive offerings or official authentication for things.

Religious features of the symbols

Symbols on seals like Sun, tree with branches, *Pipal* leaves, palm leaves, fish etc. also show the religious features of their time. Depiction of Sun symbol on seals may be related with Sun worship while fish is the symbol of *Matsyāvatāra* Vishnu. Pipal leaves, palm leaves and tree with branches indicate about the nature worship. Pipal leaves may be associated with Bhāgavatism and Buddhism while palm leaves with the worship of Balarāma.

Sealings having symbols of flower motif, crescent on hill, *Swastika, Nandipada, Purnaghata,* star and *Parashu* also throw light on their religious affairs. These symbols may be associated with Shaivism, Vaishnavism and nature worship. The sealings bearing legends like *Ramdasas* and *Gopalasayasa* arer the earliest examples of legendary Rama and Gopala in early 2nd century BCE while literary sources says that Vaishnavism was not propagated in this region till 5th century CE due to the supremacy of Buddhism and Jainism. The sealing bearing the legend *Matibharadhikaranasya* and *Chetakvihare* and having impression of *Gajabhisheka* and *Purnaghata* shows its close relation with Buddhism. Gajabhisheka is Mahamayadevi standing in the centre and upasakas are depicted on the right and left side. The legend *Chetakvihare* speaks about the existence of a Buddhist monastery which is not identified with any site it the mean time.

The impressions and legends found on the seals and sealings of Pakkakot show that Śaivism, Vaishnavism and Buddhism were propagated in this region and they flourished there side by side. In this way we can say that the art objects recovered from the ancient site of Pakkakot are capable to represent successfully the religio-artistic features of their time.

Terracotta Figurines

The terracotta figurines recovered during the present excavation at Pakkakot consist of some 44 human and 23 animal figurines. There were noticed no clay figurines in the levels of Period I, II and III A. However, the late phase of Period III marks the beginning of such pieces at the site, yielding hand-modelled specimens and in moulded form too. In few cases a perforation is seen which perhaps allowed them to be suspended with a thread. Some fragmentary figurines showing several varieties of the hand-modelled female type were found both from the levels of Period III C and Period IV. Most of the specimens are modelled figurines (Pls. XXXIX, LIV-LV).

Human Figurines

Six mould-made and hand-modelled plaques, all fragmentary, were recovered from Period IV which can stylistically be well classified under the category of Sunga-style figurines representing various types of artistic models. There is only one example of Gupta and post-Gupta plaque recovered from period V. Female figures with prominent breast were three in number which were recovered from Period III B, IV and V. In these figurines the upper and lower portions are missing with the result that details regarding human anatomy, dress and ornaments and hair style can not be reconstructed. There are seven examples of human head showing headdress with a top-knot found from period V. A class of human heads reported from various sites in north-western India and Gangetic plains have been grouped under this category because some of their facial features are Indian and at times bear physical features of the races and peoples of Western and Central Asia like the Shakas and Kushanas. Commenting upon these foreign ethnic types of human terracottas S. K. Mukherjee has noted that the figurines betraying alien and out-landish types moved from the west to the east. In other words, it may be concluded that alongwith the migrations of the alien types from the west and Central Asia and subsequent intermingling of foreigners with existing populations, the terracotta motifs ultimately got absorbed to a great extent (Mukherjee. 1990: 271-280). Only one female figure with hollow cylindrical body was recovered from period III C. In this specimen the breasts are heavy and made by appliqué technique. Similar crude figures with cylindrical body have been recorded from Ahichchhatra, Kausambi, Pataliputra, Sonpur, Vaisali, Rajghat, Narhan and Khairadih.

The so called mother-goddess type figurines, so common at other sites such as Rajghat, Kausambi and Ahichchhatra, were two in number and recovered here at Pakkakot from period III C and IV. Both figurines are crudely modelled by hand and roughly pinched in clay to the desired shape to represent a stylized human shape. Both are shaped like star-fish, flattened on the back and front with four points marking the ends of the arms and legs, and the top with rounded outline, which forms the head. The religious connotation of both figurines is not proven but in search of any better name, the nomenclature "mother goddess" has been retained by archaeologists.

Two male figures in standing posture were found from Period IV and V in which the lower portions of the body below the waist are preserved. The most important figurine is of a composite man and animal (probably *Kinnar*) form which was recovered from Period IV. It consists of a human body alongwith an animal having horse like features. It is difficult to confirm its typology because upper portion of the human body is missing.

Two specimens of female figurine of Gupta and post-Gupta period were recovered here from Period V. Several sites of the Ganga plain have yielded a large number of terracotta male and female plaques from this level showing lovely hair styles. The moulded plaques are made of single mould in moderate relief while the back is left flat and plain. These are made of finely levigated clay with no admixture of degressant and are well-baked. A majority of them represents standardized figure-models of fashionable male and female wearing a variety of gorgeous coiffures. The most favourite form of coiffure was the wig-like arrangement of hair (Gupta. 1972: 57). A female figure having lovely hair-style, rich coiffure and wig-like arrangement of the hair has been recovered from the present site from period V. At times the hair crowns the head as a semi-circular parasol with spiral locks arranged like ribs close to each other, all radiating from a top-knot. This figure has an oval, smiling face with large eyes, aquiline nose, full lips and plump cheeks.

One specimen of religious figurine was recovered from Period V while broken human figurines are eighteen in number, amongst them two were recovered from Period III B, two from Period III C, four from Period IV and ten from period V. Period-wise chart of terracotta human figurines is given below:

Table 30
Typological chart of terracotta human figurines, Pakkakot

Types	*I*	*II*	*III A*	*III B*	*III C*	*IV*	*V*	*Total*
Sunga plaques						6		6
Female figures with prominent breast				1		1	1	3
Human head					1	3	3	7
Female figures with hollow cylindrical body					1			1
Mother Goddess (hand made)					1	1		2
Standing male figure						1	1	2
Naigamesha type						1		1
Gupta and post-Gupta female figure							2	2
Gupta and post-Gupta plaque							1	1
Religious figure							1	1
Broken human figurines				2	2	4	10	18
Total				3	5	17	19	44

Animal Figurines

The excavation yielded a total number of twenty three animal figurines including six bird-shaped and two indeterminate comprising stylized figures of bull, elephant, *Nandi*, buffalo, large antelope, frog, horse, dog, snake, duck, peacock and bird. Some figures are badly broken and their fragmentary remains do not permit correct identification. All the specimens represent the technique of hand-modelling and in some cases show a skilful artistry of terracotta work. All the figurines are solid except one of duck and one of peacock which come from Period IV. These figures were perhaps used as wheeled toys. Of these, birds are numerically more prolific as they account for as many as four pieces. The second in order of frequency are elephant and horse respectively, which account for three specimens. There are two dogs recovered from period IV and two large antelopes (one from period III C and one from period IV) while bull, *Nandi*, duck, peacock, buffalo, frog and snake are represented by one specimen each (Pls. LIX-LXII).

Elephants are more popular at Hastinapur, Kausambi and Rajghat and horse was a favourite animal at Kausambi. Bull seems to be a principal animal in case of Narhan. Large antelopes and camels have also been reported from Kausambi (Sharma. 1960: 73). The figure of peacock found from this site is incised while bird figures are bright reds slipped. The anatomical details and the muscular bodies of some animals are quite realistic. A solitary figure of *Nandi*, coming from period V, displays exquisite workmanship. The stratigraphic distribution of these animal figures is given in the following table:

Table 31
Typological chart of terracotta animal figurines, Pakkakot

Types	*I*	*II*	*III A*	*III B*	*III C*	*IV*	*V*	*Total*
Bull					1			1
Elephant						3		3
Nandi							1	1
Duck						1		1
Bird						1	3	4
Indeterminate						1	1	2
Peacock						1		1
Buffalo					1			1
Antelope					1	1		2
Frog					1			1
Horse						1	2	3
Dog						2		2
Snake					1			1
Total					5	11	7	23

Terracotta and Pottery Discs

Flat circular objects of well-levigated clay and fired under oxidizing condition have been termed as discs. More than 400 specimens were recovered from Rajghat; almost half of them belong to Period-I B (600-400 BCE). Terracotta discs were also reported from Hastinapur and Atranjikhera from PGW level while at Mathura, Sravasti, Prahladpur and Masondih it was found from NBPW level. A single specimen was recovered from Kumrahar. This type of antiquity was also found from Awra, Nevasa and Brahmagiri situated in Central India, Deccan and South India but their concentration was mostly in the Gangetic plain.

Excavation at Pakkakot yielded very few specimens of terracotta discs while pottery discs or hopscotches are found 69 in number distributed in all the periods (Pls.XXXI, LXIII-LXIV). Among them 13 specimens have single perforation while unperforated pottery discs account for 56 specimens. A decorated pottery disc was recovered from Period-IV. It has 5 circular designs and 9 vertical lines on the exterior. Their periodwise distribution is given below:

Table 32
Period wise distribution of Pottery-discs, Pakkakot

Period	*BRW*	*BSW*	*NBPW*	*RW*	*RSW*	*UNS*	*Total*
I				5			5
II	1			5	2		8
III A				2	1		3
III B		2	1	7			10
III C		4		12	3		19
IV				14			14
V				8			8
Total	1	6	1	53	6	2 (RW)	67+2 (UNS) = 69

Terracotta Balls

Terracotta balls are described as marbles, pellets, sling ball etc. they are solid, handmade, well rounded and baked to a red colour. They have been found in sizeable numbers from Taxila, Rajghat, Kumrahar, and Vaishali etc. Excavation at Pakkakot yielded 128 terracotta balls from Period-III to V (Pl.LXV). No specimens were recovered from Period-I and II. These balls were made of medium to fine grained clay and baked hard in oxidizing condition. Majority of them are in bright red colour. A few of them are peeled-off at places due to weathering effect. The biggest one has diam. of 6.50 cm while the smallest one is only 1.50 cm in diam. Their periodwise distribution is as follows:

Table 33
Period wise distribution of terracotta balls, Pakkakot

Material	*I*	*II*	*III A*	*III B*	*III C*	*IV*	*V*	*Total*
Ball			4	15	52	45	12	128

Terracotta Wheels

It is a very common antiquity and is reported from various sites of the Ganga plain like Atranjikhera, Hastinapur, Kausambi, Rajghat, Vaishali, Kumrahar, Pataliputra, Manjhi, Narhan etc. in various levels. Here at Pakkakot 35 terracotta wheels were recovered. Of these 2 come from Period-II, 20 from Period-III, 10from Period-IV and 3 from Period-V (Pl. LXVI). Periodwise distribution is given below:

Table 34
Period wise distribution of terracotta wheels, Pakkakot

Material	*I*	*II*	*III A*	*III B*	*III C*	*IV*	*V*	*Total*
TC Wheel		2	1	7	12	10	3	35

Terracotta Pestles and Dabbers

The excavation yielded 9 terracotta pestles and 3 dabbers (Pl. LXVII). Their ends are slightly tapering and the longitudinal outline is convex. These pestles are pecked by excising the clay with the help of some sharp instrument. Longitudinal grooves have been made all over the body. The dabbers recovered from the site may be divided into two groups:

- Dabber with solid handle and
- Dabber with a hole in the handle

The excavation yielded 2 specimens of 1st category while the 2nd category has one specimen only. These types of dabbers are very common in mid-Ganga plain. Similar dabbers have been recovered from Period-V at Hastinapur and Atranjikhera (Lal. 1954-55: 150-151; Gaur. 1983: 89). Two dabbers have been reported from Nevasa (Sankalia.1960:384-385).

Periodwise distribution of terracotta pestles is shown in the table below:

Table 35
Period wise distribution of terracotta pestles, Pakkakot

Material	*I*	*II*	*III A*	*III B*	*III C*	*IV*	*V*	*Total*
TC Pestles					1	5	3	09

Bangles

The excavation yielded 65 bangles of which 13 made of glass, 3 each of ivory and agate and 46 of terracotta (Pl. LXVIII). Glass bangles were recovered in a good quantity in Periods-III and IV. They are mainly of sea-blue and light green in colour. Bangles of terracotta were recovered in a good number from Period-III C and IV and account for 20 and 21 specimens respectively. Periodwise and materialwise distribution is presented in the table given below:

Table 36
Period wise and material wise distribution of bangles, Pakkakot

Material	*I*	*II*	*III A*	*III B*	*III C*	*IV*	*V*	*Total*
TC				2	20	21	3	46
Glass			1	2	4	6		13
Agate					2	1		03
Ivory					1	1	1	03
Total			1	4	27	29	4	65

Terracotta Feeding Cups

Four miniature terracotta feeding cups were recovered from the excavation, 1 from Period-III B, 2 from Period-III C and 1 from Period-V (Pl. LXIX). These feeding cups are either with a short spout or without spout. They were probably used for feeding the infants or some ritualistic purpose.

Ivory Dice

In early historic period dice was made of stone, bone, ivory and terracotta. It was rectangular in shape and consists of punched circlet designs on all the four facets. Generally the incised designs engraved on it are 1, 2, 3 and 4. The dice of this denomination is reported from Period-II and V at Narhan (Singh.1994; Fig.77, Nos. 7, 8 and 11) and from Period-IV at Kumrahar (Altekar.1959, Reprint 2005: 136).

One dice of ivory was recovered from Period-V at Pakkakot. It has a peculiar engraving of 6, 10, 16 and 22 artistic circles; length is 4 cm, width and thickness is 0.9 cm.

Ivory Handle

An ivory handle of a knife or mirror was recovered from Period-III B; length is 8 cm, maximum thickness is 1.4 cm having circular cross section and shining surface. It has two small holes on both the sides for revetting the object.

Terracotta Skin Rubbers

The excavation yielded 2 terracotta skin rubbers, 1 each from Period-III C and IV. Both the specimens are rectangular in shape. Their surface has been roughened by incising criss-cross designs and simple longitudinal lines. The designs have been made on both the surface.

Terracotta Cones

The excavation yielded 28 terracotta cones from Period-III to V. They are mostly handmade and found mostly ill-fired., grey in colour. In most of the cases one end tapers. The thicker end is generally rounded and club-shaped. Similar antiquities have been reported from Period-III and IV at Kumrahar (Altekar, 1959; Pl. LXI), Period-V at Narhan (Singh. 1994; Pl. LI). Period-I at Prahladpur (Narain and Roy.1968:56) and Rajghat (Narain and Singh.1979:70).

Floral Remains

The floral remains of the site were scientifically studied by our team members Ms. Anubha Pathak and Prof. R.N.Singh. Dr. K.S.Saraswat has also given very valuable suggestions. The exhaustive collection of ancient remains of cereal, pulses, seed fruit and stem pieces was made by flotation technique for different phases particularly of Neolithic and Chalcolithic levels. The samples of organic remains from the Neolithic and Chalcolithic level could be successfully recovered from the different horizons of the habitational deposits. These comprised of more than two dozens genera. The seeds and other botanical remains were cleaned in 10 % dilute acetic acid and subsequent washing in distilled water for two or three times. Finally they were dried at normal temperature for macro data based study of morphological character with their counterpart.

From the little volume of food grains retrieved from within a fairly restricted area of excavation it has, however, been possible to obtain a good deal of information on the vegetable food available to the settlers in this region and even a glimpse of contacts beyond this region. By far the majority of grains are found in mutilated and highly distorted condition as a consequence of heat and wear, but a small fraction of the finds have permitted safe identification. The grain sample was of mixed contents. Cereal grains of wheat, barley and rice and the leguminous seeds belonging to lentil and bean in complete and broken condition. The excavation at Pakkakot, particularly of lower level, was done on a limited scale; accordingly the finds give only a limited insight into the subsistence economy. A brief note on the nature of the material and description of cultural context along with their material evidence are given in the table below:

Table 37
Description of faunal remains, Pakkakot

Sl. No.	*Archaeological Context*	*Depth in cm*	*Result*
1.	PKT-1, 14(3)	265-270 cm	Nigella sp, Brassica sp, (Mustard), Lens culinaris (Lentil), Triticum sp (Wheat), Hordeum sp (Barley), Chenopodium album (Pigweed), Trigonella occulta
2.	PKT-1, 14(3)	270-280 cm	Chenopodium album (Pigweed), Trienthema sp, Triticum sp (Wheat), Pisum sativum (Matar), Lens culinaris (Lentil), Hordeum sp (Barley), Dolichus biflorus (Bean)
3.	PKT-1, 14(4)	310-315 cm	Dolichus biflorus (Bean), Vigna sp, Oryza sativa (Rice), Chenopodium album (Pigweed), Brassica compestris (Mustard), Hordeum sp (Barley), Argemone maxicana, Trienthema sp, Pisum sativum (Matar)
4.	PKT-1, 14(4)	315-325 cm	Lens culinaris (Lentil), Lathyrus sp (Wild Pea), Hordeum sp (Barley), Triticum sp (Wheat), Chenopodium album (Pigweed), Oryza sativa (Rice)
5.	PKT-1, 14(4)	325-330 cm	Oryza sativa (Rice), Lens culinaris (Lentil), Chenopodium album (Pigweed),
6.	PKT-1, 14()	335-340 cm	Triticum sp (Wheat), Hordeum sp (Barley), Chenopodium album (Pigweed), Brassica compestris (Mustard), Lathyrus sp (Wild Pea), Nigella sp, Pisum sativum (Matar),
7.	PKT-1, 14(4)	345-350 cm	Oryza sativa (Rice), Brassica compestris (Mustard), Vigna sp, Triticum sp (Wheat), Triticum sphaerococcum, Dolichus biflorus (Bean), Lens culinaris (Lentil), Hordeum sp (Barley), Chenopodium album (Pigweed)

Detailed of identified plant remains

Neolithic context

- Triticum aestivum: The carbonized grains 4-5 in numbers have been identified. Since the seeds are mostly broken hence identification was difficult. Many caryopses have been recovered measuring 5.5-6.00 mm in length and 2.5-3.50 mm in breadth and about 2.50 mm in thickness. The grains are narrower towards both the end and thicker in the middle resemble those of bread wheat- Triticum aestivum (Pl. LXX, 1).
- Trigonella occulta: One carbonized seed has been encountered having renifirm shape with prominent beak and notched helium. Surface becomes rough due to

pressure. Its size measures 1.20 mm in length and 0.60-0.80 mm in breadth. It has been identified as Trigonella occulta (Pl. LXX, 2).

- Chenopodium album: Anumber of shiny, circular to lenticular seeds with rounded margins measuring 1.00-1.50 mm in diameter have been identified. It has resemblance with living counterpart of the genera (Pl. LXX, 3).
- Cyperus sp.: Many carbonized and semi-carbonized elongated triangular seeds measuring 1.00-1.90 mm in length, 0.75-0.95 mm in breadth and 0.60-0.80 mm in thickness have been identified as Cyperus sp. (Pl. LXX, 4).

Chalcolithic context

- Vigna radiata: Two broken cotyledon have been encountered having elongated and somewhat cylindrical in shape measuring 3.20-3.90 mm in length and 2-3 mm in breadth. Elliptical helium is situated at level of seed coat surface (Pl. LXX, 5-6).
- Hordeum vulgare: Two to three complete and broken pieces caryopsis have been recovered measuring 4.50-6.50 mm in length and 2-3 mm in thickness. The ventral furrow originates from base and gradually widen towards the upper end of the grains. The dorsal side is almost flat and embryo rests on the beak like projection. Morphologically it can be compared to living counterpart (Pl. LXX, 7).
- Lens culinaris: There are 6-7 broken carbonized and semi-carbonized seeds which have been identified. They are circular and flattened with keeled margin measuring 2.80-3.80 mm in diameter (Pl. LXXI, 8).
- Oryza sativa: Two grains of charred rice have been identified in the collection with a few broken caryopses which measure 4-5 mm in length and 1.90-2.20 mm in thickness. All grains are without husk and narrow oblong in shape, laterally flattened and much longer than broader, can be compared to Oryza sativa (Pl. LXXI, 9).
- Triticum aestivum: Pieces of the Triticum variety are highly charred and can not be identify correctly, although by appearance it can be compared to Triticum aestivum (Pl. LXIX, 1).
- Triticum spharococcum: One complete seed having smaller in size and broader in breadth than Triticum aestivum variety. Its size is 4-5 mm in length while breadth is 2.50-3.20 mm. it can be identified as Triticum spharococcum (Pl. LXXI, 10).
- Dolichus biflorus: Two to three broken ellipsoidal and somewhat kidney shaped, laterally flattened specimens have been encountered measuring 3.20-4.00 mm in length and 2-3 mm in breadth. Seed resembles to somewhat horsegram (Pl. LXXI, 11).
- Pisum sp.: Many small carbonized pieces of Pisum have been identified measuring 3.20-4.00 mm. however, no complete seed was recovered (Pl. LXXI, 12).
- Brassica sp.: Two to three semi-carbonized spherical seeds measuring 1.50-2.00 mm in diameter have been identified. Seed surface are rough with characteristic

reticulum. Morphologically it can be compared to similar looking seed of Brassica sp. (Pl. LXXI, 13).

- Nigelia sp.: Two to three carbonized slightly triangular in shape with marginal line seeds are identified having a measurement of 2.50-3.00 mm in length and 1.00-1.50 mm in breadth (Pl. LXXI, 14).
- Trienthema sp.: Three to four carbonized seeds have been identified of this species. The seeds are compressed and orbicular in shape and characteristically beaked near helium and exhibit transversely tuberculate surface. They are measured as 1.25-1.50 mm in length and 1.00-0.25 mm in breadth (Pl. LXXI, 15).
- Chenopodium album: A few shiny, circular to lenticular seeds with rounded margins measuring 1.00-1.50 mm in diameter have been identified as Chenopodium album(Pl. LXX, 3).

The occurrence of carbonized cereal, legume, oilseed and spices wood pieces throw light on the regional pattern of agriculture at Pakkakot and its vicinity. Presence of carbonized wheat, rice bordeum and legume seed clearly suggest that these are the main crop of earliest settlers. In addition, recovery of carbonized spices as Brassica, Trigonella and Nigella suggest that they also form the part of diet of the settler of the site. The presences of wild plants such as Chenopodium and Trienthema at the site which are in habitant of cold area suggest inter-regional contact of the inhabitant of the site. However, at places, Chenopodium's seed being used as food, but due to shortage of enough material, its usage at the site is uncertain. To understand properly the subsistence pattern and economy of the region, enough materials are required. The collection of plant material from the present site is quite unique which have demonstrated that during Neolithic period wheat and barley along with rice, agriculture became a firmly established economy at the site like other sites of mid-Ganga plain (Saraswat.2004-2005: 42). The find depict the traditional composition of the vegetable food available to the people. The main ingredients were cereals and legumes with occasional occurrence of fruits.

Faunal Remains

A random collection of faunal material recovered from the multi-culture site of Pakkakot was examined using standard archaeozoological methods and a protocol established at the Archaeozoology Laboratory, Deccan College, Pune by Prof P.P.Joglekar. The study revealed presence of 9 domestic species (Cattle, Buffalo, Goat and Pig), 7 wild mammals (Nilgai, Sambar, Spotted Deer, Four-horned Antelope, Blackbuck, Wild Pig and Hare), birds (Saras crane and Peafowl), reptiles (Indian Sawback Turtle and Ganga Softshell Turtle), a fresh water fish species and freshwater mussel. A total of 166 fragments were examined of which 120 were identifiable (Table-38). This high proportion of identifiable fragments is mainly because of excellent preservation of the skeletal elements. Each bone fragment was thoroughly examined to find out the impact of both pre and post-depositional factors. Bone modification signatures that were searched include intentional fractures (Sadek Kooros.1975) as well as accidental breakage of bones both in the past and after their recovery during the excavation process. The results of bone identification and where it was possible to messure bones, the measurements (Driesch, Von A.1976) were recorded in the computerized coded format used at the Deccan College. DCPARZ-computer software developed at the Archaeozoology Laboratory by Prof Joglekar in late 1980s was used to analyse the bones recorded in the standard format. Identification work was done at Archaeology Laboratory, Department of AIHC & Archaeology, Banaras Hindu University in 2011. Only a few fragments were taken to the Archaeozoology Laboratory, Deccan College for confirmation. After the analysis was over, select bones were photographed and all the studied material was restored back to the respective storage bags. Summary of faunal identification is shown in the table below.

Table 38
Summary of identified faunal specimens of Pakkakot

Period	*NISP*	*Unidentified Large*	*Unidentified Medium*	*Unidentified Small*	*Total*	*Total fragments*
I	18	1	3	6	10	28
II	4		1	1	02	06
III A	13	1	1	3	05	18
III B	11	1	2	4	07	18
III C	33	1	3	5	09	42
IV	41	3	6	4	13	54
Total	120	7	16	23	46	166

Period-I (Neolithic)

A total of 18 fragments were identifiable from Period-I (Table-38). Of these 14 fragments belonged to cattle, Buffalo and Goat (Pl. LXXII-LXXIII). The faunal material was mostly well-preserved and fragments are of large size. Only in case of a fragment of cattle femur edge was damaged, perhaps due to physical movement within the habitation deposit. A fragment of cattle humerus shaft has also preserved evidence of post-depositional damage where the surface has been cracked and some part of the bone surface has got peeled off. Impressions of Dog teeth (molars) were observed in case of two fragments-a first phalanx (PKT-27) and a second phalanx (PKT-24) of cattle. One bone tool made using metatarsal of cattle (PKT-23) was recovered from trench 9, layer-4. Tip of this tool has been fire hardened. Three fragments of wild mammals were found from this period. These were a maxilla with completely worn out tooth of spotted Deer (Axis axis), distal end of a tibia of Hare (Lepus nigricoills) with a cut mark, and a mandible fragment of wild Pig (Sus scrofa) with a broken first molar (Pl. LXXIV). A single charred fragment of carapace of the Indian Sawback Turtle (Kachuga tecta) was identified from trench 14, layer 4 (Pl. LXXV).

Period II (Chalcolithic)

Material from Period-II contained only 6 fragments of which 2 could not be identified (Table-38). Three of the identifiable fragments were antlers of Sambar (Cervus unicolor) (Pl. LXXVI). One of these was a shed antler (PKT-18) and the other was the brow tine of the main branch (PKT-19). Looking at the un-abraded edges of the shed antler, it seems that it was picked up by people just after mid-March or early April after the stag has shed it. The brow tine bearing main beam was sawed with some sharp instrument. The 3rd antler fragment (PKT-20) was of the brow tine that has been rubbed by the stag. Apart from these a large cranial fragment (interopercle bone) of the giant river cat fish (Sperata seenghala) was recovered from trench 9, layer 4. This edible fish species is commonly found in rivers of throughtout the Indian Subcontinent.

Period-III (NBPW)

A total of 78 fragments were identifiable from Period-III (Table-38) that was divided into three sub-phases: III A, III B and III C. Of these 57 fragments could be identified. Only 12 fragments of Period-III A were identifiable and except one carapace of the Ganges soft shell Turtle (Trionyx gangeticus), the rest belonged to cattle. One tool (PKT-3) recovered from trench 9 was a point that was polished. One fragment of radius bone of cattle showed marks of charring and cutting activities. Identified specimens (NISP) of the site are given in the table below:

Table 39
Identified specimens (NISP) of Pakkakot

Period	*I*	*II*	*III A*	*III B*	*III C*	*IV*
Trench	9	9/6	9	2/7	7-8/6/6	7/7/7-8
Layer	(4)	(4)/(8)	(3)	(5)/(5-6)	(3)/(9)/(11)	(1)/(2)/(1-2)
Bos indicus	5		2	0/1	3/0/0	1/0/2
Bos /Bubalus	4		9	0/6	12/0/0	0/0/9
Bubalus bubalis	2					0/0/1
Capra hircus	3				0/0/2	0/0/1
Capra/Ovis				0/1	4/0/0	0/0/12
Sus domesticus						0/0/2
B. Tragocamelus	1					0/0/1
T. quadricornis					1/0/0	
A.cervicapra					0/0/2	1/0/1
Axis axis	1			1/0	2/1/0	0/0/3
Cervus unicolor		0/3			0/1/0	0/2/0
Sus scrofa	1			0/1	4/0/0	0/0/3
Lepus nigricollis	1					0/0/1
Pavo cristatus						0/0/1
Grus antigone				0/1		
Trionyx gangeticus			1			
Kachuga tecta	1					
Sperata seenghala		1/0				
Lamellidens sp.					1/0/0	
NISP Total	19	1/3	12	1/10	27/2/4	2/2/37

Only 11 fragments were recovered from Period-III B. It was possible to identify the Spotted Deer (Pl.LXXVII), Wild Pig (Pl. LXXVIII) besides cattle and Sheep/Goat from the assemblage. One rib fragment of Cattle/Buffalo showed butchering mark (Pl. LXXIX) while a mandible fragment showed a cut mark just below the condyle. Sex identification was possible in one case-a femur fragment of cattle showed large scars for muscle attachment. An interesting find of this assemblage is femur of Saras Crane (Grus Antigone), an endemic bird species found near water bodies in North India (Pl. LXXX).

The assemblage recovered from Period-III C of the NBPW phase contained a total of 42 fragments of which it was possible to identify 33 fragments. This small assemblage is dominated by remains of domestic animals-Cattle and Goat. The wild mammals identified from this sub-phase were Spotted Deer, Sambar, Wild Pig and Four-horned Antelope and Blackbuck. A single shell of freshwater bivalve species (Lamellidens sp.) was also recovered from Period-III C context (Pl.LXXXI). Several fragments showed cut marks and a few were charred. Evidence of action of physical taphonomic factors was found in three cases. The distal end of a cattle tibia (PKT-40) showed a black patina that was not seen on any other fragments. Heavy encrustation was found on a pubic bone (ischium) of cattle recovered from the same context. The surface of an antler of Spotted Deer recovered from trench 6 showed criss-cross cracks indicating that it was exposed for a long time before getting incorporated in the deposit. Two sides of a skull of Blackbuck (PKT-49-50) with horn core were found from trench 6. Both these were cut and got deposited together (Pl.LXXXII).

Period-IV (Sunga-Kushan) (Pl. LXXXIII)

Out of 54 fragments of this period it was possible to identify 41 fragments. Several fragments of this period had signatures of impact of various pre and post-depositional modifications. For example, edges of a mandible fragment of domestic Pig (PKT-11) were abraded. In case of the distal end of a humerus of Spotted Deer, the bone surface showed heavy cracks and part of the surface has got peeled-off. Two cases of bone modifications due to scavengers were noticed. The distal end of a femur of Buffalo and the proximal end of a metatarsal of Spotted Deer were chewed by dogs. An uncommon cutting pattern was observed in case of an astragalus of Blackbuck. This bone was cut using some sharp edge but the blade has gone only through halfway towards the lateral side. Only one tool (a needle) made using either femur or humerus of Cattle/Buffalo (PKT-13) was recovered from this context. An interesting find from this phase was the proximal end of a femur (left side) of Peafowl (Pavo cristatus) that had a cut mark.

Measurements

It was possible to measure a few bones from this small assemblage (Table 23-26). It was possible to estimate the height of the cattle at the withers using the medial length of the astragalus (Zalkin.1970) and a single astragalus recovered from Period-I

(PKT-24) gave the estimate as 92.96 cm. At present this single estimate is inadequate for further comparison. Similarly, though the measurements recorded in this report can not be used for compassion with those at other sites at present. But when further study is carried out at the site in future these would be useful to obtain a size estimate of animals in various cultural phases (Joglekar 2007-2008).

Table 40
Measurements of isolated teeth from Pakkakot

Period	*Reg. No.*	*Trench*	*Layer*	*Tooth*	*Length*	*Width*	*Species*
IV	PKT-5	7-8	1-2	D2	12.00	9.95	Sus domesticus
I	PKT-28	9	4	M3	15.48	8.70	Capra hircus
III C	PKT-39	7-8	3	M3	21.67	15.87	Axis axis
IV	PKT-3	7-8	1-2	M2	25.27	24.22	B.tragocamelus
I	PKT-33	14	4	M2	21.10	22.08	B.tragocamelus

Table 41
Measurements of various skeletal elements from Pakkakot

Period	*Reg. No.*	*Context*	*Bone*	*GL*	*Bp*	*Tp*	*Bd*	*Species*
IV	PKT-9	7-8 (1-2)	HU				34.00	Axis axis
III B	PKT-52	7 (5-6)	HU				40.00	S. domesticus
IV	PKT-6	7-8 (1-2)	RA		31.02	19.47		C.hircus
III B	PKT-53	7 (5-6)	FE	114.58			11.41	Grus antigone
I	PKT-24	9 (4)	AS	53.84			36.72	B.indicus
I	PKT-27	9 (4)	HI	60.80	26.00	28.00	28.60	B.indicus

GL: Maximum length
Bp: Maximum proximal width
Tp: Proximal thickness
Bd: Maximum distal width

Table 42
Measurements of maxillae from Pakkakot

Period		*I*	*I*	*IV*
Reg. No.		PKT-34	PKT-26	PKT-2
Trench		14	9	1-2
Layer		4	4	3
Species		Bos indicus	Axis axis	Sus scrofa
P2	Length			
	Width			
P3	Length			
	Width			
P4	Length	18.00		
	Width	16.72		
M1	Length	22.00		16.66
	Width	17.00		13.53
M2	Length	25.64	15.48	22.37
	Width	21.16	12.50	16.30
M3	Length	28.31		
	Width	22.70		

Table 43
Measurements of mandibles from Pakkakot

Period		*IV*	*IV*	*III C*
Reg. No.		PKT-12	PKT-4	PKT-41
Trench		7-8	7-8	7-8
Layer		1-2	1-2	3
Species		Bos indicus	Sus domesticus	Sus domesticus
P2	Length			15.35*
	Width			9.87
P3	Length		14.95	20.88*
	Width		10.84	12.05
P4	Length			
	Width			
M1	Length			
	Width			
M2	Length			
	Width			
M3	Length			
	Width			
Condyle	Width	34.31		

* Deciduous tooth

Concluding Remarks

A careful analysis of the ceramic assemblage and other artifactual data of Pakkakot show the transition from rural to urban settlement at the site. The excavation brought to light a five-fold cultural sequence without any break in between all of them. All the five periods were characterized by their typical ceramic assemblage and other objects. Continuation of settlement is observed even in the medieval period which is evidenced by glazed ceramics and ponds and wells made of lakhauri bricks found at the site and nearby areas. Field investigation conducted by our team has observed that the inhabitants of the Neolithic culture were the first to take effective colonization at the present site. Our close observation of the ceramic assemblage shows striking similarity, both in fabric and forms, with those recovered from Imlidih Khurd, Waina, Bhunadih, Senuwar, Lahuradewa and Chirand. The cultural relics obtained from the site are ascribable from Neolithic culture to Gupta and post-Gupta period (5000 BCE-700 CE). The pottery of Cord-impressed Red Ware, plain Red Ware, Red Slipped Ware and Rusticated Ware were recovered from the site. In Cord-impressed Red Ware and Black-and Red Ware, the pots recovered are both handmade and wheelmade. The principal types in Cord-impressed Red Ware are bowls, vases and basins. These pots are made by turnnette method on slow wheel. The Cord-impressed Red Ware and plain Red Ware potteries are comparable with those of Imlidih Khurd, Waina, Bhunadih and Lahuradewa.

Agriculture was the mainstay of the economy of our research area and the concept of cultivating two crops in a year had already come in practice even in the Neolithic period datable to 5000 BCE. Cultivation of rice, wheat, barley, various types of millets, several types of pulses and oil seeds was done in the Neolithic stage. The effective colonization in the Ganga plain was done by the Black-and-Red Ware people towards the end of the Chalcolithic period some time during 2nd millennium BCE. Their settlements were sporadic and the time-span was limited as their habitational deposit does not exceed more than 50 cm (Singh.2012:153-164), but here at Pakkakot this deposit is 60 cm.

The density of population further increases in the NBPW period and new sites were inhabited. Evidence regarding dwelling houses of this period was well documented from sites like Ahichhatra, Kausambi, Hastinapur, Atranjikhera, Rajghat and Pataliputra in the Ganga basin and several other sites in the lower Ganga plain, Central India and Rajasthan. The practice of wattle-and-daub houses was followed during this period. The presence of post-holes indicates that the houses were made by using wooden or bamboo screens and floors were made of rammed earth, sometimes mixed with baked clay clods. The houses were oriented approximately along the cardinal directions. Hence, it can be presumed that they were laid according to preconceived plans. Blacksmith's furnace, potter's kilns and several open and closed mouth hearths suggest that life was well settled and specialization of crafts had already taken place by this time. The use of burnt bricks is also attested along with wattle-and-daub houses during the mid-NBPW period. A perceptible stride in the civic architecture is witnessed during the mid phase of the NBPW culture. The beginning of urbanization at the site is witnessed in Period-III B which is marked by the use of NBPW. The geographical situation of the site made it possible for its inhabitants to have commercial links with other contemporary cities like Pataliputra, Rajghat and Vaishali. The site has got the status of a full-fledged urban centre during Sunga-Kushan period. As other fortified sites like Sugh, Rangmahal, Indraprastha, Ahichhatra, Kausambi, Rajghat, Pataliputra, Vaishali, Bhita and Chirand (Ray.1984:16-22), Pakkakot is also a fortified city extended in about more than 8 hectares of area.

At present the River *Chhoti Saryu* flows about 1.5 km south from Pakkakot whiles the *Budhi* River (Lakda Nala) flows just north of the site which mingles in *Chhoti Saryu* near Chitbadagaon. The team has observed that in early NBPW period the River *Chhoti Saryu* used to flow nearby the site. It is proved by the layers of sand deposit during early NBPW period noticed in trench no. 9 and 14 of the Mound-1. In this way we may conclude that the site lies between *Chhoti Saryu* and *Budhi* River which is a unique geographical feature of the site. Contour plan of the site shows that the present mettled road from Sihachaur to Simhpur (Sronipur) was constructed on the ancient path which was used probably by traders during Sunga-Kushan period and it was continued up to medieval period. It is proved by the ponds and wells which lie on both sides of the present road.

We have recovered one sealing of baked clay of Period-V having the legends "Chetak Vihare" and "Matibharadhikaranasya" from Mound-4. To find out Buddhist site in surrounding area the team has explored neighbouring area and found a site named "Matahi" which is located about 2 kms west from the site. The name Matahi is well comparable with Matibhar. This site has a profile of a religious monument. A female figurine made of silver is a rare discovery of this site which was recovered from the pre-Mauryan level. This type of figurine is not reported from any site of Ganga plain. Although Ghosh has reported about a golden figure recovered from Laurianandangarh (Bihar) in his book *An Encyclopaedia of Indian Archaeology* but its photograph is not published and its present status is not known. A good number of terracotta seals and sealings were also recovered from the site from Period-III to V. About half dozen sealings found from the site have more than five impressions which are also not reported from any site of Ganga plain. Some of them show the antiquity of the name Ram and Gopal in 2nd century BCE. Any archaeological evidence is not yet available to prove the antiquity of both gods in Sunga period. A miniature *lota* measuring 1.1 cm long, diam of the rim 0.6 cm, was recovered from the NBPW period. Special mention may be made of two pendants, one is tortoise made of banded agate and other is a parrot made of crystal found from the NBPW level. An attractive terracotta figurine (Man and horse) is recovered from Sunga period. It is also a rare discovery and not reported from any site from this period. A sharpener of bone-point made of ivory was recovered from the NBPWlevel. Post-firing painting on Red Ware and Red Slipped Ware was for the first time recovered in Ballia district from this site. It was not reported from other sitesof Ballia like Waina, Bhunadih, Khairadih and Lakhneshwardih. Although this type of ceramics is reported from Senuwar and Chirand. We have recovered a large number of huge utensils of Grey Ware and Red Ware from the outer portion of the fortified area which indicate about community eating place. The site is extended in a wide area and not comparable to any other site in mid-Ganga plain. Further excavations may give some more important information abouit the archaeology of mid-Ganga plain.

References

Altekar, A.S. and V.K. Mishra. 1959, Reprint 2005. *Report on Kumrahar Excavations 1951-55.* Patna: K.P.Jayaswal Research Institute.

Banerjee, N.R. 1959. "The Technique of Manufacture of Stone Beads in Ancient Ujjain." *Journal of the Asiatic Society* 1 (2). Calcutta.

Chakrabarti, D. K. 2001. *Archaeological Geography of the Ganga Plain: The Lower and the Middle Ganga.* Delhi: Permanent Black.

Driesch, Von A. 1976. *A Guide to the Measurement of Animal Bones from Aechaeological Sites.* Cambridge, Massachusetta: Harvard University Press.

Dubey, S.R. *et al.* 2010. "Archaeological Investigation in Ballia District with Special Reference to Pakkakot." *Puratattva* 40. Delhi: Indian Archaeological Society.

Dubey, S.R. (Ed.). 2012. *Methodology of Numismatic Study and History-Writing*. New Delhi: Research India Press.

Gaur, R.C. 1983. *Excavations at Atranjikhera-Early Civilization of the Upper Ganga Basin.* Delhi: Motilal Banarasidas.

Ghosh, A. (Ed.). 1989. *An Encyclopaedia of Indian Archaeology.* New Delhi: Munshiram Manoharlal.

Goyal, S.R. 1995. *The Coinage of Ancient India.*Jodhpur.

Gupta, P.L. 1972. *Gangetic Valley Terracotta Art.* Varanasi.

Indian Archaeological Review 1956-57. Delhi: Archaeological Survey of India.

Indian Archaeological Review 1963-64. Delhi: Archaeological Survey of India.

Joglekar. 2007-2008. "A Fresh Appraisal of the Animal-based Subsistence and Domestic Animals in the Ganga Valley."*Pragdhara* 18. Lucknow.

Kenoyer, J. M. 1986. "Indus Beads Industry: Contribution to Bead Technology." *Ornament* 10 (1).

Kumar, B. 1978. "Bone and Ivories from Bihar." *The Journal of the Bihar Puravid Parishad* II. Patna.

Lal, B.B. 1954-55. "Excavations at Hastinapur and Other Explorations in the Upper Ganga and Sutlej Basin-1950-52. *Ancient India* 10-11.

Mackay, E.J.H. 1943. *Chanhudaro Excavations 1935-36.* Boston: Boston Museum of Fine Arts.

Mishra, Parmanand (Ed.). 1986. *Uttar Pradesh District Gazetteers: Ballia.* Rampur: Govt. Press.

Mitra, Debala. 1972. *Excavations at Tilaurakot and Kodan and Explorations in the Nepalese Terai.* Kathmandu: Govt. of Nepal.

Mukherjee, S.K. 1990. "Terracotta Figurines of the Kushan Period in the Gangetic Valley." *Historical Archaeology of India* (Eds. Amita Ray and Samir Mukherjee) New Delhi.

Narain, A.K. and T.N. Roy. 1968. *The Excavations at Prahladpur.* Varanasi: Banaras Hindu University.

Narain, A.K. and T.N.Roy. 1977. *Excavations at Rajghat, Part I.* Varanasi: Banaras Hindu University.

Narain, A.K. and P. Singh. 1979. *Excavations at Rajghat, Part III.* Varanasi: Banaras Hindu University.

Pathak, V. 1963. *History of Kosala up to the Rise of Mauryas.* Varanasi: Motilal Banarasidas.

Rajan, K. 1990. "New Light on the Megalithic Culture of Kongu Region, Tamilnadu." *Man & Environment* XV (1). Pune: Indian Society of Prehistoric and Quaternery Studies.

Rao, S.R. 1973. *Lothal and the Indus Civilization.* Bombay: Asia Publishing House.

Ray, Amita. 1984. "Secular Architecture of the Kushan Period." Paper presented in the seminar of State Museum, Lucknow.

Sadek Kooros, H. 1975. "Intentional Fracturing of Bone: Description of Criteria." *Archaeological Studies* (Ed. A.T.Clason). Amsterdam: North Holland Publication.

Sankalia, H.D. *et al.* 1960. *From History to Prehistory at Nevasa.* Poona.

Sharma, G.R. 1960. *The Excavations at Kausambi, 1957-58: The Defences and the Syenasiti of the Purushamedha,* Allahbad: Dept. of Ancient History Culture and Archaeology.

Sharma, G.R., V.D.Misra, D.Mandal, B.B.Misra and J.N.Pal. 1980. *Beginning of Agriculture: From Hunting and Food-gathering to Domestication of Plants and Animals.* Allahabad: Abinash Prakashan.

Singh, S. C. 1965. "Delimitation of the Middle Ganga Plain." *The National Geographical Journal of India* XI (2). Varanasi: Banaras Hindu University.

Singh, S.C. 1973. "Changes in the Courses of Rivers and their Effects on Urban Settlements in the Middle Ganga Plain." *The National Geographical Journal of India*. Varanasi: Banaras Hindu University.

Singh, B.P. 1986. *Life in Ancient Varanasi: An Account Based on Archaeological Evidence*. New Delhi: Sundeep Prakashan.

Singh, B.P. 1987-88. "The Chalcolithic Culture of Southern Bihar as Revealed by the Explorations and Excavations in District Rohtas." *Puratattva* 20. Delhi: Indian Archaeological Society.

Singh, B.P. 1990-91. "Excavations at Khairadih." *Journal of Bihar Puravid Parishad* IX-X. Patna.

Singh, P. 1993. "Archaeological Excavations at Imlidih Khurd-1992." *Pragdhara* 3. Lucknow.

Singh, P. 1994. *Excavations at Narhan 1984-89*. New Delhi: B.R.Publishing Corporation.

Singh, P. 1996. "Prelude to Urbanization in the Saryupar Plain." Presidential Address of the 57th Session of Indian History Congress. Chennai.

Singh, S.K. 2000-2001. "Lithic Industry of Waina, District-Ballia (UP)." *Pragdhara* 11. Lucknow.

Singh, S.K. 2012. *Settlement Pattern Urban Growth and Craft Technology in North India-An Archaeological Perspective*. New Delhi: Research India Press.

Singh, P. *et al.* 1994-95. "Protohistoric Investigations in Ballia District, UP." *Pragdhara* 5. Lucknow.

Singh, P. and A. K. Singh. 1995-96. "Excavations at Waina, District Ballia." *Pragdhara* 6. Lucknow.

Singh, A.K. and S.K. Singh. 1998. "Importance of a bead manufacturing workshop at Agiabir, Dist. Mirzapur, Uttar Pradesh." *Bharati* 24. Varanasi: Dept. of Ancient Indian History Culture & Archaeoloogy, Banaras Hindu University.

Singh, P. and A.K. Singh. 2004. *Archaeology of Middle Ganga Plain, New Perspective (Excavations at Agiabir)*. New Delhi: Aryan Books International.

Sinha, K.K. 1967. *Excavations at Sravasti, 1959*. Varanasi: Banaras Hindu University.

Tewari, Rakesh, R.K. Srivastava and K.K. Singh. 2001-02. : "Excavations at Lahuradeva, Dist.

Sant Kabir Nagar." *Puratattva* 13. Delhi: Indian Archaeological Society.

Tewari, Rakesh, R. K. Srivastava, K. S. Saraswat and K. K. Singh. 2002. "Excavations at Lahuradeva, Dist. Sant Kabir Nagar, Uttar Pradesh." *Puratattva* 32. Delhi: Indian Archaeological Society.

Tewari, R. *et al.* 2002-03. "Preliminary Report of the Excavations at Lahuradeva, Dist. Sant Kabir Nagar, Uttar Pradesh-2001-02." *Pragdhara* 13. Lucknow.

Tewari, R. *et al.* 2005. "Recently Excavated Sites in the Ganga Plain and North Vindhyas: Some Observations Regarding the Pre-Urban Content." *Pragdhara* 15. Lucknow.

Thakur, Neena and Vidula Jayaswal. 1991. "Insights into the Utilization Pattern of Osteological Remains from Senuwar." *Indian Archaeological Heritage* (Eds. C.Margabandhu *et al*, Vol. 1). Delhi.

Tosi, M.L. Bondioli & M.Vidale. 1984. "Craft Activity Areas and Survey at Mohenjo-daro." *Interim Report* 1. Aschen, RWTH ISMEO.

Tripathi, V. *et al.*2004. "Excavations at Anai (2004-05), District Varanasi, Uttar Pradesh: A Preliminary Report." *Bharati* 29. Varanasi: Banaras Hindu University.

Wheeler, R.E.I., A Ghosh & Krishna Deva.1946. "Arikamedu: An Indo-Roman Trading Station on the East Coast of India."*Ancient India* 2.

5

Archaeological Exploration in District-Nalanda: 2012-15

Nalanda district of Bihar occupies an area of 2355 sq km and the co-ordinate is 25^0 12′ 00″N latitude and 85^0 31′ 12″ E longitudes (Fig. 39). It is a part of Lower Gangatic plain except its southern part, where small hills are separated over a large area. Barh district is in the north of this district where Ganga River flows from west to east direction. Patna is located in the north- west where as Gaya and Nawadah districts lie in the south- west and south of the district respectively, where hills belonging to the Chotanagpur hills spread over in a large area. Its topography slopes towards north and most of the streams flow northward and join the Ganges as tributaries.

Figure 39: Satellite map of Nalanda District

The archaeological remains of Nalanda mahavihara lay some 11 kms north-west from Rajgir and the same distance to the south-west of Bihar Sharif, the headquarter of the district- Nalanda. It is 3 kms away from the Nalanda Railway Station and 88 Kms south-east of Patna, the metropolis of the Bihar state. Its latitude is 25^0 $8'$ N and the longitude is 85^0 $27'$ E (Kumar.1970:646-647). Historians and archaeologists identified this place with a modern village named *Badagaon* at Nalanda (Cunningham.1935:468). The term Badagaon has been taken as a corrupt form of *Viharagrama* (Dave.1967:136).

Archaeological Explorations in District-Nalanda: 2012-2015

Nalanda was certainly one of such glorious spots from which the light emitted and not only India but the neighbouring countries were also illuminated. The history of the place remained shrouded with mystery for long and despite untiring efforts made during a century and half, several layers remain concealed. There has been still a need for a comprehensive work on various aspects of Nalanda. Keeping in mind of these facts I have done archaeological exploration in the district during 2012- 2013, 2013-14 and 2015-16 along with my Research Scholar Mr. Pankaj Kumar. Archaeological Survey of India, New Delhi has permitted me for the exploration work and given license for the purpose. My objectives were as follows:

- Documentation of archaeological sites by village to village survey.
- Throw light on the artistic features of the art objects recovered during recent archaeological investigations; find out the possibility of an Art School and impact of Nalanda art on other Art centres.
- Decipher the inscribed sculptures and
- To reveal the antiquity of the settlement history of the area on the basis of recent archaeological findings.

I have started my exploration work keeping in mind the ruins of Nalanda as the main reference point (Fig. No. 40) and have surveyed more than 700 villages in

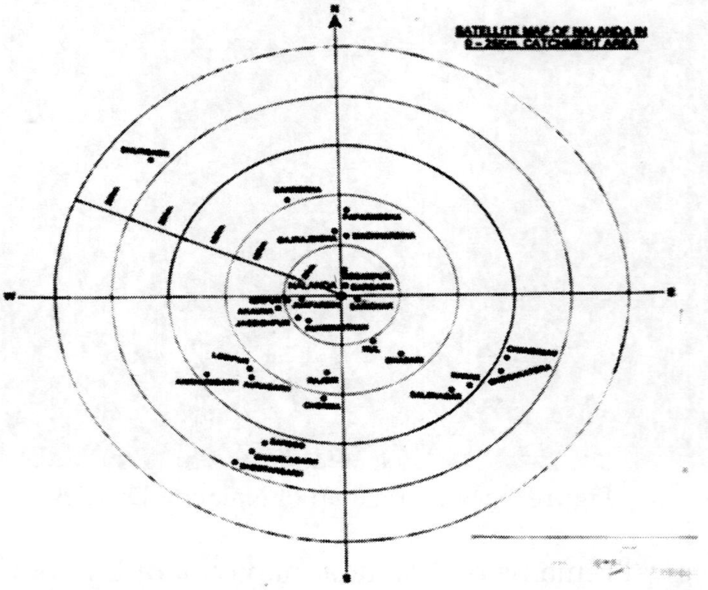

Figure 40: Archaeological sites explored in and around Nalanda

the district. Around the ruins there are 11 mounds having archaeological potential (Fig. No. 41). Three sites namely Jufardih (Excavated in 2007 by ASI,Patna circle), Rukministhan and Jagdishpur are very close to each other and located about 3 km west of the ruins of Nalanda. Explorations were also done in the vicinity of Rajgir (Fig. 42). A village to village survey was done by the team and 68 sites were found having archaeological importance.

Explored Sites

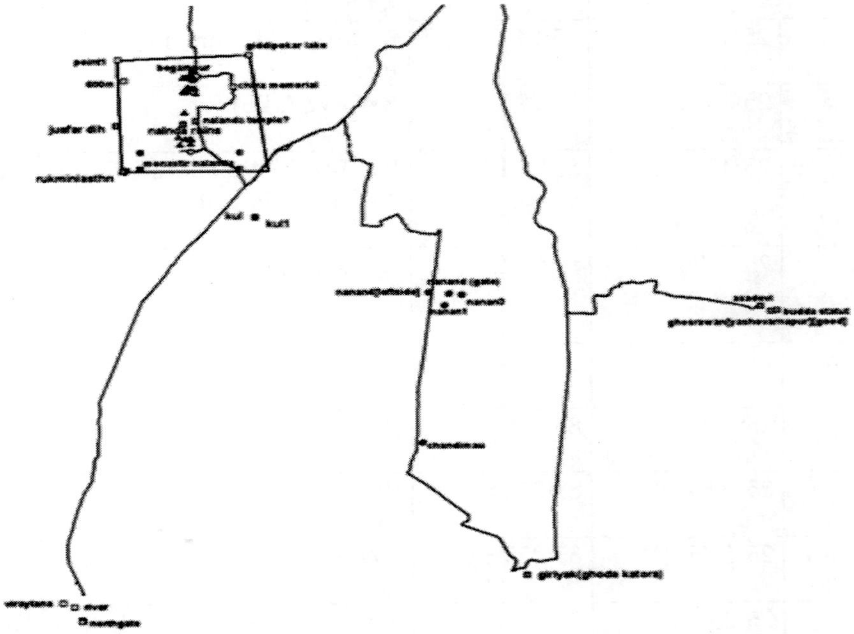

Figure 41: Archaeological sites in the vicinity of Nalanda

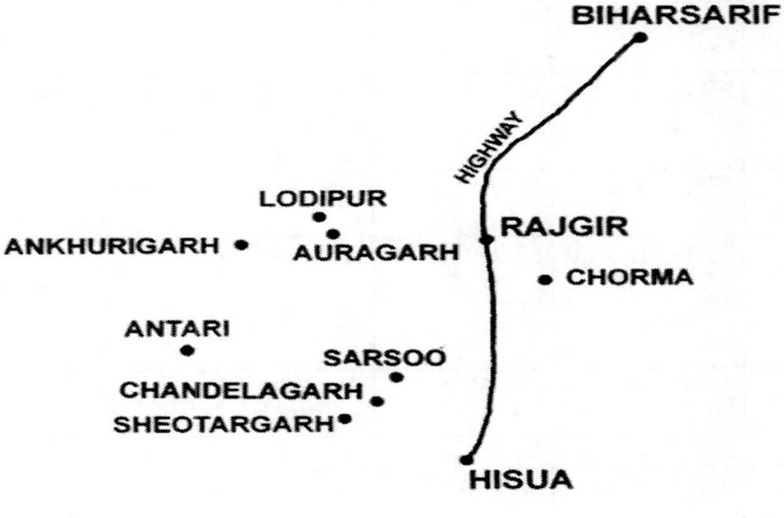

Figure 42: Archaeological sites in the vicinity of Rajgir

During exploration 68 sites were found having archaeological importance; among them only unreported sites are shown in the table below:

Table 44
New archaeological sites reporteded by the Author in dist. Nalanda

S. No.	*Name of the site*	*Latitude*	*Longitude*	*Findings*	*Nearby River*
1	Ajaypur	25°10′13″N	85°32′24″E	RW,BW,NBP & Fragments of sculptures	Paimar 1 km West
2	Ajnaura	25°13′N.	85°24′E.	Buddhist &Brahmanic sculp-tures	Paimar 1 km West
3	Aldhanna	25°15′N	85°27′E	RW,BW & BSW	
4	Arawan .	25°12′N	85°22′E	RW,BW,BSW&Buddhist &Brahmanic sculptures	Paimar 1 km East & Muhane ½ km West
5	Badauni	25°12′N	85°20′E.	RW & RSW	Muhane 2 km South & Pilch-chain1.5 km East
6	Ba□akiAat	25°11′62′N	85°24′43′ E.	Brahmanic sculptures	Paimar 1 km West &Sansi 1 km East
7	Bahadurpur	25°20′N	85°25″ E.	RW & RSW	Muhane moves West to north
8	Bara	25°6′89″N.	85°22′18″E	RW, BW &Brahmanic sculp-tures	Paimar 2 km South
9	Bara Khurd	25°14′54″N.	85°25′23′E	RW, BW &Brahmanic sculp-tures	Paimar 3 km West
10	Barah .	25°23′N.	85°29′E	RW,RSW,BW,BSW,Kushanan brickbats &Buddhist &Brah-manic sculptures	Dhoba 6 km North &Muhane 8 kmSouth
11	Barhauna	25°18′N.	85°25′E	Brahmanic sculptures	Muhane 3 km West &Sansi 3 km East
12	Beswak .	25°10′N.	85°14′E	RW,RSW,BW,BSW,TC balls &Brhmanic and Buddhist sculptures	
13	Bhui	25°10′97′N.	85°21′33″E.	Brahmanic sculptures	Paimar 1 km North
14	Birnawan	25°19′N.	85°29′ E.	RW,RSW &BSW	Muhane 4 km North
15	Chandasi	25°16′N	85°28′E.	RW &RSW	Panchane ½ km East
16	Chandaura (Silao)	25°5′21′N.	85°25′71″ E.	RW,RSW &Brhmanic and Buddhist sculptures	Paimar 300 m East
17	Charuipar	25°17′N.	85°28′E.	RW & BW	Paimar ½ km East
18	Chorsanda	25°12′54″N.	85°19′43′ E.	RW,RSW & GW	Muhane 1 km East
19	Dayalpur	25°20′N.	85°24′E.	RW &RSW	Muhane 1/2 km South &Chiraiya 1/2 km North-West

S. No.	*Name of the site*	*Latitude*	*Longitude*	*Findings*	*Nearby River*
20.	Dhurgaon	Lat. 25°14′N.	Long. 85°16′ E..	RW	
21.	Dosut	25°19′N.	85°31′E.	RW &RSW	Muhane 5 km North &Panchane 2 km East
22	Eksara	25°10′5″N.	85°23′46″ E.	RW,BW,BSW,NBP&Fragments of sculptures	Paimar 1 km East
23	Gaura	25°16′2″N.	85°19′52′ E.	RW,RSW,BW,BSW&Brhmanic and Buddhist sculptures	Nonai 2 km West &Chiraiya 2.5 km East
24	Karjara	25°6′89′N.	85°22′98″ E.	RW,RSW,BSW &Fragments of sculptures	Paimar½ km South
25	Khaira	25°10′97′N.	85°21′33′ E.	Inscribed Brhmanic and Buddhist sculptures	Paimar 1 km North
26	Kolawan	25°23′N.	85°27′E.	RW,Mud wall &Fragments of sculptures	Chiraiya ½ km West
27	Kondi	25°14′37′N.	85°26′71″E.	Fragments of sculptures	Paimar 7 km West
28	Kosnara	25°9′67′N.	85°22′54′E.	RW,RSW,BSW & Fragments of sculptures	Paimar 3 km East
29	Kundwapar	25°13′N.	85°15′E.	RW,RSW,BW & BSW	Nonai 5 km East
30	Madhopurgarh	25°20′N.	85°23′E.	RW,RSW,BW & BSW& Fragments of sculptures	Chiraiya½ km South
31	Makhdumpur (Ben)	25°8′94″N..	85°20′82″E.	RW,RSW& Fragments of sculptures	Paimar 2 km West
32	Rukhaegarh	25°19′N.	85°22′E.	RW,RSW,BW,BSW,NBP, Kushanan bricks& copper coins of medieval period	Chiraiya 1 km South-East
33	Rukministhan	25°6′N.	85°25′E.	RW,BW& Buddhist images	Paimar 3.5 km West
34	Sahri	25°11′29″N.	85°22′21″ E.	Brhmanic sculptures	Muhane 1 km West &Etaua 2 km East
35	Sakrau□ha	25°10′97′N.	85°25′ 62″E.	RW&Brhmanic and Buddhist sculptures	Paimar5oo m West
36	Sonchari	25°11′24′N.	85°19′91′ E.	RW,RSW &Brhmanic and Buddhist sculptures	Muhane½ km East
37	TazuBigha	25°8′91′N.	85°25′ 29″E.	RW, BW,NBP & inscribed Buddha image	Paimar 2.5km West
38	Telmar	25°26′N.	85°26′E.	RW	Dhoba 2 km North
39	Tungi	25°10′13′N	85°32′24′E	RW,BW,BSW&Brhmanic and Buddhist sculptures	Gordhoba 1 km West

A brief report of all 68 sites is given below. I have also given a very brief report of two excavated sites *i.e.* Juafardih located 3 km south-east to the ruins and Ghorakatora 7 km east of Rajgir whose findings show that settlement history of Nalanda is going back to 10th to 12th century BCE.

Ajaypur (Lat. 25⁰ 10′13″N, Long. 85⁰ 32′24″E)

This village is 14 km north-west from the ruins of Nalanda and 12 km west from the district headquarter on Bihar Sharif-Ekangar Sarai Road. The River *Paimar* flows 1 km west to the village. There is a mound to the south of the village covering an area of 100x90 mts with an extant height of 6 mts. Pot-sherds of Red Ware, Black Ware and NBP Ware were recovered during exploration. Fragment of sculptures are kept in Raja Jaipal Sthan and Goraiya Sthan of the village.

Ajnaura (Lat. 25⁰ 13′N, Long. 85⁰ 24′E)

It is about 13 km north- west to the ruins of Nalanda and about 11 km west from Bihar Sharif. The *Paimar* River flows 1 km west to the village. A large number of Brahmanic and Buddhist sculptures are scattered in the middle and the southern portion of the village.

Aldhanna (Lat. 25⁰ 15′N, Long. 85⁰ 27′E)

This village is 18 km north from the ruins of Nalanda and 13 km north-west from the district headquarter of Bihar Sharif. There is a mound in the middle of the village covering an area of 100x60 mts with an extant height of 6 mts. Pot-sherds of Red Ware, Black Ware and Black Slipped Ware were recovered during the exploration.

Arawan (Lat. 25⁰ 12′N, Long. 85⁰ 22′E)

This village is about 16 km south- west from the ruins of Nalanda and 18 km east from the district headquarter on Bihar Sharif-Ekangarsarai Road. The mound extended into 25x20 mts with an extant height of 9 mts is located to the south of the village yielding Red Ware, Black Ware and Black Slipped Ware. At Brahma Sthan, located to the north-east of the village, a number of Buddhist and Brahmanic images are kept under worship.The River *Paimar* flows 1 km east while the *Mohane* flows ½ km west to the village which presents a unique geographical scenario.

Atma (Lat. 25⁰ 8′ N, Long. 85⁰ 19′ E)

The village Atma is 22 km west from the ruins of Nalanda and 20 km south- west from the district headquarter of Bihar Sharif. The *Paimar* River flows 1 km east to the village. To the south of the village there is a mound extended into 50x60 m with an extant height of 15 mts yielding Red, Black, Black Slipped and NBP Ware.To the east of the village a few Brahmanic sculptures made of black basalt are kept in Biharimal temple and Radhe Shyam Thakurbari (Pl.LXXXIV-LXXXV).

Aungari (Lat. 25⁰ 12′ N, Long. 85⁰ 15′ E)

The village Aungari is 34 km north- west from the ruins of Nalanda and 33 km west from the district headquarter of Bihar Sharif. The *Nonai* River flows 1 km south to the village. To the south-west of the village there is a Sun temple. A large number of Brahmanic and a few Buddhist sculptures made of black basalt are kept in and around the temple among which some are inscribed (Pl.LXXXVI-LXXXVIII).

Badagaon (Lat. 25⁰ 8′78″N, Long. 85⁰ 26′64″E)

It is situated adjacent to the north of the ruins. Towards north-east corner of the village there is a mound which roughly covers an area of 105x100 mts with an extant height of 8 mts. The size of exposed bricks in the section of the mound is 46x25x5 cm. A modern temple is constructed over the mound in which a sculpture of Mahishasuramardini made of black basalt is installed. An another mound to the west of the village is extended into 35x67 mts with an extant height of 1.5 mts yielding Red Ware pottery.Special mention may be made of two sculptures of black basalt kept in the south of the village; one is about 8 ft high Buddha in *Bhumisparsha mudra* locally known as Teliabhandar and another one is Buddhist tantric goddess Marichi (Pls.LXXXIX-XC).There is another temple of Sun god inside the village where several Brahmanic and Buddhist sculptures of Pala period are kept. Special mention may be made of a crowned image of Buddha and a panel showing Siddhartha's *Mahābhiniṣkramaṇa* (Pls.XCI-XCII).

Badaki Aat (Lat. 25⁰ 11′62″N, Long. 85⁰ 24′43″ E)

The village Baḍaki Aat is 10 km west from the ruins of Nalanda and 13 km south-west from the district headquarter of Bihar Sharif. The *Paimar* River flows 1 km west to the village while the River *Sansi* flows 1 km east to the village. The village lies between two rivers which presents a unique geographical scenario. The mound is totally occupied by the present inhabitants. Sculptures made of black basalt are kept at Goraiya Sthan and Nakta Baba Sthan of the village. Pot-sherds of Red Ware were collected from the surface.

Badauni (Lat. 25⁰ 12′N, Long. 85⁰ 20′ E)

Vedagram was the ancient name of village Badauni which is located19 km north- west from the ruins of Nalanda and 18 km west from the district headquarter of Bihar Sharif. It is said that in ancient times Vedas were studied here. The *Mohane* River flows 2 km south to the village. The *Pilchchain* River, a tributary of the *Mohane*, flows 1.5 km east to the village. To the east of the village there is a mound extended into 12 acres with an extant height of 3 mts yielding Red and Red Slipped Ware. A broken carved pillar made of black stone is kept on the mound.

Bahadurpur (Lat. 25⁰ 20′N, Long. 85⁰ 25′ E)

This village is situated on the eastern bed of *Mohane* River. It is about 36 km north to the ruins of Nalanda and 24 km north- west from the district headquarter. The mound extended into 100x70 mts with an extant height of 4 mts is located to the south of the village yielding Red and Red Slipped Ware.Building of a primary school is built on the mound.

Bara (Lat. 25^0 06′89″N, Long. 85^0 22′18″E)

This village is 8 km south-west from the ruins of Nalanda and 18 km west from the district headquarter on Bihar Sharif-Ekangar Sarai Road.The mound extended into 200x200 mts with an extant height of 12 mts is located to the south of the village yielding Red Ware and Black Ware.The river *Paimar* flows 2 km south to the village. Sculptures are kept at Thakurbari and Brahma Sthan located to the east and south of the village respectively.

Bara Khurd (Lat. 25^0 14′54″N, Long. 85^0 25′23″E)

This village is 13 km north-west from the ruins of Nalanda and 15 km north from the district headquarter of Bihar Sharif. The river *Paimar* flows 3 km west to the village. To the south of village there is a small mound measuring 25x20 mts in area with an extant height of 6 mts yielding Red Ware and Black Ware. A carved pillar measuring 95x23 cm is kept on the mound. To the south of the village there is a Shiva temple in which a large number of sculptures made of black stone are kept.

Barah (Lat. 25^0 23′N, Long. 85^0 29′E)

Located on the border of Nalanda and Patna districts this village is about 38 km north from the ruins of Nalanda and 26 km north-west from the district headquarter. The mound situated to the east of the village is extended into 70x50 mts with an extant height of 5 mts (Pl.XCIII) yielding Red, Red Slipped, Black and Black Slipped Ware. Kushana and Gupta brick-bats are noticed in the section. Remains of 21 steps are still intact to climb on the mound. It is said by the present inhabitants that actual number of steps was thirty one. At Mahadeva Sthan a few Brahmanic and Buddhist sculptures made of black basalt are kept under worship (Pl.XCIV). The River *Dhoba* flows 6 km north while *Mohane* flows 8 km south to the village.

Badhauna (Lat. 25^0 18′N, Long. 85^0 25′E)

The village Badhauna is 21 km north-west from the ruins of Nalanda and 18 km north-west from the district headquarter of Bihar Sharif. The *Mohane* River flows 3 km west while River *Sansi* flows 3 km east to the village. The mound situated to the north of the village is extended into 70x50 mts with an extant height of 5 mts. A few sculptures of black stone are kept to the south of the village at Mahadeva Sthan. Mention may be made of an image of Uma-Maheshwar.

Begampur (Lat. 25^0 8′25″N, Long. 85^0 26′55″E)

There is a huge mound towards south of the village Begampur located 1 km north to the ruins. It is extended in 300x300 mts with an extant height of 5 mts from the surrounding plain yielding Red Ware pottery. Remains of brick walls are also noticed. The site was excavated in 2007-08 by ASI, Patna Branch-III.

Beswak (Lat. 25^0 10′N, Long. 85^0 14′E)

The village Beswak is located 37 km north-west from the ruins of Nalanda and 36 km south-west from the district headquarter of Bihar Sharif. The *Mohane* River flows ½ km east to the village. There are two mounds in the village. Mound-I situated towards the east of the village is extended into 200x150 mts with an extant height of 6 mts while Mound-II is located to the south-east of the village extended into 75x75 mts with an extant height of 3 mts. Pot-sherds of Red Ware, Red Slipped Ware, Black Ware and Black Slipped Ware along with a few terracotta sling-balls were collected during exploration. A large number of Brahmanic and Buddhist sculptures of black stone are kept in to Thakurbari, Goraiya Sthan and Mahadeva Sthan (Pl.XCV-XCVII).

Bhadari (Lat. 25^0 6′39″N, Long.85^0 28′43″E)

Situated on a small mound measuring 10x7 mts with an extant height of 4 mts, this village is about 1.5 km east of Kool and 4.5 km south-east of the ruins and 12 km south from Bihar Sharif. It seems that it is a corrupt form of the word *Bhadra Arya* which means auspicious. As referred in the Pali text *Mahavagga,* the first meeting of Buddha with Sariputra and Moggallana held here. Only trial trench can be initiated. Pot-sherds of Red and Black Ware were recovered during exploration.

Bhui (Lat. 25^0 10′97″N, Long. 85^0 21′33″ E)

This village is about 12 km south- west from the ruins of Nalanda and 21 km south from the district headquarter of Bihar Sharif. The mound extended into 30x30 mts with an extant height of 5 mts is located to the south-east corner of the village. A Mosque is built by the present settlers on the mound. A few sculptures of black stone are kept in the Brahma Sthan, located to the north of the village. The River *Paimar* flows 1 km south to the village.

Birnawan (Lat. 25^0 19′N, Long. 85^0 29′ E)

This village is about 26 km north-east from the ruins of Nalanda and 23 km north-west from the district headquarter. The mound extended into 110x90 mts with an extant height of 5 mts is located to the south of the village yielding Red, Red Slipped and Black Slipped Ware. River *Mohane* flows 4 km north to the village.

Chandasi (Lat. 25^0 16′N, Long. 85^0 28′E)

The village Chandasi is 15 km north to the ruins of Nalanda and 12 km north-west from the district headquarter of Bihar Sharif. The *Panchane* River flows 1/2 km east to the village. The mound situated to the north-east of the village is extended into 70x50 mts with an extant height of 5 mts. Pot-sherds of Red and Red Slipped Ware were collected from the surface of the mound.

Chandaura (Silao) (Lat. 25^0 5′21″N, Long. 85^0 25′71″ E)

Located near Silao the village Chandaura is 8 km south-east from the ruins of Nalanda and 16 km south from the district headquarter of Bihar Sharif. The *Paimar* River flows 300 m east to the village. To the south of the village there is a mound extended into 50x30 m with an extant height of 7 mts yielding Red and Red Slipped Ware.To the north of the village a few Buddhist and Brahmanic sculptures made of black basalt, among which some are inscribed, are kept (Pl.XCVIII).

Chandi Mau (Lat. 25^0 5′44″N, Long. 85^0 30′15″E)

This village is located about 10 km south-east from the ruins of Nalanda and about 14 km south-west from Bihar Sharif. The mound is extended into 5 acres with an extant height of 6 mts and located south-east to the village.The River *Panchane* flows ½ km east to the village.Ceramics of Red Ware, Black-and-Red Ware associated with NBPW were recovered during exploration. To the south of the village there is a temple containing Brahmanic and Buddhist sculptures of Gupta and Pala periods.In 2000-01 an area of 70x60 sq m was excavated and declared a single culture site of Pala period. Remains of brick-built Buddhist temple and Votive stupa was found along with stone sculptures of Brahmanic and Buddhist deities and terracotta plaques, sealings and votive *stūpa* (Pls. XCIX-CIV).

Charuipar (Lat. 25^0 17′N, Long. 85^0 28′E)

The village Charuipar is 19 km north to the ruins of Nalanda and 16 km north-west from the district headquarter of Bihar Sharif. The *Paimar* River flows 1/2 km east to the village. The mound situated to the east of the village is extended into 60x50 mts with an extant height of 3 mts. Pot-sherds of Red and Black Ware along with a few terracotta beads were collected from the surface of the mound.

Chorsanda (Lat. 25^0 12′54″N, Long. 85^0 19′43″ E)

This village is 22 km west from the district headquarter on Bihar Sharif-Ekangar Sarai Road. The river *Mohane* flows 1 km east to the village. The mound extended into50x50 mts with extant height of 4 mts is located to the south of the village yielding Red Ware, Grey Ware and Red Slipped Ware.

Dayalpur (Lat. 25^0 20′N, Long. 85^0 24′E)

The village Dayalpur is 28 km north-east to the ruins of Nalanda and 25 km north-west from the district headquarters of Bihar Sharif. The *Mohane* River flows 1/2 km south while *Chiraiya* flows ½ km north-west to the village. The mound situated to the east of the village is extended into 90x80 mts with an extant height of 5 mts. Pot-sherds of Red and Red Slipped Ware were collected from the surface of the mound. To the south-east of the village a few fragments of black stone are kept at Goraiya Sthan (Pl. CV).

Dhurgaon (Lat. 25⁰ 14′N, Long. 85⁰ 16′E)

The village Dhurgaon is 30 km north-west to the ruins of Nalanda and 28 km west from the district headquarters of Bihar Sharif. The *Nonai* River flows 3 km east to the village. To the south of the village there is a mound extended into 40 *bigha*. Towards south of the mound there is a tank of 12 *bighas* locally known as *Giddhi Pokhar*. Fragments of sculptures are kept in Mahadeva and Devi Sthan respectively. Few sculptures such as Buddha, Tara, Ganesh, Vishnu etc. along with some intact earthen ware of Red Ware were recovered during digging the tank by the villagers and presently kept in the High School, Dhurgaon (Pls.CVI-CIX).

Dosut (Lat. 25⁰ 19′N, Long. 85⁰ 31′E)

The village Dosut is 29 km north to the ruins of Nalanda and 26 km north-west from the district headquarters of Bihar Sharif. The *Mohane* River flows 5 km north while *Panchane* flows 2 km east to the village. The mound situated to the south of the village is extended into 100x100 mts with an extant height of 10 mts. Pot-sherds of Red and Red Slipped Ware were collected from the surface of the mound.

Dumari (Lat. 25⁰ 13′N, Long. 85⁰ 19′ E)

This village is about 15 km north-west from the ruins of Nalanda and 21 km north-west from the district headquarter. The mound extended into 40x30 mts with an extant height of 5 mts is located to the west of the village yielding Red Ware.

Eksara (Lat. 25⁰ 10′5″N, Long. 85⁰ 23′46″ E)

The village Eksara is 7 km north-west from the ruins of Nalanda and 15 km south-west from the district headquarter of Bihar Sharif. The *Paimar* River flows 1 km east to the village. The south-west portion of the mound is inhabited by the present villagers. Pot-sherds of Red Ware, Black Ware, Black Slipped Ware and NBP Ware (Silver and Golden) were recovered during exploration. A few sculptures made of black basalt are kept in the Goraiya Sthan and Thakurbari, among them a broken image of Marichi is noticeable (Pl. CX).

Gajrajbigha (Lat. 25⁰ 10′N, Long. 85⁰ 26′E)

It is situated on a small mound about 3 km north of the ruins and completely occupied by modern settlers. A trial digging may be taken.

Gaura (Lat. 25⁰ 16′2″N, Long. 85⁰ 19′52″ E)

This village is about 21 km north-west from the ruins of Nalanda and 24 km north-west from the district headquarter. The mound extended into 60x50 mts with an extant height of 8 mts is located to the south-west of the village yielding Red Ware, Red Slipped Ware, Black Ware and Black Slipped Ware along with a few terracotta objects. To the south of the village at Goraiya Sthan a large number of Brahmanic and Buddhist sculptures are kept.

Ghorakatora (Lat.25^0 2′ N, Long.85^0 32′E)

This village is located 18 km south-east to the ruins of Nalanda and 23 km south from the district headquarters of Bihar Sharif (Pl. CXI; Fig. No.43). There is a huge mound covering an area of 250x200 mts with an extant height of 15 mts situated on the eastern bank of the River *Panchane*. About 1 km east to the mound the famous *Indra Shila* cave (Pl. CXII) is located on the southern face of the Giriyak hill which was mentioned by Fahien and Hiuen-tsang and identified by Broadly, Cunningham and Kittoe. It is said that here Indra had put 32 questions before the Buddha.

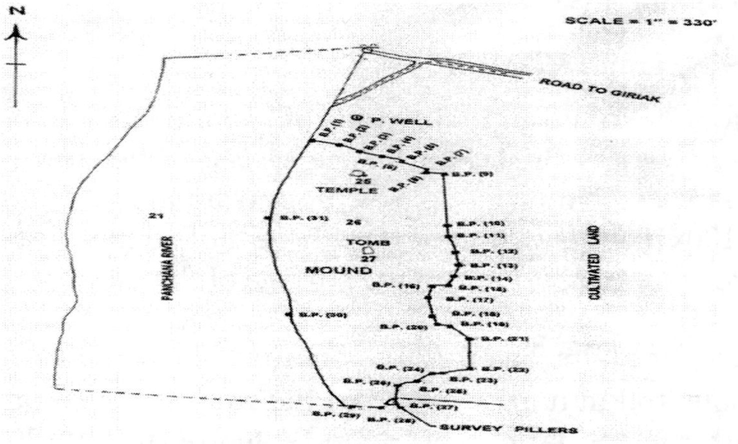

Figure 43: Site-plan, Ghorakatora

A large number of Ring Wells and remains of brick-walls are noticed on the mound (Pl.CXIII). During my exploration Pot-sherds of Red Ware, Red Slipped Ware, Black Ware, Black Slipped Ware, NBPW and Grey Ware along with terracotta balls and pottery discs were collected (Pl.CXIV). A few terracotta and stone sculptures made of black basalt are kept on the northern side of the mound (Pl. CXV). On the basis of the pottery and antiquities recovered from the site its antiquity may be dated earlier than 10th century BC.

Ghosrawan (Lat. 25^0 6′N, Long. 85^0 34′ E)

This village is about 16 km south-east from the ruins of Nalanda and 12 km south-east from the district headquarter. The River *Jirain* flows 2 km east to the village. To the west of the village there was a large mound extended into 350x200 mts having an extant height of 17 mts measured by A. Cunningham in 1875 but presently most of the part was cut-ploughed for agricultural purposes.Pot-sherds of Red and Black Ware were collected during exploration. A few Brahmanic and Buddhist sculptures are kept in the Asha Devi temple located west of the village (Pls.CXVI-CXXVI).

Jagdishpur (Lat.25^0 7′61″N, Long.85^0 25′32′E)

The mound of Jagdishpur is situated 500 mts south-west of the village Jagdishpur and $11^{1/2}$ km south-west of the ruins of Nalanda Mahavihara. The mound is extended into

50x50 mts with an extant height of 7 mts from the surface. Ceramics of Black Slipped Ware, Black Ware and Red Ware were collected from the surface.

Juafardih (Lat.25^0 8′ N, Long.85^0 27′E)

The ancient mound of Juafardih covering an area of 105x100 mts with an extant height of 15 mts is located 3 km south-west of the ruins of Nalanda and 15 km south-west of Biharsharif,the present headquarter of district- Nalanda and 93 km south-east of Patna, the capital of Bihar. The site is located on the ancient bed of the River *Paimar*. The river has shifted its course further west to a distance of 2.5 km from the site. A good no. of NBPW, Black Slipped Ware, Black-and-Red Ware, Grey Ware and Red Ware were found on the surface along with burnt bricks measuring 36x27x6 cm. Similar kind of ceramics had been recovered during excavation at Rajgir (Ghosh.1959:27). The site might have been associated with the ancient Nalanda Mahavihara. The site was excavated in 2006-07 by ASI Patna Circle and revealed three cultural periods:

(i)	Chalcolithic	1600-1200 BCE
(ii)	NBPW Period	1200-400 BCE
	Early Phase	1200-900 BCE
	Middle Phase	900-600 BCE
	Late Phase	600-400 BCE
(iii)	Sunga-Kushana	100 BC-100 CE

A mud stupa was also exposed built during the NBPW phase (Pl.CXXVII). The most important contribution of Juafardih excavation is the early date for NBPW period supplied by Birbal Sahni Institute of Paleobotanical Research, Lucknow which goes as early as 1200 BCE.

Pottery

Period I : Chalcolithic Culture

Black & Red Ware, Grey Ware, and Red Ware

Period II: Northern Black Polished Ware Culture

NBPW.Black Ware, Black Slipped Ware, Grey Ware, and Red Ware

Period III: Post NBPW Culture-Mixed Pottery

Besides ceramics, mention may be made of objects made by terracotta, stone, silver, copper and iron (Pls.CXXVIII-CXXXII).

Karjara (Lat. 25^0 06′89′N, Long. 85^0 22′98′ E)

This village is about 10 km west from the ruins of Nalanda and 21 km north-west from the district headquarter. The mound extended into 30x25 mts with an extant height of 5 mts is located to the west of the village yielding Red Ware, Red Slipped Ware, Black Ware and Black Slipped Ware. At Goraiya Sthan a few sculptures made of black basalt are kept under worship. The River *Paimar* flows ½ km south to the village.

Kewaideeh (Lat. 25⁰13′N, Long. 85⁰ 28′ E)

The village Kewaideeh is 9 km north from the ruins of Nalanda and 8 km north-west from the district headquarter of Bihar Sharif.The *Paimar* River flows 2.5 km west to the village. To the south of the village there is a mound presently used for agricultural purposes and locally known as *Dihas*. Pot-sherds of Red, Red Slipped, Black and Black Slipped Ware are recovered from the mound.

Khaira (Lat. 25⁰ 10′97″N, Long. 85⁰ 21′33″ E)

The village Khaira is 16 km north- west from the ruins of Nalanda and 17 km west from the district headquarter of Bihar Sharif on Ekangarsarai-Bihar Sharif Road. The *Paimar* River flows 1 km north to the village. Some Buddhist and Brahmanic sculptures, among which one is inscribed, made of Black basalt are kept to the north of the village at Brahma Sthan (Pl.CXXXIII) Pot-sherds of Red Ware were collected from the surface.

Khirauti (Lat. 25⁰ 14′N, Long. 85⁰ 22′ E)

The village Khirauti is 15 km north- west from the ruins of Nalanda and 4 km north from Nishchalganj Bazar on Bihar Sharif-Ekangar Sarai Road. The *Nonai* River flows 3 km west to the village. To the south of the village there is a mound extended into 100x70 mts with an extant height of 10 mts yielding Red Ware, Red Slipped Ware, NBPW, Black Ware and Black Slipped Ware. There is evidence of moat around the mound. Sculptures made of black basalt are kept at Vishnu Sthan and Mahadeva Sthan of the village.

Kolawan (Lat. 25⁰ 23′N, Long. 85⁰ 27′E)

The village Kolawan is 36 km north to the ruins of Nalanda and 33 km north-west from the district headquarters of Bihar Sharif. The *Chiraiya* River flows ½ km west to the village. Remains of mud-wall are noticed in the southern section of the mound. To the west of the village a few fragments are kept at Goraiya Sthan (Pl. CXXXIV).

Kondi (Lat. 25⁰ 14′37′N, Long. 85⁰ 26′71″E)

It is about 10 km north to the ruins of Nalanda and about 12 km north-west from Bihar Sharif. The *Paimar* River flows 7 km west to the village. Fragment of sculptures are kept in the southern and western portion of the village (Pl.CXXXV).

Korai (Lat. 25⁰ 8′N, Long. 85⁰ 29′E)

This village is about 6 km east from the ruins of Nalanda and 9 km south from the district headquarter Bihar Sharif. The mound locally known as Garh par extended into 100x70 mts with an extant height of 5 mts is located to the west of the village. Pot-sherds of Red, Red Slipped and Black Ware were collected from the surface of the mound. The River *Panchane* flows 1 km east to the village.

Kosnara (Lat. 25^0 9′67′N, Long. 85^0 22′54″E)

It is about 10 km west to the ruins of Nalanda and about 17 km south-west from Bihar Sharif. The *Paimar* River flows 3 km east to the village. There is a mound to the south of the village covering an area of 35x25 mts with an extant height of 7 mts. Pot-sherds of Red Ware, Black Ware and Black Slipped Ware were recovered during exploration. A few sculptures are kept in the Shiva temple and Jagdamba Sthan of the village.

Kul (Lat.25^0 6′76″N, Long.850 27′54″E)

The village Kul is located about 3 km south-east of the ruins of Nalanda and about 12 km south-west from Bihar Sharif.The mound located in the village measuring 115x65 mts with an extant height of 3 mts is still barren and used by villagers during harvesting. Several sculptural fragments are kept at four places and are under worship (Pls.CXXXVI-CXXXVIII). Pot-sherds of Red Ware were recovered during exploration. Scholars of Buddhism claim that Moggallana, one of the chief disciples of Buddha belong the village named Kolita and perhaps Kool is its corrupt form. The site needs to be excavated vertically to know the cultural sequence.

Kundwapar (Lat. 25^0 13′N, Long. 85^0 15′E)

The village Kundwapar is 29 km north-west to the ruins of Nalanda and 28 km west from the district headquarters on Bihar Sharif-Ekangar Sarai Road. The *Nonai* River flows 5 km east to the village. The mound (Pl. CXXXIX) situated to the east of the village is extended into 150x100 mts with an extant height of 3 mts. Pot-sherds of Red, Red Slipped, Black and Black Slipped Ware along with a few terracotta beads were collected from the surface of the mound (Pl. CXL).

Machhaldiha (Lat. 25^0 10′N, Long. 85^0 27′E)

This village may be identified with *Machhalgama* referred in *Jatakas*, commentary of *Dhammapada* and *Sumangalavilasini*. It is situated on a small mound about 3 km north of the ruins and 11 km south-west to Bihar Sharif. There are some fragments made of black stone kept at Devi Sthan. One of them is a broken image of Buddha in *Abhaya mudrā* having an inscription of one line which is under decipherment.

Madhopurgarh (Lat. 25^0 20′N, Long. 85^0 23′E)

This village is 29 km north to the ruins of Nalanda and 26 km north-west from the district headquarter. There are two mounds extended into 100x80 mts with an extant height of 4 mts located to the south of the village yielding Red, Red Slipped, Black and Black Slipped Ware. To the east of the village a few fragments of black stone are kept at Mahadeva Sthan. The River *Chiraiya* flows ½ km south to the village.

Makhdumpur (Ben) (Lat. 25^0 8′94″N, Long. 85^0 20′82′E)

Located near Ben this village is about 12 km west to the ruins of Nalanda and about 22 km south-west from Bihar Sharif. The *Paimar* River flows 2 km west to the village. There is a mound in the middle of the village. Fragment of sculptures made by black basalt are kept at Mahadeva Sthana (Pl.CXLI). Red and Red Slipped Ware were collected from the surface.

Maniyawan (Lat. 25^0 8′N, Long. 85^0 29′ E)

The village Maniyawan is 9 km east from the ruins of Nalanda and 12 km south-west from the district headquarter of Bihar Sharif.The *Paimar* River flows 2.5 km west to the village. The southern part of the village is situated on the mound yielding pot-sherds of Red, Red Slipped, and Black Ware.A few fragments made of black basalt are kept in Mahadeva Sthan. Mention may be made of a stone plaque showing Navagrah, an image of Surya measuring 31′x 161/2′ and an image of Parvati (Pl.s.CXLII-CXLIV). The River *Panchane* flows 1/2 km east to the village.

Mustafapur (Lat. 25^0 8′N, Long. 85^0 26′ E)

It is situated about 2 km north from the ruins of Nalanda and 14 km south-west from the district Headquarter Bihar Sharif. The mound having brick structures is extended into 30x25 mts with an extant extant height of 2.5 mts. There is an image of Buddha with *Muchalinda Naga* having an inscription of two lines on the pedestal which is under decipherment. The river *Paimar* flows about 7 km west to the village.

Nanan (Lat. 25^0 5′44″N, Long. 85^0 30′15″E)

It is situated about 3 km south-east of Kul-Bhadari, 7 km south-east from the ruins and 11 km south from Bihar Sharif. The mound located in the middle of the village is extended in to 5 acres with an extant height of 1.5 mts. Scattered potsherds of Red Ware and Black Ware indicates its archaeological importance. Fragments of sculptures are kept at Goraiya Sthan (east of the village) and at Shiva temple (north of the village). A few medieval remains are also noticed. The name Nanan may be identified with ancient *Nalakagama*, where Sariputra was born and eventually passed away. The River *Panchane* flows 1 km east of the village.

Nona (Lat. 25^0 7′N, Long. 85^0 27′E)

Located on a small mound it is 2 km south from the ruins and 12 km south-west from Bihar Sharif. Fragment of sculptures are kept in various places of the village (Pl. CXLV-CXLVIII).

Opa (Lat. 25^0 13′N, Long. 85^0 18′ E)

The village Opa is 21 km north-west from the ruins of Nalanda and 22 km west from Bihar Sharif. The *Nonai* River flows 2 km west to the village. To the south of the village there is a mound extended into 150x120 mts with an extant height of 10 mts. Pot sherds of Red Ware, Black Slipped Ware and Black-and-Red Ware are found on the surface.

Paparnausa (Lat. 25^0 8′86″N, Long. 85^0 26′77″E)

Settled on a small mound the village is located about 4.5 km north of the ruins and about 10 km south-west from Bihar Sharif.The mound is extended into 40x25 mts with an extant height of 4 mts yielding Red Ware and brick- bats. A few fragments made of black stone are kept at Jagdamba Sthan located in the south-west of the village near Kudwa Pokhar. *Paimar* River flows 5 km west to the village.

Raitar (Lat. 25^0 3′N, Long. 85^0 32′ E)

The village Raitar is 15 km south-east from the ruins of Nalanda and 17 km south from the district headquarter of Bihar Sharif.The *Panchane* River flows 2 km west to the village. To the west of the village there is a mound extended into 200x100 mts with an extant height of 4 mts yielding pot-sherds of Red and Red Slipped Ware.

Rukhaegarh (Lat. 25^0 19′N, Long. 85^0 22′E)

The village Rukhaegarh is 29 km north to the ruins of Nalanda and 26 km north-west from the district headquarters of Bihar Sharif. The *Chiraiya* River flows 1 km south- east to the village. There are two mounds situated to the south of the village extended into 100x100 mts with an extant height of 15 mts (Pl.CXLIX). Pot-sherds of Red, Red Slipped, Black, Black Slipped and NBP Ware were collected from the surface of the mound. Kushan bricks are also noticed in the section. A few stone sculptures are scattered at various places in the village (Pls.CL-CLII). Four copper coins having legends of medieval and British period recovered from the mound were shown by the villager Mr. Chandramauli Prasad Shukla,

Rukministhan (Lat.25^0 6′N, Long. 85^0 25′ E)

The mound of Rukministhan is located about 2 km south-west of the ruins of Nalanda and 500 mts east from Jagdishpur mound covering an area of 90x50 mts with an extant height of 6 mts from the surrounding area. Pot –sherds of Red Ware was collected during exploration. The eastern portion of the mound is comparatively higher than the other portion where a modern temple had been constructed to enshrine a life-size image of Buddha measuring 2.92x1.98x0.85 mts in *Bhumisparsha mudra* made of black stone of Pala period. There is a depiction of the life-history of Buddha by intricate engraving on the outer surface of the image (Pl.CLIII). One another image of Buddha is also found in the same posture but the head is broken.

Sahri (Lat. 25^0 11′29″N, Long. 85^0 22′21″ E)

This village is about 15 km north-west from the ruins of Nalanda and 15 km south-west from the district headquarter on Bihar Sharif-Ekangarsarai Road. A few Brahmanic sculptures of black stone are kept in the Goraiya Sthan located to the east of the village. The River *Mohane* flows 1 km west to the village.

Sakraudha (Lat. 25^0 10′97″N, Long. 85^0 25′ 62″E)

The village Sakraudha is located about 8 km north from the Nalanda ruins and about 15 km south-west from Bihar Sharif.There is a mound in the south of the village extended into 60x40 mts with an extant height of 4 mts yielding Red Ware only. A few fragments of black stone are kept at Goraiya Sthan. One of them is a broken statue of Buddha in *Dhyān mudrā* (Pl. CLIV). The river *Paimar* flows just 500 mts west to the village.

Saure (Lat. 25⁰ 8′N, Long. 85⁰ 24′ E)

The village Saure is 7 km west from the ruins of Nalanda and 16 km south-west from Bihar Sharif. The *Paimar* River flows 1.5 km east to the village. To the south of the village there is a mound extended into 70x50 mts which is presently used for agricultural purposes. Pot sherds of Red Ware and Red Slipped Ware are found on the surface. Sculptures made of black basalt are kept at Devi Sthan, Mahavir Sthan, Goraiya Sthan and Mahadeva Sthan of the village.

Shankar Garh (Lat. 25⁰ 14′N, Long. 85⁰ 21′ E)

The village Shankar Garh is about 25 km north- west from the ruins of Nalanda and 22 km west from Bihar Sharif. The *Paimar* River flows 8 km east to the village. To the south of the village there are two mounds yielding pot-sherds of Red Ware, Red Slipped Ware and Black Ware.

Silao (Lat. 25⁰ 5′21″N, Long. 85⁰ 25′71″ E)

Silao is 8 km south- east from the ruins of Nalanda and 16 km south from the district headquarter of Bihar Sharif. The *Paimar* River flows 300 m east to the village. To the south of the village there is a mound extended into 50x30 m with an extant height of 7 mts yielding Red and Red Slipped Ware.To the north of the village a few Buddhist and Brahmanic sculptures made of black basalt are kept in a temple known as Mahadeva Sthan among them some are inscribed. Special mention may be made of a standing image of Buddha and an inscribed broken sculpture of Buddha's chief disciple-Mahakashyap (Pl.CLV).

Inscription as deciphered inscribed on the image of Mahakashyapa made of black basalt is as follows: The inscription was first deciphered by Puranchanda Nahar in 1835 and subsequently by B.C. Chhabra in 1837. Recently the inscription was read by Prof. Suman Jain of my department as follows:

Line 1 (Left side)- "Siddham (Symbol-i) Nirvivachhedam Surapatirabhūtsapta Vārān Purā Yah Praptam Martye Sumahani Kule Janma Ye-

Right side-NtāmitardhoI Hemābhikhyāmamitajavano........Prāvrājīdah

Line 2 (Left side)-Purasavapuşań Kāpileyam Vihāya II[1] Dinānādhānugatamanaso Yasya Natyānyadevāyā

Right side-Nti Dvaidhań Bhagavati Jine Yasca (śca) Bhaktyā Natoabhūt I Nirvvānprādādapi Ca Sugatah Svi-

Line 3 (Left side)-Yasańhātikādīr Yasmai Vau (Bau) ddha Pravacanavridā Yena Gītāsca (śca) Dharmah II [211] Nivritah Svamdhişthāya De-

Right side- Hań Satvār (Ttvam) dhameva Yah I Gurupāde Girau Ramye Soayamābhāti Kāśyapah II [311].

Sonchari (Lat. 25^0 11′24″N, Long. 85^0 19′91″ E)

Sonchari is 19 km north-west from the ruins of Nalanda and 21 km west from the district headquarter of Bihar Sharif on Bihar Sharif-Ekangarsarai Road. The *Mohane* River flows ½ km east to the village. To the south of the village there is a mound extended into 100x30 m with an extant height of 8 mts yielding Red and Red Slipped Ware. To the west of the village a few Buddhist and Brahmanic sculptures made of black basalt are kept at Bauddha Baba (Pl.CLVI).

Tazu Bigha (Lat. 25^0 8′91″N, Long. 85^0 25′ 29″E)

This village is 6 km north-west from the ruins and 15 km south-west from Bihar Sharif situated on a small mound. Pot-sherds of NBPW, Red Ware and Black Ware were recovered during exploration. An image of Buddha measuring 25x20 inch in *Dhyana mudra* is kept outside the Shiva temple having an inscription of one line on the pedestal which is under decipherment (Pl.CLVII). River *Paimar* flows 2.5 km west to the village.

Telmar (Lat. 25^0 26′N, Long. 85^0 26′E)

The village Telmar is 40 km north to the ruins of Nalanda and 37 km north-west from the district headquarters of Bihar Sharif. The *Dhoba* River flows 2 km north to the village. The mound situated to the east of the village is extended into 70x50 mts with an extant height of 3 mts. Pot-sherds of Red Ware were collected from the surface of the mound.

Tetrawan (Lat. 25^0 6′N, Long. 85^0 36′E)

The village Tetrawan is 16 km east to the ruins of Nalanda and 10 km south-east from the district headquarters of Bihar Sharif. The *Jirain* River flows ½ km east to the village. The village is situated on the mound. A large number of Buddhist and Brahmanic sculptures made of black basalt are kept in the Bhagwati temple located to the south of the village. About 100 mts ago a huge stone image of Buddha in *Bhumisparsha mudra* having inscriptions on the lotus petals on which Buddha is seated is kept in Gautam Buddha Sthan (Pls.CLVIII-CLIX).

Tulsigarh (Lat. 25^0 21′N, Long. 85^0 25′E)

The village Tulsigarh is 30 km north to the ruins of Nalanda and 27 km north-west from the district headquarters of Bihar Sharif. The *Mohane* River flows ½ km east to the village. There is a mound to the south of the village extended into 70x50 mts having an extant height of 16 mts yielding Red Ware only. A large number of fragments of sculptures are kept at Goraiya Sthan (Pls. CLX-CLXIV).

Tungi (Lat. 25^0 10′13″N, Long. 85^9 32′24″E)

This village is 16 km east from the ruins of Nalanda and 5 km south-east from the district headquarter of Bihar Sharif. There are two mounds to the south of the village covering an area of 100x70 mts with an extant height of 3mts. Pot-sherds of Red Ware,

Black Ware and Black Slipped Ware along with terracotta objects were recovered during exploration. A large number of fragments made of black stone are kept in the Sun temple, Thakurbari and Naga Sthan (Pls.CLXV). The river *Gordhoba* flows 1 km west to the village.

References

Cunningham, A. 1935. *Ancient Geography of India*. Varanasi: Indological Book House.

Dave, J.H. 1967. *Immortal India* III.Bombay: Bharatiya Vidya Bhavan.

Kumar, N. 1970. *Bihar District Gazetteers*. Patna: Government of Bihar.

Pandey, Mithila Sharan. 1963. *The Historical Geography and Topography of Bihar*. Delhi: Motilal Banarasidas.

Archaeological Survey of India Annual Report: 1921-22. Delhi: Archaeological Survey of India.

Archaeological Survey of India A Review: 1922-23. Delhi: Archaeological Survey of India.

Archaeological Survey of India Annual Report : 1923-24. Delhi: Archaeological Survey of India.

Archaeological Survey of India Annual Report : 1924-25. Delhi: Archaeological Survey of India.

Archaeological Survey of India Annual Report : 1926-27. Delhi: Archaeological Survey of India.

Archaeological Survey of India Annual Report : 1927-28. Delhi: Archaeological Survey of India.

Archaeological Survey of India Annual Report : 1928-29. Delhi: Archaeological Survey of India.

Archaeological Survey of India Annual Report : 1929-30. Delhi: Archaeological Survey of India.

Archaeological Survey of India Annual Report : 1930-34. Delhi: Archaeological Survey of India.

Archaeological Survey of India Annual Report : 1934-35. Delhi: Archaeological Survey of India.

Archaeological Survey of India Annual Report: 1935-36. Delhi: Archaeological Survey of India.

Cunningham, A.1935.Ancient *Geography of India.*Varanasi: Indological Book House.

Dave, J.H.1967.*Immortal India III*. Bombay: Bharatiya Vidya Bhavan.

Indian Archaeology A Review: 1955-56. Delhi: Archaeological Survey of India.

Indian Archaeology A Review: 1973-74. Delhi: Archaeological Survey of India.

Indian Archaeology A Review: 1975-76. Delhi: Archaeological Survey of India.

Indian Archaeology A Review: 1982-83. Delhi: Archaeological Survey of India.

Kumar, N.1970. *Bihar District Gazetteers*. Patna: Government of Bihar.

Smith, V.A.1914.*Early History of India*. Oxford: Clerendon Press.

Chaudhary, B.K.2008. "Identifying the surroundings of Nalandas Mahavihara".*Puratattva* 38.Delhi: Indian Archaeological Society.

Ghosh, A. 1959 (4th edition).*Nalanda.* Delhi: Archaeological Survey of India.

Memoirs of Archaeological Survey of India.1999. Delhi: Archaeological Survey of India.

Memoirs of Archaeological Survey of India 66. Delhi: Archaeological Survey of India.

Sankalia, H.D. 1972(2nd edition).*The University of Nalanda.* Delhi.

Saran, S.C. *et al.*2008. "Excavations of Juafardih and its identification with Kulika". *Puratattva* 38.Delhi: Indian Archaeological Society.

Sharma, Arvind Kumar.2012.*The Pala Art in Bihar*. Patna: Janaki Prakashan.

6

Documentation and Iconographical Study of Scattered Art Objects in District-Nalanda and its Vicinity: 2012-15

Iconography is an interesting and at the same times a difficult subject. It requires not only knowledge of art, but of widely dispersed literatures both secular and religious. Images are mute spectators of the past ages. Their fine craftsmanship, beauty and polish convey much more than their values. Till date the sculptures of Nalanda are related to Pala School of Art or Magadhan Art. As we are aware that the Gandhara, Mathura and Sarnath School of Art are named after their places where these specific art forms were developed. The impact of the Sarnath School was felt in India's peripheral areas. Its influence reached as far east as the present Bangladesh and Assam and to the west in Ajanta and in the north-west up to Mirpur Khas. Being nearer to Sarnath, Nalanda also experienced its impact. But when the Sarnath idiom passed through Nalanda, it received certain Nalanda orientations. The Brahmanic and Buddhist sculptures found scattered in district-Nalanda and its vicinity support the contention of Art Historians and Archaeologists that the region could be reckoned as the cradle of Indian iconography (Sharma. 2012:42).

What is interesting to note here is that along with its religious and theological activities, Nalanda also developed into a great centre of Buddhist art. This is indeed written in an inscription of the time of Yashovarmadeva (MASI 1999: 27). There was definitely a workshop of art at Nalanda where images of gods and goddesses were made and molded on the advice of expert architects and sculptors (Sankalia 1972: 267). Here I would like to quote Havell's remark- "The University of Nalanda was a school of art and crafts. Nalanda has yielded some hundreds of sculptures in stone and bronzes. It is almost impossible to have so many sculptures without a regular school of art and crafts. Nalanda had not only dispatched religious ambassadors to south-east and far-east but also spread the divine massage of Buddha through its stone, metal, terracotta and stucco images".

Nalanda is not surrounded by any hill but hilly areas are there in the adjourning areas of Rajgir and Gaya. But interestingly enough, the sculptures of Nalanda are not all made with the same stone available at Rajgir or Gaya. Some of the sculptures of Nalanda were carved on Andalusite-biotite quartz-muscovite seri cite schist. A number of sculptures were made from Chlorite muscovite. These rocks consists micaceous minerals and therefore it was easy to carve intricate designs on them. Some of the images at Nalanda have also been made on dark grey Graphite phyllite stone which was quarried from south of Ganga river in Bihar. A number of images at Nalanda were carved in basalt. This stone was either quarried from Rajmahal hills at Bhagalpur or from the hills at Kharagpur in Munghyr.

During exploration done by the author with his Research Scholar Mr. Pankaj Kumar during 2012-15, he found hundreds of sculptures scattered on various sites unprotected and unpreserved. I have seen more than 50 inscribed Brahmanic and Buddhist Sculptures. I have taken help from Prof. Arvind Kumar Singh, Jiwaji University, Gwalior and Prof. Suman Jain of my department to decipher these inscriptions. Most of the Buddhist sculptures are inscribed with famous Buddhist creed-"Ye Dhamma Hetuppabhava...." It is noted that the number of Brahmanic sculptures is not less than Buddhist sculptures. It is also observed that these Brahmanic sculptures belong to Shaiva, Vaishnava and Saur (Sun) cult. Hence, my purpose is to attract attention of the Art Historians and Archaeologists to find out the possibility to establish Nalanda School of Art.

Brahmanic Sculptures

During archaeological investigations a number of Brahmanic images were found at Nalanda which proves that followers of Buddhism and Brahmanism used to live side by side at the place. Continuity and popularity of Vaishnava sect results with the discovery of several images of Vishnu and his consorts Lakshmi and Saraswati in Eastern India during post-Gupta period and subsequently in the Pala-Sena period. Nalanda also witnessed the tradition. During later Gupta period images related to Shaiva sect were also carved. During Pala-Sena period images of Uma-Maheshvara were carved. Goddess Uma is shown seated on the lap of Maheshvara in such images. Worship of Shakti also took place during this period and images of Durga and *Saptamātrikas* were carved on a broad level.

It is a sad thought to note that iconoclasts invaded Nalanda and carried destructive activities, arson and loot. Nalanda is now in ruins. It is however, strange to note that in spite of such wanton damages inflicted upon Nalanda; quite a good number of sculptures survived the onslaughts of invading iconoclasts. These images are mostly preserved in different museums in India and abroad. Some of these are in personal collections while a few are still in situ. I am describing only about those images which are found scattered on various sites during my exploration still unprotected and giving invitation for vandalism.

Shaiva Sculptures

During my exploration I noticed that the whole family of Shiva is represented through images. Apart from Linga (Phallus), images of Shiva were made in human form too (Shiva alone and with Parvati i.e. Uma-Maheshvara form) along with Ganesha and Nandi. These images were made mostly by black basalt. Shiva lings were found at Afsad, Aungari, Barah, Beswak, Ghosrawan, Tetrawan, Paparnausa, Tazu Bigha, Nanan, Ajnaura and Kosnara while Ek Mukh lings were found at Afsad and Ghosrawan. Images of Shiva in human form were found scattered at Aungari, Ghosrawan, Maniyawan and Kosnara while Uma-Maheshwar form were recovered from Afsad, Aungari, Barah, Badhauna, Ghosrawan, Kolawan, Tetrawan, Kondi, Ajaypur, Ajnaura, Eksara and Kosnara sites. It is interesting to note that images of Parvati is found only at two places *i.e.* Dayalpur and Nanan while sculptures of Mahishmardini Durga were recovered from so many sites like-Afsad, Aungari, Barah, Ghosrawan, Tetrawan, Tulsigarh, Nanan and Ajnaura. Ganesha images were found at Dhurgaon, Ghosrawan, Maniyawan, Ajaypur, Ajnaura, Eksara and Kosnara. Sculptures of Nandi were found at Afsad, Barah, Ghosrawan, Kul, Nanan, Kondi, Ajnaura, Eksara and Kosnara.

Vaishnava Sculptures

Images of Vishnu, Lakshmi, Saraswati, Varah and Dashavatara made of black basalt and *Ashtadhatu* were found scattered at various sites in the district. Vishnu images were found at Aungari, Barah, Beswak, Dhurgaon, Ghosrawan, Samas, Tulsigarh, Paparnausa and Ajnaura. Special mention may be made of the statue of Samas which is about 6 feet high made of *Ashtadhatu* recovered during the digging of nearby pond. Only one statue of Saraswati is noticed at Ghosrawan. Images of Lakshmi were found from Afsad, Barah, Dhurgaon and Ghosrawan. A 6 feet high image of Varah was installed in a newly built temple. A stone plaque showing the images of *Dashavatara* was found from Kondi.

Saur (Sun) Sculptures

The images of Sun god were made by black basalt and are found in two forms:

1. With his chariot 7 horses symbolizing 7 rays of the Sun which follows the Pauranic tradition.
2. Without his chariot putting on boots. This form was developed by Maga Brahmans during Kushan period.

These images were found at Afsad, Aungari, Barah, Beswak, Dayalpur, Ghosrawan, Tetrawan, Maniyawan and Kondi.

Other than these sculptures of Brahmanic deities images of Kuber were found at Afsad, Barah, Dayalpur, Dhurgaon, Ghosrawan and Maniyawan. Fragment of sculptures of Brahmanic deities were found at Afsad, Aungari, Barah, Beswak, Badhauna, Dayalpur, Dhurgaon, Ghosrawan, Kolawan, Madhopur, Tetrawan,

Samas, Paparnausa, Tazu Bigha, Nona, Maniyawan, Kondi, Bara Khurd, Aldhanna and Ajaypur. Present status of the scattered Brahmanic sculptures in the district is shown in the Table No. 45.

Table 45
Showing Scattered Brahmanic Sculptures, Nalanda

Sl. No.	*Type of Sculptures*	*No. of Sites*	*No. of Sculptures*
1.	Linga (Phallus)	11	19
2.	EkMukha Linga	02	02
3.	Shiva	04	07
4.	Uma-Maheshwara	12	18
5.	Parvati	02	02
6.	Mahishmardini Durga	09	14
7.	Ganesha	07	12
8.	Nandi	09	10
9.	Vishnu	09	15
10.	Lakshmi	04	06
11.	Sarswati	01	01
12..	Dashavatara	01	01
13.	Varah	01	01
14.	Sun	09	20
15.	Kuber	06	07
16.	Fragment of Brāhmaṇic images	20	180
	Total	107	315

Buddhist Sculptures

The evolution of Tantric Buddhism introduced many images of gods and goddesses and their worship. A sizeable number of such images were carved at Nalanda in stone and metal that subsequently formed the major subject matter of Nalanda sculptures (Bhattacharyya.2008:32). During my exploration I found a great number of Buddhist sculptures made of black basalt scattered on various sites unprotected. Some of them are intact and very beautifully carved the life-scenes of Buddha. More than 50 images were found inscribed and most of them were read as the famous Buddhist creed-"Ye Dhamma Hetuppabhava..."Among these images mention may be made of images of Buddha, Bodhisattvas, Varahi and Trailokya-Vijay. A great number of fragments were also found on various sites.

Images of Buddha

Images of Buddha were found at Aungari, Beswak, Aiyer, Dhurgaon, Ghosrawan, Jethian, Parvati, Rukhaegarh, Tulsigarh, Mustafapur, Paparnausa, Tazu Bigha, Kul, Nona, Rukministhan, Maniyawan, Chandi Mau, Kondi, Eksara and Kosnara.

Images of Bodhisattvas

Sculptures of Bodhisattvas were found at Afsad, Aungari, Beswak, Dayalpur, Dhurgaon, Ghosrawan, Tetrawan, Paparnausa, Kul and Ajnaura.

Other Buddhist deities

Images of Marichi were noticed at two sites *i.e.* Eksara and Ghosrawan. Only one broken image of Trailokya-Vijay was found at Jethian. Fragment of Buddhist sculptures were found at Afsad, Aiyer, Dhurgaon, Ghosrawan, Jethian, Parvati, Rukhaegarh, Tetrawan, Tulsigarh, Begampur, Mustafapur, Paparnausa, Tazu Bigha, Kul, Nanan, Rukministhan, Nona, Chandi Mau, Kondi, Bara Khurd, Aldhanna, Ajnaura and Kosnara. Present status of the scattered Buddhist sculptures in the district is shown in the Table No. 46.

Table 46
Showing Scattered Buddhist Sculptures, Nalanda

Sl. No.	*Type of Sculptures*	*No. of Sites*	*No. of Sculptures*
1.	Buddha	20	48
2.	Bodhisattva	10	20
3.	Marichi	02	02
4.	Trailokya- Vijaya	01	01
5.	Fragments of Buddhist Deties	23	177
	Total	56	248

A few misinterpreted sculptures

The sites of Bargaon, Telhara and Versiyawan needs special mentioned because unique sculptures recovered from these sites are misinterpreted by local inhabitants. An image of Buddha in *Bhumisparsha mudra*, made of black basalt recovered from Bargaon is locally known as Telia Bhandar. According to local belief if a pregnant woman offer mustered oil to that image she will get a healthy baby. Another image of Buddhist tantric goddess Marichi is called Dhelwa Baba. It is believed that if a person is going to do a good work he must hit the image by a brick-bat. A stone slab on which the scene of Siddhartha's *Mahabhinishkramana* is depicted is installed on the pedestal of the Sun god and interpreted as Arjuna of Mahabharata. The image of Buddha in *Bhumisparsha mudra* recovered from Tetrawan is known as Bhairav Baba while the Buddha image of Versiyawan is called Gachchfar Baba. The word gachch is used for a tree. Actually the image was hidden between two trees. During a strong storm both trees were fell down and the image came out, so it is named Gachchfar Baba. During my exploration I noticed following facts:

- Brahmanic images are not less in number in comparison to Buddhist Sculptures.
- More than 50 Buddhist images are found inscribed either around the hallo or on the pedestal. Most of them have been read as the famous Buddhist creed-*Ye dhamma hetuppabhava*...
- Shaiva, Vaishnava and Saur sects of Brahmanism were prevalent in the region.
- Buddhist and Brahmanic faiths were developing side by side and there was no rivalry in between them.
- Quantity and Art form of Nalanda Sculptures compelled us to consider it as Nalanda School of Art.

The number of Brahmanical images is more than the Buddhist sculptures. This reveals that Brahmanism was also surviving in a better condition with the proper support of either of central power or local kings or society while Buddhism was facing its down phase in spite of having patronage of Pala Kings. Why the Magadha got so much importance that it started imperialism and why the Buddha and Mahavira philosophy originated or formulated here? What was the reason behind the rise of NBPW as dates are of much older than the Buddha and Second Urbanization? Very less number of BRW sites has been reported in the region which demands a proper understanding of Culture of Pre-Buddhist era. Series of researches have been made on several aspects in this region but lots of work is inviting us to execute in a scientific way. If we study the region scientifically after excavating several sites of the region a strong opinion will certainly come and this will help us to study the region in new dimension.

Aesthetic Evaluation

Nalanda yielded one of the richest collections of sculptures in stone, bronze and stucco. These sculptures were images of gods and goddesses of Buddhist and Brahmanic pantheon. A few Jain images were also discovered from the district. The images of Nalanda are mostly dated to the Pala period (8th -12th century CE), but there are instances, although, fewer in number at Nalanda, are dated to pre-Pala period. After carefully examining these pre-Pala specimens, Ray, very aptly observed that the *Prachya* country, which had inherited a culture and ethnic character different from those of *Aryavarta*, endowed the subtle delicacy and spiritual refinement of Sarnath sculptures with a warmth of emotion and sensual appeal(Ray.1931:523). This is evident in some of the Buddha images from Nalanda. A few of these sculptures on stylistic ground are dated in Gupta and late-Gupta period (5th and 6th century CE). Of these images, mention may be made of a few stucco specimens (Ghosh.1959:18).

In the Nalanda Museum collection there is a detached female head which was discovered at Site No. 4 and has been stylistically dated to the 5th century CE. The ovoid face, very finally carved eye-brows, lotus petal like eyes, soft and sensitive lips and curls in the hairs, are some of the features that connect this face with the classical Gupta faces. The same holds good about a detached and partially eroded and damaged head of the Buddha in stucco, which is in the collection of the Nalanda Museum. The face reminds us its intimate relation with the Sarnath School in the Gupta period. The elongated ears, the half opened eyes as if looking inward and withdrawing itself from the surroundings nearby, the movement of the eye-brows, the heavy lower lip and the face like a hen's egg, are all present here. However, the stylization of hair and the *urna* on the forehead are the two features which place it somewhat later in the 6th century CE. Another stucco image of the contemporary period was discovered in a niche on the wall of staircase of *Stupa* No. 3 at Nalanda. This image delineates an emphatic representation of Bodhisattva Avalokiteshvara, who is shown standing in *tribhanga* posture within a shallow niche. This nimbate Bodhisattva displays by his right hand an attitude which looks almost like *varada mudra* and his left hand which is placed on his left thigh holds the stalk of a stylized lotus. He looks down as his name suggests (Avalokit), his matted locks on the head has been carefully arranged and some of his hairs are allowed to fall down on his shoulder. Halo behind his head is without any ornamentation. He wears *ekavali* (a single beaked neckless) and a pair of wristlets. He also wears diaphanaous drapery just like the Buddha images of Sarnath. The anatomical perfection and careful treatment of the different plains of his bodies and the soft plastic qualities are related to late 6th century sculptures of Sarnath idom.

To the North of the North-East corner of *Stupa* No.3, in a votive *stūpa* installed within a niche, an image of a Bodhisattva has been carved in such a way that there could be a wonderful play of light and shade which would ultimately enhance its divine beauty. However, this seated Bodhisattva has enough proves to indicate the evident exhaustion of the classical grace in it. The sculptures of this period were intended to convey the same spiritual grace as the Sarnath sculptures did. The refinement in carving continued in the late 6th-7th century sculptures of Nalanda. These sculptures imbibed inspirations definitely from Sarnath idom. The introduction of jewelery in the figure of Lokanatha points to a later date of manufacture. The treatment of the lips and the upper eye-lids in such figures place them in a somewhat post-Gupta period (Huntington.1984:110).

The modelling as well as the mannerism of certain bronze images of Nalanda made subsequently an impact on some of the Kashmiri bronze Buddhas, resulting a close stylistic similarity that may have resulted due to the import into Kashmir both of sculptures and artists from Bengal. However, the impact of Eastern Indian Art on the art of Kashmir was not the one way traffic. The Kashmiri art had spread in Bihar and Bengal as a result of political and cultural intercourse during the reign of king Devapala. The style of Kashmiri Avalokiteshvara in the 8th century is said to have served as a prototype for a number of sculptures in Bihar and Bengal including Nalanda.

Although Nalanda School imbibed inspiration from Sarnath School of Art, but it could not maintain the classical grace and beauty for years. If the sculptures of Nalanda dated 6th-8th century CE are carefully examined, it is easily noticed that the classical grace evaporated and a meaningless and drowsy heaviness characterize the sculptures produced in this time bracket (Ray.1931:640-47). Mention may be made of a standing Buddha image of Nalanda Museum collection dated to the 7th century CE carved in basalt shows *Abhaya mudra* by his right hand and holding the end piece of his scarf (*Sanghati*) by his left hand. The image represents a coarse plastic surface and outline looses its fluidity. The face has completely lost the classical charm and the plasticity of the body was very summarily executed. A drowsy heaviness predominates in this image (Mukherjee.1959:4-5).

A few Brahmanic images also yielded during this period; for instance, mention may be made of a *vedibandha* which includes a seated figure of Parvati made of granite which was recovered from the Temple Site- 2 and placed to the 7th century CE. A contemporary image of Shiva installed within a *vedibandha* was also found from the same site. Besides these figures mention may be made of images of Kartikeya, Gaja-Lakshmi and Kubera. The drowsy heaviness in plasticity prevailed upon these deities. The presence of Brahmanical images, predominantly at a Buddhist site is somewhat intriguing. The existence of such images appears to have been tolerated by the Buddhists at Nalanda (Ghosh.1959:49-50).At the same time it is to be noted that Nalanda also produced a few such Buddhist images where Brahmanical gods such as Indra, Brahma, Vishnu, Shiva and Ganesha were categorically belittled. Thus the place exhibited religious animosity as well as compromise at a given time (Bhattacharya.2008:62).

From the aesthetic point of view if we compare the images of Guptan period with the images of 7th century CE, carved at Nalanda we could find the noticeable difference.The seated figure of Kartikeya dated 5th century CE and the standing image of the same deity dated 6th century CE in Bharat Kala Bhawan, one could find the degeneration in the case of Nalanda image of Kartikeya that took place within a span of a century. In fact, in the 7th century CE Nalanda was incorporating in its plastic diction, certain local characteristics and prejudices along with somewhat different regional, social and religious ideals in it, which ultimately led to certain changes. The image of Kuber and Shiva when considered in terms of their sculptural qualities one finds that the stone carvers were more concerned about their iconographical details and were less interested to concentrate on the plastic qualities. They depict heavy and coarse features and evince complete indifference of the sculptor with regard to the proportion, modelling and plastic rhythm. The etymological meaning of the term Kubera is of course Ku-bera *i.e.*, the ugly body. But when Gupta sculptor fashioned an image of Kubera they tried to project it in a much disciplined manner. The same type of image could not be produced at Nalanda in the 7th century CE. The images of 7th-8th century CE at Nalanda faintly reminds us of their distant connection with the Gupta idoms. One of the reasons for the discontinuance of the Gupta plastic conception, grace and refinement was the absence of political cohesion after the Guptas in Northern India and certain phenomenal changes in Indian iconography in general.

The sculptors at Sarnath preferred to carve large stone images and concentrated on minute details and careful executions while the Nalanda sculptors went for smaller statues and the same holds good not only for stone images but the metal sculptures as well. The images of Nalanda mostly date from the Pala period. During this period the religious life of Eastern India came into the grip of Tantra cult. It also affected the religio-artistic features of Nalanda (Datta.1944:267-68). As a result a large number of Tantric gods and goddesses evolved and worshiped. During this period artists introduced a greater variety of images and also a number of *mudras, asanas* and other technical details. It appears that a large number of artists were commissioned to meet the larger demands for images and a result of which sculptures with varying degrees of skill and training were produced. The sculptors between 8th -12th centuries went for cult images mainly and they carved the images strictly according to formulas enunciated as in *Sadhanamala, Nishpannayogavali, Advyavajra Sangraha* etc.The Buddhist sculptures of Nalanda tried to maintain in varying degrees a certain amount of dignity and serenity in their bearing and yet their charm and sensuousness have a spell of allurement that is at once physical and spiritual in the 9th century and onwards. The images of Hariti and Jambhala when compared with the figures of the Bodhisattvas of 6th -7th centuries at Nalanda appear less integrated and united. Both images are shown seated on the similar type of throne with the leogryphs on either side. The structure and preparation of the thrones, the lions at the corners and the halos mark a different treatment in form and composition. The artists introduced in the halo behind two separate bands of beaded chain and circular flames which was not seen earlier. This motif became very common in the images of the contemporary period.

Metal images of Nalanda were cast in brass, bronze and octo alloy (ashtadhatu). These images were made in large quantity and are available from the post-Gupta period. Metal casting as a technique developed to a great extent at the place and this appears to have been included into the regular curriculam of the Mahavihara.

Possibility of Art School at Nalanda

On the basis of the iconographical study if we analyse the possibility of Nalanda School of art then we come at a conclusion that it was a continuous process of centuries which was developed in a broad area including other local art styles. Art objects since Gupta to Pala-Sena period were recovered from Nalanda. Sculptors made Buddhist images in stucco, stone and bronze and also expressed their art skills in paintings since 6th century to 12th century CE. During Gupta period Indian artists have given material form to the Indian life style which was a mixture of materialistic world and spirituality.Excellent art works of this period were recovered from Sarnath, Mathura and Deogarh while terracotta figurines and small art objects were reported from every excavation done in north India (Chauley.). During this period a number of art centers were developed at Pataliputra and its vicinity which was named as Pataliputra Art School by R.D.Banarjee (Banarjee.1933:17). In the beginning these art centers were influenced by the Gupta Art of Sarnath School, such as strait eyebrows, curled hair style and special type of *Ushnisha* but the upper and lower dresses and tucked style was shown by tradional lining (Banarjee. 1933:17). According to Banarjee two speciality of Pataliputra art style differenciate it from Sarnath School but to whom Banarjee named Pataliputra art School, actually it was not limited only in Pataliputra but it was extended up to Nalanda, Rajgrih, Bodh Gaya and other art centers of Magadh. As Agrawal says that during this time the art activities were extended in the southern area of the Ganga such as- Rajgrih and Nalanda and in the west up to Bodh Gaya (Agrawal.1965:296). Since this time, Nalanda which was a famous Buddhist centre like Sarnath became growing as a centre of art and in later times the art and culture of Nalanda spread in north and soth-east Asian countries.

Archaeological investigations in the region of Nalanda and its vicinity were started in 1838 and still it is going on. A number of images made of terracotta, stucco, stone and bronze were recovered during the excavations of the Nalanda Mahavihara which are installed in the site museum, Patna museum, National museum, New Delhi, Indian museum, Kolkata, British museum, London etc. Apart of these a number of images, intact and in fragments, are still scattered in the district and its vicinity which was documented by the author during his village to village survey in 2012-13, 2013-14 and 2015-16. An excavation was also carried out by the author and his team during 2015-16 at Rukhaegarh, Chandi, Nalanda. During archaeological investigation in the district and its vicinity it was noticed that sculptors used to made Buddhist as well as Brahmanic images too. Most of the scattered images were built during Pala-Sena period and the material was mainly black basalt.

The quantity of images recovered from the region till date proves that there must be a centre of art in this place. Now the question arises that is the manufacturing of images in the region was only the contribution of Pala emperors? Because the art developed at Nalanda and its vicinity is named as Pala School of Art but making of sculptures was prevalent in the region before Palas. Although the number of Gupta images at Nalanda is less in comparison to Pala period. Chauley defended it in following points:

- In early period of Mahayanism the worship was done collectively, so that the necessity of image making was not realized.
- Unavailability of stone pieces in the region
- Due to fame of stucco images followers of Buddha donot felt the need of stone or metal images.

In this way we can say that Nalanda was developed as a centre of Art since Gupta period. Sankalia also supported this theory and told that during Gupta period Nalanda became a centre of sculpture making (Sankalia, 1972: 261). Local sculptors of Nalanda adopted the special characteristics of the art schools of pre-Mauryan, Greeko-Bactrian, Persian, Mathura, Amaravati and other art schools and produced a number of Buddhist images under a new art style which was different from the earlier art styles (Coomaraswami. 1914: 74). It was done during Gupta period because without a regular centre of art it is impossible to recover such a huge number of images from the region (Sankalia. 1972: 261). Making of sculptures was done here at local level because it is impossible to impoprt images in such a huge quantity. Local sculptors have given a new dimension to the Nalanda art under the skillfull direction of Dhiman and Bitapal.

Images of temple site no. 2 of Nalanda are datable to 6-7th century CE. It was the time of later guptas. During this time stucco figures were made on a grand level. A number of stucco images were recovered from the 5th layer of main *stūpa* no. 3 which was almost Buddhist upon which local impact may be seen. After that stone images were being made for which raw material was supplied from the nearby hills of Rajgir and Munghyer, so that a large number of stone images were built at Nalanda. According to Huttington Nalanda Buddha has its own speciality. Among Buddhist images here veriety of images were made which is larger in quantity in comparison to any other Buddhist site and also able to express the local religious sentiments. Whereever presence of the images of Brahmanic deties shows religious harmony in between them but attempts were also made to show them inferior to Buddhist deties. Such as Indra, Brahma, Vishnu, Shiva and Ganesha were shown trampled underfoot by Buddhist deties which also proved the local impact on the art.

The facts analyzed above shows that a centre of art was already developed and images were made without any interruption at Nalanda long before the Palas so it is useless to connect it with Pala School of Art. So it is a narrow minded thought to link up it with a dynasty. As Sarnath, Mathura, Gandhara art schools were named after their birthplace so that the art form which was developed at Nalanda and was given a different form must be known as "Nalanda School of Art".

Decline of the Centre of Art

When we study about the iconography of Nalanda we found that during early Pala period commendatory manifestation of tenderness is noticed in sculptures. Later the sculptors showed extraordinary skill in ornamentation and decoration of the halo (Singh. 1958: 149) but the images made during the last phase of Pala period seems apathetic due to restrictions and conservatism. During 11-12th centuries the whole halo was full of various types of carvings and painted sceneries and the size of the images were made very big. During this time the iconography of Nalanda has taken a fixed shape in which classical rules must be obeyed, so that lack of livelihood is noticed in the images of this period. Abide by classical rules the sculptors of Nalanda trimmed their wings of art and the art abide with restrictions has taking his last breath (Singh. 1958: 150). Being alive any art it is necessary to give a free environment to the sculptors so that they may express their skills in the stone and give tangible form to their imaginations but just opposite the classical laws of iconography became so unliberal and very harsh at Nalanda.The sculptors of Nalanda were compelled to make sculptures as per harsh rules so that they became unable to give perceptible form to their imaginations. Fixed form of postures and stiffness of the body became obstacles in the development of iconography. The sculptors of Nalanda has given consolation to themselves by fine carving of the halo of the images, so that the main subject of the iconography became subsidiary and the period of its development was also completed.

Skill of art and reverential belief was dedicated only to the main statue in the early Nalanda images but sculptors of 11-12th century have found satisfaction in carving the halo, throne and ornamentation of the image because it was impossible to them to oppose the harsh classical rules. There is lack of natural flexibility and movement in the images of this period but it was full of fine carvings and ornamentation. Various postures of the arms, bending status of the neck and the *tribhanga* posture of the whole body is unable to express the natural movement. It seems that the sculptors intentionally moved the parts of the body of the images in unproper way (Singh.1958:151). Preceding to downfall this Art School was finally destroyed by the

Muslim invasion. Apart from Nalanda other art centres like Vikramshila, Bodh Gaya, and Kukkutapadagiri etc. were also demolished during this period. Decline of these Mahaviharas also affected the art centres running under them. When the sources were dried up to promote these art centres then it was natural that its conservation and preservation became a dream and the luxuriant growth of the crop suddenly burnt up (Singh. 1958: 150).

Fusion on other Art traditions

Iconography is an interesting and at the same times a difficult subject. It requires not only knowledge of art, but of widely dispersed literatures both secular and religious. Images are mute spectators of the past ages. Their fine craftsmanship, beauty and polish convey much more than their values.

Till date the sculptures of Nalanda are related to Pala School of Art or Magadhan Art. As we are aware that the Gandhara, Mathura and Sarnath School of Art are named after their places where these specific art forms were developed. The impact of the Sarnath School was felt in India's peripheral areas. Its influence reached as far east as the present Bangladesh and Assam and to the west in Ajanta and in the north-west upto Mirpur Khas. Being nearer to Sarnath, Nalanda also experienced its impact. But when the Sarnath idiom passed through Nalanda, it received certain Nalanda orientations. The Brahmanic and Buddhist sculptures found scattered in district-Nalanda and its vicinity support the contention of Art Historians and Archaeologists that the region could be reckoned as the cradle of Indian iconography. (Sharma. 2012: 42).

The evolution of Tantric Buddhism introduced many images of gods and goddesses and their worship. A sizeable number of such images were carved at Nalanda in stone and metal that subsequently formed the major subject matter of Nalanda sculptures (Bhattacharyya.2008:32). Nalanda attained prominence as an important *Mahāyānist* centre during the time of imperial Guptas. Pala art is preponderant here occupying the same remarkable position as held by Sarnatha and Mathura of the Gupta Age. The availability of carved bricks, pillars, gold coins, inscriptions, stuccos, fragments of grey sandstone-figures along with the names of those Gupta rulers, responsible for the construction of Nalanda Mahavihara as stated by Hiuen-tsang, are some of the definite archaeological evidences of the Gupta settlement of Nalanda. The extant remains of sculptures are very few in this period. During this period worship was purely a community type of ritual, used to be practiced by the worshippers in groups, that is why many images were not required, neither worship of images by individuals within the monastic cell was developed (Beal. 1973: 39). Monasteries were also very few in the beginning. The non-availability of the suitable rocks in the nearby regions and craftsmen may be another reason for the absence of art center at Nalanda as during Gupta era. The stuccos were most inexpensive material, used mostly in decorative purposes and even the colossal images within the sanctum sanctorum were also made of stuccos, as a result of which necessity of stone images were not felt by the devotees.

A remarkable change is marked in the later period which followed immediately after the Guptas. Due to the passage of time and the growing popularity of Mahayana Buddhism, worship of images by individuals became predominant, as a consequence of which a greater demand was felt in the society which paved the way for the establishment of independent Art centers like Nalanda, Kurkihar and Bodhgaya, during the Pala period. By imbibing tantric ideas and incorporating a number of deities, the Eastern Provinces created a vast pantheon of their own by freely incorporation into their pantheon several of the Brahmanic deities under different names and also with certain modifications.

A number of deities belonging to the regular Brahmanical pantheon was assimilated into Mahayanic worship viz. Saraswati, Ganesha and the Saptamatrikas. Brahmanic deities like Surya, Vishnu, Kubera etc., came to be incorporated into Buddhism as Marichi, Lokeshvara, and Jambhala etc. Heruka, Singhnada, Nilkantha and Vajrahunkara are but adaptations of the benign and the malignant aspect of Bhairava and Shiva. A comprehensive study of many of the Brahmanical icons and the corresponding group of Mahayana or Vajrayana Buddhist images will enable us to see the transference of the attributes of Indra to Vajrapani, of Brahma to Manjusri and of Vishnu to Avalokiteshvara etc. (Bhattacharyya. 2008: 141).

A few artistic works came in vogue at Nalanda in between the transition phase, *i.e.* the end of the Gupta period and the beginning of the Palas. The style and other decorative details show a stylistic affirmation with those of the Gupta workmanship on the one hand and a sharp regional feature manifest in the physiognomy style of drapery and ornaments concerned. It is problematic to determine their date because they were produced of grey sandstone in stead of black basalt in which almost all the inherent qualities of the Gupta workmanship are to be noticed. Excavations at Nalanda have yielded also coarse and lifeless images of Brahmanic and Buddhist pantheon which reveals untiring efforts of a group of local artists to model them in pursuance of the Gupta idiom (Patil. 1963: 328). Such type of images was described by Banerjee in *Eastern Indian School of Medieval Sculptures* as pre-Pala in origin and cited examples from the collection of Indian Museum, Kolkata. The existence of such types of images definitely testifies the fact that a regular centre of art had already been established at Nalanda in the post-Gupta period. On the recovery of sculptural remains at Nalanda, Havell remarked-"The University of Nalanda was school of art and craft. The remark becomes true from the discovery of hundreds of sculptures in stone and bronze. It seems almost impossible to have so many sculptures without a regular school of arts and crafts".

It is a sad thought to note that iconoclasts invaded Nalanda and carried destructive activities, arson and loot. Nalanda is now in ruins. It is however, strange to note that in spite of such wanton damages inflicted upon Nalanda; quite a good number of sculptures survived the onslaughts of invading iconoclasts. These images are mostly installed in different museums in India and abroad. Some of these are in personal collections while a few are still in situ. The site during the span of last hundred years yielded not only the ruins of stupas and viharas in course of explorations and excavations but has also laid bare innumerable number of stone and bronze sculptures and stucco figurines. The number of artifacts discovered so far from Nalanda, has led certain scholars to infer that, perhaps, the carving of stones and the moulding of metal images were included in the regular curriculam of the Mahavihara otherwise it could not be possible either by Dhiman or Bitpala alone or even by a dozen of their disciples to produce such a large number of icons at Nalanda. The available writings do not give an overall view about the nature and content of Nalanda's sculptures. In fact, a systematic and comprehensive survey of Nalanda Art as a whole has been long over due.

Fusion on Indian Art

Afsad

A large temple at Afsaḍ has its plinth decorated with stucco reliefs. There are also several stone images of 7th-8th century CE. The stucco panels illustrate *Ramayana* scenes. They are placed within alternating rectangular and keyhole-shaped niches of approximately 36″X20″ separated from one another by pilasters corresponding to Nalanda Site-3 pilasters very closely.The surfaces of the Afsad temple are more highly ornamented, probably indicating a somewhat later date. The stuccoes of Afsad show no evidence of the Sarnath influence that was so prominent in the sculptures of the Nalanda region. As to their precedents the Rajauna pillars and the reliefs of Patharghat may be mentioned here (Sinha: 53).

Akota (Pl.CLXVI)

It is an interesting feature that the pointed halo of Vajrapani (11th century CE) from Nalanda is seen in the attendant figures of Rishabhanath from Akota of 8th century CE (Shah.1955:11).. Similar halo is seen in the bronzes representing Sarvanubhuti Yaksha and Ambika Yakshi from Akota of 10th century CE. Bronze image of Jivantasvami (Late 6th century CE) has eyes inlaid with silver, fan-shaped projections of its crown, *urṇā*, strands of hair-locks arranged in stages, two ends of the waist-band, large loop, incised lines on *dhoti*, vertical folds between the legs, broad chest with rounded shoulders are found in Nalanda images of 8th-9th century CE (Shah.1955:27). Beaded halo of the sculptures from Nalanda of the same period is seen in the Akota bronzes of Jivantasvami of 6th century CE. The throne of the bronze images of Ambika (7th century CE) from Akota shows ornamental cross-bar with *amalaka*-shaped ends, pointed halo and fabulous *vyalakas* flanking its sides. These features are present in bronze *Jatamukuta* Lokeshvara and Vajrapani from Nalanda. Beaded halo placed on beaded throne, crocodile-beads on the ends of the cross-bar, *vyalakas* on sides of the throne, couchant lions supporting the throne, ornamental cloth hanging over the pedestal are the special features of a bronze image of a Jina (8th century CE) found from Akota. Similar features are noticed in the sculptures of Nalanda dated 8th-9th century CE. The *Chamaraḍharini* image of Akota (8th century AD) has large string loops hanging from waist-band with ornamental vertical ends between the legs which are seen in the image of Khadiravani Tara from Nlanda. An image of Ambika from Akota (8th century CE) shows folds of flesh below her breasts. Similar device is seen in the early sculptures of Mahasaraswati and Mahamayuri of Nalanda.

Kurkihara

In so far as silver-inland eyes, *urna*, drapery, lotus-seat and the pedestal are concerned, bronze images of Buddha recovered from Nalanda (9th century CE) are very much similar to the bronze Buddha with Brahmanical gods as attendants found from Kurkihara and kept in Patna museum (Shah.1955:62). The *ushnisha* of the Kurkihara image shows a high flame. The oldest bronze images of Buddha of Kurkihara are not earlier than 8th century CE (Sinha: 54). Similar bronzes of Nalanda are more in number. During the Pala period the number of dated bronzes from Kurkihara is greater than those of Nalanda (Pls.CLXVII-CLXIX).

A number of scholars think that Kurkihara bronzes are very close to those of Nalanda and belong to the same period but there are certain differences in between them. The Kurkihara bronzes are more elaborate than those of Nalanda.In some of the Kurkihara bronzes the Bodhi tree is superimposed over the halo which is never the case with the Nalanda bronzes representing the Buddha in *Bhumisparsha mudra*. Kurkihara has yielded several bronzes of the Buddha with flamed *ushnisha* but no such bronze is known from Nalanda although in one stone image of 13th century CE representing standing figure of the Buddha there is high *ushnisha* with a pointed flame. In a Buddha image of Kurkihara the lower part of the body is stout and its drapery seems to be very heavy. No such elaboration is reported in the Nalanda bronzes. The Kurkihara bronzes show comparatively much use of precious stones as is evident from lamp-shaped sockets seen from top to bottom. If such a socket surmounts a bronze, it should not necessarily belong to Nalanda. In a Kurkihara bronze the outer border is composed of these sockets only. In certain Buddha images from Kurkihar, the lower portion is almost static and wood-like. This feature is absent in Nalanda. In some of the Kurkihara bronzes the flamed border is carved very minutely and the flames are set very closely. This is not the general rule at Nalanda. Some of the Kurkihara bronzes surpass the Nalanda bronzes in beauty. Some have fully open staring eyes with pointed ends and a central small depression marks on teir pupil. This depiction is also known at Nalanda.

Sirpur

There are basic similarities as well as local varients when we compare Nalanda bronzes with those from Sirpur (Pl.CLXX). Asher thinks that Sirpur bronzes apply fine linear details while the Nalanda bronze leave unadorned surfaces. It may be also noticed in haloes and thrones (Sinha:85).

Telhara

A Buddha image of Telhara (Tiladhak Mahavihara) has a motif of alternating diamond and circles seen on some niches of the plinth at Nalanda Site-2 (Pl.CLXXI). A pair of small standing Buddhas flanks its halo as seen attending the Preaching Buddhas at Sarnath of Gupta period (Asher.1980:51).

Tetrawan

A standing Buddha image recovered from Tetrawan is similar to the Nalanda images. A seated Buddha image (Late 7th century CE) recovered from Tetrawan (Tendadigram) shows a superb assimilation of the styles that prevailed at Nalanda and Bodh Gaya (Asher.1980:78). It is comparable with stucco Buddha images of Nalanda Site-3 and a Buddha image in *Bhumisparsha mudra* (8th century CE) recovered from Bodh Gaya.Its face, shape of eyes and long arched incised eye-brows recall the Muchalinda Buddha of Bodh Gaya of the same date. Its body resembles that of the Afsad stone figure of the same date.

Fusion on Foreign Art

Bangladesh (Fig. 44)

The origin of the name Bengal (known as *Bangla* and *Bongo* in Bengali language) is unknown. One theory suggests that the word derives from "Bang", a Dravidian tribe that settled the region around 1000 BCE. The word might have been derived from the ancient kingdom of *Vanga* (or *Banga*), which came from the Austric word "Bonga" meaning the Sun-god. The Indo-Aryan suffix *"desh"* is derived from the Sanskrit word *desha* (region, province, country). The earliest reference to "Vangala" (*Bangla*) has been traced in the Nesari plates (805 CE) of Rashtrakuta Govinda III which speak of Dharmapala as the king of Vangala. The records of Rajendra Chola I of the Chola dynasty, who invaded Bengal in the 11th century, speak of Govindachandra as the ruler of Vangaladesa.

The early history of Bengal featured a succession of city-states, maritime kingdoms and pan-Indian empires. The Buddhist Samatata kingdom emerged in east Bengal after 232 BCE. The Mauryan and Gupta empires ruled much of the region between 200 BCE-550 CE. The Pundravardhana region encompassed much of north-western Bengal. The Harikela state ruled the north-east and coastal areas. The Hindu leader Shashanka founded the Gauda kingdom in the 7th century. The Buddhist Chandra dynasty rose to power in the southeast.

After a period of civil war, the Bengali Buddhist Pala Empire was established circa 750 CE. Its rulers were followers of the Mahayana school of Buddhism. The Palas ushered an age of stability and imperialism. They patronized many universities and temples. Pala sculpture and painting are considered among the most finest of ancient Asian art. The Pala dynasty ruled for four hundred years, reaching its peak under Dharmapala and Devapala.

The present-day borders of Bangladesh took shape during the Partition of Bengal and British India in 1947, when the region came to be known as East Pakistan, as a part of the newly formed state of Pakistan. It was separated from West Pakistan

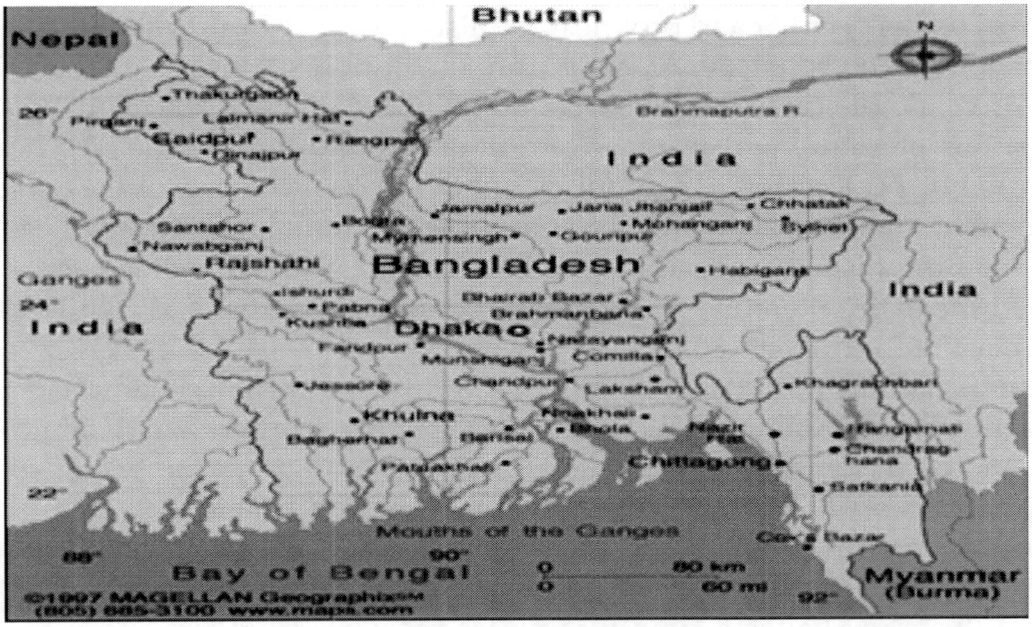

Figure 44: Map of Bangladesh

by 1,400 km of Indian Territory. Due to political exclusion, ethnic and linguistic discrimination and economic neglect by the politically dominant western wing, nationalism, popular agitation and civil disobedience led to the Bangladesh Liberation War and independence in 1971. After independence, the new state endured poverty, famine, political turmoil and military coups. The restoration of democracy in 1991 has been followed by relative calm and economic progress.

Impact of Tantrayana

The Tantric Buddhist scholars like Chandragomin, Shantideva, Shantirakshita, Jetari (junior), Atisha (Dipankara Srijnana), Jnanasrimitra, Abhayakaragupta, Divakarachandra, Kumarachandra, Kumaravajra, Danashila, Putali (or Puttali), Nagarjuna (the Alchemist and Mystic), Tankadasa (or Dangadasa), Prjnavarman, Bodhibhadra, Mokshakaragupta, Vibhutichandra, Subhakara, Vanaratna, and the like had unique contributions, literary and otherwise in the development of the Buddhist Tantric movement in Eastern India. By their zeal and constant endeavour this movement was spread in Tibet and Nepal and was firmly rooted in those countries, especially in Tibet. It is learnt that most of the Tantric scholars, as mentioned above, hailed from Bengal. In the Pala period, the entire Bengal was flooded with the tremendous flow of the Buddhist Tantric movement which was characterized by the belief that "the realization of the absolute was possible through the non-dual state of union of the female and the male aspects of the absolute—*Prajna* (wisdom) and *Upaya* (method)". Apart from the religious side, this movement was responsible for the growth of enormous Tantric literature in Sanskrit in the eastern part of India, especially in Bengal. It will be seen that Bengal had a very large share in the cultivation and spread of this peculiar and prolific Buddhist and allied Tantric literature, which in all probability received encouragement from the Buddhist kings of the Pala dynasty. But it is remarkable that with the advent of the Sena kings, who had Vaishnavite leanings, this literature and culture went underground for all time. We hear of no suppression or persecution of Buddhism under the overlordship of the Senas, but it was probably a part of their policy to encourage Brahmanical studies as a reaction against the Buddhistic tendencies of the Pala kings. Fortunately, however, Tibet has preserved the entire literature in *Bstan-hgyur*, and now we have to recollect this lost Indian treasure from Tibet.

In the Sena and Post-Sena periods the Buddhist Tantric scholars had to make adjustment with the Brahmanical Tantra of the period in order to maintain their very existence in their homeland. As a result we find the origin of the *Shaktistic* form of Tantric Buddhism—*i.e.* literal union of the male and the female took the place of the transcendental union of *Prajna and Upaya* in order to realize the absolute happiness (mahasukha). Some scholars are of opinion that the Buddhist Tantric Yogis passed from Buddhism to Shaivism simply to please their heretic rulers and gain political favours. But actually the Tantric Yogis did not pass from Buddhism to Shaivism, so to say; rather they adopted many Shaiva-tantra-elements in their own principles. As a result, we find the origin of various Shaiva-Buddhist mixed cults in Eastern India like the *Kaula, Natha, Avadhuta, Sahajiya* and *Baul*. The promoters and successors of these mixed Tantric cults were known as Siddhas or Siddhacharyas (whose traditional number was eighty-four). Kukkuri-pada, Shabari-pada, Lui-pa, Matsyendranatha, Goraksanatha, Jalandhari-pada, Viru-pa, Tilo-pa, Naro-pa, Kanha-pa, Saraha etc. were some of the distinguished Siddhas, most of them hailed from Bengal. These Siddhacharyas were responsible for the growth of wonderful literatures like *Doha-kosha, Charyapada* and the like, which are regarded as the earliest sources of Bengali language. The *Doha-kosha* and the *Charyapada* were composed mostly in *Shauraseni Apabhramsa* and Old Bengali, which were translated into Tibetan Bstan-hgyur. These literatures were mainly composed in the period 950-1200 CE (De.1927: 384). It is however; very difficult to trace the history of the rise of these later Tantric movements, but in the words of P.C. Bagchi "It is probable that they were indistinguishable from each other in the transitional stage. They gradually developed their distinctive character, and the transition seems to have been over by the 13th century. The Sahajiya appeared many years before the advent of Sri Chaitanya (1486-1534). Its progress could not be checked by the protagonists of the Chaitanya movement, although they tried their best to do so. On the other hand, it was the Chaitanya movement which in course of time, became deeply influenced by the Sahajiya." The Mainamati Copper Plate inscription of the 13th century tells us that in Pattikeraka in Tippera there were followers of this particular religious sect originating from the Buddhist Sahaja-yana (De.1927:423). The ideas of Sahajiya may be known from the old songs on Lord Sri Krishna written by Badu Chandidasa. The Bauls (religious enthusiasts) emerged from Sahaja-yana, and they were more orthodox than the Sahajiyas. Even today the remants of the *Bauls* are found in West Bengal, and if one can minutely study their songs, it will be discovered that the basic themes of these songs comprise the fundamental Buddhist doctrines of *Anitya, Dukkha and Anatma* (*Indian Historical Quaterly* IX :282). In west Bengal there is another small community which has preserved some Buddhistic elements in its cult, known as the Dharma Cult.

We may, therefore, come to the conclusion that Buddhism did not entirely disappear from Bengal, but it transformed itself into those living forces which inspired and guided the religious and literary life in Bengal for centuries even after the disappearance of its distinctive features.

Artistic Impact of Nalanda on Bangladesh

The fusion of Nalanda Art on the art tradition of Bangladesh may be studied under four categories:

(i) **Chittagaon Art**

(ii) Lalmai-Mainamati (District-Comilla) Art

(iii) Mahasthangarh (District-Bogra) Art

(iv) Rajshahi and Maldah Art

Mahayana Buddhism was prevalent in the region from 8th -9th century CE. Images of Buddha, Padmapani, Tara and other deties are found in Pandita Vihara ascribed to 9th -12th century CE. The bronze images are similar in workmanship to the Nalanda bronzes. Inscribed Buddhist bronze images discovered in the Chittagaon district range in date from 9th -12th century CE engraved on their back-slabs and pedestals are preserved in the Chittagaon monastery. Although Buddhist images have been found in the region as stray examples, some more finds prove the existence of a local centre of Buddhist art forming a link in the chain of its development and its migration to Myanmar. Some of these specimens show clear affinities to the bronze images of the Nalanda School, certain others Burmese bronzes.

According to Huttington there is general resemblance between the Nalanda metal images and thosae of Jhewari in Chittagaon although the Jhewari objects carry a strong local tradition (Huttington.1984:190-93). She observes in three seated images *i.e.* Akshobhya, Vairochana and Amitabha bear an almost startling resemblance to a seated Buddha from Nalanda which probably dates from the mid 9th century. Therefore, the Jhewari specimen would seem to have been made during the same time and was obviously a product of a school closely related to that of Nalanda. The Jhewari Buddhas have smiles on their faces. A number of images may be ascribed to mid 9th century. Although the Jhewari images have ties with Nalanda images, they suggest that they are products of local south-eastern Bengali workshops. She concludes that Mitra informs that the hoard of Jhewari bronzes in Chittagaon district is preserved in Indian Museum, Kolkata (Mitra.1982:8). She has studied photographs of some of the images of the Temple monastery of Chittagaon. In total she has studied 86 icons, a miniature metal temple and a metal *stupa*. Many of these sculptures reveal the exixtence of a distinctive local school with an individuality of its own.The school appears to have flourished during 9th -10th century CE, though images continued to be made long afterwards also. The centre of metal-casting was at Pandita Vihara near Chittagaon (Mitra.1982:1). She is of the opinion that some of the Jhewari bronzes show clear affinity to the bronzes of Nalanda School while others to Burmese bronzes (Mitra.1982:15). Dixit also found that the Jhewari bronzes are closely allied to the products of the Magadha School and they are similar in workmanship to the Nalanda bronzes. One bronze Buddha image has a circular seal on its back as in Nalanda images with Buddhist creed. The crown of the Maitreya figure shows fan-shaped ends of ribbon projecting from two sides.

Debala Mitra describes a bronze miniature *Rekha* temple. She says that it belongs to 10th century CE and cannot be regarded as a miniature replica of the Mahabodhi temple which has only one entrance to the sanctum-sanctorum of the ground floor. She informs that from Jaipur also a metal miniature temple has been found which resembles that from Jhewari. She adds further that the corner shrines of the Mahabodhi temple are products of 19th century CE and that the corner-structures were originally stupas like the 5th temple site of Nalanda. A miniature metal stupa from Jhewari has been ascribed by her to 9th -10th century CE. It consists of platform, drum, *harmika, chhatravali* and a crowning member. This *stupa* has a low-shouldered dome, solid squarish *harmika and a chhatravali* of five gradually diminishing *chhatras* with a narrow space in between. The Jhewari images possess a number of unusual characteristics. Some of them are related to types recovered at Nalanda and Kurkihara (Pl.CLXXII).

Ramachandran says that the Buddhist images found at Jhewari ascribing 9th -13th century CE are, however, marked by a ruggedness and constraint, though they are but provincial variations of the Pala School and are akin to the School that flourished in Myanmar and Assam during the period.

Lalmai-Mainamati (District-Comilla) Art

Metal images numbering about one hundred are reported from the Salban Vihara located at Lalmai-Mainamati hills in south-east Bengal mostly belonging to 7th -8th century CE. According to Huttington a seated Bodhisattva figure from Mainamati is very close to the image of Sarvavani in style and bears resemblance with a Nalanda figure of the same period. A seated figure of Manjusri from Salban Vihara compares well with Nalanda figures of early to mid 9th century CE. Its features are refined execution on lotus petals, relaxed care of the main figure and detailing of the elephants and lions on its seat are typical of the time of Devapala and compare well with the work from Nalanda of about the same time (Huttington.1984:18). The treatment of the outer rim of the halo with its several rows of detailed decoration appears to be of the local style which is found in the art of Jhewari also. Another image from the Comilla district is that of the Sitatapatra of late 9th century CE. It compares with a figure of Chunda from Nalanda of the same date. According to Huttington the Nalanda specimen has a raised pedestal and is much more three dimensional in form.

Mahasthangarh (District-Bogra) Art

According to Huttington a metal image of Manjusri found from Saralpur village near Mahasthangarh is comparable with a Bodhisattva image of Nalanda in so far as facial features, hair-style, simplicity of garments and lack of jewellery are concerned. Similar facial features are found in the Sarvavani figure.

Rajshahi and Maldah Art

A metal image of Brahmanic deity Vishnu recovered from Kumarpur in Rajshahi district ascribable to 8th century CE having a square body, much use of bead motif and with general simplicity and crudeness, has a bulbous appearance as seen in early images of Nalanda. Its crown is of an early type and its four arms shown in a downward direction mark a feature associated with pre 9th century Vishnu images. Huttington concludes that in respect of the Bengal School of metal sculptures, it is easy to detect the relationships of those schools to others, such as that of Nalanda certain elements earmark the local trends. The use of the solid halo found so frequently in south eastern Bengal is not generally present in Nalanda images. In fact, while a few metal sculptures from Nalanda with this feature are known. It is possible thet they were brought to the site from another place of manufacture.

China (Fig. 45)

Buddhism was not likely to get a warm reception from the Chinese at the first stage. It was more or less considered as an object of curiosity. The foreign missionaries had to work hard in order to create in China an interest in Buddhism. The first two missionaries, Kashyap Matanga and Dharmaraksha, translated a number of works into Chinese in order to give the people a general idea of Buddhism. A great impetus was given to the propagation of the contemplative aspect of Mahayana by an Indian teacher whose personality has become almost mythical in the Far East. This was Bodhidharma, commonly known in China as *Ta-mo* (Dharma). No other Indian monk attained such fame in China as Bodhidharma. From the beginning of the 7th century century Buddhism was entering a new phase in China. When the Tang dynasty came in power and unified the whole of China after long centuries of internal strife, Buddhism entered upon the most glorious period of its history in China.

Buddhism soon entered into a new phase in China, till then altogether unknown in that country. It was the mystic phase. Buddhism was slowly changing in India. An esoteric Buddhism was growing under the influence of Brahmanism. It is generally known as Tantrayana, but it included various forms of mysticism known as Vajrayana, Kalachakrayana, and Sahajayana etc. Nalanda was no less a centre of this new forming of Buddhism. It did away with all earlier practices and introduced the cult of many new gods and goddesses. The form of worship was also very mystic and involved some form of Yoga, use of mystic gestures and formulae, contemplation on the mystic value of sound, etc. This form of Buddhism was taken to China by Vajrabodhi, developed and extensively preached by his disciple, Amoghavajra (Legge. 1886:73-78).

Figure 45: Map of China

Fusion on Chinese Art

Chinese art was also influenced by Nalanda art. Gilt bronze images of Shakyamuni from China (8th century CE) shows the Buddha seated cross-leged in *Bhumisparsha mudra* keeping left hand on lap (Pl.CLXXIII-CLXXIV). Except the face which shows short eyes in meditation, flat nose and thin lips, the entire body appears to have been influenced by the art form prevailed at Nalanda. The double leaves of the lotus seat are typically belonging to 11th -12th century CE. A clay figure representing Amitayus from China appears to be a youthful figure seated in cross-legged posture in *Samadhi mudra*. The ends of *dhoti* are shown in a fan-shaped manner in front of the cross-legged portion. Lotus petals are of 11th -12th century CE. These features are common in Nalanda sculptures also. In another clay figure representing Manjusri from China, *Gaja* and *Vyala* motif, a feature of 9th century CE sculptures of Nalanda is noticed. Its back-slab has a flamed border and is rounded at the top. These features are also present in the Nalanda sculptures of 9th-10th century CE. A stone image of Maitreya from China shows an elongated back-slab with a border of flames which are similar to the flames employed in several Nalanda images.

Indonesia (Fig. 46)

Indian colonization of south and south-east Asian countries was started from 3rd century BCE and the credit goes to Emperor Ashoka who sent his religious ambassadors Mahendra, and Sanghamitra in Tamraparni (Sri Lanka) and Sona and Uttara to Suvarnadvipa (Myanmar). The Indian traders also played an important role to promote Indian culture in this region. By the tremendous effort of kings, traders and religious ambassadors every aspect of Indian culture was introduced in this region.

India's cultural contact with Indonesia begins in 1st century CE. Java (Yavadvipa), Sumatra (Sri Vijay), Bali and Borneo (Varuna dvipa) are the main islands of this country. Borobudur Stupa is the world famous architectural monument of this country. Indonesia like much of South-east Asian countries was influenced by Indian culture. Indonesian students flocked to Nalanda Mahavihara for the higher study of Buddhist texts and after the completion of their studies they used to take away small Buddhist bronze images as mementoes to theie native land. In this way the art tradition of Nalanda reached in this country.

Indonesia is an archipelagic country of 17,508 islands (6,000 inhabited) stretching along the equator in South East Asia. The area of Indonesia is populated by peoples of various migrations, creating a diversity of cultures, ethnicities, and languages. Fossilised remains of Homo erectus and his tools, popularly known as the "Java Man", suggest the Indonesian archipelago was inhabited by at least 1.5 million years ago. Austronesian people, who form the majority of the modern population, are thought to have originally been from Taiwan and arrived in Indonesia around 2000 BCE. From the 7th century CE, the powerful Srivijaya naval kingdom flourished bringing Hindu and Buddhist influences with it. The Buddhist Shailendra and Hindu Mataram dynasties subsequently thrived and declined in inland Java. The last significant non-Muslim kingdom, the Hindu Majapahit kingdom, flourished from the late 13th century, and its influence stretched over much of Indonesia.

Figure 46: Map of Indonesia

Artistic features of Nalanda in Indonesia

The art of Indonesia once remind us of their ancestry and their closeness with Nalanda School of Art. But the question is, one has to trace beyond any doubt the routes through which the artistic idioms went to Indonesia from Nalanda. The migration of art, to a certain extent, was made possible by the visiting religious teachers specialized in the art and architecture of India. Dharmapala, a teacher of Nalanda stayed for a while in ancient Indonesia. Kumarghosha, Vajrabodhi and his desciple Amoghavajra on their way to China halted for some time at Sri Vijay (Sumatra-a territory of Indonesia). It appears that they were mainly responsible for preaching various aspects of Buddhism there (Ghosh.1959: 21). Scholars believe that ancient Sri Vijay possibly served as the media through which Buddhist traditions of India penetrated ancient Indonesia.

A.Ghosh thinks that Nalanda played a significant role in transmitting Indian religion and religious art to Indonesia. I-tsing, the Chinese traveler was in Sri Vijay in the second half of the seventh century. He recorded that-thousands of monks, scholars and pilgrims were studying Sanskrit texts which were translated into other local languages. In this connection it may be stated that the ports of Tamralipti in Bengal, Palur in Orissa and Bhrigukaccha in Gujrat served as the gateways through which Gupta and Pala artistic traditions flowed down to Indonesia. It appears that the artistic trends from Indian mainland were introduced to Indonesia through small sized bronze and terracotta images because these were easily portable and in all probability these were carried back to Indonesia to a large extent by the Indonesian pilgrims and students who came to India considering it as a holy land and on their way back they took with them the sacred mementoes on their visit to India. Images of Prajñāpāramitā and Buddha recovered from Indonesia shows the impact of Nalanda art (Pls. CLXXV-CLXXVI). This explains the introduction of Mahayana-Tantrayana iconography and art in Indonesia. In this connection mention must be made of a large copper-plate grant of Sri Devapaladeva (Majumdar. 1990: 52) in which the King granted five villages and apparently built a new monastery at Nalanda at the instance of Shailendra King Balputradeva for the students hailing from Suvarṇadvipa. The above references are sufficient to prove that how early Indian religions and art spread in Indonesia and made its impact felt in the religion and religious art of that country.

Now I would like to analyze some bronze and stone images of Indonesia and their close association with Nalanda. Buddha images which are found to be carved on sectional stones in Borobudur (Yavadvipa-Java) are curiously enough met with certain standing images of Buddha at Nalanda (Pl.CLXXVII). The image of Buddha in the Leiden Museum, Holland (No. 1403-2844) also needs a detailed analysis in order to estimate its iconographic and stylistic indebtedness to Buddha images of Nalanda. The Buddha is shown seated in *Bhdrasana* on an artistically conceived throne. A circular halo encircles his head. The halo is plain in the middle and its edges all along moulded and decorated with scalloped designs. At the bottom of this halo and almost behind the neck a few flames still survive which state that the halo was originally surrounded with flames. The enthroned image of the Buddha is placed on a *tri-ratha* pedestal. In front of the central projection of the base there appears a four spoked wheel which is flaked on either side by the profiles of two deers. On other side of the throne on which the Buddha is shown seated, a decorative motif has been very carefully and artistically adjusted.The motif includes at its bottom a couchant elephant profile, a dwarfish-rider on it in the middle and the latter is surmounted by a standing *Simha-vyala*. A knobbed crossbar from the back rest of the throne projecting to the left has suffered multilation. From the right side knobbed projection hangs a narrow and designed strip, which is devided into three registers inscribed with a common motif which, however, is difficult to identify.

These elements in their decorative details betray strong Indian affiliation. The wheel between the two deers is a well known Indian symbol and the parallel is taken from the clay seals of the Pala period (Kempers. 1933: 67). The knobbed crossbar projected on either side of the throne is very commonly found designed on Pala bronzes at Nalanda (Buddha image in Patna Museum, Acc. No. 4859 and Hariti image in National Museum, New Delhi, Acc. No. 681712). The *Simha-vyala* or *Simha* standing on a couchant elephant is also noticed in Nalanda bronzes. The flames that encircle the halo of the bronze Buddha were noticed in many Pala bronzes (Nalanda Buddha in Patna Museum, Acc. No. 8459). The impact of the Sarnath crossed boundaries of India and made its impact felt in Sumatra and Java. However, this migration of Sarnath idiom could be made possible through Nalanda. When the Sarnath idiom passed through Nalanda, it received certain Nalanda orientation. As a result certain characteristics of Nalanda sculptures went to Indonesia.

Myanmar (Fig. 47)

Literary and archaeological evidence shows that the entire culture and civilization of Myanmar was borrowed from India. Many Burmese inscriptions are written in Sanskrit and Pali. Many religious structures having the images of Indian gods and goddesses have been found in Myanmar. The art of the country was so much influenced by the Indian art that it was said about the Ananda temple that although it was built in the Burmese capital, it was an Indian temple. Everything in the temple from *Shikhara* to basement has the stamp of Indian genius and craftsmanship. According to the chronicles of Myanmar, Tagaung was founded by the Hindu prince Abhiraja in the ninth century BCE. An ancient prince of Banaras is said to be the first ruler of the kingdom of Arakan. Indian influence in Myanmar was in such proportion that the Burmese applied Indian names to their localities. For example, Sravasti, is identified with Tharawaddy, and Aparantaka, which is identified as a district of western India, the scholars identify with upper Myanmar, Utkala, the place where Tapassu and Bahllika, the two merchants who first saluted the Buddha after his enlightenment, is usually identified with Orissa in India, but the Burmese tradition locates it in Myanmar, thus the system of mythical geography arose.

Regarding the character of early Burmese Buddhism, Theravada, as known from the inscriptions on the golden plates and tiles, found near the ancient site of Prome and which was deciphered by Finot. They consist of Theravada religious formulae: Pali is the language; the alphabet is of a south Indian type and said to resemble closely that use in the inscriptions of the Kadamba dynasty. Myanmar and Sri Lanka are said to have been visited by the Buddha himself and imparted even some of his power to the celebrated image which is now in the Arakan Pagoda at Mandalay. It is also stated that Ashoka's missionaries went to lower Myanmar. Sona and Uttara were dispatched to Suvarnbhumi is stated by the *Dipavamsa*, and it is identified with the district of Thaton which seems to be a corruption of Saddhammapura and this tradition is accepted in Myanmar. Thus the statement of the *Dipavamsa* is significant and the work was composed in the 4th century CE and taken from older chronicles which evidently proves that lower Myanmar was a Buddhist country. In the eleventh century when Aniruddha conquered the Tailangs, Buddhist monks and Tripitaka were found there. Aniruddha's conquest resulted in the religious exchange of embassies with Sri Lanka. Communication, with the east coast of India, is confirmed by the presence of Sanskrit words in Old Tailang, and mention of Kanchipuram and the great commentator Dharmapala and other learned men. Analogies have also been traced between the architecture of Pagan and Southern India and such communication by sea must have brought not only Hinayanist Buddhism but also Mahayanist and Tantric Buddhism and Brahmanism from Bengal and Orissa, all of whose influence is seen or present in the ancient buildings and sculptures of the country. Thus, taken together, *i.e.* writing's character, knowledge of Kanchipuram etc. indicate that lower Myanmar had accepted Theravada before the 6th century and before contacts with southern India. However, contact with Bengal and Orissa might have imported Mahayanism. During Aniruddha's period, the religion of Upper Myanmar was the same as of Lower Myanmar except, that changed it by reference to Sri Lanka. After 1200, if not earlier, the idea prevailed that the Mahavihara was the standard of orthodoxy and the Tailang church, which had some Mahayanist features, fell below it and in the 15th century, this view was universally accepted and separate existence of the Tailang church came to an end.

Impact of Nalanda Art on Myanmar

It seems that artists from different centers of Magadha migrated to Pagan, the capital of Myanmar during 10th-12th century CE and produced a large number of stone and bronze sculptures there. The images from Pagan are assigned by Vogel to Magadha of 11th -13th century CE. A bronze image of Tara ascribable to 9th -10th century CE is said to have been imported from India. It is presently preserved in the Pagan museum. Several Buddha and Bodhisattva images of Indian origin have been foud at Pagan (Pls.CLXXVIII-CLXXIX). A Buddha image seated in *Samadhi mudra* from Nalanda of 10th century CE has a bronze head, halo, *chhatra* and pedestal, and has its body in carnelian. It is called as a composite figure by Kamini Sinha. This is the only figure of its kind of Nalanda. It appears to be one of the sources for the Buddha figures in Nepal in view of its short, round and flat face. Burmese kings of Pagan were intimately

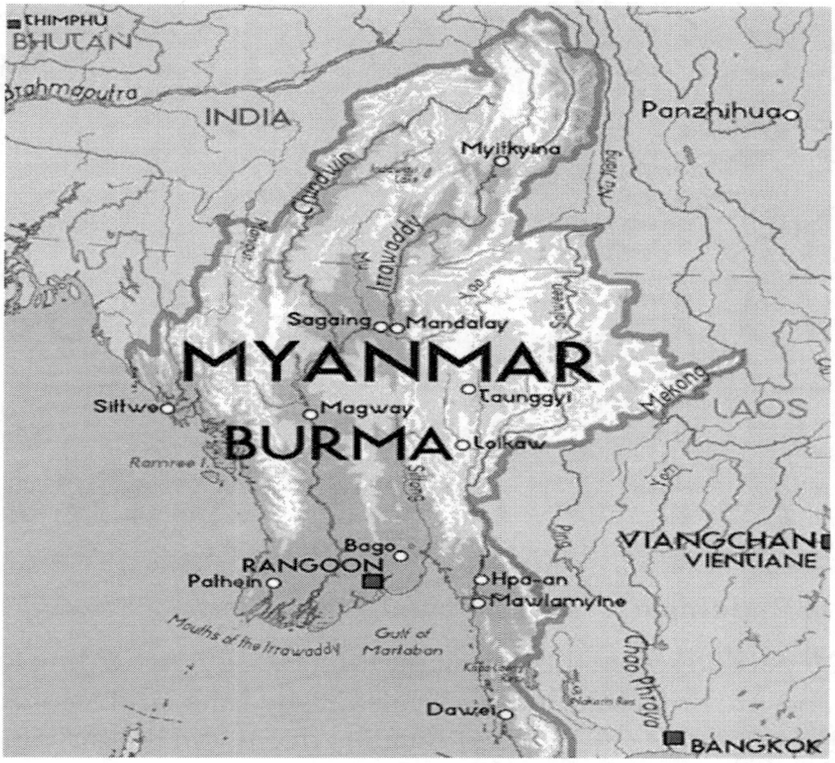

Figure 47: Map of Myanmar

connected with Bodh Gaya and Nalanda. This contact lead to a new image of the Buddha of the Sthaviravada School, which found its way from Myanmar in to north Thailand and became there a fore-runner of the Thai School of art.

Nepal

Nepal extended in the form of an elongated rectangle between the longitudes of 80^0-15^0 West and 88^0-15^0 East and latitudes of 26^0-15^0 and 30^0-30^0 North. It is bounded on the north by the China occupied Tibet and on the east, south and west by the Indian territories of Sikkim, West Bengal, Bihar and Uttar Pradesh (Fig.48).The total area of the country is 800 km east-west and its breadth varies from 144 to 240 km north-south. Watered by the *Kali, Karnali, Bheri, Seti, Rapti, Gandaki, Bagmati, Kosi* and *Mechi* rivers and their numerous tributaries and decked with a large number of glacial-impounded lakes, the land of Nepal has been divided into six geographical zones:

1. The Tibetan Tethys Zone
2. Himalayan Gneiss Zone
3. Main Central Thrust Zone
4. Midland Zone
5. *Mahabharata* Zone and
6. Shiwalik Zone (Arita *et. al.*1982:29).

Figure 48: Map of Nepal

Introduction of Buddhism

Buddhism in Nepal dates from the time of Buddha himself. According to legends many Bodhisattvas and previous Buddhas have also visited the land. Monuments to these Buddhas can be seen in the valley. It is difficult to document the early Buddhist history of Nepal, but we know that the region became a great meeting point for Indian and Tibetan Buddhist scholars. During their visit to Tibet the great Acharyas of Nalanda Mahavihara Shantarakshita, Padmasambhava and Kamalsheel spent some time in Nepal and propagate the Dhamma. Nagarjuna, the great Madhyamika philosopher and many others visited, lived and taught the people of Nepal. Stone inscriptions and colophons provide clear evidence that a strong lineage of Mahasanghika nuns existed in the 7th century CE. The country became a repository of Buddhist Sanskrit literature and famous for its production of fine Buddhist art and scroll paintings. Buddhism in Nepal includes Theravada, Mahayana and Vajrayana traditions. According to legends Buddha set forth Three Wheels of Law to suit varying degrees of intelligence and receptivity:

1. At Rishipatana Mrigadava (Deer Park) near Varanasi (Saranatha), Buddha turned the First Wheel of Law which constituted the doctrines of the Four Noble Truths and Eight-fold Path and it is designated as Sravakayana.
2. At Griddhakuta hill (Vulture Peak) near Rajgir (Dist. Nalanda, Bihar), the Buddha turned the Second Wheel of Law which constituted the doctrines of Emptiness and Selflessness of the person and phenomena. These doctrines are vividly preserved in *Prajnaparamita* and *Vaipulya* sutras. This approach was later known as Mahayana or Path of the Bodhisattva.
3. At Vaishali, on the other hand, the Buddha turned the Third Wheel of Law which constituted the doctrines of Buddha-nature as described in *Tathagatagarbha sutra*, *Mahaparinirvana sutra* and *Dharanisvaraja sutra*.At various places such as Dhanyakataka, Sriparvata, Kamakhya, Sirihatta, Purnagiri, Oddiyana etc. the

Buddha revealed the path of Mantra to his highly gifted disciples as a shorter path to attain enlightenment. This approach was termed as Vajrayana, which integrates all three vehicles (Mitra.1971:73).

Art

Nepal has a time-honoured tradition of art and culture embedded with Buddhism. In fact, the artistic tradition of Nepalese peoples is instrumental in elevating the status of Nepal in the world. In the past Nepalese artists produced many excellent images and were sent to Tibet, China, Japan and Mongolia. The bronze statue of Akshobhya (in Lhasa at Ramochhe temple) is considered to be one of the most excellent images ever produced by the artist of Nepal, which was taken to Lhasa by Nepalese princess Bhrikuti Devi(wife of the Tibetan king Srong-btsan-sGampo) in the seventh century. Although the artistic heritage has come a long way through the lives and lifestyle of Nepalese people, the exact meanings and implications as regard to the different images or deities relating to Vajrayana Buddhism has slowly gone out of focus during the passage of time. Even today there are many sculptors, artists and painters who can meticulously carve or paint such images or deities with excellent results, but the incumbent meanings however cannot be found with ease.

Impact of Nalanda Art on Nepal

I am trying to provide some facts, materials and information on Buddhist Iconography gathered through extensive study of canonical texts relating to Vajrayana Buddhism prevailing in Nepal and some from Tibet albeit in a humble way. It describes important deities and images especially relevant in Nepalese context along with their functions, utility, virtues and wisdom in the path to enlightenment.

According to Ramchandran, the Nalanda and Kurkihara Buddhist bronzes of divinities are the sources of inspiration of Nepalese copper gilt images. A bronge image of Vajrapani from Nalanda appears to be imported from Nepal. An image of the Buddha from Kathmandu in the niche of the votive stone *stupa* stands on left leg keeping the right leg loose.It grants *Varada mudra* with right and holds the hem of garments with upraised left hand against shoulder. The *Ushnisha* resembles that of the Pala period Buddha images. Its waist-band shows bow-shaped ends. The *Chivara* is transparent and its lower part recalls that of the Sultanganj copper image. The figure may be attributed to 8th century CE on the stylistic grounds. It resembles an 8th century figure of Lokanatha and the stucco figures of Site-3 from Nalanda. A stone image of Bhrikuti stucco figures carries the tradition of stucco figure of Nagi from Maniyaramatha, Rajgir; but on account of its profuse decoration, pointed halo, prominent flames on its back-slab and a manuscript fastened to its left ear, it has to be ascribed to 11th century CE. The head of a stone image stucco figure resembles that of an 8th century Avalokiteshvara figure from Nalanda. A Maitreya image made of silver from Nepal is one of the choicest icons. The deity is seated loosely in cross-legged posture carrying a miniature stupa in the crest and holding a *Kundika* in the left hand

and *Nagakesara* held in the right hand and is deeply wrapt in meditation. The lotus petals are of 11th -12th century CE. In the specimen from Nalanda stupa, in the crest *Nagakesara* and lotus-seats are seen but *Kundika*, an earlier feature of Maitreya figures from Mathura and Gandhara is absent. Sculptures of Avalokiteshvara, Buddha and Vishnu from Nepal preserved in the Boston Museum are much nearer to that of the Gupta period (Pls. CLXXX-CLXXXI). Images similar to these may have been seen at the great university of Nalanda when it was visited by Hiuen-tsang and I-tsing.

Sri Lanka (Fig. 49)

Sanskrit Simhala (Pali Sihala), perhaps alluding to the lions (Simha, Siha) (Mallalsekhara.1928:2). In Indian literature, Ceylon is called Lanka and *Tamraparni* (Tambapanni), separate from the subcontinent only by a narrow stretch of sea, open to influences originating in India. The connection of India with Sri Lanka can be traced back to the time of *Ramayana*, when Rama attacked Lanka to rescue Sita. The regular colonization of Sri Lanka began after the conquest of the island by Vijaya. He laid the foundations of the Simhalese dynasty. In the third century BCE Mahendra and his sister, Sanghamitra were sent to Sri Lanka by Ashoka and as a result, Buddhism was introduced into Sri Lanka (Mallalsekhara.1928:27). The ruler of the country was converted to Buddhism. Slowly, Buddhism sepread all over the island. It was on account of the spread of Buddhism that the cultural and political relation between India and Sri Lanka became very intimate. We come across a large number of Buddhist monasteries all over the country. The colossal recumbent Buddha images in stone appear in several Buddhist sites, indicating *Mahaparinibbana*. A colossal seated image of the Buddha in the vicinity of Anuradhapura is one of the outstanding achievements of Ceylonese art. The iconography of the images leaves no doubt of their Mahayanistic character (Coomaraswamy.1914:31). The earliest known images, life-size or more than life-size, were set up in shrines for adoration.

Artistic impact of Nalanda on Sri Lanka

Buddha images found from Anuradhapur and Mihintale are very close to the Nalanda images (Pls. CLXXXII-CLXXIII). The bronze image of Jambhala from Nalanda is similar to the bronze figure from Sri Lanka ascribed to 8th century CE. The pedestal of Vajrapani made of copper from Sri Lanka of 9th century CE and probably originally gilded resembles that of a bronze image of Buddha found at Nalanda (Ashar.1980:26). It also resembles the bronze image of Vishnu from Nalanda belonging to 10th century CE.

Tibet

Before the advent of Buddhism Tibetans have faith in Bon Religion which was founded by Shen-rub in 5th century CE. Followers of this religion believe in Demi-gods, Yaksha, Heaven, Nagloak and sacrifice. They believe that with the help of chanting secret mantras and by pleasing gods and goddesses' one can achieve the pleasure of heaven.

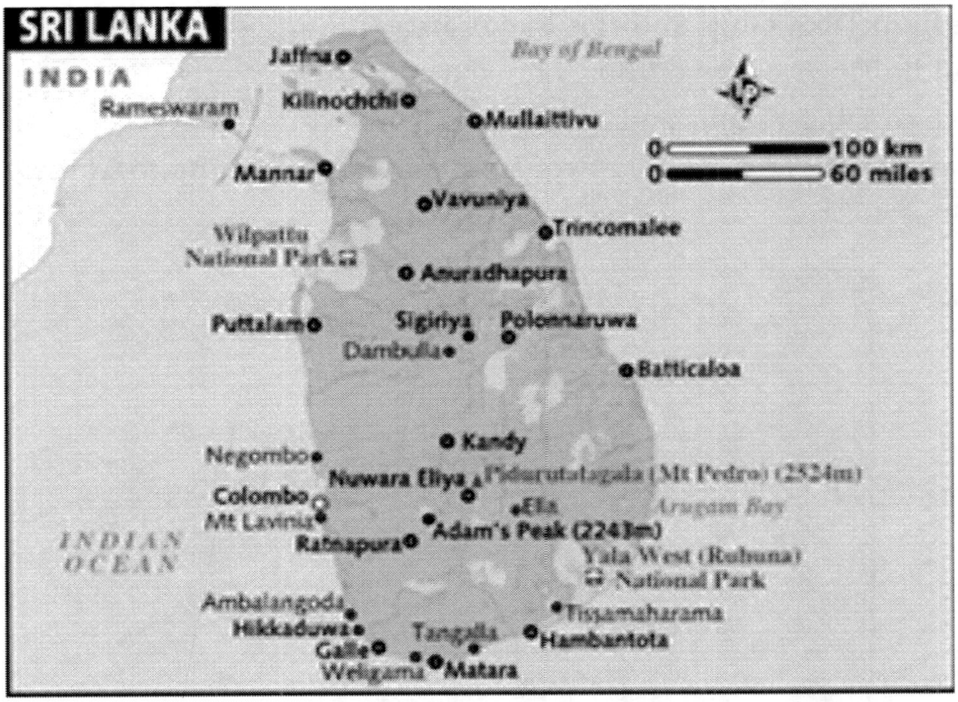

Figure 49: Map of Sri Lanka

India's cultural contact with this region begins in 7th century CE. The then Tibetan emperor Srong-bstan-sgampo who was married with Chinese princes Wu-Kong and Nepali princes Bhrikuti, the daughter of King Anshuverman became a devout Buddhist due to his both Buddhist wives. He sent his minister Thonmi to India to learn Indian script. The credit goes to Thonmi who made a script for Tibetan language on the basis of Guptan Brahmi. Srong-bstan-sgampo established a temple at Jokhang and installed the image of Akshobya in the honour of Nepalese Princess Bhrikuti with whom the king married. In 8th century CE during the reign of emperor Khri-srong -lde -btsan two acharyas of Nalanda Mahavihara Santarakshita and Padmasambhava were invited to propagate Buddhism in Tibet. Samye, the first monastery of Tibet was constructed during his reign and Tibetan peoples were ordained as Buddhist monks. With religion the Indian art tradition, especially the art of Nalanda also introduced in this Himalayan region.

Geographical Scenario

Located at 10,000-16,000 feet high from the Sea-level Tibet is known as "The Roof of the World" spread over 50,000 sq mile. The river Brhamputra (Tsang-po) is the lifeline of Tibet. In the north lies the Kuen-Lun and Tang-La Mountain Ranges of China, Himalayan Ranges of India is in the south, in the west lies the Karakoram and Ladakh region while in the east is China (Fig. 50). Maximum Rainfall is 5″-15″. There is a great difference in temperature between day and night. In summer day temperature is recorded 26-29^{0} C while at night it goes down below 0^{0} C. Millet and *Kodon* are the main crops. Tibet is divided into four zones:

- Western Tibet-Guge and sPu-Rangs area
- Middle Tibet-gChang, dBus, Lho-kha and Kong-po area
- Eastern Tibet-Khams and Am-do area
- Byang-thang area- Spread over from mid-west Tibet up to Chinese Turkistan (Xin-Xiang)

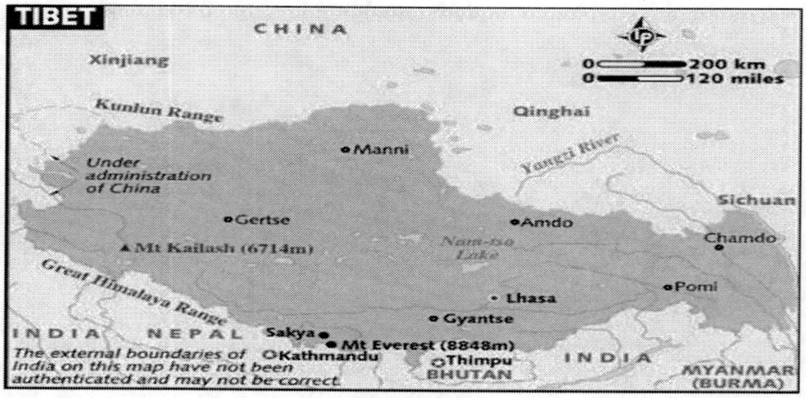

Figure 50: Map of Tibet

Architectural Remains

Samye Monastery: Imitation of Odantapuri Mahavihara (Pl. CLXXXIV)

With the growth of Buddhist samgha, the number of monks also increased in Tibet. They needed dwelling to live in. It was an urgent necessity. An idea of the monastery thus crept in for their living. So that the King Khri- srong-lde-btsan built a monastery named-*bSam-ye*. This monastery was built near Lhasa, the capital of Tibet after the model of Odantapuri Mahavihara close to Nalanda.

Samye, the first Buddhist monastery of Tibet constructed during 8th century CE was just the imitation of the Odantapuri Mahavihara. It is located on the northern bank of *Yarlung Zambo* River. It was listed as a key cultural relic under state protection in 1996. It was also approved as a state A-class scenic spot in 2005.With a history of more than 1000 years, Samye Monastery is the most famous and oldest monastery among the Tibetan historical and cultural relics. There are rich and precious relics collected in Samye Monastery (Pl.CLXXXV), including the historical and religious documents, various statues and murals. It has been praised as one of the oldest library which stored the ancient culture of Tibet.

Historicity

According to tradition, the Indian monk Shantarakshita made the first attempt to construct the monastery while promoting his sutra-centric version of Buddhism. Finding the Samye site auspicious, he set about to build a structure there. However, the building would always collapse after reaching a certain stage. Terrified, the construction workers believed that there was a demon or obstructive thought form in a nearby river making trouble.When Shantarakshita's contemporary Padmasambhava arrived from northern India, he was able to subdue the energetic problems obstructing the building of Samye. According to the Fifth Dalai Lama, Padmasambhava performed the *Vajrakilaya* dance and enacted the rite of 'thread cross' or *namkha* to assist King Khri-srong-lde-btsan and Shantarakshita clear away obscurations and hindrances in the building of Samye.The great religious master Padmasambhava performed this dance in order to prepare the ground for the Samye Monastery and to pacify the malice of the Lha [local mountain god spirits] and srin malevolent spirits in order to create the most perfect conditions. He went on to say that after Padmasambhava consecrated the ground he erected a thread-cross — a web coloured thread woven around two sticks — to catch evil. Then the purifying energy of his dance forced the malevolent spirits into a skull mounted on top of a pyramid of dough. His tantric dance cleared away all the obstacles, enabling the monastery to be built in 779 CE. The dance was memorialized by the construction of *Vajrakilaya* stupas — monuments honouring the ritual *kilya* (*phurba*) daggers — at the cardinal points of the monastery, where they would prevent demonic forces from entering the sacred grounds. The above mentioned quotation makes reference to the relationship of the *Vajrakilaya/Phurba* to the stupa and mentions *torma* and *namkha*. Moreover, the building of Samye marked the foundation of the original school of Tibetan Buddhism, the Nyingma. This helps to explain how Padmasambhava's tantric-centric version of Buddhism gained ascendance over the sūtra-based teaching of Shantarakshita. When Padmasambhava consecrated Samye Monastery with the *Vajrakilaya* dance, he tamed the local spirit protector, Pehar Gyalpo, and bound him by oath to become the head of the entire hierarchy of Buddhist protective spirits. Pehar, later known as Dorje Drakden, became the principal protector of the Dalai Lamas, manifesting through the *Nechung* Oracle. The Construction of the temple started in the year 779 under the able supervision of Tibetan King Khri- srong-lde-btsan. It was then handed over to the famous Buddhist master Padmasambhava continued the construction of the monastery. On the day of the foundation ceremony, King Khri- srong-lde-btsan gave permission to seven descendants for staying in the temple and for cultivation in it. They were the first group of monks ever to stay in the Samye Monastery. They came to be known as 'Seven Enlightened Disciples of Samye'. Since then, the monastery has become a national treasure and is now under the care of the government.

An exact replica of the Universe

If you wish to see the Universe, you must see the Samye Monastery. The whole temple is build as an exact replica of the Universe mentioned in the Sutras. In the center, the majestic central hall depicts Mount Meru, which is considered to be the starting point of the world. Similar to the position of Sun and Moon in the Universe, the Sun and Moon Chapel are constructed in north and south respectively. One may find four large halls and eight smaller one symbolizing the four large and eight small continents of the world. There is a circular wall all round the temple depicting the boundary of the World. This is just the outlay of the temple. Inside these halls you are bound to find many more amazing things

Layout

Its layout resembles the *Mandala* of the Esoteric Buddhism. Mandalas are usually symmetric with series of concentric circles and squares. The centre point is the residence of the resident deity, from whom the *Mandala* is identified. Lines are drawn from the centre until they intersect and form circles and squares. The finished Mandalas have four gates, which symbolize a culmination of the four virtues: compassion, kindness, sympathy and equanimity. Other Buddhist auspicious symbols can also be included in the design. Form and colour application techniques are strictly followed in the process of creating a *Mandala* to show religious meanings.

Architectural features

Samye Monastery is noted for its large scale and integrated architectural style. The magnificent and unique central hall is the main hall of the temple, representing the central world Mount Meru. It is three-storied combining Chinese, Tibetan and Indian architectural styles. The first floor is of the Tibetan architectural style, the second the Han style and the third the Indian style. Hence the monastery is also called the "Three-styled Temple". On the top floor of the central Hall is the best place to enjoy Samye Monastery's ingenious layout.

When you start your scintillating journey through the temple and come across the central hall, you'll come to know why this monastery is called the 'Three Styled Temple'. The hall is divided into three layers, all with different styles, the lowest in Tibetan style, middle one in Han style and the topmost in Indian style. On the middle layer of hall, historical records of Tibet are inscribed on the walls which contain the religious history of Tibet. A circular wall surrounds the temple as if marking the periphery of the world stacked by 1008 tiny *chortens* (1008 is a sacred number in Buddhism). There are many captivating murals that are hanging on the wall that show the history of Samye monastery apart from the biography of the legendary master Padmasambhava. Also look at a pair of spectacular lion sculpture and the first bell made in the history of Tibet.

The Sun and Moon chapels in the north and south stand as the Sun and Moon in the universe. In the four corners of the central hall lie the White, Red, Black and Green stupas guarding the Dharma like the Four Heavenly Kings, who are guardians of the Universe. Four larger halls and eight smaller halls are distributed around all sides of the central hall, symbolizing the four large continents and eight small ones. The halls in the monastery house many statues and murals, and the monastery has bronze bells, carved marble lions and tablets marking the development of Buddhism. All these are valuable cultural relics. In the monastery there is a pair of white marble statues, their shapes are simple and with a carving style of Tang Dynasty. They are the most precious remaining stone sculptures in the monastery. Besides, there is a rare bronze bell with ancient Tibetan script on it. According to the record, this is the first bell cast in Tibet. Today Samye Monastery is still an active monastery and important pilgrimage destination. It's one of the main scenic spots of the state-level scenic area – the *Yarlung* River Scenic Area.

Cultural Relics

The murals in Samye Monastery are of abundant contents and various stories. Among which the most famous one is the Record of Tibetan History. It is 92 meters long and presented the religious description of Tibet and some ancient legends. There is also the famous Biography of Padmasambhava and panorama of Samye Monastery, as well as the murals presented the folk customs of ancient Tibet. There are a lot of statues related to the history of Samye Monastery, including Padmasambhava, Khri-srong-lde-btsan, Shantarakshita and Srong-bstan-sgampo. They are still being highly respected since they did great contribution to the construction and development of Samye monastery. There are also other valuable cultural relics in Samye Monastery, such as the bronze bells carved with beats and the tablets recorded the development and history of Buddhism.

Doomsday

The original buildings have long disappeared. They have been badly damaged several times — by civil war in the 11th century, fires in the mid 17th century and in 1826, an earthquake in 1816, and in the 20th century, particularly during the Cultural Revolution. As late as the late 1980s pigs and other farm animals were allowed to wander through the sacred buildings.

Reconstruction

Samye monastery experienced several restorations after several fire disasters. Its original buildings have long disappeared. Most of the existing buildings in the monastery were built by the Seventh Dalai Lama. The prosperity of Samye Monastery is greatly due to the efforts of the 10th Panchen Lama. Each time it has been rebuilt, and today, largely due to the efforts of the 10th Panchen Lama from 1986 onward, it is again an active monastery and important pilgrimage and tourist destination. So you may imagine what the importance of Odantapuri Mahavihara was? If we may able to discover the ruins of this monastery it will be a great tribute not only to the field of Archaeology and Art and Architecture but to the entire Buddhist world.

The Odantapuri Mahavihara was the main center of Buddhist Tantric tradition during Pala period. It is a great matter of sorrow that the ancient seats of wisdom like Nalanda and Vikramshila were already identified and excavated. Recently the Tiladhak Mahavihara is also exposed during the excavations of Telhara, Nalanda (Pls, CLXXXVI-CLXXXVII) but Odantapuri is still unidentified and its shrouded mystery is waiting to be solved. Historians suggest that it was situated whether on Badi Pahari or on Garh Par, both located in Bihar Sharif, the district headquarter of Nalanda.

Keeping in mind this fact during my archaeological explorations (2012-13, 2013-14 & 2015-16) in the district I had visited both the sites. At Badi Pahari a few structural remains of medieval period were noticed on the top of the hill (Pl.CLXXXVIII). Any type of pot-sherds or antiquity was not found. At Garh Par two small mounds are still remaining (Pls.CLXXXIX-CXC) but both are highly occupied for residential purposes. Pot-sherds of Red Ware and a few terracotta antiquities were recovered from the surface (Pl. CXCI). A wall made of Kushanan bricks was noticed in the section of a mound (Pl.CXCII). Kushanan brick-bats were also found scattered on both of the mounds. Only trial trench may be taken.

In the month of October, 2014 I came to know that some construction work is going on at Nalanda College Campus, Garh Par, Bihar Sharif, Nalanda and during digging by JCB a Stone wall, Pot-sherds of Red and Black Ware along with a few stone sculptures were found (Pls. CXCIII-CXCVII). Findings of my exploration suggest that Garh Par was the actual site of Odantapuri which is still extended into 3x3 km area having height of about 10 mts from the surrounding area. But the whole area is occupied for habitation purposes and there is no space for extensive excavation which may reveal the structural remains of the Odantapuri. Only trial trenches may be taken at few places. Keen interest of historians as well as archaeologists may be able to solve the mystery of the Odantapuri Mahavihara.

Tson-kha-pa Sumatikirti (1357-1414 CE) and his desciples established large colleges on the model of Nalanda Mahavihara in Tibet where thousands of the Mongols studied (Sankrityayan: 428). In the Lhobrak valley of Tibet there is a shrine on the model of Nalanda (*JBORS* IX: 22) under the direction of Acharya Padmasambhava (Chatterji.1933:41). A Nalanda Monastery built west of Lhasa near the Tibetan-Nepalese border is about 350-400 years old (Korosi.1957: 188). Beyond the hills, to the north of Lhasa, a monastery was constructed after the name of Nalanda during the 14-15th century CE for about 2500 students (Sankrityayan.1952:418; Mishra.1998:267). Nalanda being the richest centre of art was not only closely interwoven with the neighbouring centres of art in Magadha but was connected with the art centers of the outside world like Tibet (Mishra.1998:343).

Fusion of Nalanda Art on Tibet

In the history of Buddhist art in India, Nalanda occupies a special place. It not only added a few interesting facets but also a general polish of its own. Such was the fame of the School that its influence can be seen in Pan-Asian Buddhist art as well (Pal.1972: XVII). The Nalanda School of Art emerged as a full-fledged School with the establishment of Pala rule in Magadha and most of the creative workmanship on stones and bronzes falling within the Pala age along with remarkable iconographic development. Nalanda during its glorious career extending over four centuries had intimate cultural links with the neighbouring countries viz. Nepal, Tibet and South-east Asian countries. Scholars from these countries flocked to the great seat of learning to receive instructions at the feet of its great acharyas. Scholars from Nalanda also went to these countries on cultural and religious missions. It might be assumed that along with them the Nalanda School of Art travelled to those far off countries and inspired the artistic efforts of those regions(Chauley.2002:38).The art of Tibet is the logical prolongation of the art of the Palas (750-1060 CE). The Tibetan sculptures are based on the Pala style of metal imagery (Pls. CXCVIII-CXCIX).

The tradition transmitted by the Tibetan scholar Lama Taranatha, which probably derives from the older source of Nepalese origin, indicates that the Tibetans received their artistic training from the Indian masters. The monastery of Nalanda was the focal point from which the Buddhist culture spread in Tibet, and gave not only form to the religion but also inspired the art of Tibet. Taranatha informs that under King Dharmapala of the Pala dynasty, two famous artists, Dhiman and Bitpala, father and son were credited with famous painting and modeled statues. They were the founders of the schools in cast metal images, sculptures and paintings in 9th century CE during the rteigns of Dharmapala and Devapala (Chauley.2002:87).

The Tibetan sculptures are based on the Pala styles of metal imagery. An ivory Buddhist trinity from Tibet recalls the bronzes of Nalanda for its linear dropery. The face of umbrella-bearing Indra to the left of Buddha's image is typical Pala (Pott.1951:270). Ferocious Yamantaka of Tibet is known at Nalanda also during 10th century CE. In an 18th century CE Padmapani (Pott.1951:13) figure from Tibet several features of Pala sculptures are seen; meditative face, scarf across the body, standing in *tribhanga*, luxuriant lotus-stock, short drawers, late medieval type of petals as also seen in ạ number of Nalanda sculptures (CBAE.1956). Two stone figures of Simhanada Manjusri from Nalanda (NM 595/57-58 and 0032/7-1) resemble a bronze figure of the same god from Tibet (Getty.1978: XVII). A Tibetan bronze figure representing Shyama Tara (Getty.1978: XXXVIII) is quite close to certain female deities from Nalanda (1-692 and 10767/1-434-bronze).

The motif of elephant, lion and *Vyalaka* which was used from 9th century CE onwards at Nalanda, reached Tibet decorating the thrones of statues. The Dhyani Buddhas decorate the crowns of Bodhisattvas at Nalanda; but in Tibet they are depicted round the body of the *stūpas*. The images of Manjusri seated in easy posture as a youthful person with hair arranged in plates, a necklace with tiger's claws with heavy kuṇdalas were most probably popularized over a vide area from Nalanda.The mantra *"Om Mani Padme Hum"* on a Nalanda figure (9th century CE) represents the male and female principals in mystic union. The letters a.u.m. stands for Buddha, Dharma and Sangha respectively, thus representing the male, female principles and the product of theie union. This technique reached Kashmir also. Alice Getty observes that the Tibetans borrowed the styles of sculptures (12th -14th century CE) from Nepal.

A Tibetan bronze image of Siṁhanada is seated in *Ardhaparyanka mudra*. The couchant fabulous lion looks towards the deity. An *ajinavastra* goes across the trunk. The right hand of the deity is placed on the right knee and the left hand in vertical posture holds the lotus-stalk, on which there is a sword. The lotus petals represent the 11th-12th century CE type. Alice Getty says that the forms of Avalokiteshvara and Manjusri are united in order to conceive the form of Simhanada Lokeshvara. According to the *Sadhana* the five Dhyani Buddhas emanate from the body. However, the Tibetan bronze is aesthetically very poor. A stone image of seated Avalokiteshvara resembles a bronze figure of Avalokiteshvara from Tibet in sitting posture with both of the legs on the seat in *Maharajalilasana,* vertically placed left hand holding the lotus-stalk, rounded halo, double lotus-seat, pedestal supported byliond at corners and a cloth covering the central part of the pedestal. Two stone sculptures of Simhanada Manjusri from Nalanda (NM 595/57-58 and 00032/7-1) resemble a bronze figure of the same deity from Tibet, such as the sitting posture in *Ardhaparyankasana Dharmacakra mudra,* book on lotus, couchant lion, lotus petals of 11th -12th century CE, left leg pendent and resting on lotus cushion etc. A bronze image found from Fatehpur, Gaya is nearest to the Tibetan bronze in body, posture, lotus-stalk, lotus petals etc. A Tibetan bronze image representing Shyama Tara is quite close with certain female deities made of bronze from Nalanda (1-692 and 10767/1-434).

References

Agrawal, V.S. 1965. *Studies in Indian Art*. Varanasi: Prithivi Prakashan.

Anguttarnikaya. 1956. London: Pali Text Society

Archaeological Survey of India Annual Review: 1921-22.

Archaeological Survey of India Annual Review: 1922-23

Archaeological Survey of India Annual Review: 1923-24

Archaeological Survey of India Annual Review: 1924-25

Archaeological Survey of India Annual Review: 1926-27

Archaeological Survey of India Annual Review: 1927-28

Archaeological Survey of India Annual Review: 1928-29

Archaeological Survey of India Annual Review: 1929-30

Archaeological Survey of India Annual Review: 1930-34

Archaeological Survey of India Annual Review: 1934-35

Archaeological Survey of India Annual Review: 1935-36

Arita, K. et al. 1982. "Geology and Structure of the Pokhara-Piuthan Area, Central Nepal", *Journal of Nepal Geological Society* 2 (Special Issue).

Asher, F.M. 1980. *The Art of Eastern India*. Minnesota.

Banarjee, R.D. 1933. *The Age of the Imperial Guptas*. Varanasi: Banaras Hindu University.

Beal, S. 1973. *The Life of Huien-tsang by Shaman Hwai Li*. New Delhi: Munshiram Manoharlal Publishers Pvt. Ltd.

Bhattacharya. 1949. *Nishpannayogavali of Mahapandita Abhayakargupta*. Baroda: Oriental Institute.

Bhattacharyya, Benoytosh. 2008 (Reprinted). *The Indian Buddhist Iconography*. New Delhi: Aryan Books International.

Bhattasali, N.K. 1929. *Iconography of Buddhist and Brahmanic Sculptures in the Dacca Museum.* Cambridge.

CBAE 1956

Chatterji, B.R. 1933. *India and Java.* Calcutta: IJ.

Chaudhary, B.K. 2008. "Identifying the surroundings of Nalandas Mahavihara".*Puratattva* 38.Delhi: Indian Archaeological Society.

Chauley, 2002. *Art and Architecture of Nalanda.*

Chavannes, E. (Ed. & Tr.) *Memoire Religieux Eminents Par I-tsing.*

Coomaraswami, A.K. 1914. *Bronzes from Ceylon.* Colombo.

Cunningham, A. 1935. *Ancient Geography of India.* Varanasi: Indological Book House.

Dave, J.H. 1967. *Immortal India III.* Bombay: Bharatiya Vidya Bhavan.

De, N.L. 1927 (2nd edition). *The Geographical Dictionary of Ancient and Medieval India.* London: Luzac and Company.

Dutta, B.N. (Tr.). 1944. *Mystic Tales of Lama Taranath.* Calcutta: Ram Krishna Vedanta Matha.

Epigraphica Indica II. Delhi: Archaeological Survey of India.

Epigraphica Indica XX. Delhi: Archaeological Survey of India.

Getty, A. 1978. *The Gods of Northern Buddhism.* New Delhi.

Ghosh, A. 1959 (4th edition).*Nalanda.* Delhi: Archaeological Survey of India.

Ghosh, A.1959 (4th edition) *Nalanda.* Delhi: Archaeological Survey of India.

Huntington, S.L.1984. *The Pala-Sena Schools of Sculptures.* Leiden.

Indian Archaeology A Review: 1955-56

Indian Archaeology A Review: 1973-74

Indian Archaeology A Review: 1975-76

Indian Archaeology A Review: 1982-83

Indian Historical Quaterly VI

Indian Historical Quaterly IX

Journal of Bhandarkar Oriental Research Society IX

Kempers, A.J.B. 1933. *The Bronzes of Nalanda and Hindu-Javanese Art.*Leiden:E.J.Brill.

Korosi, A.C. 1957. *The Life and Teachings of Buddha.* Calcutta: Susil Gupta India Pvt. Ltd.

Kumar, N. 1970. *Bihar District Gazetteers.* Patna: Government of Bihar.

Legge, James. 1886. *Travels of Fahien.*Oxford.

Majjhimnikaya I. 1899. (Eds. Trenchner, V. and R. Chalmers). London: Pali Text Society

Majumdar, R.C. (Ed.). 1955. *The Age of Imperial Kanauj (History and Culture of Indian People)* Vol. IV. Bombay.

Mallasekhara, G.P. 1928. *Pali Literature in Ceylon.*

Memoirs of Archaeological Survey of India 66. Delhi: Archaeological Survey of India.

Memoirs of Archaeological Survey of India.1999. Delhi: Archaeological Survey of India.

Mishra, B.N. 1998. *Nalanda* in 3 Vols. Delhi: B.R.Publishing Corporation.

Mitra, Debala. 1982. *Bronzes from Bangladesh:A Study of Buddhist images from district Chittgaon.* Delhi: Agam Kala Prakashan.

Mitra, R.L. 1970 (Reprint).*The Sanskrit Buddhist Literature of Nepal.* Calcutta: Sanskrit Pustak Bhandar.

Mukherjee, Radha Kamal. 1959. *The Culture and Art ofg India.* London: George Allen amd Unwin Ltd.

Pal, Pratapaditya (Ed.). 1972. *Aspects of Indian Art.*Leiden

Pandey, Mithila Sharan. 1963. *The Historical Geography and Topography of Bihar.* Delhi: Motilal Banarasidas.

Pandey, R.N. 2008. *Nepal through the Ages.* NewDelhi: Adroit Publishers.

Patil, D.R. 1963. *Antiquarian Remains From Bihar.*Patna:K.P.Jayaswal Research Institute.

Pott, P.H. 1951. Introduction *to the Tibetan Collection of the National Museum of Ethnology.* Leiden.

Ray Chaudhury, H.C. (Ed.). 1931. *Dynastic History of Northern India.* Calcutta.

Ray Chaudhury H.C. 1938 (4th edition). *Political History of Ancient India.* Calcutta.

Sankalia, H.D. 1972 (2nd edition).*The University of Nalanda.* Delhi.

Sankrityayan, Rahul. 1952. *Buddhacharya.* Sarnath: Mahabodhi Sabha.

Saran, S.C. *et al.* 2008. "Excavations of Juafardih and its identification with Kulika". *Puratattva* 38.Delhi: Indian Archaeological Society.

Shah, U.P. 1955. *Studies in the Jain Art.* Banaras.

Sharma, Arvind Kumar. 2012. *The Pala Art in Bihar.* Patna: Janaki Prakashan.

Sinha, Kamini. *Early Bronzes of Bihar.*

Sircar, D.C. "The Kailan Copper Plate Inscription opf King Sridharan Rata of Samatata". *Indian Historical Quaterly* XXIII.

Smith, V.A. 1914. *Early History of India.* Oxford: Clerendon Press.

Waddel, L.A. 1974. *Buddhism and Lamaism of Tibet.*New Delhi.

Waters, Thomas. 1988. *On Yuan Chwang's Travels in India* II

7

Archaeological Exploration in the Vicinity of Nalanda District: 2012-15

During the exploration work carried out during 2012-2015 by the author with his Research Scholar Mr. Pankaj Kumar in district-Nalanda it was decided to explore its vicinity, so was done in the year 2015-16 and a number of sites having archaeological importance were reported. A brief report of few important sites is mentioned below:

1. Afsadha (District-Nawadah; Lat. 25^0 09′N, Long.85^0 31′E): The site is located on the border of Nalanda and Nawadah districts. It is 40 km south-east to the ruins of Nalanda and 42 km south-east from the district headquarters of Bihar Sharif. The *Sakri* River flows 4 km west to the village. The mound situated to the south of the village is extended into 60x50 mts with an extant height of 8 mts (Pl.CC). Brick walls are noticed in the section of the mound. Several Brahmanic and Buddhist images are kept in Varaha Sthan, Shiva temple and Devi Sthan. Special mention may be made of images of Varaha, an incarnation of Vishnu, Ekmukhi Linga, Ashtabhuji Durga and Mahishmardini Durga (Pls. CCI-CCIV).

2. Aiyer (District-Gaya; Lat. 23^0 74′N, Long.85^0 95′E): This site is located on the border of Nalanda and Gaya districts. It is 37 km south-west to the ruins of Nalanda and 49 km south-west from the district head quarters of Bihar Sharif. To the south-west of the village there is a hill having two natural grottos. To the west of the village a few Buddhist sculptures made of black and sand stone are kept at Devi Sthan. Mention may be made of a stone panel of stupa worship which is inscribed both on upper and lower portion with famous Buddhist creed "Ye Dhamma hetuppabhava" (Pl.CCV).

3. Parvati (District-Nawadah; Lat. $29^0$97′N, Long.$76^0$83′E): This site is also located on the border of Nalanda and Nawadah districts. It is 34 km south-east to the ruins of Nalanda and 38 km south-east from the district headquarters of Bihar Sharif. The site was situated on the ancient bed of *Sakri* River; at present its course changed about 10 km west to the village. To the south-west of the

village an intact image of Buddha in *Dharmacakrapravartan mudra* made of black stone is kept at Baba Sthan (Pl.CCVI). A hill known as Parvati having a natural grotto named Indra-Shila is located to the south-west of the village (Pl.CCVII). Pot-sherds of Red Ware and Kushana brick-bats are noticed on the hill. A newly built Ram-Sita temple is located on the hill.

4. Samas (District-Shekhapura; Lat. $25^{0}17'$N, Long.$85^{0}71'$E): This village is located on the border of Nalanda and Shekhpura districts. It is about 40 km east to the ruins of Nalanda and about 31 km north-east from Bihar Sharif. The River *Sakri* flows 15 km south to the village. There is a mound to the south of the village near an ancient tank spread over on 26 acres. A large image of Vishnu in *Sthanak mudra* is kept in a temple nearby the tank. On the pedestal of the image an inscription of one line is inscribed which is under decipherment (Pl. CCVIII).

An exploration work was carried out at Kurkihar and its vicinity, district- Gaya (Fig. 51), Bihar by the author himself and his team during the month of May, 2016. Kurkihar lies on Nalanda-Gaya road. It was a great centre of art during Pala period. A number of Buddhist images made of stone and bronze were recovered from the site. The site lies on the ancient path followed by the Buddha. So the site and its peripheral area have a great archaeological importance. Keeping in mind this fact my team decides to make a village to village survey.

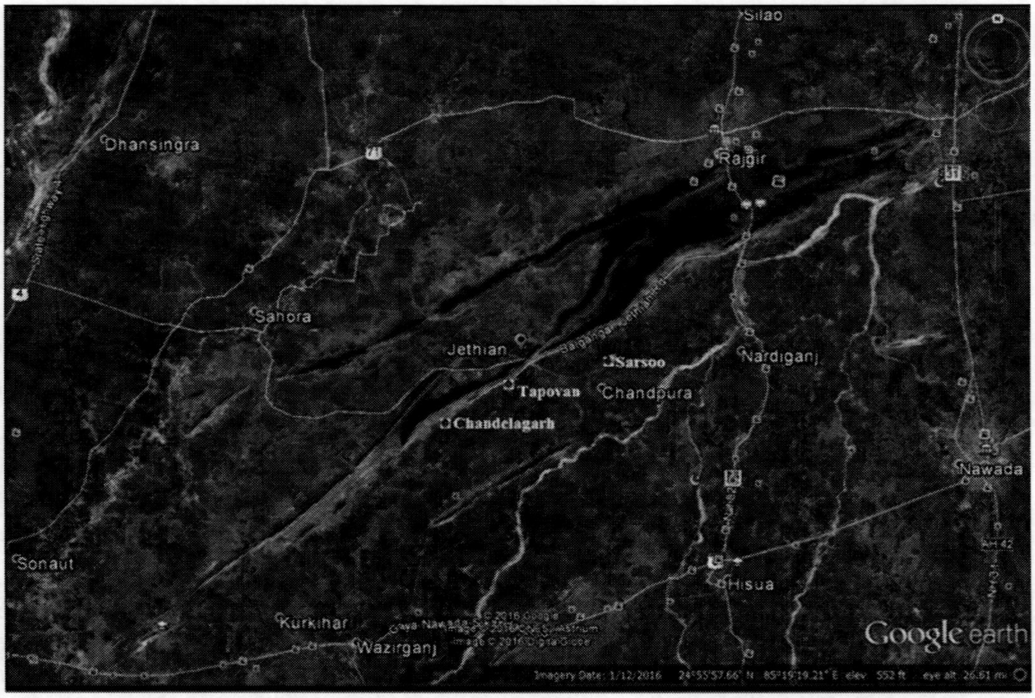

Figure 51: Satellite map of Kurkihar and its vicinity

Prime objectives of our explorations in the region are documentation of Buddhist sites in the area; re-assess the present conditions of the earlier reported sites, comparative study of the ceramics and antiquities collected during explorations along with other sites of the lower Ganga plain and also to assess the ancient trade-route. With the above objectives, a village to village survey in the region was conducted. In the process, about two dozen villages were surveyed. But only four sites having archaeological potential namely Jethian, Tapovana, Chandelagarh and Sarsoogarh are significant as per our present objectives. A brief report of these sites is given below:

Chandelagarh (24⁰ 54′ 14″ N, 85⁰ 18′8.99″E)

This huge mound extended into 500 x 200 mt (Pl. CCIX) is located about 1.5 km south-east from Tapovan hot-springs and 10 miles south-east from Rajgir at the foothills of Jethian on the bank of perennial river *Mangura,* which flows west to east. The height of the mound is approx 40′ to 50′ from the river bed of *Mangura.* The surface study of the mound indicates that the site was first inhabited by the Black and Red ware culture people followed by Northern Black Polished Ware Culture, Mature NBPW, degenerated NBPW, Sunga-kushana, Gupta and up to Pala period respectively. The above chronology is based on the classification of potteries collected from the surface. A number of fragments of sculptures found scattered on the top of the mound made of black stone of Pala period.

Jethian (Lat. 24⁰ 56′N, Long. 85⁰ 20′E)

The site was first reported in 1871 by Cunningham, who identified Jethain with *Yashtivana.* It is well connected by train and road with Rajgir and Gaya. This cultural zone is divided into two pockets *i.e.* Valley area and Dam area. Being located on the old route from Gaya to Rajgir, Buddha had passed through this valley several times. As stated in *Mahaparinibbana sutta* once King Bimbisara had received the Buddha near *Yashtivana* and after hearing his preach he became his disciple. The place is well protected by the hills on two sides, and a forest towards north-east of Rajgir. Hiuen -tsang refers to a rich bamboo- forest in this area, from which the name *Yashtivana* or modern Jethian is derived and even as late as 1871, Cunningham heard the name of *Jakhtiban.* He, however, did not fully explore the area; but in about 1899, Stein visited various places in the valley and on the hills and described about the ancient remains. Recently A.K.Prasad (2011) has published an article on this area. A brick structure like terraced shape *stupa* is noticed below the Shiva temple at dam area (Pl.CCX). Some fragments of sculptures of Brahmanic and Buddhist deities and broken door jambs etc. are found in the dam area, among them special mention may be made of an image of Buddha in Pralambapada mudra (Pl.CCXI). Some bricks are exposed varied in sizes ranging 48x28x5 cm, 50x 30x7 and 23x20x16 cm. Pot sherds of BRW and NBPW are found on the surface.

Tapovan (Lat. 24⁰ 54′45″N, Long. 85⁰ 18′50″E)

The site is located on Rajgir-Gaya road. It was noticed initially by Buchanan in about 1900 CE. Quoting a tradition he said that it was the birth-place of the famous epic king

Jarasandha. He had also mentioned the names of the hot-springs as *Chanda-kaushik, Hansatirtha, Purna-Hansa* and *Sanatan-kundan-dasanak-tirtha*. After Buchanan, A. Stein visited Tapovan and described about the ruins. He, however, names only the largest spring as *Sanat-kumar-kund*. All these springs are enclosed by stone walls with stone-built steps leading down to the water. The images of Shiva, Vishnu and Hara-Gauri are kept inside the holy tanks. Stein noticed a large mound representing a *stūpa* in between the largest spring and the modern temple on the west measuring 75′ to 81′ in diameter at the base, about 45 ′square at top having height of about 10′ from the surface. He suggests that this was the *stupa* which lies on the walking-path of the Buddha as marked by Hiuen- tsang. Hiuen-tsang further informs that people from far and near used to flock here for holy-bath, after which chronic diseases were healed. Scattered images around the springs are unprotected inviting thieves and antique smugglers.

Sarsoo (24^0 55′ 55.4′ N, 85^0 21′72 E)

This site is in Atari Police Station, Gaya located on the Rajgir-Jethian road, 10 km south-east from Rajgir covering 12 km of area having height of 12 to 50 m. There is a circular-shaped mound which seems like a *stupa*. A number of Brahmanic and Buddhist images including Ganesha, Vishnu, Buddha and Tara are kept inside a modern temple (Pls. CCXII-CCXIV). On the basis of the study of potteries and antiquities recovered from the surface of the mound it can be assumed that the site belongs to Pre-Mauryan to pala period. To the east of the village there is another modern temple in which an Uma-Maheshwar image is installed in a niche measuring 70 x 43 x 17 cm which may belong to post- Gupta period. Three Shiva-lingas with Yonipitha are kept in the western most side of the village

Our exploration indicates that Jethian and Tapovan are the larger settlements might have some connectivity to each other. Tapovan is also connected with the epic king Jarasandha. Buddha used this path while traveling from Bodh Gaya to Kushinagar. The images found in this region are almost made of basalt and belong to the Pala period. On the basis of above investigations it can be said that the region is full of archaeological potential and need to explore other remaining area of the region. Recent excavations done at Rajgir and its vicinity indicates its Chalcolithic feature and approximately datable to 1200 BCE. Without proper investigation and excavation in the hilly areas of the region the settlement pattern and its connection with Rajgir could not be traced.

Referemces

Chaudhary, B.K.2008. "Identifying the surroundings of Nalandas Mahavihara". *Puratattva* 38.Delhi: Indian Archaeological Society.

Ghosh, A. 1959 (4th edition). *Nalanda.* Delhi: Archaeological Survey of India.

Memoirs of Archaeological Survey of India.1999. Delhi: Archaeological Survey of India.

Memoirs of Archaeological Survey of India 66. Delhi: Archaeological Survey of India.

Sankalia, H.D. 1972 (2nd edition).*The University of Nalanda.* Delhi.

Saran, S.C. *et al.*2008. "Excavations of Juafardih and its identification with Kulika". *Puratattva* 38.Delhi: Indian Archaeological Society.

Sharma, Arvind Kumar.2012.*The Pala Art in Bihar*. Patna: Janaki Prakashan.

8

Small Scale Excavation at Rukhaegarh, District-Nalanda: 2014-15

The very name of Nalanda invokes us a deep sense of reverence and a perpetual sense of pride for it. This is because the place has gone deep down into Indian psyche as the greater and the best seat of learning of which humanity can ever dream of Nalanda mahavihara, was unique in more ways than one. Student's all-round development-moral, intellectual and spiritual was the sole motive of education at Nalanda. But the best part of it was the imparting of practical learning; what were taught in theory (*Pariyatti*) were practiced (*Patipatti*) in life.

Etymology

The etymology of the word Nalanda is uncertain. Different derivations have been proposed. Hiuen-tsang, a Chinese traveller who visited and studied at Nalanda in the seventh century AD, discusses various theories as to the origin of the name. He says that "to the south of Nalanda sangharam, in the middle of a mango grove (*Ambavana*), there was a tank where dwelt a dragon (Naga) called Nalanda. By the side of it is built the sangharam which therefore, takes the name of the Naga (Beal.1911:167). However, this was a legendary account, I-tsing, another Chinese traveller who visited India after Hiuen-tsang thinks that Nalanda derived its name from the Nagananda (Takakusu. 1896: 571). We can not understand why the travellers should disagree regarding the name of the Naga. It seems I-tsing is giving the original name of the Naga, whereas Xuan-Zang gives the name which Naga came to acquire afterwards. The Naga, therefore, must have been in course of time came to be called, the Naga of Nalanda. But this discussion does not lead us to anywhere. At least it does not tell us how the place came to be known as Nalanda. That there was a mango grove, a tank and perhaps the Naga too is beyond doubt. Buddha in his tours always stayed under a grove of trees and Nalanda must have had also one. As to the tank etc. we have the testimony of Cunningham who explored the place and carried on some excavations there in the last of the 20th century "That is still existing immediately to the south of the ruined monastery, a small tank called *Kargidya pokhar* (presently known as Giddhi pokhar), which exactly answers to the position of the Nalanda tank and is identical place of the Naga (*IAR*.1988-89:30).

The second account which Xuan-Zang puts forth carried greater authenticity. He says "But the truth is that Tathagata in old days practiced the life of a Bodhisattva here and became the king of a great country and established his metropolis in the land. Moved by pity for living things he delighted in continually relieving them. In remembrance of this virtue he was styled "clarity without intermission" and the Sangharam was called in perpetuation of his name (Beal.1911:167). The reason why Xuan-Zang considers the latter account as true can be easily explained. He was a devout Buddhist and when he wrote this account he only voiced the feelings of a Buddhist who had invented a legend to explain the name of Nalanda. The story sounds like one of the Jataka tales which describes the previous lives of Buddha. We cannot, however, give credence to this explanation for the simple reason that even Buddha was alive; the place was called by the same name (*Mahaparinibban Sutta*: 87-89). Dharmaswami, a Tibetan monk who visited Nalanda in 1236 CE gives the name as Nalanda which meant in Tibetan Lord of men and ads that it was built by a former king because of which, it is given this name (Roerich: 90). Hirananda Sastri thought that the name was derived from Nala meaning "lotus-stalks" because then, as even today, it had a large number of lotus-ponds. It would then mean the giver of lotus-stalks (Sastri.1930:04). Lotus is a symbol of wisdom and da meaning to give. Thus Nalanda means giving wisdom. A. Ghosh is of opinion that Nala, Nalaka Gramaka and Nalanda found in different contexts as place names are all variants of the same place name (*Epigraphica Indica*. 1829:27).

To resume the history of the name Nalanda Samual Beal has put forward one etymological analysis of the name suggested by Hiuen-tsang's interpretation (Beal. 1911:168). In a footnote on the phrase "charity without intermission" he says the word Nalanda would thus appear to be derived from Na-alamda, not giving enough or not having enough to give. But this interpretation rather goes against the one given by the traveller, though it is quite correct literally. If, however, we take 'na-alamda' as an interrogative sentence requiring a positive or affirmative reply: alam dātum (for da) viz. that there is sufficient to give, we can say that the phrase na-alam-datum (for da) though negative emphatically supplies positive evidence that the place was rich enough to provide for all. The position of 'na' in the senctence 'alamdatum' na is not so objectionable because it can as well be put in front: Na-alam-datum because in Sanskrit the position of words does not matter so long as the sense is conveyed by an emphasis put on the words, which in the present case would naturally be put on the word 'na'. In short the name conveyed the idea that the place was rich and prosperous.

The early history of the place bears sufficient testimony to its claim to be rich and prosperous city. Various Buddhist texts tell us that the place in the days of Buddha was a prosperous village (*Majjhim Nikaya*. 1951: 377). It is said that Lepa, one of the citizen of Nalanda, was rich and famous and had large houses, vehicles, gold and silver, possessed of useful and necessary things—owning many male and female slaves, cows, buffaloes and sheeps (*Sutrakritanga*: 420). Even the Buddha had partaken of Lepā's hospitality. Lepa offered his rich bathing hall to the enlightened one who gladly accepted it and delivered a long discourse which had the effect of converting him to Buddhism. *Sutrakritanga*, a Jain text book, also tells us that Nalanda contained hundreds of buildings (Beal. 1911: 420). Even before Buddha Nalanda finds mention in certain Jain works. According to Jain tradition Mahavira met Gosala at this very place. Buddha recurrently visited the place and stayed at its mango-groves. Ananda believed it to be a better place for *Nirvana* than Pataliputra.

Historicity

The humanity has always aspired for achieving something higher and it is this vision which makes it distinct from rest of the living beings on this planet. This has fructified in two ways i.e. the exterior development, noticed through multiple scientific and technological achievements and secondly the interior growth visualized through the discipline of mind and other faculties to search within and gradually open the gate of self realization or spiritual elevation. The first path is called *Preya* (pleasing) and the second is known as *Sreya* (benevolent). It is the second course which has been opted by India and several experiments were made with excellent results. The science of diffusing this process is known as philosophy but the term conveying true sense gifted by Indian seers is darśana which in the common parlance stands for seeing deity or divinity. The system of realizing divinity in one own self is the realm of darshana. While the material progress is appreciated through eyes the inner blossoming is beyond the range of the optical vision. One has to close his eyes to be detached from the world to search within him. This is the prerequisite of darśana and then there open a number of channels to reach the goal. The option of a particular channel depends on one's own training and tuning and Indian seers and sages have offered various solutions to this puzzle. Their contribution has been laudable and the world has been immensely benefited through their knowledge. It is the reason that this land was known as *Vidyaguru*.

The tradition of collecting, preserving and furtherance of Jnana (wisdom) was maintained for long and even after the demise of exponents or propounders; it was continued by their illustrious disciples who established the seats of learning. Seekers of knowledge thronged from distant quarters even crossing the geographical barriers and stayed for several years to persue their studies and returned to their respective countries with great sense of satisfaction and glow. They commanded high respect at home and made their own contribution in further dissemination of their learning. This is how the innumerable lamps were lit by those few who had the courage and aspiration to quench their thirst of darshana at the very fountain of knowledge.

Nalanda was certainly one of such glorious spots from which the light emitted and not only India but the neighbouring countries were also illuminated. In or before 6th century BCE it was a prosperous town providing congenial environment to religious, social and academic activities. This must have been a sub-urban place situated not far from Rajgriha, which has a hoary past and associated with several mythical kings from the time of *Ramayana* and *Mahabharata*. In the reign of Bimbisara (C 543-491 BCE) it developed as a capital town and hills around commanded respect for being religiously sacred. Nalanda was sanctified in the 6th century BCE through the visits of the Buddha, Mahavira and their preachings during the course of long stay in the rainy season (Vassavasa). The Pali Tripitakas record the place as a favourite resort of seers. When the Buddha visited and gave Ten Discourse, Nalanda was already a center of religious activities. A local wealthy merchant Pavarika gifted a mango grove to the Buddha and it was named Pavarika Ambavana. He also constructed some resting places for the Buddha and his disciples. As per record of *Sutrakritanga*, Lepa was another merchant who donate his riches and became a devout follower. It was here that the Enlightened One preached *Kevatta sutta* and *Upali sutta*. The *Majjhimnikaya* appreciated Nalanda to be a prosperous town with thick population (Ayari Nalanda Idha Cheva Feeta Cha Bahujana Achinna Manussati). Similarly, *Digha* and *Samyutta Nikaya* refer to the place with a sense of admiration not forgetting the mango grove (Ekam samyam Bhagva Nalandayam Viharati Pavarikamba Vane). The visits and preachings of the Tathagata bestowed greater fame and sanctity to the place. At the same time, two important disciples Dhammasenapati Sariputta and Mahamoggalana belonged to this area. The former was born at Nalaka and the later at Kulika. Name Nalanda is suggested to be derived from Nalak. It is also interesting to note that Sariputta was born and expired also at the same spot. Later Ashoka is said to have built a stūpa in his memory. During one of the vassāvāsas at Nalanda a follower of Mahavira, Makkhaligosala sought the shelter in the samgha.

On the solid foundation of dhamma, darshana and charity, the monastic establishment of Nalanda rose brick by brick till it ushered into a great mahavihara in the mid- Gupta period and continued to flourished for six centuries. Besides the religious and the spiritual background and the majestic campus, what attracted the students and others most, were its fame for imparting the best education and the great acharyas associated from the beginning to the end. The *Nikayasamgraha* tradition informs that those monks who were discarded in the 3rd Buddhist Council met at Nalanda and formed a separate group of Mahasanghika which were later known as Mahayanists. While the Buddhist theology and particularly the Mahayana philosophy formed the major portion of prospectus, other subjects like Sankhya (system of philosophy), Hetuvidya (logic), Tantra (magic), Shabdavidya (grammar), Chikitsavidya/ Ayurveda (Medicine and treatment) were taught and the Vedic studies were also not ignored. Familiarity with Brahmanical texts was necessary for the canonical combat (Shastrartha). Archaeologists and art historians observe that the production of fine quality of stone sculptures and excellent bronzes would not have been possible without proper training by the expert artists. We do find a term

Shilpavidya which must have covered art, icons, crafts and architecture. Thus the early Nalanda Mahavihara offered multiple options of subjects.

No doubt the Vihara initially aimed at guiding and assisting the Buddhist mendicants to practice the dhamma, but by the passage of time, higher studies in different subjects were found necessary and the Vihara developed into a Mahavihara i.e. large academic institution, corresponding to the present day university. When Fa-hien visited the place in the 4th century CE, he saw only a stupa which must have been in existence probably from the time of Ashoka but the pilgrim did not notice the large complex of mahavihara which has been so elaborately mentioned by Hiuen-tsang in the early 7th century CE. We can therefore safely conclude that the campus took shape between the 5th and 6th century and continued to be enlarged as per requirement.

Nalanda magnificently contributed to the world culture in different ways. The students from different countries arrived and stayed at Nalanda and not only pursued their studies in the disciplines taught in India but conduct wise also they were moulded in the Indian style of life which laid emphasis on good conduct. On their return to the respective lands they spread the same message and sacraments of Indian Culture and Buddhism which they had followed in India and taught at Nalanda. These naturally resulted in diffusion of Buddhism and Indian culture in neighbouring countries. Secondly, some of the works authored by the great ācāryas of Nalanda were carried by them on their return to their native places. These were either translated in local languages or were rendered in dialects of the region for easy understanding of the people. The feeling of respect and adoption of contents in conduct helped in spreading the Buddhism. I-sting informs that while opening the sheets of a manuscript in the library of Nalanda he read on the colophon that it was written by a Korean monk Hwai Ywui. This leads to different speculations, i.e. the Korean monk came before I-sting and wrote it or he brought it from Korea which may not be possible, or he copied an old book for his use at mahavihara.

Thirdly, some of the acharyas either went of their own or were invited by the kings or noblemen of the foreign lands. Those who should specially be mentioned are Asanga, Dinganaga, Shantarakshita, Kamlashila, Dharmapala, and Padmasambhava. All these great acharyas made tresmendous contribution in disseminating the basic elements of Indian culture through the message of the Buddha in the vast region which is known as the Buddhist world. The place justified its name as Naladna i.e. offering limitless knowledge.

Nalanda remained in the stage of dormancy for about seven centuries in the reign of Sungas, Kushanas and early Gupta kings either due to political conditions or the aptitude of rulers. Sungas and early Guptas although ruled in Magadha with capital at Pataliputra, yet they were either, Vedic and Bhagvata or Shaiva. From the time of Shakraditya identified as Kumargupta I (415-455 CE), the trend changed with adoption of flexibility and Nalanda received royal patronage and the mahavihara started emerging. In the later Gupta rule, Nalanda continued to ascend and the mahavihara took the final shape and the students thronged from distant parts.

During the post-Gupta, Vardhana/ Maukhari and early Pala period the fame of the mahavihara crossed barriers of land and seekers of knowledge arrived even from the foreign countries, like Hiuen-tsang (629-645 CE) and I-tsing (617-695 CE) from China and Chag-chos-rje-dpal (Dharmasvami-1236 CE) from Tibet. Not only the campus expanded to accommodate the swelling number of students but also the teachers required to handle multiple disciplines. The number of students at its prime phase differs from authority to authority but it was certainly more than ten thousand and some put it even larger. The number of teachers was one thousand five hundred. There were three hundred rooms and several monasteries.

The spreading glory resulted in huge rush of seekers of admission to the mahavihara and the dvarpandits were deputed to test the new arrivals. This was some sort of Entrance Test which ascertained quality of academic standard and also ensured the proper use of resources available with the growing mahavihara. Restrictions in admission must have necessiated finding a parallel mahavihara at Vikramshila. The graph of glory of Nalanda continued to raise upto the end of the 8th century but the point of saturation also reached. Some what laxity in studies and conduct crept in. Tantricism started overpowering the Vinaya and Sheela. Followers of Shankaracharya protested against the monks and their mystic rituals, confronting deities' like Aparajita and Parnashabari further polluted the religious harmony. The mahavihara was cracking by the pressure of loose administration and lack of public support as the academic lusture was fading. Under these precarious situations the doomsday also came when Bakhtiar Khilji attacked fiercely in the early thirteenth century. Not only the great mahavihara and its monasteries were demolished but the large libraries, like Ratnasagara, Ratnodadhi and Ratnaranjaka, housing thousands of volumes were also set ablaze. Dynamism and dignity were reduced to death dust and once the multistoried wonderful grand mahāvihāra complex transformed into heaps of mounds to be forgotten for six centuries.

Sir Alexander Cunningham, the first Director General of the Archaeological Survey of India visited the site in 1861 and identified it as old Nalanda on the basis of the travel accounts of Hiuen-tsang. Although Francis Buchanan had earlier seen the place in 1812, but he could not identify it. Regular excavations started in 1916 under the direction of Spooner and with the untiring efforts of Hirannda Shastri for two decades, the mighty majestic Nalanda resurfaced from the womb of earth.

Geographical Background

Indians has a rich cultural heritage and a glorious past which is reflected in almost all fields of life educational, cultural, social, political, economic and more so in the spiritual. If we peep into the rich Buddhist literature we get a panaromic view of India of the sixth century BCE and of later period particularly of the area known as *Majjhimdesha*, middle land. If we browse in Nalanda in particular we find that the literature refers that the present Nalanda, situated 88 kms south-east of Patna, the metropolis of the state of Bihar had a glorious past. It was a center of activity of two great luminaries— Buddha and Mahavira and their other contemparires. Later on Nalanda flourished as a great center of higher learning. In due course of time Nalanda and the present ruins (archaeological site of ancient Nalanda mahavihara) became almost synonymous with each other. Among the entire Buddhist educational center in Ancient India, Nalanda claims to be the foremost. It was such a distuinguished center for higher Buddhist education that scholars used to steal the name of Nalanda to glorify themselves as a student. In fact, Nalanda mahavihara existed for at least six centuries as a great center for higher studies.

About Nalanda mahavihara, which has been explored and unearthed partially, our knowledge is still limited. The more we know about the splendor of Nalanda mahavihara the more we wonder. The mahavihara of six *sangharamas* (convert house) was an institute of learning with fame for its academic creating values. Sankalia (1934) rightly epitheted the Nalanda mahaviahara, because the materials available so far, are not yet exhaustive to estimate how the four major facets of the Indian people's culture had been accumulated and assimilated through centuries from one generation to other. Nalanda spread therefore Indian wisdom (*Prajna*) in multiple dimensions as Taxila had once flourished by the life time of the Buddha. Altekar (1965), Dutta (1954), Ghosh (1965), Mukherjee (1947) dealt already some aspects of Nalanda and her environment with its educational management and technology. Barnet Kempers (1933) explored some data and specimens of cross-cultural negotiations in the bronze arts of Nalanda with South-east Asian countries while Nalanda had been an expertise in bronze. Temple of magnificent design is said to have been built at Nalanda by the ruler of Kannauja, Harshavardhana (606-647 CE).

The very name of Nalanda conjures up before our mind's eye all that is best and most excellent in education. In other words, it has become synonymous with the best kind of education that humanity can be proud of. There are very good universities in different parts of the world today. Some of them like Sorbonne or Paris University in France and Oxford and Cambridge in United Kingdom have been in existence for a very long time. There are others like Harvard, Wisconsin and Philadelphia in United States of America and yet others in other parts of the world but none commands as much respect as Nalanda did, none has got that prestigious and privileged position as it still enjoys today, although the Nalanda mahāvihāra was demolished as far back as in the beginning of the thirteenth century CE.

Topography

The archaeological remains of Nalanda mahāvihāra lay some 11 kms north-west from Rajgir and the same distance to the south-west of Bihar Sharif, the headquarter of the district Nalanda. It is 3 kms away from the Nalanda Railway Station and 88 Kms south-east of Patna, the metropolis of the Bihar state. Its latitude is 25^{0} 8′ N. and the longitude is 85^{0} 27′ E. (Kumar.1970: 646-647). Historians and archaeologists identified this place with a modern village named Badagaon at Nalanda (Cunningham.1924: 468). The term Badagaon has been taken as a corrupt form of *Viharagrama* Dey. 1927: 136).

Physical Division

Nalanda district of Bihar occupies an area of 2355 square kilometer and the co-ordinate is 25^0 12′ 00″ N latitude and 85^0 31′ 12″ E longitudes. It is a part of Lower Gangatic plain except its southern part, where small hills are separated over a large area. Barh district is in the north of this district where *Ganga* River flows from west to east direction. Patna is located in the north- west where as Gaya and Nawadah districts lie in the south- west and south of the district respectively, where hills belonging to the Chotanagpur hills spread over in a large area. Its topography slopes towards north and most of the streams flow northward and join the Ganges as tributaries.

Climate and Environment

As this district lies on 25^0 12′ 00″ North latitude, it enjoys sub tropical monsoon type climate indicating the impact of its location in sub tropical belt and the monsoon winds. Climate of this district is characterized by highly variable weather condition and divided into four distinct seasons:

1. Cold weather season (from mid December to mid March) with temperature ranging from 7^0 c to 17^0 c but in rare case it decreases to the freezing point,
2. Hot dry weather season (mid March to the end of May) with temperature ranging from 26^0 c to 36^0 c and temperature rarely goes below the 26^0 c rather some time exceed the temperature up to 40^0 c,
3. Wet season (from June to September), and
4. The season of retreating monsoon (from October to mid December).

Rainfall

The average annual rainfall in the district is 992.0 mm (39.05″). The rainfall during the south-west monsoon season constitutes about 87 % of the annual rainfall. August is the month with the highest rainfall. The variation from year to year of the annual rainfall is not large. On an average there are 47 rainy days *i.e.* days with rainfall of 2.5 mm-10 cm or more. Analysis of the rainfall in the district is given in table-47:

Table 47

Rainfall in the district, Source: DAO Office, Biharsharif, Nalanda

Rainfall	*Normal RF (mm)*	*Normal Rainy days*	*Normal Onset*	*Normal Cessation*
SW monsoon (June-Sept.	899	41	3rd week of June	3rd week of Oct.
NE monsoon (Oct.-Dec.)	65	03		
Winter (Jan.-Feb.)	28	03		
Summer (March-May)	44	03		
Annual	1036	50		

Soil

The district lies in the Lower Gangatic plain having one of the fertile lands of the world. The whole district is covered with alluvial soil except some southern part where black soil is found predominantly. Description of the soil quality of the district is given in table-48:

Table 48
Soil quality of the district, Source: DAO Office, Biharsharif, Nalanda and NABARD, Nalanda

Major Soils	*Area('000 ha)*	*Total %*
Sandy Soils	44.756	18.61
Coarse Sandy Loam Soils	40.538	16.86
Fine Sandy Loam Soils	62.171	25.86
Clayey Soils	92.908	38.65
Saline Calcareous Soils	0.00	0.00

Agriculture

District Nalanda is divided into the hills in the south and the low country to the north. The whole district is intersected by streams, which in the hot and cold weather contain little or no water, but at the time of heavy rain are filled from bank to bank. The greater part is provided with a system of irrigation works intended to store and distribute the water. Reservoirs called *ahars* are built, some of which are filled with rain water and natural drainage, while others are replenished by damming the rivers. A number of artificial channels convey the water from the rivers to the reservoirs, and other small channels conduct it to the fields of the cultivators. These irrigation works protect the greater part of the district from any general failure of the crops by drought, but there are two exceptions to the general rule, viz., the Islampur Thana (116 square miles) in the extreme south-west, and the south-east corner of the Bihar Thana. The former Thana contains few officient irrigation works, and the river *Phalgu*, which traverses this area, has silted up. Much of the land is high and sandy; while some of it consists of sterile soil, impregnated with carbonate of soda. The latter tract, which is comprised within the Asthawan Thana, has also lost the means of irrigation which it formerly possessed, owing to the silting up of its river channels.

Agricultural operations normally start during *Rohini Nakshatra* (last week of May to last week of June) when *Bhadai* crops are sown. Paddy seedlings are sown in early *Adra* (middle of June) and transplantation of paddy normally starts in *Purva Nakshatra* (middle of July) and ends by the end of August. The rains have to be adequate right from the time when seedlings are sown in the field till transplantation is over and then light showers should be intermittent and ultimately the *Hathia Nakshatra* should give plenty of rain to enable paddy crops to mature and also give sufficient moisturw to land so that *Rabi* crops may be sown in it. Periodic rains from December to February are also essential for a good *Rabi* harvest.

The principal crops of the district fall under three main harvests, The *Aghani*, *Bhadai* and *Rabi*. The *Aghani* is the winter crop which is harvested in the month of *Aghan* (November-December) and is composed mainly of winter paddy. The *Bhadai* is the early or autumn crop reaped in the month of *Bhado* (August-September) consisting of the variety of 60 days paddy (Sathi), sugarcane, marua, maize, millets and other less important grains. The *Rabi* crop includes cold weather crop like wheat, barley, gram and pulses etc. Analysis of agricultural land use is given in table-49.

Table 49
Agricultural land use in the district, Source: DAO Office, Biharsharif, Nalanda

Agricultural land use	*Area('000 ha)*	*Cropping intensity %*
Net sown area	191	150.2 %
Area sown more than once	95.9	
Gross cropped area	287	

Irrigation

Rains are the universal source of irrigation and success of crops largely depends on their adequacy and even distribution throughtout agricultural operations. The district receives on an average 1036 mm of rain during a normal year. Out of this, the south-west monsoon accounts for about 899 mm while remaining is winter rain. Rainfall cannot be depended upon as an unfailing source of irrigation. Therefore, artificial irrigation supplements rainfall in varying degreefor the success of agriculture. The water resources of the district consist in rivers; most of them almost dry up in summer, artificial reservoirs (Ahars), channels (Pains), embankments and wells including tube-wells. The soil of a large portion of this district does not retain moisture well. The slope of the district, from south to north, makes the rain water run into the *Tal*. In the post-Independence period with the development of power in rural areas electrically operated tube-wells have become a major source of irrigation. Analysis of irrigation in the district is given in table-50.

Table 50
Irrigation in the district Source: DAO Office, Biharsharif, Nalanda

Irrigation	*Area ('000 ha)*
Not irrigated area	93.5
Gross irrigated area	134.1
Rainfed area	97.5

Sources of irrigation available in the district are given in table-51.

Table 51
Sources of irrigation available in the district, Source: DAO Office, Biharsharif, Nalanda

Sources of irrigation	*Number*	*Area ('000 ha)*	*% of total irrigated area*
Canals		10.4	11.1
Tanks		01.2	01.2
Open wells		50.8	54.4
Bore wells		31.1	33.4
Pump sets	30172		
Total irrigated area		107.296	100

Hill areas and Water Resources

There are five hills in Rajgir named-*Vaibhara, Pandava, Vepulla, Griddhakuta and Rishigiri* (Pandey.1963:35). *Panchane, Paimar, Jirayan, Sakri, Mohane, and Dhoba* are the main rivers of this district which are basically seasonal rivers and are fed by rains during monsoon and join the *Ganga* as tributaries.

Mineral Resources

The only commercial minerals found in the district are sand of the rivers and stone-chips of Rajgir hills. Sulpher is also found in Rajgir hills but it is still waiting for its commercial use.

Demography of Nalanda district

Table 52
Source: Census of India, 2011, Nalanda

Total Population	*Male population*	*Female population*	*Male child (0-6)*	*Female child (0-6)*	*Sex ratio*	*Child Sex ratio*	*Literacy*	*Male literacy*	*Female literacy*
2872523	1495577	1376946	259703	241343	921	924	66.41%	77.11%	54.76%

Table 53
Population Ratio- 1: Rural, 2: Urban, Nalanda

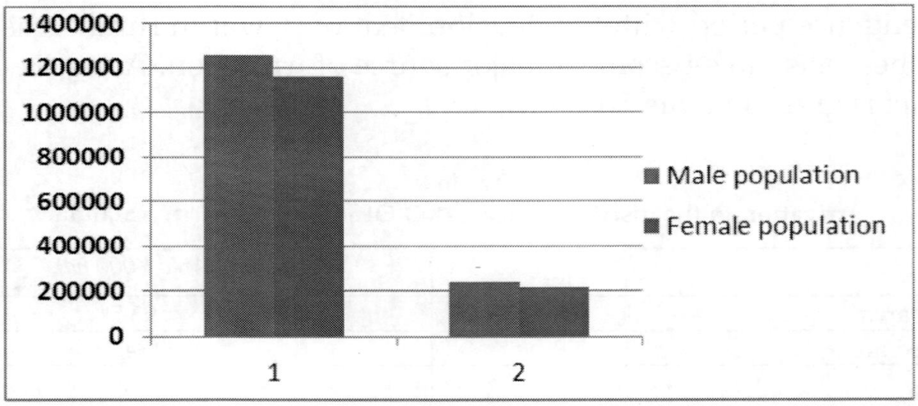

Table 54
Sex Ratio, Nalanda

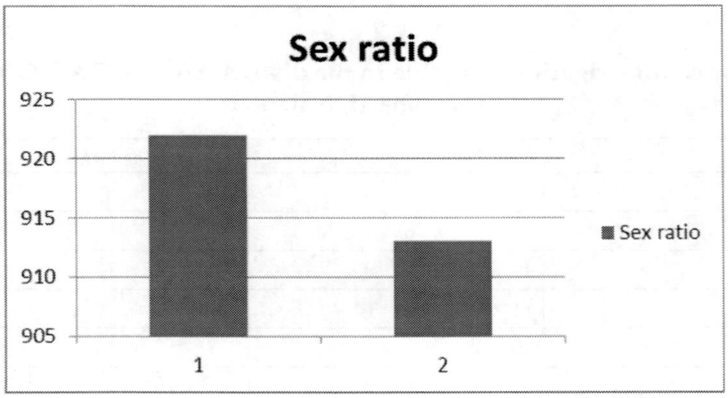

Table 55
Literacy Ratio, Nalanda

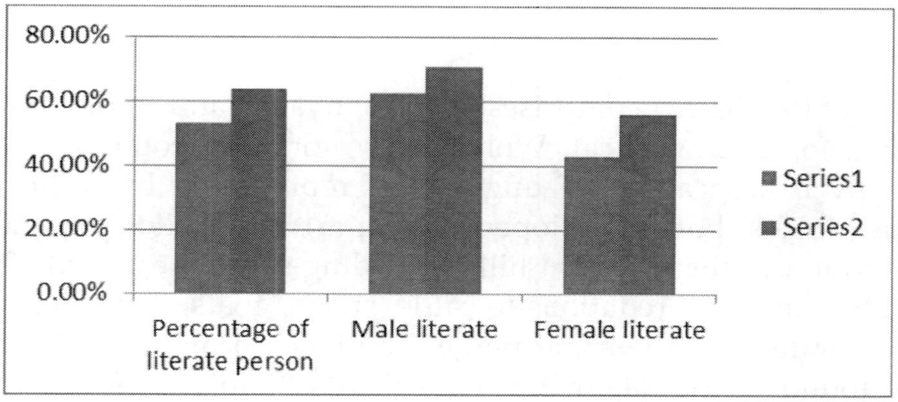

Flora

In the alluvial area of the district rice, wheat, pulses, sugarcane and a great ariety of other crops are extensively grown and the area not under cultivation is bare vor dotted over with clumps of bamboos and mango orchards. Farther from the river the country is more diversified, and sometimes a dry scrub forest is met with, of which the principal species are *glochidion* and other *euphorbiaceous shrubs, butea* and other *leguminous* trees, besides various examples of *ficus, schleichera, wendlandia, gmelina, wrightia, adina* and *stephegyne*. Throughout this tract the mango (mangifera indica), *pipal* (ficus religiosa) and banyan (ficus indica) are common. The other principal trees being the *bel* (aeglemarmelos), *neem* (melia azadirachta), *siris* (mimosa sirissa), jack-fruit (arlocarpus-integrifolia) and rerd cotton tree (bambaz malabaricum).

Except for some forests in the Rajgir hills the district is devoid of forest wealth of any consequence. The forests constitute less than 1 % of the total area of the district and the worst thing is that some afforestation work is still going on in the Rajgir hills. The tops of the hills and the rugged percipitious side are covered with a scrub-jungle interspersed with small trees like *Boswellia serrate, Cleistanthus collinus, Sterculia urens, Cassia fistula, Lannea coromandelina, Diospyros melanoxylon, Cochlospermum religiosum, Bridelia tomentosa, Cordia dichotoma,* and *Mitragyna parvifolia;*and shrubs like *Hamiltonia suaveclans, Securinaga virosa, Gardenia latifolia, Ficus lacor, Carissa pausinerva and Murrava paniculate;* with climbers like *Bridelia stipularis, Acaciacanscens, Zuzyphus oenoplia, Olax scandens* and *Ichnocarpus frutescens*. In the crevices of the rocks in the lower regions of the hills grow shrubby specimens of *Murraya paniculata, Dendrocalamus strictus, Acacia canescens, Nyclanthes arbortristis, Pavetia indica, Indigofera elliptica, Holarrhena antidysenterica, Heliceeres isora, Diospyros Montana, Carissa opaca* with scramblers like *Combrelum decandrum*, and *Acacia spp* and herbs like *Desmodium gangeticum, Anisochilus carnosus, Acrua Sanguino lenta, Waltheria indica, HibiscusMicranthus, Celosia argentea* and a few grasses. The vegetation of the valley is predominantly of the thorn-scrub forest type with *Dendrocalamus stricius*. With it are associated *Copparis zavlanica, Zizyphus mauritiana, Gymnosporia spinosa* and *Streblus asper*. These sgrubs grow in clumps separated from each other by coarse grasses, *Helicteres isara* and the irregular pathways.

Fauna

The carnivore of the district comprises leopard, hyaena and some smaller animals, such as jackal, fox and wild cat. Wolves were formerly common but they have now practically disappeared.The ungulate is represented by *nilgai* (bose'aphus tragocamelus), black buck (antilope cervicapra) and wild pig. Leopards are occasionally found in the southern hills extending south-westwards from Giriyak and they confine their depredations to cattle, sheep, goats, dogs and small ponies. Hyaenas are common in the same range. The black bear (ursus labiatus) is also occasionally found in the Rajgir hills.He subsists mainly on forest fruits; but he comes out into the level country at night to raid the maize and sugarcane crops, and to climb the toddy palms to drink *tādi*, fermenting in the pasis pots, or in the early hot weather, when the *mahua* flowers are falling, to feast on the freshly fallen flowers under thr trees. Wild pig is seen in this neighbourhood. *Nilgais* are common in the large *chars* and in the mango groves and among the high crops. Hares are numerous in the drier parts; jackals are common throughout the district; and porcupines and foxes are occasionally seen.

The game birds in the hills consist of pea-fowl, jungle-fowl, grey partridge, black partridge, and bush quail. In the plains grey quail, rain quail, and button quail make their appearance every year. Green pegeons are common and rock pegeons also visit the plains during harvest time. Red and yellow hilled geese, red headed pochard and white-eyed pochard, pintail and gadwall are found on the river beds and on the large tanks by the middle of the November. Besides these, the shoveller and Brahmani duck and different verieties of teal and comb duck visit the district. With them come the white and the black ibis, curlew, whimbrel, jack snipe, smaller snipe of six varieties, locally known as *batara, ghotra, bagodhia, surma, sarghai* and *bhurka*; golden plovers, and waders. Other cold-weather birds are the cranes locally known as *kurkura* (Anthropaedus Virgo), *kulung* (Grus communis), and various storks, the most noteworthy among them being a gigantic stork called lohaserang (Xenorphynohus asiaticus).

Rivers of the district contain a great number of edible fish, such as *buari, tengra, naini* and *rohu*. Fishing practically begins in October with the subsidence of the floods, and the busy season is from November to March, the largest hauls being made during December to February. Fish of all kinds and all sizes are caught, but the most valuable belong to the carp family, such as *rohu* and *katla*; rohu are caught up to the weight of 40 pounds. Crustaceous fish are common and prawns (jhingra) are caught in large numbers.

Among reptiles tortoises are common. Various species of snakes are found all over the district, cobra and *karait* being poisonous ones. Among the non-poisonous dhamin, dorwa and hurhura may be mentioned.

Previous Archaeological Investigations

Sir Alexander Cunningham, the first Director General of the Archaeological Survey of India visited the site in 1861 and identified it as old Nalanda on the basis of the travel accounts of Hiuen-tsang. Although Francis Buchanan had earlier seen the place in 1812, but he could not identify it. Regular excavations started in 1916 under the direction of Spooner and with the untiring efforts of Hirannda Shastri for two decades, the mighty majestic Nalanda resurfaced from the womb of earth.

The archaeological remains of Nalanda mahavihara lay some 11 kms north-west from Rajgir and the same distance to the south-west of Bihar Sharif, the headquarter of the district Nalanda. It is 3 kms away from the Nalanda Railway Station and 88 Kms south-east of Patna, the metropolis of the Bihar state. Its latitude is 25^0 8′ N. and the longitude is 85^0 27′ E. (Kumar.1970:646-647). Historians and archaeologists identified this place with a modern village named Badagaon at Nalanda (Cunningham.2006:468). The term Badagaon has been taken as a corrupt form of *Viharagrama* (Dave.1967:136).

Archaeological investigations at Nalanda has undertaken in various phases and periods. The archaeological sites in district-Nalanda have been extensively explored and excavated time to time. As a result, a large number of structures have been exposed. Most of these are in ruins but these structures even today, glorify the ancient seat of learning. The structures include dilapidated monasteries, temples, stupas and ancient avenues. Most of them belong to the Pala period *i.e.* 8th-12th centuries CE, but some structures belong even to pre-Pala period. Archaeological investigations done previously by the pioneers in the field such as Buchanan (1839), Kittoe, Cunningham (1871, 73, 80, 82 and 83) and Broadley (1872) are extremely important for the purpose.

Before Independence

First of all the site was surveyed, explored and partially excavated by Broadly and Cunningham. In course of explorations, Cunningham discovered beautiful sculptures which were shifted to Indian Museum, Kolkata. Cunningham referred in his report that the remains of Badagaon consisted of numerous masses of brick ruins, the prominent of which was a row of lofty conical mounds running between north and south. These high mounds were considered as remains of a huge temple attached to Nalanda monastery.The systematic explorations and excavations of the site began in 1915-1916 by Spooner, but the task of excavations was continued thereafter by J.A. Pege and G.C.Chandra.

The great monastery of Nalanda covered an area of 1600 x 400 ft. This open space, most probably, served as the courtyard for the six smaller monasteries; also find reference in the travelogue of Hiuen-tsang. To the south of the monastery, there was a tank which is still there and known as *Giddhi Pokhar* (Cunningham.1935:30). Cunningham followed the travelogue of Hiuen-tsang and identified certain ruins accordingly. Cunningham detected a temple outside the western wall of the monastery. It was 53 ft in height and 65-70 ft in thickness near the top. Hiuen-tsang referred to this spot as a place where Buddha stayed for 3 months and explained the law for the benefit of the gods. This mound is also known as *Pumwa* mound, since it is situated in the east of *Pumwa* tank. Cunningham excavated the mound up to 17 ft and exposed a strait wall of a temple. He also discovered a small stupa to the south of the mound. This is the spot where a pious mendicant, from a far country performed *panchanga* in honour of Buddha (Cunningham. 1935:31). Cunningham found the ruins of a *stūpa* outside the western wall of the monastery close to a tank where Buddha was questioned by a hierarch on the topic of life and death. The highest and the largest mound was 200 ft in height originally and when it was discovered, it was still 60 ft from the surrounding area. It might be the same temple which was built by Baladitya and referred by Hiuen-tsang. An image of Buddha was installed in this temple (Cunningham.1935:32). The mound was subsequently excavated by Marshall (Cunningham.1935:33). The temple stood on a plinth 12 ft high above the level, forming a terrace 15 ft wide all around. The inner room was 20 ft square with an entrance hall on the east side. Fragments of sculptures were found in the entrance hall.

Cunningham found remains of several small stupas in dark blue stone of various sizes, ranging 10 to 30 ft in height in the north-east corner of the temple. The ornamental carvings on these stupas were in good order and many of them were very elaborate. The basement and the body of each stupa were built of separate stones and were joined together with iron for greater durability. Cunningham also discovered a temple in which an image of Avalokiteshvara was installed. There was a monastery built by Baladitya to the north of this temple which contained a statue of ascetic Buddha. About 2000 ft north of this monastery and to the east of *Suraj Pokhar* he discovered the ruin of a huge temple (Cunningham.1935:34). This may be the same temple where a lofty statue of Tara was once installed.

During 1915-16 explorations and excavations at Nalanda were done under the supervision of Spooner. Thereafter, the task of the excavations was taken up by Page except for a short period when Shastri took the charge of the operations. The conservation works of the ruins of Nalanda was first taken over by Page to identify each stratum very systematically which contributed to a large extent to unfold the cultural history of Nalanda.Under the supervision of Page, debris was cleared during which remains of early brick pavement and plastered platform were brought into light. Certain fragmentary remains were conserved and support was given to the old structures. In monastery no.-1, the exposed platform was found inset with the representations of *Kinnar* (ASI AR.1921-22:19). Spooner and Page also studied the layers of ashes, potsherds, heavy brick debris and natural earth-accumulation in order to record the events of fire and destruction and of the abandonment and subsequent reoccupations of the site. Further excavations were undertaken in monastery no.1 and 9 during 1922-23. Successive levels were identified and dated between 6th to 12th centuries CE. Images of Brahmanic and Buddhist deities were discovered during excavations which prove the presence of eclecticism among the people in the later medieval period which was further established by Hiuen-tsang' s reference to the study of the Vedas by the monks at Nalanda (*ASI AR*.1922-23:107). During this period, two very fine stone sculptures of the Buddha seated in *Bhumisparsha mudra* surrounded by scenes depicting the principal events of his life were discovered. A large number of seals and sealings, earthen pots and vases were discovered (*ASI AR*.1922-23:150). Page refers to the discovery of a Shaivite sculpture of this period. Another important discovery was a gaming die that suggests that the Buddhist were not altogether above the amusements of less austere humanity. Such materials were recovered from monasteries no. 1 and 1-A, as well as from many other Buddhist sites (*ASI AR*.1923-24:74). Page referred to the discovery of a group of a little votive *stūpas* and fragments of stupa pedestals in the annual report of 1924-25. A few of them were made of stone and were decorated with Buddha images in rows one above the other forming a specific pattern. For instance, while one row represents the Buddhas in *Bhumisparsha mudra*, the next row shows Buddha images in *Dhyana mudra* while a third one presents Buddha with *Abhaya mudra* and the fourth row depicts Buddha in *Dharmachakrapravartana mudra*. In a few little *stūpas* eight conventional life scenes of the Buddha are found to have been delineated in a succession of panels. Among the discovered stupas, four bear dedicatory inscriptions datable to 9th century CE. One of them has reference to the reign of Mahendrapaladeva, the Gurjara Pratihara king of Kannauj which proves that the said ruler must have extended his sway as far east as Magadha (Smith:1914:402). Discovery of an inscribed image of Hariti of the reign of king Devapaladeva (*ASI AR*.1924-25:135) and a female image holding a *vajra* identified as Vajra Tara were also reported (*ASI AR*.1924-25:136).

Excavation work was continued around the north-west and eastern portion of the site in 1926-27 which revealed a great flight of steps which was flanked by step walls profusely ornamented with the stucco images of Buddhas and Bodhisattvas. Apart from these an inscribed copper plate of king Devapaladeva was recovered from the ruins of the so called 3rd monastery. A metal image of Balarama inscribed with Devapala's name was also discovered from the same area. From site no. 4 another inscribed metal image identified as Tara was discovered. During excavations a bronze image of Bodhisattva seated on a lotus flower was discovered from site no.1. Another metal image of Vajrapani, seated in cross-legged posture has been also reported. A very interesting stone disc has been recovered from site no.1 on which an image of Kubera seated in the middle of a circle, surrounded by eight other Kuber figures in similar posture was depicted. A bronze figure of Avalokiteshvara was also found from the same site near Devapala monastery (*ASI AR*.1926-27:218-19).

During excavations of 1927-28 seven images including Buddha, Maitreya, Avalokiteshvara, Vajrapani and Vishnu were discovered from monastery site no.1. One of the Buddha images is complete with halo, seated in *Bhumisparsha mudra*; another is nearly complete but there is no back Stella; third one is shown seated in *Bhadrasana* in *Dharmachakrapravartana mudra* flanked by a male and female figure. Maitreya and Avalokiteshvara images are shown two handed; their right arm display *Varada* and left arm carry lotus stalks. The image of four handed Vishnu is in standing posture holding his usual attributes. Vajrapani is shown seated cross-legged holding a *vajra* in his left hand and *chauri* in the right hand. A stone image of Avalokiteshvara seated in *Lilasana* along with a large bronze image with detached head was discovered from monastery site no.6. A small image of Kubera is also reported from monastery no.1 (*ASI AR*.1927-28:160-61).Images of two four handed deities flanked by a lion and a bull at the foot were discovered from the same site. Two hands of these images are in *Varada* and *Abhaya mudra*; third one bearing a *Trishul* and a *Linga* on *Yoni* in the fourth hand. These images were identified as goddess Parvati. A small image of four handed Ganesha holding his usual attributes like axe, lotus etc. seated in *Lilasana* with his mount rat seen below his feet was discovered from the same area (*ASI AR*.1927-28:161).

While editing the excavation report of Nalanda during 1928-29, H.Hargreaves has reported about a bronze image of Buddha seated on a lotus in *Bhumisparsha mudra* discovered from monastery site no.4. Apart from this image, a seated bronze image of Avalokiteshvara, a standing bronze image of Tara, a seated bronze image of Kubera under an umbrella, an inscribed stone image of Buddha and a tiny seated image of Buddha were recovered from this stratum. A gold coin of Kumaragupta I was found below this stratum. During the period a few sculptures were yielded from monastery site no.7. Among them mention may be made of a bronze image of seated Kubera, a partially damaged stone panel showing the life scenes of Buddha and a fragment of an inscribed stone (*ASI AR*.1928-29: 144-45).

Kuraishi reported the discovery of a beautiful stone image found near the eastern side of the main shrine during 1929-30 (*ASI AR*.1929-30:136). Besides this, six bronze sculptures of Buddha and Bodhisattvas were recovered from the north-west corner of the site. A gilt image of Buddha in seated *Bhumisparsha mudra* on a lotus under a Bodhi tree was recovered. A small gilt figure of Buddha in the same posture was also found. Special mention may be made of an image of Buddha seated on a *Vishvapadma*, shaded by triple umbrella. Gilt figures of Tara, Avalokiteshvara, and Bodhisattva Padmapani seated in *Dhyan mudra* were also yielded from this period. A beautiful stone image of Avalokiteshvara was discovered from monastery no.8. A gilt image of Buddha in *Bhumisparsha mudra*, and an image of Bodhisattva Padmapani seated on *Vishvapadma* were discovered from monastery site no.1 (*ASI AR*.1929-30:201-02).

Excavations were continued during 1930-34 and the reports were prepared by Kuraishi and Chandra. During the period a large mound located to the north of site no.3 was excavated yielding stone slabs and column bases in front of a shrine. A few stucco images of Buddha and Kubera were also discovered from this area. From monastery site nos.10 and 11 and *Chaitya* site no.1, 12, 83 and 87 objects came out respectively. Mention may be made of the figures of Buddha, Bodhisattva, Tara, Vajrapani, Jambhala and Trailokyavijaya in different forms and attitudes discovered from these sites (*ASI AR*.1930-34:278). Among them an image of Simhnada Manjusri, a stone image of Revanta on a horse back attended by followers, a reclining female figure, a standing Buddha image in *Abhaya mudra* and a bronze figure of *Kinnara* holding a lute in his hands may needs special mention.

During 1934-35 excavations were done of monastery site no.11 yielding 87 images. Special mention may be made of a bronze figure of Mayadevi standing under an Ashoka tree, a bronze miniature stupa and a Buddha image, made partially in bronze and in stone (*ASI AR*.1934-35:40). During 1935-36 Chandra reported about four dozen antiquities recovered from site no.13. Among them 11 were stone images and a few in bronze. One of the bronze images shows seated Buddha on a lion throne in *Bhumisparsha mudra* (*ASI AR*.1935-36:51). The back of the image is found to be inscribed with the Buddhist creed. During this period a number of standing bronze Buddha figures were found, of which two were moulded in *Abhaya* and *Vrada mudra* respectively. During this period a beautiful bronze image of Tara with superb modeling and perfect finishing was also discovered (*ASI AR*.1935-36:51). Archaeological investigations done in the district before independenceis shown in Table 56:

Table 56
Showing Archaeological investigations done in district-Nalanda before independence

S. No.	*Year*	*Name of the site*	*Investigator*
1	1838	Nalanda	First reported by F.Buchanan
2	1861	Nalanda	Identified by A.Cunningham
3	1905-06	Rajgir	Archaeological Investigation by John Marshall
4	1913-14	Rajgir	Scientific clearance of Bimbisara Jail and Maniyar Math by V.H.Jackson
5	1915-1937	Excavation of Ancient Nalanda University ruins	1915-1916 to 1935-1936:Excavation conducted by A. Sunder, H. Sastri and Later on by J.R.Page

After Independence

After independence there have been certain very useful explorations in the region (Sharma 1987 and Tripathy 1998). During 1955-56 in course of a general clearance, a Jain sculpture of medieval period was found (*IAR*.1955-56:37). Excavations done during 1973-74 a large number of images were discovered belonging to the Pala period. Sculptures of Vishnu, Surya, Haragauri, Buddha, Tara, Marichi, Chaturmukha linga and Ganesha were discovered from the village of Badagaon located north to the ruins. Images of Avalokiteshvara, Buddha in *Bhumisparsha mudra,* Vishnu and Haragauri were discovered from the village of Surajpur adjacent to Badagaon. At Machchaldiha, just south to Badagaon, sculptures of Dhyani Buddha, Maitreya, Avalokiteshvara and Vishnu along with a few votive stupas were discovered. Sculptures of Buddha were also recovered from Mirchaiganj and Mohammadapur located north to Badagaon. A number of images including a crowned Buddha in *Bhumisparsha mudra,* a panel showing life-scenes of Buddha, tripal faced Marichi, Tara and Jambhala were discovered from Pachwara located south-west to Badagaon. A crowned Buddha image from Lodipur and a seated image of Avalokiteshvara from Tazubigha were also reported (*IAR*.1973-74:50). A number of beautiful sculptures including Uma-Maheshvara, Tara, Bodhisattva, Marichi etc. came to light during clearance of the eastern part of the Sarai mound of the ruins (*IAR*.1973-74:67).

An interesting inscription of 7th-8th century CE was discovered at Sarai mound during excavations of 1975-76 which referred to a bronze image of Buddha being installed by king Purnavarmana (*IAR*.1975-76:8). During this year a heavy stone slab probably used as a part of a door in the entrance of a temple, was recovered. A partially exposed stone pedestal of a garbhagriha revealed remnants of paintings in red, black and white pigments. This painting shows an unidentified seated person with one hand raised and a standing elephant (*IAR*.1975-76:9). The excavations also revealed stone votive stupas, Buddha images in *Bhumisparsha* and *Dharmachakra mudras* and a few other deities related to the Buddhist pantheon (*IAR*.1975-76:9).

Sporadic excavations were done after 1976 by the mid-eastern circle of Archaeological Survey of India. Mention may be made of a figure of Vagishvari sitting on a standing lion during excavations of 1981-82. During 1982-83 an image of Surya and a panel of Dhyani Buddha were exposed (*IAR*.1982-83:25). Archaeological investigations done in the district after independence are shown in Table 57:

Table 57
Showing Archaeological investigations done in district-Nalanda after independence

S. No.	*Year*	*Name of the site*	*Investigator*
1	1950	Excavation near the Cyclopean wall, Rajgir	A.Ghosh
2	1953-1955	Scientific clearance at Jivak Amarvan, Rajgir	D.R.Patil
3	1961-63	Rajgir	R.Singh
4	1974-1982	Excavations of Sarai mound at Ancient Nalanda University Ruins (Pl.I)	ASI
5	1999-2001	Excavation of *Stūpa* at Banganga,Rajgir (Pl II)	ASI
6	2001-2002	Excavation at Chandi Mau, Silao (Pls. III-VI)	ASI
7	2004-2005	Scientific clearance behind Temple No.3, Nalanda revealed temple on wheels at four corners – Gupta period (Pl.VII)	ASI
8	2006-2007	Excavation at Juafardih, Nalanda (Pls.VIII-XIII	ASI
9	2006-2007	Excavation at Begumpur, Nalanda	ASI
10	2008-2009	Excavation at Ghora Katora, Giriyak (Pls.XIV-XVI	ASI
11	2008-2009 & 2012-13	Excavation at Telhara, Ekangar Sarai Revealed *Tilādhak* Monastery (XVII-XVIII)	ASI
12.	2012-13	Village to village exploration in the district	Bythe author (BHU,Varanasi)

S. No.	*Year*	*Name of the site*	*Investigator*
13.	2013-14	Village to village exploration in the district	Bythe author (BHU,Varanasi)
14.	2014-15	Excavation at Rukhaegarh,Chandi,Nalanda	Bythe author (BHU,Varanasi)
15.	2015-16	Exploration in the peripherial area of Nalanda District	Bythe author (BHU,Varanasi)

Recent Archaeological Investigations

Since 1999 up to 2014 a few excavations were conducted by the Archaeological Survey of India and successfully revealed some architectural remains in the district like- Stupas and Votive Stupas, Temple-complex and Monasteries. A brief report is given below:

Stupas and Votive Stupas

Recently a few Stupas and Votive Stupas were discovered at Nalanda and its Vicinity. These were made of mud, bricks and terracotta also.

1999-2001

During 1999-2001 excavations were done at Banganga Valley, Rajgir, Nalanda in which a brick Stupa constructed in terrace -form was discovered.

2001-2002

In 2001-2002 excavations were done at Chandi Mau (Lat. 25^0 3′N, Long.85^0 30′ E). It is 10 km south-east of the ruins and about 8 km south-east of Silao on Bihar Sharif-Rajgir Road. The mound located to the south-east of the village is extended into 3 acres with an extant height of 6 mts. The excavations yielded Black and Red Ware pottery associated with NBP Ware and revealed remains of brick-built Buddhist temple and Votive Stupas. Besides these, Stone sculptures of Buddhist deities and Plaques, Sealings and Votive Stupas made of terracotta were also recovered. To the south of the village there is a temple containing a number of Buddhist and Brahmanic images of Gupta and Pala period.

2006-2007

The ancient mound of Juafardih (Lat.25^0 8′ N, Long.85^0 27′E) covering an area of 105x100 mts with an extant height of 15 mts is located 3 km south- west of the ruins of Nalanda and 15 km south-west of Bihar Sharif, the present headquarter of district-Nalanda and 93 km south-east of Patna, the capital of Bihar. The site is located on the ancient bed of the River *Paimar*. The river has shifted its course further west to a distance of 2.5 km from the site. A good no. of NBPW, Black Slipped Ware, Black-and-Red Ware, Grey Ware and Red Ware were found during exploration along with burnt bricks measuring 36x27x6 cm. Similar kind of ceramics had been recovered during excavation at Rajgir (Ghosh.1959:96). The site might have been associated with the ancient Nalanda Mahavihara.

In 2006-2007 excavations were held at Juafardih and Begumpur, Nalanda. A mud-stupa was exposed built during the NBPW phase at Juafardih. Apart of this pottery of NBPW, Black Slipped Ware, Black-and-Red Ware, Grey Ware and Red Ware along with terracotta, stone and iron objects were found during excavations. Copper and Silver coins are the other important recoveries. The most important contribution of Juafardih excavation is the early date for NBPW period supplied by Birbal Sahni Institute of Paleobotanical Research, Lucknow ranging from 1200-400 BC. It is interesting to bring forth that there are four C^{14}dates which have given early dates for NBPW levels (Saran *et.al.*2008:71).

Table 58
Showing C^{14}dates of NBPW Period of Juafardih excavation, 2006-07

Sl. No.	*Sample No./ Depth*	*Layer*	*B.S. No.*	*Age of the sample based on the value of half life 4470#30 years*	*Calibrated Age*
1.	3527,JFD-5/4.36 m	13	2705	3100+110 B.P.	1354 BC
2.	3528, JFD-3/2.25-2.28 m	8	2706	3010+90 BP	1259 BC
3.	3529,JFD-2/2.05 m	7	2707	3280+90 BP	1562 BC
4.	3525, JFD-6/2.7-3.26 m	6	2703	2850+80 BP	1002 BC
5.	3526, JFD-8/2.15m	8	2704	2740+100 BP	857 BC

During my exploration some Votive Stupas made of black stone were found on the surface from Karjara, Nanan and Tungi. A brief report is given below:

The village Karjara (Lat. 25^0 06′89″N, Long. 85^0 22′98″ E) is about 10 km west from the ruins of Nalanda and 21 km north- west from the district headquarter. The mound extended into 30x25 mts with an extant height of 5 mts is located to the west of the village yielding Red Ware, Red Slipped Ware, Black Ware and Black Slipped Ware. At Goraiya Sthan a few sculptures made of black basalt are kept, among them fragment of a Stupa made of black basalt is noticed. The River *Paimar* flows ½ km south to the village.

The village Nanan (Lat. 25^0 5′44″N, Long. 85^0 30′15″E) is situated about 3 km south-east of Kul-Bhadari, 7 km south-east from the ruins and 11 km south from Bihar Sharif. The mound located in the middle of the village is extended into 5 acres with an extant height of 1.5 mts scattered potsherds of Red Ware and Black Ware indicates its archaeological importance. Fragments of sculptures are kept at Goraiya Sthan (East of the village) and at Shiva temple, among them a Votive Stupa made of black basalt are noticed to the north of the village. A few medieval remains are also noticed. The name Nanan may be identified with ancient *Nalakagama*, where Sariputra was born and eventually passed away. The River *Panchane* flows 1 km east of the village.

The village Tungi (Lat. 25^0 10′13″N, Long. 85^0 32′24″E) is 16 km east from the ruins of Nalanda and 5 km south-east from the district headquarter of Bihar Sharif. There are two mounds to the south of the village covering an area of 100x70 mts with an extant height of 3 mts. Pot-sherds of Red Ware, Black Ware and Black Slipped Ware were recovered during exploration. A large number of fragments made of black stone are kept in the Sun temple, Thakurbari and Naga Sthan, among them a Votive Stupa made of black basalt is noticed. The River *Gordhoba* flows 1 km west to the village.

Temple

During 2004-2005 scientific clearance behind Temple No.3 of Nalanda ruins revealed temple on wheels at four corners of Gupta period.

Monasteries

Apart from Nalanda Mahavihara which was already identified and partly excavated, there were some other monasteries in the district. Recently ruins of *Tiladhak* Mahavihara were exposed at Telhara. The ancient *Odantapuri* Mahavihara is still unidentified.

Tiladhak Mahavihara

The ancient site of Telhara (Lat. $25^0$13′N, Long. $85^0$11′E) is 28 km west-northwest of the ruins and 4 km west of Ekangar Sarai on Ekangar Sarai-Jehanabad Road. A mound known as *Bilandi* is situated in the south-west of the village with an extant height of 7 mts. A number of Buddhist and Brahmanic images were found lying at various places of the village. Due to the archaeological importance of the site Cunningham was eager to excavate the site but his wish was not fulfilled.

It is indeed a great pleasure that the Archaeological Survey of India is now able to fulfill the task and since 2008 up to 2013 excavations were conducted at Telhara which revealed the ruins of *Tiladhak* Mahavihara which is mentioned in Xuan-Zang's travelogue. In one of the Nalanda seals the place is mentioned as *Tilakanda* Vihara (*MASI* 66:37). It was a great tantric seat.

Odantapuri Mahavihara

In the month of October, 2014 suddenly I came to know that some construction work is going on in Nalanda College Campus, Bihar Sharif, Nalanda and during digging by JCB a Stone wall along with Pot-sherds of Red and Black Ware along with a few stone sculptures were found. Immediately I rushed to the site and saw the human vandalism and reported to the DG, ASI with photographs.

To know the historical importance of Garh Par, Bihar Sharif, Nalanda where the Nalanda college is situated, one has to remember about ancient *Odantapuri* Mahavihara. This Mahavihara was the main center of Buddhist Tantric tradition. It is a great matter of sorrow that the ancient seats of wisdom like Nalanda and Vikramshila were already identified and excavated. Recently the *Tiladhak* Mahavihara mentioned above is also exposed but *Odantapuri* is still unidentified and its shrouded mystery is waiting to be solved. Historians suggest that it was situated whether on Badi Pahari or on Garh Par, both located in Bihar Sharif, the district headquarter of Nalanda. Keeping in mind this fact during my archaeological exploration (2012-14) in the district I had visited both the sites. At Badi Pahari a few structural remains of medieval period were noticed on the top of the hill. Any sign of pot-sherds or antiquity was not found. At Garh Par two small mounds are still remaining but both are highly occupied for residential purposes. Pot-sherds of Red Ware and a few terracotta antiquities were recovered from the surface. A wall made of Kushanan bricks was noticed in the section of a mound. Kushanan brick-bats were also found scattered on both of the mounds. Only trial trench may be taken. Keen interest of historians as well as archaeologists may be able to solve the mystery of the *Odantapuri* Mahavihara. It is interesting to know that the first Buddhist monastery of Tibet-the *Samye* monastery constructed during 8th century CE was the copy of the *Odantapuri* Mahavihara.

Apart of these findings in 2008-09 a few Palaeolithic tools and Microliths were also collected from Banganga Valley of Rajgir during exploration.The excavation at Ghorakatora done in 2008-09 had brought out a pre-NBPW horizon. Investigations done at Ghorakatora are shown in the table given below:

Table 59
Previous Archaeological Investigations at Ghorakatora

S.No.	*Year*	*Archaeological Investigations*
1	1811-12	Francis. Buchanan
2	1847	Kittoe
3	1861-62	A. Cunningham
4	1872	A. M. Broadley
5	1940	Declared protected Archaeological Site of National Importance by Central Government of India in 1940
6	1987	K.K.Sharma
7	2007	P.K.Mishra

B.K. Choudhary, Director, K.P. Jayaswal Research Institute, Patna has reported 52 sites of archaeological importance in and around Nalanda (Chaudhary.2008:91-101) which is shown in Table 60:

Table 60
Sites reported by B.K.Chaudhary in dist. Nalanda, *Puratattva*-38.

S.No.	*Name of the Site*	*Latitude*	*Longitude*
1.	Baragaon	25^{0}8'N.	85^{0}26'E.
2.	Begampur	25^{0}8'N	85^{0}26'E.
3.	Surajpur	25^{0}8'N	85^{0}26'E.
4.	Daman Khanda	25^{0}8'N	85^{0}26'E.

S.No.	*Name of the Site*	*Latitude*	*Longitude*
5.	Mustafapur	25°8'N	85°26'E.
6.	Nakphullichak	25°9'N	85°26'E.
7.	GajrajBigha	25°10'N	85°26'E.
8.	Machchaldiha	25°10'N	85°27'E.
9.	Paparnausa	25°10'N	85°26'E.
10.	Sarichack	25°7'N.	85°27'E.
11.	Maniyawan	25°8'N	85°29'E.
12.	Kool	25°6'N	85°27'E.
13.	Bhadari	25°6'N	85°28'E.
14.	Kapatia	25°8'N	85°27'E.
15.	Nona	25°7'N	85°27'E.
16.	Muzaffarpur	25°8'N	85°27'E.
17.	Jagdishpur	25°8'N	85°26'E.
18.	Saure	25°8'N	85°24'E.
19.	Kewaideeh	25°13'N	85°28'E.
20.	Parasi	25°17'N	85°30'E.
21.	Koraideeh	25°8'N	85°29'E.
22.	Dharahara	25°6'N	85°29'E.
23.	Nanan	25°6'N	85°31'E.
24.	Chandimau	25°3'N	85°30'E.
25.	Raitar	25°3'N	85°32'E.
26.	Nohsa	25°8'N	85°22'E.
27.	Atma	25°8'N	85°19'E.
28.	Bele	25°11'N	85°18'E.
29.	Jamuawan	25°11'N	85°17'E.
30.	Shankardeeh	25°14'N	85°21'E
31.	Pilichcha	25°14'N	85°21'E
32.	Khirauti	25°14'N	85°22'E
33.	Tulsi	25°21'N	85°25'E
34.	Jiyar	25°11'N	85°37'E
35.	Tetrawan	25°6'N	85°36'E
36.	Ghosrawan	25°6'N	85°34'E
37.	Mubarakpur	25°7'N	85°10'E
38.	Islampur	25°8'N	85°12'E
39.	Ichchaus	25°8'N	85°12'E
40.	Sanda	25°8'N	85°26'E
41.	Beswak	25°11'N	85°14'E
42.	Aungari	25°12'N	85°13'E
43.	Telhara	25°13'N	85°11'E
44.	Dumari	25°13'N	85°19'E
45.	Opa	25°13'N	85°18'E
46.	Kurtha	25°15'N	85°18'E
47.	Juniar	25°16'N	85°15'E
48.	Dhurgaon	25°14'N	85°15'E
49.	Chamhera	25°15'N	85°15'E
50.	Mandachcha	25°16'N	85°11'E
51.	Chandi	25°19'N	85°24'E
52.	Dayalpur	25°21'N	85°24'E

Choudhary claims that there are several sites in the region whose antiquity is as old as, or even earlier than, that of Juaferdih.

Nalanda has perhaps received the highest amount of scholastic attention till date than any other Archaeological site in India. The history of Nalanda remained shrouded with mystery for long and despite untiring efforts made during a century and half, several layers remain concealed. It must be admitted, however, that in spite of receiving so much of attention from the scholars, there are still certain areas of the culture of Nalanda that have not yet been properly attended.

Rukhaegarh Excavation: 2015-16

The ancient settlement of Rukhaegarh (Lat. 25^0 19′N, Long. 85^0 22′E) is located 29 km north to the ruins of ancient Nalanda Mahavihara and 26 km north-west from Bihar Sharif the district headquarters of Nalanda, Bihar. The village Rukhaegarh lies on the route from Rajgir to Patna, the present capital city of Bihar (Fig. 52). The distance between Nalanda to Patna is near about 90 kms; Rukhae is about 30 kms from the ruins of Nalanda, so it seems natural that the site was a halting-place for the Buddhist pilgrims. A number of fragments of Buddhist sculptures of Pala-Sena period made of black basalt were scattered at various places in the village.

The site is surrounded by three rivers *i.e. Nonai, Chiraiya and Mohane*. The river *Nonai* flows about 2 km west while the other two rivers flow 1 and 2 km east to the village respectively showing uniqueness of the site (Fig.7). There is a moat in the west of the mound. The site is not only extended in about 2x1 km of area, but its catchment area extends in about 4 kms having 16 villages including a number of sites having archaeological importance around the periphery of the river banks. The maximum height of the mound is about 10 meters (Pl.-CCXV).

The ancient settlement of Rukhaegarh is situated to the south of the village. During exploration in 2012-14 several brick walls were noticed in the section of the mound. It was observed that ancient bricks of the mound have been used in a number of modern houses. The people are rapidly destroying the cultural remains of the site. During exploration it has been noticed that half of the mound was cut by JCB and the soil was used to construct the new four-lane road. Before the site loses its archaeological significance, the author and his team members (Prof. R.N.Singh, Mr. A.K.Pandey, Mr. Amit Kumar and Mr.Pankaj Kumar) have decided to excavate the site with the kind approval of the Archaeological Survey of India; so was done in 2015-16 at the site.

Aims and objectives

1. To know the cultural sequence of the site.
2. Comparative study of ceramics and antiquities found during excavations with other sites of Lower Ganga plain
3. Find out the linkages of the site with the ancient Nalanda Mahavihara and other sites of the Region.
4. To know the settlement pattern of the site.

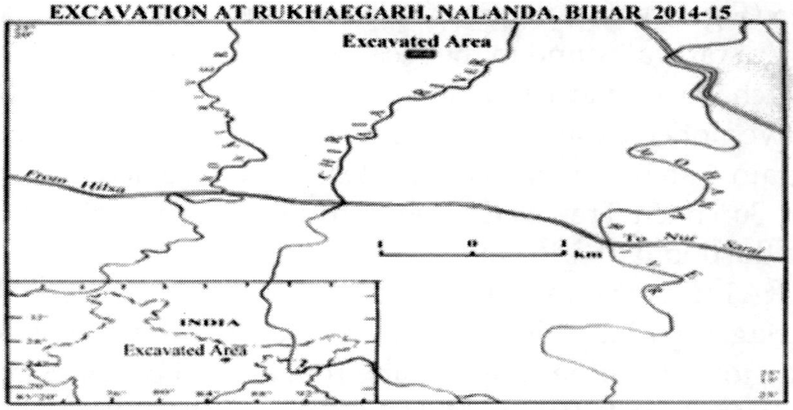

Figure 52: Excavated area of Rukhaegarh

The Cutting and Stratigraphy

We have measured coordinates of the main mound as. Lat. 25^0 19.566′ N, Long. 85^0 22.355′ E and height was 146′. But we could not lay out any trench at the top up of the mound because of modern settlements. However, we could excavate in the field just adjacent to the main mound where five vertical trenches *viz.* A1, E5, XA1, Y1 and Y2 measuring 3x3 meters were laid out for digging. Amongst them two trenches *viz.* Y1 and Y2 were found disturbed due to agricultural activities of the present inhabitants. We were able to reach up to the natural soil in the rest of the three trenches. In addition to the above, five section scraping were done in the western and southern part of the mound to know the complete cultural sequence of the mound.

In Trench A1, (Lat. 25^0 19.547′ N.; Long. 85^0 22.340′ E., elevation 118′,) the humus deposit was 35 cm thick because of recent agricultural activities. However, a rammed floor of pot-sherds and burnt clay plastered by fine riverine clay was traced at the depth of 45 cm. After cutting the floor we recovered NBPW sherds along with Red and Black slipped ware sherds. The percentage of NBPW is less than other associated wares. At the depth of 60 cm we found a pit on the slope which continued up to 1.29 m. After that we found a layer of 16 cm of mature NBPW; again 19 cm was disturbed and then we found a layer of 38 cm of Deluxe NBPW and finally the natural soil (Fig. 53).

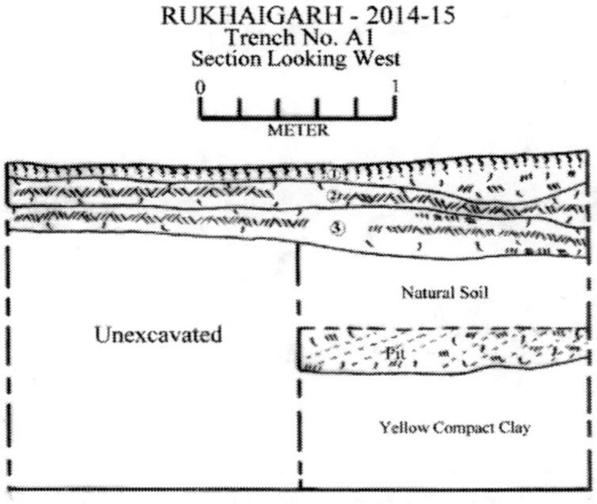

Figure 53: Trench no. A I

In Trench E5 (Fig. 54) after digging 7 cm of humus we found a 20 cm thick layer of Deluxe NBPW; a pit was found in the west corner. In order to recover some datable materials and archaeobotanical remains, wet floatation were done for the NBPW deposits. We have noticed some grains at the depth of 23 cm. In addition to AMS dating of the grains, archaeobotanical studies will be carried out by the specialist. At the depth of 30 cm in Trench E5, the natural soil was noticed but the digging continued up to the depth of 1.10 cm.

The Trench XA1 (Fig. 55) was laid down on the western slope of the mound, (Lat. 25⁰ 19.574′ N, Long. 85⁰ 22.283′ E, elevation 118′). This trench was found disturbed up to layer-4 due to water-pipe connection. From layer-5 potteries of Sunga-Kushan period were recovered while layers 6 and 7 belongs to NBPW period attested by the potteries of NBPW and associated wares. The people of the NBPW period were settled on the natural soil.

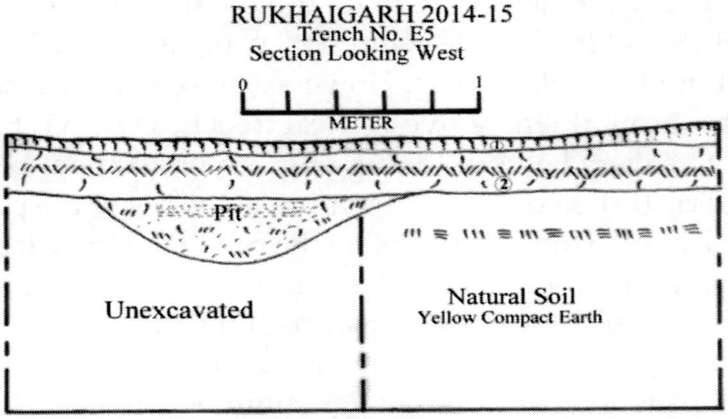

Figure 54: Trench no. E 5

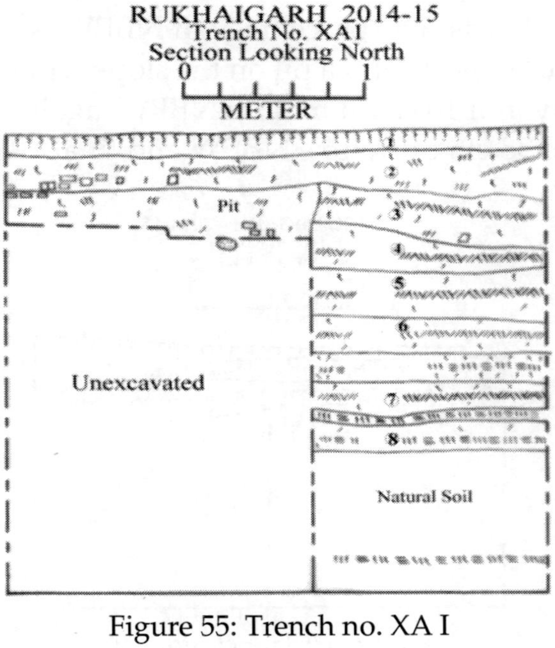

Figure 55: Trench no. XA I

In addition to excavations at five trenches mentioned above, section scraping were done at five localities in the western and southern part of the mound which exposed a Ring Well (just west to Trench A1) of Kushan period (Pl. CCXVI). The Ring well was dug up to the deposits of the NBPW level; two wells of Sunga period (one was exposed up to 17 courses to the south of Trench A1 with an extant height of 89 cm having diameter of 90 cm full of filling materials like ashes, pot-sherds and loose earth and other up to 37 courses just west to Trench. E5, diameter is 4 ft made of wedge-shaped burnt bricks measuring 23 cm in length and width is 20 and 16 cm respectively while thickness was 5 cm, sealed by 4 courses of Mauryan bricks measuring 48x28x5 cm) were also exposed (Pls. CCXVII-CCXVIII). In addition, 10 courses of Sunga-Kushan brick wall showing plan of five rooms along with another six courses of brick-wall measuring 52x30x5 cm was also recorded (Pl. CCXIX).

Cultural Sequence

The limited excavation brought to light four-fold cultural sequence *i.e.* from NBPW Culture to Early Medieval period without any break in between all of them. Period I is NBPW Culture; the cultural deposit of this period is 1.25 meter, which was recorded in trench nos. AI and XAI. Period II represents Sunga-Kushan period while Period III is Gupta-Post-Gupta and Period IV is Early Medieval period. All the four periods were characterized by their typical ceramic types and other antiquities. The features of these periods are described below:

Period I-NBPW Period

The deposit of earliest habitation was found in trenches E 5, A1 and XA 1 represented by 1.25 m of cultural deposit. The ceramics of this period comprises of deluxe quality of NBPW, Black slipped ware, Grey ware, Red ware, Red slipped ware and Cord-impressed red ware (Pl.CCXX). The other finds include a copper cast coin, beads of terracotta and bone.

Period II-Sunga-Kushan period

Remains of period II were recorded from trenches E 5, A1 and XA 1. This period is characterized by the absence of NBP ware. Black slipped ware and Red ware are the dominant ceramic industry of this period (Pl. CCXI-CCXXII). Structural remains were noticed by section-scraping in the western and southern parts of the mound. The structures have two phases *i.e.* Sunga and Kushan periods. Small finds of this period comprised copper and iron objects, terracotta beads, figurines and discs.

Period III-Gupta and post-Gupta period

Both slipped and unslipped variety of Red ware was recovered (Pl.CCXXIII). Among antiquities mention may be made of terracotta figurines, pestles, sling balls, beads etc. No structural activity was noticed in this period during section-scraping at five places.

Period IV-Early medieval period

The site continued to be occupied during early medieval period as well. Glazed pottery was recovered from the surface and a few copper coins of this period were also found and kept in the collection of Mr. Chandramauli Shukla who is presently residing on the mound.

Findings of the Excavation

The excavation yielded pot-sherds of Northern Black Polished Ware, Black Ware, Black Slipped Ware, Red Ware, Gray Ware and Glazed Ware along with 71 antiquities of copper, iron, bone, terracotta etc. Some structural activities were also noticed by scrapping on various places of the main mound. A brief description is given below:

The ceramic assemblage

The ceramic assemblage of Period I comprised of Black, Black slipped, Grey, Red slipped and NBP ware. The NBP ware has been recovered in different shades like black, silvery, golden and dark brown. Bowls and flanged bowls were found in majority. In Black slipped ware dishes are the principal type followed by knife edged bowls. The fabric and core of these vessels are very thin and light. The fine and medium fabric bowls, dishes, basins and vases have been recovered in Red ware. The common types are bowls with straight sides and inverted rim, knife edged bowls, dishes with incurved rim and sagger base and vases of varying sizes. In Grey ware, the pottery types of NBPW and Black slipped ware continues.

The pottery of Period II is Red, Black and a few course variety of Grey ware. In comparison to the pottery of period I, the ceramic industry has declined in the clay quality (fabric), surface treatment and firing. The important shapes are ink-pot and knobbed lids, sprinklers, bottle necked jars and pans with elongated loop handle and bowls with inverted rims.

The Period III is characterized by the occurrence of Red ware only. The application of lustrous red slip was also applied in the pottery of this period. Big sized vases, knobbed lids, large sized basins etc. are recovered from this period. Vases with out-turned long featureless rim and short concave neck and splayed out rim with expanding body are the other important shapes.The occurrence of glazed pottery from the surface suggests the existence of Period IV at the site.

The potteries are important assets for archaeologists to bridge the gaps in human cultural past. It is the key constituent of materials unearthed during excavations and helps us to define, distinguish, demarcate and delineate a culture. The ceramic assemblage of Rukhaegarh has been studied period wise.

Period I

The ceramic assemblage of period I comprised of Black, Black slipped, Grey, Red slipped and NBP ware. The NBP ware has been recovered in different colours like black, silvery, golden and dark brown. Bowls and straight sided bowls were found in majority. The fabric and core of these vessels are very thin and light. The fine and medium fabric bowls, dishes, basins and vases have been recovered in Red ware. The common types are bowls with straight sides, dishes with incurved rim and sagger base and vases of varying sizes. In Grey ware, the pottery types of NBPW and Black slipped ware continues.

Period II

The pottery of period II is Red, Black and a few course variety of Grey ware. In comparison to the pottery of period I, the ceramic industry has declined in the clay, surface treatment and firing. The important shapes are ink-pot and knobbed lids, sprinklers, bottle necked jars and pans with elongated loop handle and bowls with inverted rims.

Period III

This period is characterized by the occurrence of Red ware only. The application of lustrous red slip was also applied in the pottery of this period. Big sized vases, knobbed lids, large sized basins etc. are recovered from this period. Vases with out-turned long featureless rim and short concave neck and splayed out rim with expanding body are the other important shapes.

Period IV

Only glazed pottery was recovered from the surface.

Antiquities (Pls.CCXXIV-CCXXX)

A total of 71 antiquities were recovered from our limited excavations at Rukhaegarh. These included five copper objects including a copper coin, five iron objects, twelve beads including ten of terracotta and of bone and glass (one each), sling ball, wheel, gamesman, discs, terracotta figurines and other objects.

The excavation yielded five copper objects distributed in period I, II and III. They comprise a cast coin, an antimony Rod, a broken bangle, broken part of a bowl and an unidentified object due to heavy erosion. In addition to copper objects, five iron objects were recovered from period II and III; among them mentioned may be made of three Nails and one Chisel.

The limited excavation of Rukhaegarh yielded only twelve beads including ten made of terracotta. Bone and glass beads account only one specimen respectively; bone bead is spherical-shaped while glass bead is square in shape. Terracotta beads are *Ghata*, Areca nut and Cylindrical shaped and present in period II and III. *Ghata* shaped beads have been treated with bright red slip. They were fired under oxidizing conditions resulting in a red colour. Areca nut shaped beads are made of fine clay on a fast wheel and baked very hard at a high temperature. Perhaps these beads were fired in closed kilns under reducing condition, resulting in a black or smoky grey surface. The excavation yielded only two terracotta pendants which show exquisite craftsmanship. They are of circular and cylindrical in shape.

The excavation at the site yielded only one copper cast coin from the Trench XA I at the depth of- 1.05 m in Stratum- 5 from the upper level of NBPW Period. The coin is made of Copper, circular-shaped having a diameter of 1.3cm, its weight is 1.80 gram and thickness is 0.23 cm. Obverse of the coin showing Crescent on three arched hills. On the Reverse side of coin an elephant is depicted. This type of coins is reported from Mathura, Kaushambi and also from Pakkakot.

The terracotta figurines recovered during the present excavation consist of four human and six animal figurines from period I, II and III. They were hand modeled and in molded form too. Among human figurines three were male and only one is female. Animal figurines are of snake, dog and buffalo. Other figures are badly broken and their fragmentary remains do not permit correct identification. All the specimens are solid and represent the technique of hand-modeling.

Among other terracotta objects mentioned may be made of discs, hop-scotches, lamps, gamesman, wheels, dabbers, cones etc. The excavation yielded very few specimens of terracotta discs. They are only three in number. A single specimen of similar type was also reported from Kumrahar excavations. Hop-scotches are made of waste pieces of pottery and have a rough circular shape. Some of the hop-scotches have single perforation in the centre. All these specimens are distributed in period I, II and III.

The excavation also yielded nine sling-balls including one made of stone from period II and III. They are solid, hand made, well rounded and baked to red colour. They have been found in sizeable numbers from Kumrahar and Vaishali. These balls were made of medium to fine grained clay and baked hard in oxidizing condition. Majority of the specimens are in bright red colour. The present excavation yielded four specimens of terracotta wheels distributed in period II and III. Such wheels are quite common in this area and reported from Pataliputra, Kumrahar and Vaishali.

The excavation yielded two stone and one terracotta pestle from period II and III. Stone pestles are broken while terracotta pestle is intact and pecked by excising the clay with the help of some sharp instrument. One terracotta dabber was recovered from period III having a solid handle. Two broken bangles and one specimen of ring were recovered from period II and III. In additions, five cones and three gamesman of terracotta were recovered also from period II and III. They are handmade and black in colour. Similar antiquity has been reported from Kumrahar

Samples of grains were collected by flotation process. Animal bones were also collected during excavations. Analysis of these remains is under study.

Our limited excavation revealed that-the pre-NBPW culture might be the first to make effective colonization at the site since during explorations several Black and Red ware sherds were collected. However, we could not trace their cultural deposit in the excavations. The limited excavation brought to light a four-fold cultural sequence from NBPW to early medieval period without any break in between them. All the four periods were characterized by their typical ceramic industries and other antiquities. The structural remains show that during Sunga-Kushan period the site was fully developed and compelled us to think that there might be a Buddhist monastery but due to lack of funding we couldn't able to reveal it.

The unique geographical situation of the site considers us to think that it was possible for its inhabitants to have commercial links with other contemporary cities like Rajgriha, Nalanda and Pataliputra. The site might be destroyed by flood activity during pre-NBPW period because more than 2 meters sand-deposit was found after NBPW level up to the natural soil in trench nos. A1 and XA1; still the site is surrounded by three rivers *i.e. Nonai, Chiraiya* and *Mohane.* Recovery of a good number of bowls and flanged bowls of deluxe variety of NBPW show that these ceramics might be used by Buddhist monks for alms. Considering the location of the Rukhaegarh situated between Nalanda and Pataliputra, it seems natural that the site was a halting-place for the Buddhist pilgrims. A number of fragments of Buddhist sculptures of Pala-Sena period made of black basalt were scattered at various places in the village. Black and Red Ware pot-sherds were also found from the pit but not from a stratified layer. The horizontal excavations in future may be able to reveal a pre -NBPW level at the site.

Metal objects

Copper

The excavation yielded seven copper objects distributed in period II and III. They comprise an antimony Rod, broken bangles, rings etc. Some of the objects are not identifiable due to heavy erosion; hence these specimens are placed under the indeterminate category.

Iron

Only four iron objects were recovered from period II and III; among them mentioned may be made of Nails and a Sickle.

Coin

The antiquity of the use of coins in India has been a subject of controversy among historians and numismatists since a long time. It is beyond doubt that coins existed in India in 6th century BCE. The testimony of the early Buddhist literature, the *Ashtadhyayi* of Panini and other texts including the archaeological evidence for the Punch-marked coins prove it conclusively (Goyal.1967:87). The excavation at the site yielded only one cast copper coin from NBPW level.

Beads and Pendants

Beads and pendants of various raw materials are the important constituents of the assemblage of the antiquities recovered from any excavation. The limited excavation of Rukhaegarh yielded only twelve beads including ten made of terracotta. Bone and stone beads account only one specimen respectively; bone bead is spherical-shaped while stone bead is square in shape. Terracotta beads are *Ghata,* Areca nut and

Cylindrical shaped and present in period II and III. *Ghata* shaped beads have been treated with bright red slip. They were fired under oxidizing conditions resulting in a red colour. Areca nut shaped beads are made of fine clay on a fast wheel and baked very hard at a high temperature. Perhaps these beads were fired in closed kilns under reducing condition, resulting in a black or smoky grey surface. The excavation yielded only two terracotta pendants which show exquisite craftsmanship. They are circular and cylindrical in shape.

Terracotta objects

Terracotta Figurines

The terracotta figurines recovered during the present excavation consist of four human and six animal figurines from period I, II and III. They were hand modeled and in molded form too. Among human figurines three were male and only one is female. Animal figurines are of snake, dog and buffalo. Other figures are badly broken and their fragmentary remains do not permit correct identification. All the specimens are solid and represent the technique of hand-modeling.

Discs and Hop scotches

Among other terracotta objects mentioned may be made of discs, hop scotches, lamps, gamesman, wheels, dabbers, cones etc. The excavation yielded very few specimens of terracotta discs. They are only three in number. A single specimen is also reported from Kumrahar in Bihar. Hop scotches are made of waste pieces of pottery and have a roughly circular shape. Some of the hop scotches have single perforation in the centre. All these specimens are distributed in period I, II and III.

Terracotta and Stone Sling-balls

The present excavation yielded nine sling-balls including one made of stone from period II and III. They are solid, hand made, well rounded and baked to red colour. They have been found in sizeable numbers from Kumrahar and Vaishali in Bihar. These balls were made of medium to fine grained clay and baked hard in oxidizing condition. Majority of the specimens are in bright red colour.

Terracotta Wheel

It is a very common antiquity and reported from Pataliputra, Kumrahar and Vaishali in Bihar. The present excavation yielded four specimens distributed in period II and III.

Pestles and Dabbers

The excavation yielded two stone and one terracotta pestle from period II and III. Stone pestles are broken while terracotta pestle is intact and pecked by excising the clay with the help of some sharp instrument. One terracotta dabber was recovered from period III having a solid handle.

Bangles and Rings

Two broken bangles and one specimen of ring were recovered from period II and III.

Cones and gamesman

Five cones and three gamesman were recovered from period II and III. They are handmade and black in colour. Similar antiquity has been reported from Kumrahar (Altekar and Misra.1959:Pl.LXI).

Structural remains

Five section scraping were done in the western and southern part of the mound which exposed a Ring Well (just west to Trench no. A1) of Kushan period continued up to the NBPW level, two wells of Sunga period (one was exposed up to 17 courses to the south of Trench no. A1 with an extant height of 89 cm having diameter of 90 cm full of filling materials like ashes, pot-sherds and loose earth and other up to 37 courses just west to Trench no. E5, diameter is 4 ft made of wedge-shaped burnt bricks measuring 23 cm in length and width is 20 and 16 cm respectively while thickness was 5 cm, sealed by 4 courses of Mauryan bricks measuring 48x28x5 cm), 10 courses of Sunga-Kushan bricks showing plan of five rooms along with another six courses of brick-wall measuring 52x30x5 cm.

Floral and Faunal Remains

Samples of grains were collected by flotation process. Analysis of these remains is under study. Prof. P.P.Joglekar of the Deccan College of Archaeology, Pune is analyzing the samples of faunal remains.

Epilogue

Nalanda attained prominence as an important Mahayanist centre during the time of imperial Guptas. Pala art is preponderant here occupying the same remarkable position as held by Sarnatha and Mathura of the Gupta Age. The availability of carved bricks, pillars, gold coins, inscriptions, stuccos, fragments of grey sandstone-figures along with the names of those Gupta rulers, responsible for the construction of Nalanda Mahavihara as stated by Hiuen-tsang, are some of the definite archaeological evidences of the Gupta settlement of Nalanda. The extant remains of sculptures are very few in this period. During this period worship was purely a community type of ritual, used to be practiced by the worshippers in groups, that is why many images were not required, neither worship of images by individuals within the monastic cell was developed (Beal. 1973:39). Monasteries were also very few in the beginning. The non-availability of the suitable rocks in the nearby regions and craftsmen may be another reason for the absence of art center at Nalanda during Gupta era. The stuccos were most inexpensive material, used mostly in decorative purposes and even the colossal images within the sanctum sanctorum were also made of stuccos, as a result of which necessity of stone images were not felt by the devotees.

A remarkable change is marked in the later period which followed immediately after the Guptas. Due to the passage of time and the growing popularity of Mahayana Buddhism, worship of images by individuals became predominant, as a consequence of which a greater demand was felt in the society which paved the way for the establishment of independent Art centers like Nalanda, Kurkihar and Bodhgaya, during the Pala period. By imbibing tantric ideas and incorporating a number of deities, the Eastern Provinces created a vast pantheon of their own by freely incorporation into their pantheon several of the Brahmanic deities under different names and also with certain modifications.

A number of deities belonging to the regular Brahmanical pantheon was assimilated into Mahayanic worship viz. Saraswati, Ganesha and the Saptamatrikas. Brahmanic deities like Surya, Vishnu, Kubera etc., came to be incorporated into Buddhism as Marichi, Lokeshvara, and Jambhala etc. Heruka, Simhanada, Nilkantha and Vajrahunkara are but adaptations of the benign and the malignant aspect of Bhairava and Shiva. A comprehensive study of many of the Brahmanical icons and the corresponding group of Mahayana or Vajrayana Buddhist images will enable us to see the transference of the attributes of Indra to Vajrapani, of Brahma to Manjusri and of Vishnu to Avalokiteshvara etc. (Bhattacharyya.2008:141).

A few artistic works came in vogue at Nalanda in between the transition phase, *i.e.* the end of the Gupta period and the beginning of the Palas. The style and other decorative details show a stylistic affirmation with those of the Gupta workmanship on the one hand and a sharp regional feature manifest in the physiognomy style of drapery and ornaments concerned. It is problematic to determine their date because they were produced of grey sandstone in stead of black basalt in which almost all the inherent qualities of the Gupta workmanship are to be noticed. Excavations at Nalanda have yielded also coarse and lifeless images of Brahmanic and Buddhist pantheon which reveals untiring efforts of a group of local artists to model them in pursuance of the Gupta idiom (Patil. 1963:328). Such type of images was described by Banerjee in Eastern Indian School of Medieval Sculptures as pre-Pala in origin and cited examples from the collection of Indian Museum, Kolkata. The existence of such types of images definitely testifies the fact that a regular centre of art had already been established at Nalanda in the post-Gupta period. On the recovery of sculptural remains at Nalanda, Havell remarked-"the University of Nalanda was school of art and craft." The remark becomes true from the discovery of hundreds of sculptures in stone and bronze. It seems almost impossible to have so many sculptures without a regular school of arts and crafts. The Nalanda School of Art emerged as full-fledged Art School during Pala reign in Magadha and most of the creative workmanship on stones and bronzes falling within this era along with remarkable iconographic development.

The limited excavation at Rukhaegarh revealed that-

- During exploration I observed that the authors of the pre-NBPW culture might be the first to make effective colonization at the site. After excavation the settlement pattern of the site proved it. The limited excavation brought to light a four-fold cultural sequence from NBPW to early medieval period without any break in between them. All the four periods were characterized by their typical ceramic industries and other antiquities.

- The structural remains show that during Sunga-Kushan period the site was fully developed and compelled us to think that there might be a Buddhist monastery but due to limited excavation we couldn't able to reveal it.
- The unique geographical situation of the site considers us to think that it was possible for its inhabitants to have commercial links with other contemporary cities like Rajgriha, Nalanda and Pataliputra.
- The site might be destroyed by flood activity during pre-NBPW period because more than 2 mts sand-deposit was found after NBPW level up to the natural soil in trench nos. A1 and XA1; still the site is surrounded by three rivers *i.e. Nonai, Chiraiya* and *Mohane.*
- No weapons were recovered made by bone, stone or metal which shows that the inhabitants of the site have faith in non-violence. Iron objects recovered from the site are agricultural equipments.
- Recovery of a good number of bowls and flanged bowls of deluxe variety of NBPW show that these ceramics might be used by Buddhist monks for alms.
- The distance between Nalanda to Pataliputra is near about 90 kms; Rukhae is about 30 kms from the ruins of Nalanda, so it seems natural that the site was a halting-place for the Buddhist pilgrims. A number of fragments of Buddhist sculptures of Pala-Sena period made of black basalt were scattered at various places in the village.
- Black and Red Ware Pot-sherds were also found from the pit but not from a stratified layer. Horizontal excavation on broad level may be able to reveal a pre -NBPW horizon and also huge structural remains of Sunga-Kushan period.

Recent archaeological investigations done in the district compelled us to rethink about its antiquity. It seems that the settlement history of the area may go back earlier than the times of Buddha. The excavation at Juafardih done in 2006-07 and at Ghorakatora in 2008-09 had brought out a pre-NBPW horizon. It is interesting to note that apart from the findings of these two sites a few Palaeolithic tools and Microliths were also collected during exploration from Banganga Valley of Rajgir which opens the door of pre-historic research in the district.

References

Altekar. A. S. and V.K. Mishra. 1959. *Report on Kumrahar Excavation 1851-55.* Patna: K.P.Jayaswal Research Institute.

Beal, S. 1973. *The Life of Hiuen-tsang by Shaman Hwai Li.* New Delhi: Munshiram Manoharlal Publishers Pvt. Ltd.

Bhattacharya, Benoytosh. 2008. (Reprinted). *The Indian Buddhist Iconography*. New Delhi: Aryan Books International.

Goyal, S.R. 1967. *A History of the Imperial Guptas. Allahabad: Central Book Depot.*

Patil, D. R. 1963. *Antiquarian Remains of Bihar*. Patna: K.P.Jayaswal Research Institute.

Cunningham, A. 1935. *Ancient Geography of India*. Varanasi: Indological Book House.

Dave, J. H. 1967. *Immortal India* III.Bombay: Bharatiya Vidya Bhavan.

Kumar, N. 1970. *Bihar District Gazetteers*. Patna: Government opf Bihar.

Pandey, Mithila Sharan. 1963. *The Historical Geography and Topography of Bihar*. Delhi: Motilal Banarasidas.

9

Archaeological Exploration along the Panchakroshi Road, Varanasi: 2016-17

Varanasi and its adjacent area is located between the latitude 25^0 15′ 0″ N- 25^0 20′ 22″ N and longitude 82^0 56′ 44″ E- 83^0 4′ 10″ E. The area is located about 50 km north of the Vindhyan ranges demarcating the southern limit of the Ganga basin and forming the northern flank of the peripheral craton (Fig. 56). Varanasi city and its environs are located at an average height of about 76 m above the mean sea level and by and large have largely even topography with a low relief in kilometre scale undulations. The *Ganga* is the principal river of Varanasi flowing incised into its narrow valley from south to north direction. Geomorphologically the area is located in the Central Ganga basin of the Indian subcontinent. Its climate is tropical with a marked monsoonal effect. The area receives about 80 % of itsannual rainfall of 1020 mm from the south-west monsoon during the months of July-August. In summer the maximum temperature rises to 47^0 C and in winter the minimum temperature drops to 4^0 C with the average annual temperature being 24^0 C.

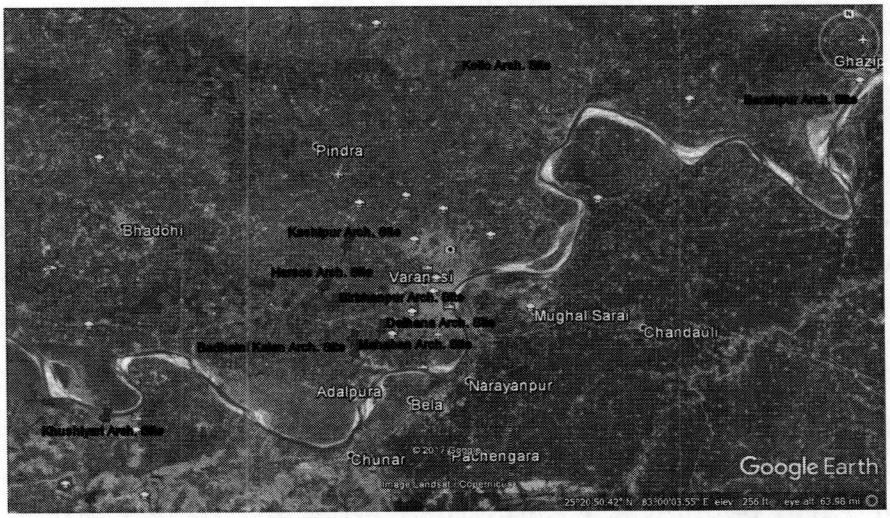

Figure 56: Satellite map of Varanasi and its vicinity

Historicity

The sacred city of Varanasi, the city of light, is a place of spiritual liberation. It is also said to be one of seven cities that bestow *moksha*, including Ayodhya, Mathura, Haridvar, Kanchi, Ujjain and Dvaraka. The city of Varanasi situated on the left bank of the River *Ganga* between the River *Varuna* on the North-East and the *Asi* on the South-West. It was the capital of the Kashi kingdom and was encompassed by the walls. It was one of the principal cities of the Central India or mid Ganga plain. According to Epic and Pauranic tradition, the said capital city was founded by Divodasa, one of the celebrated kings of Kashi, on the northern bank of the *Ganga* and the southern side of *Gomati* (*Mahabharata*.31, 15-17). *Mahabharata* says that the city had the semblance of Amravati of Indra. It is said to have been populated by the Brahmanas, Kshatrityas, Vaishyas and Shudras (*Mahabharata*.31, 16-18). The city is described in several Puranas (*Bhagvata* X, 66, 41; *Padma Purana* 35, 87). From both the Pauranic and Jataka records it appears that the city was known by different names in ancient times (*Vsshnu Purana*, V. 34,14, 21-40; *Brahmanda Purana*, 3,67, 26-62; *Jataka*, IV, 15, 119-20). Before the rise of Buddhism it had an extent of 12 leagues or Yojana i.e. about 85 miles (*Jataka*, VI, 160). The township actually grew in Buddha's time. Varanasi continued to be the capital of the kingdom of Kashi during the days of the Buddha. From Buddhist literature, both Pali and Sanskrit Buddhist texts, it distinctly appears that it was magnificent, extensive, prosperous and populous city at that time (*Digha Nikaya*, II, 220, 235; *Anguttara Nikaya*, I, 213; *Divyavadana*, 73; *Lalitavistara*,405-6). The city is frequently referred in the Jataka records where it is said to have been over 2000 miles in circuit (*Jataka*, 442). Many Jatakas testify to the unsurpassed glory of the city. In one of the Pali chronicles, Varanasi is included in eight principal capital cities of India (*Mhavamsa*. Comm., 67). The *Vinay Mahavagga* (X, 2, 3) also bears testimony to the former greatness and prosperity of the city which can be corroborated by the evidence furnished in the commentary on the Vinay (*Samantapasadika*, I, 201). There are abundant reference to the city in Buddhist sources as a great centre of both internal and external trade and commerce and indigenous industry. It had also a town-hall for the transaction of public business. It flourished as a political, commercial and religious centre. The city is also mentioned in the Jain Puranas (*Mahapurana*, 16, 151; *Hvarivansha Purana*, 3, 3; *Padma Purana*, 6,317). Panini also mentions the Kashi kingdom (IV, 2,116) and its capital Varanasi in a gana (IV, 2, 97). Ptolemy's *Kassida* has been equated with Kashi which is also used as a name for Varanasi. His Erarasa, a metropolis, has been identified by Saint Martin with capital Varanasi. But this identification seems to be of doubtful nature as it has not been supported by other scholars.

In the early 5th century CE, Varanasi was a flourishing city, as stated by Fa-hien. On the basis of an eye-witness account of Hiuen-tsang it can be further added that in the 7th century CE the capital city on the western side of Ganga was about 18 Li (3 miles) in length and from 5 to 6 Li (1 mile) in breadth. The inhabitants were very numerous and had boundless wealth. There were above 30 Buddhist monasteries with more than 3000 monks and above 100 temples with more than 10000 professed adherents' of the sects, the majority being devotees of Shiva. Within the capital there were 20 temples. They had towers of many stories and magnificent chapels built of stones elaborately carved and of wood richly painted.

Archaeological Excavations

The ancient city of Varanasi was situated on the place which is identical with the ruins of the fort of Rajghat. An extensive excavation was carried out at Rajghat first by A.K.Narain of the Banaras Hindu University in 1957 (*IAR* 1957-58:86) and then jointly by him and T.N. Roy in 1960-61 which revealed the various phases of settlement at the site. The most notable discovery was that of enormous clay rampart dating back to the earliest occupation of the site (*IAR* 1960-61:35-37). The dates assigned to the different periods of occupation at Rajghat are as follows:

Ia C. 800 BCE-600BCE.

Ib C. 600 BCE-400 BCE.

Ic C. 400 BCE-200 BCE.

II C.200 BCE to the beginning of the Christian era.

III From the beginning of the Christian era to C. 300 CE.

IV C. 300 CE-700 CE.

V C. 700 CE -1200 CE.

VI C. 1200 CE-1700 CE.

Further excavation was carried out in 1962-65 ((*IAR* 1963-64:16; 1964-65: 17). The archaeological evidence shows the earliest occupation of the site early in the 1st millennium BCE. D.L.Eck on the basis of the excavations carried out at the site in the mid 1960s also supports the view that the old city wall is datable to the 9th century BCE. The city was in the flourishing state in the Kushan period. By CE 300 it reached the zenith of progress. The uppermost phase of the settlement at the site could be dated to the 17th century CE. Recently the site was again excavated by B.R.Mani and Vidula Jayaswal whose report is awaited.

Apart from Rajghat Excavations were made at Aktha, Ramnagar and Shultankeshwar by Vidula Jayaswal but reports are still awaited.

Exploration: 2016-17

Noticing the archaeological importance of Varanasi and its Vicinity the author and his team including Prof. R.N. Singh, Mr. A. K. Pandey, Mr. Dhirendra Pratap Singh, Mr. Amit Ranjan and Mr. Bipin Kumar Singh has decided to do a village to village survey and document the remaining sites having archaeological importance with the kind permission of the Archaeological Survey of India. The exploration work was done during 2016-17 and a number of sites were discovered having archaeological importance.

Objectives

Prime objectives of our exploration in the region were documentation of archaeological sites in the area, comparative study of the ceramics and antiquities collected during exploration with other sites of the middle Ganga plain and find out the ancient trade-route.

Explored Sites

The exploration work carried out in Varanasi and its peripheral area by the author and his team during the month of March-April, 2017 had revealed a number of sites having archaeological importance, among them following sites were found very important:

Bhadaini Kalan (25⁰ 13′81″N, 82⁰ 52′43″ E)

The site is located 150 yards west to the road which leads to another site named Mahavan. It is extended in an area of 100x200 mts having a mound of 30x30 m whose height is 3.5 m from the surface. The shape of the mound is roundish while the top is flat. A section exposed by the villagers in the west shows a pit below 1.5 m along with potteries. Two broken glass bangles (yellow and green) were recovered from the exposed pit. Pot-sherds of Red Ware in different shapes were collected from the surface (Pl. CCXXXI). Agricultural practices are going on around the mound which will destroy the site very soon.

Barah (21⁰ 10′N, 82⁰ 23′ E)

It is approximately 18 km south-west to Gazipur and 58 km north-east to Varanasi located on the northern bank of River Gomati (Pl.CCXXXII). Pot-sherds of Red Ware, Black Slipped Ware and NBPW along with brick structure were noticed on the surface (Pl. CCXXXIII).

Birbhanpur (25⁰ 16′59″N, 82⁰ 51′ 43″E)

The site is located about ½ km north to the canal by crossing a small bridge covering ½ km of area (Pl.CCXXXIV). It is totally occupied by the villagers for agricultural purposes. The closest water resource is the canal and a pond. Another site named Harsos is 3 km north to the site. Pot-sherds of Red Ware, Black Slipped Ware and Gray Ware were collected from the surface (Pl. CCXXXV).

Delhana (25⁰ 14′93″N, 82⁰ 54′84″ E)

It is 50 m north from the road. The mound is 100X70 m having height of 2.5 m from the surface (Pl.CCXXXVI). Kushanan bricks and a few fragment of sculptures made of black basalt were noticed below a pipal tree. The mound is completely destroyed for the agricultural purposes. Pot-sherds of Red Ware were collected from the surface (Pl. CCXXXVII).

Harsos (25⁰ 18′24″N, 82⁰ 50′54″ E)

The site is located on the main road which goes from Raja Talab to Babatpur. This mound is extended into 300X200 m having height of 1 m from the surface. It is used for agricultural purposes. Pot-sherds of Red Ware were collected from the surface (Pl. CCXXXVIII).

Kashipur (25⁰ 15′16″N, 82⁰ 53′16″ E)

The site is located 50 m east to the Nandikeshwara Mahadeva temple on Panchkroshi Road. The mound covers an area of 150X50 m and its height is 2.5 m from the surface (Pl. CCXXXIX). The mound is fully encroached by the villagers. Pot-sherds of Red Ware along with a few broken TC animal figurines were collected from the surface (Pl. CCXL).

Khusiyari (25⁰ 14′25″N, 82⁰ 54′32″ E)

This intact mound is covering an area of 400X300 m having height of 2.5 m from the surface. A pond is located on the north and the site of Delhana is 3 km North-East to it. Pot-sherds of Red Ware, Gray Ware and Black Slipped Ware along with TC hopscotch were collected from the surface (Pls. CCXLI--CCXLIV).

Koilo (25⁰ 56′66″N 83⁰ 01′12″ E)

This site is located at Varanasi-Jaunpur border extended on more than half km (Pl. CCXLV). The River Gomati flows to the north of the site creating a narrow crescent. The height of the mound from the river bed is more than 12 m. During exploration Pot-sherds of BRW, NBPW, BW, BSW and RW were collected from the surface (Pls. CCXLVI-CCXLVIII).

Mahavan (25⁰ 13′71″N, 82⁰ 51′43″ E)

This large mound is extended in an area of 700X500 m having height of 1 m from the surroundings (Pl.CCXLIX). Kushanan bricks and a few fragment of sculptures made of black basalt are laying on the surface. Pot-sherds of Red Ware, Gray Ware and Black Slipped Ware were collected from the surface (Pl. CCL).

Apart from Varanasi the author explored few another sites on Varanasi-Chandauli border with his Research Scholar Mr.Sanjay Kumar Kushwaha who is presently Assistant Professor in a college affiliated to Allahabad University. A brief description is given in the table below:

Table 61
Archaeological sites on Varanasi-Chandauli border

S. No.	*Name of the Site*	*Location*	*Longitude/Latitude*	*Pottery*	*Other remains*	*Water resources*
1.	Anjania Baba (Derhgawana)Pl. CCLI	Tehsil-Sakaldiha, Dist. Chandauli	25⁰ 22′51″N. ; 83⁰ 19′34″ E.		Fragment of sculptures	

S. No.	*Name of the Site*	*Location*	*Longitude/Latitude*	*Pottery*	*Other remains*	*Water resources*
2.	Bhagvati Mai Kot (Saiyadraja) Pl. CCLII	Tehsil-Chandauli , Dist. Chandauli	25^{0} 15′29″N. ; 83^{0} 21′19″ E.	Red and Red Slipped Ware	Burnt-bricks	River *Karmanasha*
3.	Bhagvati Mai Kot (Dharahra) Pl. CCLIII	Tehsil-Sakaldiha, Dist. Chandauli	25^{0} 21′6″N. ; 83^{0} 15′22″ E.	Red and Red Slipped Ware	Structural remains	*Ban-Ganga* River
4.	Bhundadih (Onawal) Pl. CCLIV	Tehsil-Sakaldiha, Dist. Chandauli	25^{0} 21′49″N. ; 83^{0} 19′15″ E.	Red, Red Slipped and Black Slipped Ware	Ancient Well,Burnt-bricks	*Lehra-Manehra* Nala
5.	Devarapur Pl. CCLV- Pl. CCLVI	Tehsil-Sakaldiha, Dist. Chandauli	25^{0} 21′30″N. ; 83^{0} 15′29″ E.	Red and Red Slipped Ware	Burnt-bricks and Fragment of sculptures	*Suraj Kund* Pond
6.	Devarapur Kot	Tehsil-Sakaldiha, Dist. Chandauli	25^{0} 23′57″N. ; 83^{0} 15′29″ E.	Red and Red Slipped Ware	Burnt-bricks and Fragment of sculptures	*Suraj Kund* Pond
7.	Karjara Kot Pl. CCLVII	Tehsil-Chandauli , Dist. Chandauli	25^{0} 24′39″N. ; 83^{0} 6′39″ E.	Red, Red Slipped and Black Slipped Ware	Burnt-bricks and TC Pestle	River *Ganga*
8.	Keshavpur Pl. CCLVIII	Tehsil-Sakaldiha, Dist. Chandauli	25^{0} 24′39″N. ; 82^{0} 15′47″ E.	Red, Red Slipped and Black Ware	Ancient Well and structural remains	*Ban-Ganga* River
9.	Khandwari Kot Pl. CCLIX	Tehsil-Sakaldiha, Dist. Chandauli	25^{0} 24′40″N. ; 83^{0} 12′39″ E.	Red, Red Slipped and Black Slipped Ware	Ancient Well and structural remains	*Ganga* River
10.	Maheshi (Naul) Pl. CCLX- Pl. CCLXI	Tehsil-Sakaldiha, Dist. Chandauli	25^{0} 23′57″N. ; 83^{0} 17′52″ E.		Stone Sculptures	
11.	Manni Patti Chatti Pl. CCLXII	Tehsil-Chandauli, Dist. Chandauli	25^{0} 25′23″N. ; 83^{0} 26′52″ E.	Red, Red Slipped and Black Ware		*Ganga* River
12.	Misrapuram Pl. CCLXIII	Tehsil-Sakaldiha, Dist. Chandauli	25^{0} 21′6″N. ; 83^{0} 15′17″ E.	Red and Red Slipped Ware	Stone fragments	

S. No.	*Name of the Site*	*Location*	*Longitude/Latitude*	*Pottery*	*Other remains*	*Water resources*
13.	Prahladpur Kot	Tehsil-Chandauli , Dist. Chandauli	$25^0 26'24''$N. ; 83^0 27'17'' E.	Red, Black Slipped and NBP Ware	Ancient Well, structural remains and TC Objects	*Ganga* River
14.	Prahladpur Shivala	Tehsil-Chandauli , Dist. Chandauli	$25^0 26'41''$N. ; 83^0 27'3'' E.	Red and Black Slipped Ware	Structural remains and remains of ancient temple	*Ganga* River

An important site named Mundher (Pls. CCLXIV-CCLXX) was also explored in District-Chandauli wherefrom pot-sherds of RW, BW, NBP and associated wares alongwith a few terracotta and copper objects were collected from the surface. A few stone fragments of Brahmanic sculptures were also found on the surface.

Concluding remarks

A comparative study of pot-sherds and antiquities recovered from these sites shows that they may be ascribable from Chalcolithic to early medieval period. Sites of Mahavan and Koilon are very rich in the sense of archaeological potential. Horizontal excavations of both the sites may be able to throw light on various aspects and give a new dimension to the archaeology of mid Ganga plain.

References

Anguttar Nikaya I, 213.

Anusasana Parva, 31, 16-18.

Bhagvat Purana, X, 66, 41.

Brahmanda Purana, 3, 67, 26-62.

Digha Nikaya II, 220,235.

Divyavadana, 73.

Harivamsa Purana, 3, 3.

Indian Archaeology A Review 1957-58:86. Delhi: Archaeological Survey of India.

Indian Archaeological A Review 1960-61:35-37. Delhi: Archaeological Survey of India.

Indian Archaeological A Review 1963-64:16. Delhi: Archaeological Survey of India.

Indian Archaeological A Review 1964-65:17. Delhi: Archaeological Survey of India.

Jataka, IV, 15, 119-20.

Jataka VI, 160.

Lalitavistara, 405-6.

Mahabharata, Anusasana Parva, 31, 15-17.

Mahapurana, 16, 151.
Mahavamsa Commentary, 67.
Matsya Purana, 183, 62.
Padma Purana, 35, 87.
Samantapasadika I, 201.
Vishnu Purana, V, 34, 14, 21-40.

10

Archaeological Exploration at Sakas, Sasaram (Rohtas), Bihar: 2017-18

The Neolithic site of Sakas (24^0 54′ 10.46″ N, 83^0 56′45.00″ E) is located in the Kaimur hills of District Rohtas, Sasaram, Bihar.It is approximately 10 km South-West from Sasaram, 3 km West of the village Sikaria and 6 km South-East of the Neolithic settlement of Senuwar. The Kaimur hill ranges are further located 2-3 km South-East of the settlement. A small stream flows 2-3 km away from the site. It is a small low mound having an occupational deposit of 4 mts (Pl. CCLXXI). The site can be approached by Sasaram-Darigaon pitch road. The site was first reported by Birendra Pratap Singh, Department of AIHC & Archaeology, Banaras Hindu University while excavating the archaeological site of Senuwar (*IAR* 1985-86:12-14) and subsequently published by him (*Pragdhara*. 1996-97: 67-75; *Excavations at Senuwar*. 2004:1-9).

After the discovery of the Neolithic site Chirand in Bihar, it was desired to obtain details regarding the nature of the settlement and distribution pattern of sites particularly of the Neolithic-Chalcolithic phases in Bihar. The fieldwork done by Birendra Pratap Singh in the region revealed a number of Neolithic sites, like Senuwar, Sakas, Malaon, Badalgarh, Daindih Akorhi etc. Among these sites Senuwar was excavated horizontally by Birendra Pratap Singh.

To understand the nature of settlement, social systems and relationship between the inhabitants and the environment in the hinterland of Senuwar during Neolithic, Chalcolithic and NBPW periods and also evaluate the processes that occurred in the rise of urbanization in the region a reconnaissance survey was done by the author in association with Prof. R. N Singh, Dr. Vikas Kumar Singh, Mr. A.K.Pandey, Mr. Dhirendra Pratap Singh and Mr. Bipin Kumar Singh of the Department of AIHC & Archaeology, Banaras Hindu University in the month of April, 2017.

During exploration a good variety of pot-sherds along with a few antiquities were collected from the surface. Among antiquities mention may be made of two broken TC wheels, one bead of agate and one made of steatite along with one copper bangle (Pl. CCLXXII). Apart of these stone blades, scrappers and flakes along with some raw materials were also recovered (Pls.CCLXXIII-CCLXXVI). Among potteries mention may be made of Corded Red Ware, Corded Black and Red Ware, Red Ware, Black and Red Ware, Black Ware, Red Slipped Ware, Red Ware and Black and Red Ware with appliqué design, Burnished Red Slipped Ware, Red Slipped Ware, NBP Ware, Burnished Black and Red Ware, Burnished Black Ware and Burnished Red Ware. Main shapes of these potteries are bowl, vase, basin, lipped basin, beaker, beveled dish etc. (Pls.CCLXXVII-CCLXXIV). Surface finds suggests three distinct cultural periods, viz. Neolithic, Chalcolithic and NBPW culture. However, probability of Mesolithic deposit may be postulated because of recovery of a few microliths alongwith, cores and raw materials. The site appears to be small hamlet of Neolithic and Chalcolithic phase which was possibly reoccupied during the NBPW phase. The team has assessed that the site is ideal for horizontal excavations.

Since the surface finds of Sakas is very rich, we will discuss it in detail. Among surface finds pottery constituted the most prominent trait. Important features of the pottery associated with the respective cultural phases are discussed below:

Neolithic Culture

During exploration Burnished Red Ware, Cord Impressed Pottery, Rusticated Ware and Red Ware were collected from the surface which proves the Neolithic feature of the site.

Burnished Red Slipped Ware

The clay used to make this coarse pottery is not well levigated. It is heavily tempered with organic and mineral contents. The core is gritty and porous. It is either complete black or major portion of the pottery is black leaving a thin red zone on either side thereby suggesting that the firing was also insufficient. The ware is invariably slipped with thick paste ranging in shade from bright red to dark red and burnished in varying degrees. In few potteries burnishing is of high order and produces a gloss on the surface. Such vessels looks graceful which show even application of the slip. The thick paste applied on the vessels is mainly with a view to cover the coarse surface of the pots. In cases of bowls and other small sized pots it is noted both on the outside and the inside while on vases only on the outside. The ware occasionally shows blotchy surface. The fabric of the pottery is medium and thick.Fabric of varying sizes of bowls is medium while vases are thick.The shapes are same as found at Senuwar, Period I (Singh.1990:28-33). It included convex sided bowls with featureless rim, channeled bowl with faint traces of rim painting in ochre colour in post-firing condition, flat based pots, vases with flaring small rim, with long rim, basin with an out-curved rim and beveled dishes.

Corded BRW and Red Ware

This coarse ware is distinguished by bold cord impressions on the exterior of the pots. The cording strokes are vertical, slanting and horizontal. The clay used is not well levigated, heavily tempered with organic contents and ill-fired. The pottery is found without surface treatment and colour is dull red or mat red. A few numbers of sherds are found internally treated with red slip. The slip on the outer surface is noted up to rim or slightly below it and the remaining exterior is covered by cord marks. Main shapes are bowls and vases. Such pot-sherds are reported from Senuwar from the overlapping layers of IB and Period II which continue to occur in the latter period (Singh. 1977: 79).

Rusticated Ware

A few fragmentary sherds of rusticated ware have been collected from the surface of the site. This red ware is extremely coarse and crude in fabric. The exterior is roughened by a coarse grained paste. This ware shows remarkable identity with those recovered from Senuwar Period I (Singh.1977:79).

Red Ware

This coarse pottery is heavily tempered, ill fired and devoid of any surface treatment. Main shapes are vases with incurved rim, bowl lid with pinched lip, lid with pointed knob, with straight knob having flat top, flat based pot, convex sided bowl, lipped bowl etc. The shapes represented are those found in the corresponding level at Senuwar.

Chalcolithic Culture

The main ceramic assemblage of this period is Black and Red, Black Slipped and Red Wares.

Black and Red Ware

A good number of Black and Red Ware,both plain and paintedwere recovered from the site which may be divided into following groups:

- Topped black and red ware
- Highly burnishedand slipped on both the sides
- Internal surface is treated with bright black slip and external with thin red slip.

Main shapes are convex sided bowl showing multiple grooves externally near the rim, deep bowl, channeled bowl and basin.

Black Slipped and Red Wares

Black slipped is found in small number represented by sherds of medium fabric. Main shapes include dishes and bowls with convex and corrugated side.Among Red Ware important shapes are vase with flared rim and carinated neck, basins and perforated footed bowls.

NBPW Culture

It is represented by NBP Ware along with associated wares likeRed, Black Slipped and Grey Wares. Vases, dishes and bowls are the common shapes of the pottery.

Concluding Remarks

Location of the ancient settlement of Sakas was advantageous in many ways, viz., availability of vast alluvial plains facilitating agriculture, pastures for animals, stone for manufacturing tools and artifact, hunting, fishing etc. The Kaimur hills, overgrown with shrubs and trees, are an ideal home for games, variety of edible roots and fruits. R.S.Pappu in his study "Catchment Analysis" in relation to Senuwar suggested that settlement like Sakas was not only related to the parent settlement of Senuwar but was completely depended on that. He is of the view that "this was temporary seasonal settlement set up in such favourable place where it could carry out number of activities such as collection of wild plants, pastoral activity, hunting, artifact manufacturing etc., in the vicinity of raw material."

Our knowledge about the Neolithic pottery of mid Ganga plain is insufficient. The evidence obtained from Chirand, Taradih, Maner and Chechar-Kutubpur showed close resemblance and suggests widespread and long lived cultural facies. The ceramic assemblage and other cultural traits from Sakas as compared with the excavated materials of Senuwar, it showed the repetition of the same cultural sequence and close identity with the material remains of Neolithic, Chalcolithic and NBPW Culture. However, probability of Mesolithic deposit may be postulated because of recovery of a few microliths along with, cores and raw materials.

Reference

Pal, J.N. 1986. *Archaeology of Southern Uttar Pradesh: Ceramic Industries of Northern Vindhyas.* Allahbad.

Singh, Birendra Pratap. 1977. "Neolithic and Chalcolithic Pottery of the Middle Ganga Plains: A Case Study of Senuwar". *Ancient Ceramics Hisatorical Enquiries and Scientific Approaches* (Ed. Pant, P.C. and Vidula Jayaswal).

Singh, Birendra Pratap. 1990. "Early Farming Communities of Kaimur Foot-Hills". *Puratattva* 19. Delhi: Indian Archaeological Society.

Sinha, Bindeshwari Prasad. 1970. "Neolithic Culture in the Gangetic Valley." Paper presented at the International Congress of Orientalist held at Canbera.

Bibliography

Agrawal, V. S. 1965. *Studies in Indian Art*. Varanasi: Prithivi Prakashan.

Altekar, A. S. And V. K. Mishra. 1959, Reprint 2005. *Report on Kumrahar Excavations 1951-55*. Patna: K. P. Jayaswal Research Institute.

Anguttarnikāya. 1956. London: Pali Text Society

Anusasana Parva, 31.

Archaeological Survey of India Annual Review: 1921-22.

Archaeological Survey of India Annual Review: 1922-23

Archaeological Survey of India Annual Review: 1923-24

Archaeological Survey of India Annual Review: 1924-25

Archaeological Survey of India Annual Review: 1926-27

Archaeological Survey of India Annual Review: 1927-28

Archaeological Survey of India Annual Review: 1928-29

Archaeological Survey of India Annual Review: 1929-30

Archaeological Survey of India Annual Review: 1930-34

Archaeological Survey of India Annual Review: 1934-35

Archaeological Survey of India Annual Review: 1935-36

Arita, K. *et al*. 1982. "Geology and Structure of the Pokhara-Piuthan Area, Central Nepal", *Journal of Nepal Geological Society* 2 (Special Issue).

Asher, F. M. 1980. *The Art of Eastern India*. Minnesota.

Banarjee, R. D. 1933. *The Age of the Imperial Guptas*. Varanasi: Banaras Hindu University.

Banerjee, K. D. 1987. "Stone Age Migrations in India. " *Archaeology and History*. Edited by D. P. Chattopadhyay. New Delhi.

Banerjee, N. R. 1959. "The Technique of Manufacture of Stone Beads in Ancient Ujjain. "*Journal of the Asiatic Society* 1 (2). Calcutta.

Beal, S. 1973. *The Life of Hiuen-tsang by Shaman Hwai Li*. New Delhi: Munshiram Manoharlal Publishers Pvt. Ltd.

Bhagvat Purana, X, 66, 41.

Bhattacharya, Benoytosh. 1949. *Nishpannayogavali of Mahapandita Abhayakargupta*. Baroda: Oriental Institute.

Bhattacharyya, Benoytosh. 2008 (Reprinted). *The Indian Buddhist Iconography,* New Delhi: Aryan Books International.

Bhattasali, N. K. 1929. *Iconography of Buddhist and Brahmanic Sculptures in the Dacca Museum.* Cambridge.

Brahmanda Purana, 3, 67, 26-62.

Brown, Coggin J. 1909. *Journal of Asiatic Society of Bengal* . New Series V.

CBAE 1956

Chakrabarti, D. K. 2001. *Archaeological Geography of the Ganga Plain: The Lower and the Middle Ganga.* Delhi: Permanent Black.

Chakrabarti, D. K. , R. N. Singh, D. K. Lahiri and R. Tewari. 2006. "Further Thoughts on the Harappan Issue in Western UP: Sites in Saharanpur-Muzaffarnagar-Hartidwar Area. *South Asian Studies* 22.

Chatterji, B. R. 1933. *India and Java*. Calcutta: IJ.

Chaudhary, B. K. 2008. "Identifying the surroundings of Nalanda Mahavihara". *Puratattva* 38. Delhi: Indian Archaeological Society.

Chauley, 2002. *Art and Archiotecture of Nalanda.*

Chavannes, E. (Ed. & Tr.) *Memoire Religieux Eminents Par I-tsing.*

Coelho, V. H. 1970. *Sikkim and Bhutan*. Vikas Publications. New Delhi.

Coomaraswami, A. K. 1914. *Bronzes from Ceylon*. Colombo.

Cunningham, A. 1935. *Ancient Geography of India*. Varanasi:"Indological Book House.

Dave, J. H. 1967. *Immortal India III*. Bombay: Bharatiya Vidya Bhavan.

De, N. L. 1927 (2nd edition). *The Geographical Dictionary of Ancient and Medieval India*. London: Luzac and Company.

Digha Nikaya II, 220,235.

Divyavadana, 73.

Driesch, Von A. 1976. *A Guide to the Measurement of Animal Bones from Aechaeological Sites.* Cambridge, Massachusetts: Harvard University Press.

Dubey, S. R. (Ed.). 2012. *Methodology of Numismatic Study and History-Writing*. New Delhi: Research India Press.

Dubey, S. R. , A. K. Singh & G. K. Lama. 2010. Archaeological Investigation in Ballia District with special reference to Pakkakot. *Puratattva.* 40. Delhi: Indian Archaeological Society.

Dubey, S. R. , A. K. Singh & G. K. Lama. 2012. *Pakkakot: Some New Archaeological Dimensions of Mid-Ganga Plain*. Rishi Publications: New Delhi.

Dutta, B. N. (Tr.). 1944. *Mystic Tales of Lama Taranath.* Calcutta: Ram Krishna Vedanta Matha.

Epigraphica Indica II. Delhi: Archaeological Survey of India.

Epigraphica Indica XX. Delhi: Archaeological Survey of India.

Gaur, R. C. 1983. *Excavations at Atranjikhera-Early Civilization of the Upper Ganga Basin.* Delhi: Motilal Banarasidas.

Getty, A. 1978. *The Gods of Northern Buddhism*, New Delhi.

Ghosh, A. 1959 (4th edition). *Nalanda.* Delhi: Archaeological Survey of India.

Ghosh, A. (Ed.). 1989. *An Encyclopaedia of Indian Archaeology*. New Delhi: Munshiram Manoharlal.

Goyal, S. R. 1967. *A History of the Imperial Guptas. Allahabad: Central Book Depot.*

Goyal, S. R. 1995. *The Coinage of Ancient India*. Jodhpur.

Gupta, P. L. 1972. *Gangetic Valley Terracotta Art*. Varanasi.

Harivamsa Purana, 3, 3.

Huntington, S. L. 1984. *The Pala-Sena Schools of Sculptures*. Leiden.

Indian Archaeology A Review: 1955-56. Delhi: Archaeological Survey of India.

Indian Archaeological –A Review 1956-57. Delhi: Archaeological Survey of India.

Indian Archaeological –A Review 1957-58. Delhi: Archaeological Survey of India.

Indian Archaeology -A Review1958-59. Delhi: Archaeological Survey of India.

Indian Archaeological –A Review 1960-61. Delhi: Archaeological Survey of India.

Indian Archaeological-A Review 1963-64. Delhi: Archaeological Survey of India.

Indian Archaeological –A Review 1964-65. Delhi: Archaeological Survey of India.

Indian Archaeology -A Review: 1973-74. Delhi: Archaeological Survey of India.

Indian Archaeology- A Review: 1975-76. Delhi: Archaeological Survey of India.

Indian Archaeology -A Review: 1982-83. Delhi: Archaeological Survey of India.

Indian Historical Quaterly VI.

Indian Historical Quaterly IX.

Jataka, IV, 15.

Jataka VI, 160.

Joglekar. 2007-2008. "A Fresh Appraisal of the Animal-based Subsistence and Domestic Animals in the Ganga Valley. "*Pragdhara* 18.

Joshi, J. P. , M. Bala and J. Ram. 1984. "The Indian Civilization: Reconsideration on the basis of distribution maps. " *Frontiers of the Indus Civilization* (Eds.) B. B. Lal and S. P. Gupta. Delhi: Books & Books.

Journal of Bhandarkar Oriental Research Society IX

Kempers, A. J. B. 1933. *The Bronzes of Nalanda and Hindu-Javanese Art*. Leiden:E. J. Brill.

Kenoyer, J. M. 1986. "Indus Beads Industry: Contribution to Bead Technology. " *Ornament* 10 (1).

Korosi, A. C. 1957. *The Life and Teachings of Buddha*. Calcutta: Susil Gupta India Pvt. Ltd.

Kumar, B. 1978. "Bone and Ivories from Bihar. " *The Journal of the Bihar Puravid Parishad* II. Patna.

Kumar, N. 1970. *Bihar District Gazetteers*. Patna: Government of Bihar.

Lal, B. B. 1954-55. "Excavations at Hastinapur and Other Explorations in the Upper Ganga and Sutlej Basin-1950-52. " *Ancient India* 10-11.

Lalitavistara.

Legge, James. 1886. *Travels of Fahien.* Oxford.

Mackay, E. J. H. 1943. *Chanhudaro Excavations 1935-36.* Boston: Boston Museum of Fine Arts.

Mahabharata, Anusasana Parva, 31, 15-17.

Mahapurana, 16, 151.

Mahavamsa Commentary, 67.

Majjhimnikāya I. 1899. (Eds. Trenchner, V. and R. Chalmers). London: Pali Text Society

Majumdar, R. C. (Ed.). 1955. *The Age of Imperial Kanauj (History and Culture of Indian People)* Vol. IV. Bombay.

Mallasekhara, G. P. 1928. *Pali Literature in Ceylon.*

Matsya Purana, 183, 62.

Memoirs of Archaeological Survey of India 66. Delhi: Archaeological Survey of India.

Memoirs of Archaeological Survey of India. 1999. Delhi: Archaeological Survey of India.

Mishra, B. N. 1998. *Nalanda* in 3 Vols. Delhi: B. R. Publishing Corporation.

Mishra, P. K. 2008. *Archaeological Exploration in Sikkim.* Sundeep Prakashan. New Delhi.

Mishra, Parmanand (Ed.). 1986. *Uttar Pradesh District Gazetteers: Ballia.* Rampur: Govt. Press.

Mitra, Debala. 1972. *Excavations at Tilaurakot and Kodan and Explorations in the Nepalese Terai.* Kathmandu: Govt. of Nepal.

Mitra, Debala. 1982. *Bronzes from Bangladesh: A Study of Buddhist images from district Chittgaon.* Delhi: Agam Kala Prakashan.

Mitra, R. L. 1970 (Reprint). *The Sanskrit Buddhist Literature of Nepal*, Calcutta: Sanskrit Pustak Bhandar.

Mukherjee, Radha Kamal. 1959. *The Culture and Art of India.* London: George Allen amd Unwin Ltd.

Mukherjee, S. K. 1990. "Terracotta Figurines of the Kushan Period in the Gangetic Valley. " *Historical Archaeology of India* (Eds. Amita Ray and Samir Mukherjee) New Delhi.

Narain, A. K. and T. N. Roy. 1977. *Excavations at Rajghat, Part I.* Varanasi: Banaras Hindu University.

Narain, A. K. and P. Singh. 1979. *Excavations at Rajghat, Part III.* Varanasi: Banaras Hindu University.

Narain, A. K. and T. N. Roy. 1968. *The Excavations at Prahladpur.* Varanasi: Banaras Hindu University.

Padma Purana, 35, 87.

Pal, J. N. 1986. *Archaeology of Southern Uttar Pradesh: Ceramic Industries of Northern Vindhyas.* Allahbad.

Pal, Pratapaditya (Ed.). 1972. *Aspects of Indian Art.* Leiden

Pandey, Mithila Sharan. 1963. *The Historical Geography and Topography of Bihar.* Delhi: Motilal Banarasidas.

Pandey, R. N. 2008. *Nepal through the Ages*, New Delhi: Adroit Publishers.

Pathak, V. 1963. *History of Kosala up to the Rise of Mauryas*. Varanasi: Motilal Banarasidas.

Patil, D. R. 1963. *Antiquarian Remains From Bihar*. Patna:K. P. Jayaswal Research Institute.

Pott, P. H. 1951. Introduction *to the Tibetan Collection of the National Museum of Ethnology*. Leiden.

Rajan, K. 1990. "New Light on the Megalithic Culture of Kongu Region, Tamilnadu. " *Man & Environment* XV (1). Pune: Indian Society of Prehistoric and Quaternery Studies.

Rao, S. R. 1973. *Lothal and the Indus Civilization*. Bombay: Asia Publishing House.

Ray Chaudhury, H. C. (Ed.). 1931. *Dynastic History of Northern India*. Calcutta.

Ray Chaudhury, H. C. 1938 (4th edition). *Political History of Ancient India*. Calcutta.

Ray, Amita. 1984. "Secular Architecture of the Kushan Period. " Paper presented in the seminar of State Museum, Lucknow.

Risley, H. H. 2010 Rep. *The Gazetteer of Sikkim*. B. R. Publishing Corporation. New Delhi.

Sadek Kooros, H. 1975. "Intentional Fracturing of Bone: Description of Criteria. " Archaeological Studies (Ed. A. T. Clason). Amsterdam: North Holland Publication.

Samantapasadika I, 201.

Sankalia, H. D. 1972(2nd edition). *The University of Nalanda*. Delhi.

Sankalia, H. D. *et al*. 1960. *From History to Prehistory at Nevasa*. Poona.

Sankrityayan, Rahul. 1952. *Buddhacharya*. Sarnath: Mahabodhi Sabha.

Saran, S. C. *et al*. 2008. "Excavations of Juafardih and its identification with Kulika". *Puratattva* 38. Delhi: Indian Archaeological Society.

Shah, U. P. 1955. *Studies in the Jain Art*. Banaras.

Sharma, Arvind Kumar. 2012. *The Pala Art in Bihar*. Patna: Janaki Prakashan.

Sharma, G. R. , V. D. Misra, D. Mandal, B. B. Misra and J. N. Pal. 1980. *Beginning of Agriculture: From Hunting and Food-gathering to Domestication of Plants and Animals*. Allahabad: Abinash Prakashan.

Sharma, G. R. 1960. *The Excavations at Kausambi, 1957-58: The Defences and the Syenasiti of the Purushamedha*, Allahbad: Dept. of Ancient History Culture and Archaeology.

Sharma, T. C. 1980. *The Neolithic Pattern of India*. Paper presented at IAS and ISPQS at Allahabad.

Shinde, V. , Toshiki Osada, M. M. Sharma, Akinori Uesugi, T. Uno, H. Maemokui, P. Shivalkar, S. Deshpandey. 2008. "Exploration in the Ghaggar Basin and Excavations at Giradwad, Farmana (Rohtak) and Mitathal (Bhiwani district), Haryana. " *Linguistics, Archaeology and the Human Past* 3. Kyoto: RIHN.

Singh, A. K. and S. K. Singh. 1998. "Importance of a bead manufacturing workshop at Agiabir, Dist. Mirzapur, Uttar Pradesh. " *Bharati* 24. Varanasi: Dept. of Ancient Indian History Culture & Archaeoloogy, Banaras Hindu University.

Singh, B. P. 1977. "Neolithic and Chalcolithic Pottery of the Middle Ganga Plains: A Case Study of Senuwar". *Ancient Ceramics Hisatorical Enquiries and Scientific Approaches* Ed. Pant, P. C. and Vidula Jayaswal.

Singh, B. P. 1986. *Life in Ancient Varanasi: An Account Based on Archaeological Evidence*. New Delhi: Sundeep Prakashan.

Singh, B. P. 1987-88. "The Chalcolithic Culture of Southern Bihar as Revealed by the Explorations and Excavations in District Rohtas. " *Puratattva* 20. Delhi: Indian Archaeological Society.

Singh, B. P. 1990. "Early Farming Communities of Kaimur Foot-Hills". *Puratattva*19. Delhi: Indian Archaeological Society.

Singh, B. P. 1990-91. "Excavations at Khairadih. " *Journal of Bihar Puravid Parishad* IX-X. Patna.

Singh, P. 1993. "Archaeological Excavations at Imlidih Khurd-1992. " *Pragdhara* 3. Lucknow.

Singh, P. 1994. *Excavations at Narhan 1984-89*. New Delhi: B. R. Publishing Corporation.

Singh, P. 1996. "Prelude to Urbanization in the Saryupar Plain. " Presidential Address of the 57th Session of Indian History Congress. Chennai.

Singh, P. , A. K. Singh and Brahmanand Singh. 1994-95. Protohistoric Investigations in Ballia District, *Pragdhara*, No. 5.

Singh, P. and A. K. Singh. 1995-96. "Excavations at Waina, District Ballia. " *Pragdhara* 6. Lucknow.

Singh, P. , A. K. Singh and R. N. Singh. 1996-1997. Explorations along the *Chhoti Saryu* River, *Pragdhara*, No. 7.

Singh, P. and A. K. Singh. 2004. *Archaeology of Middle Ganga Plain, New Perspective (Excavations at Agiabir)*. New Delhi: Aryan Books International.

Singh, S. C. 1965. "Delimitation of the Middle Ganga Plain. " *The National Geographical Journal of India* XI (2). Varanasi: Banaras Hindu University.

Singh, S. C. 1973. "Changes in the Courses of Rivers and their Effects on Urban Settlements in the Middle Ganga Plain. " *The National Geographical Journal of India*. Varanasi: Banaras Hindu University.

Singh, S. K. 2000-2001. "Lithic Industry of Waina, District-Ballia (UP). " *Pragdhara* 11. Lucknow.

Singh, S. K. 2012. *Settlement Pattern Urban Growth and Craft Technology in North India-An Archaeological Perspective*. New Delhi: Research India Press.

Sinha, Bindeshwari Prasad. 1970. "Neolithic Culture in the Gangetic Valley. " Paper presented at the International Congress of Orientalist held at Canbera.

Sinha, K. K. 1967. *Excavations at Sravasti, 1959*. Varanasi: Banaras Hindu University.

Sinha, Kamini. *Early Bronzes of Bihar*.

Sircar, D. C. "The Kailan Copper Plate Inscription opf King Sridharan Rata of Samatata". *Indian Historical Quaterly* XXIII.

Smith, V. A. 1914. *Early History of India*. Oxford: Clerendon Press.

Tewari, Rakesh, R. K. Srivastava, K. S. Saraswat and K. K. Singh. 2002. "Excavations at Lahuradeva, Dist. Sant Kabir Nagar, Uttar Pradesh. " *Puratattva* 32. Delhi: Indian Archaeological Society.

Tewari, R. *et al.* 2002-03. "Preliminary Report of the Excavations at Lahuradeva, Dist. Sant Kabir Nagar, Uttar Pradesh-2001-02. " *Pragdhara* 13. Lucknow.

Tewari, R. *et al.* 2005. "Recently Excavated Sites in the Ganga Plain and North Vindhyas: Some Observations Regarding the Pre-Urban Content. " *Pragdhara* 15. Lucknow.

Thakur, Neena and Vidula Jayaswal. 1991. "Insights into the Utilization Pattern of Osteological Remains from Senuwar. " *Indian Archaeological Heritage* (Eds. C. Margabandhu et al, Vol. 1). Delhi.

Tosi, M. L. Bondioli & M. Vidale. 1984. "Craft Activity Areas and Survey at Mohenjo-daro. " *Interim Report* 1. Aschen, RWTH ISMEO.

Tripathi, V. *et al.* 2004. "Excavations at Anai (2004-05), District Varanasi, Uttar Pradesh: A Preliminary Report. " *Bharati* 29. Varanasi: Banaras Hindu University.

Vishnu Purana, V, 34, 14, 21-40.

Waddel, L. A. 1974. *Buddhism and Lamaism of Tibet*. New Delhi.

Walsh, E. H. G. 1904. A Note on stone implements in the Darjeeling district, *Journal of Asiatic society of Bengal* 3.

Waters, Thomas. 1988. *On Yuan Chwang's Travels in India* II.

Wheeler, R. E. I. , A Ghosh & Krishna Deva. 1946. "Arikamedu: An Indo-Roman Trading Station on the East Coast of India. "*Ancient India* 2.

Pl.I: Unfinished Harvester, Adampool Basti (East Sikkim)

Pl.II: Neolithic Celt, Aho (East Sikkim)

Pl.III: Neolithic Perforated Celt, Namche Bung (East Sikkim)

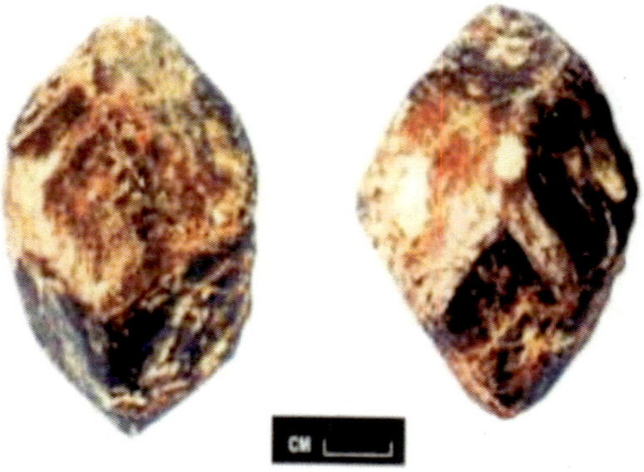

Pl.IV: Neolithic Unfinished Sling Ball, Penglong La (North Sikkim)

Pl. V: General view of the Neolithic site Phaungma, EastSikkim

Pl. VI: Close-up view of the Neolithic site Phaungma, East Sikkim

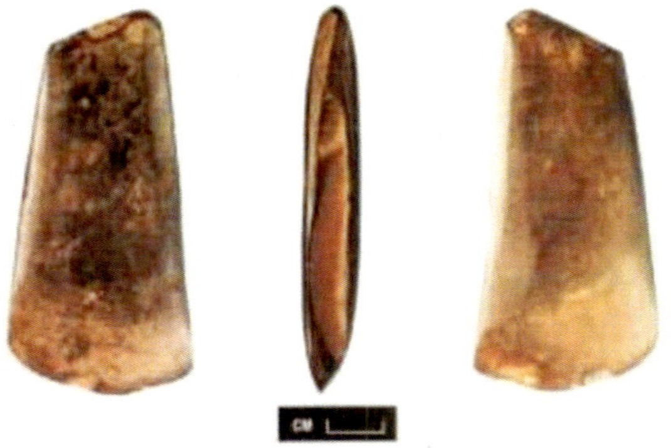

Pl.VII: Neolithic Axe, Phaungma (East Sikkim)

Pl.VIII: Neolithic Adze,RankaRaigaon(East Sikkim)

Pl.IX: Neolithic Celt, Sandur (East Sikkim)

Pl.X: Neolithic Adze, Sangkhola (East Sikkim)

Pl.XI: Neolithic Celt, Upper Sandur (East Sikkim)

Pl. XII: General View of the Alamgirpur Mound, Meerut

Pl. XIII: Mound of Bulandakhera, Gautam Buddha Nagar

Pl. XIV: General View of the Sirsalgarh Mound, Baghpat

Pl. XV: Mound of the Pakkakot

Pl. XVI: General view of the excavated trenches 1, 2, 3 and 4, Mound-2

Pl. XVII: General view of the excavated trenches 5, 7, and 8, Mound-2

Pl. XVIII: Burnt brick structures of Period III C

Pl. XIX: Burnt brick structures of Period IV

Pl. XX: Post-holes and furnace of Period III

Pl. XXI: Section of trench 6, Mound-2

Pl. XXII: Burnt brick structures of Period IV and V

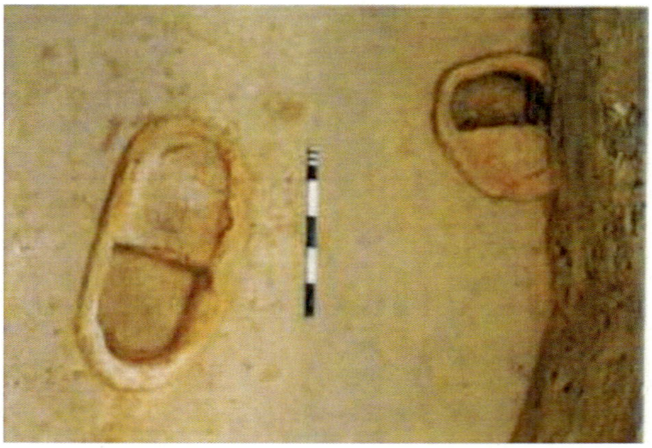

Pl. XXIII: Ovens of Period IV

Pl. XXIV: Section of trench 9, Mound-1

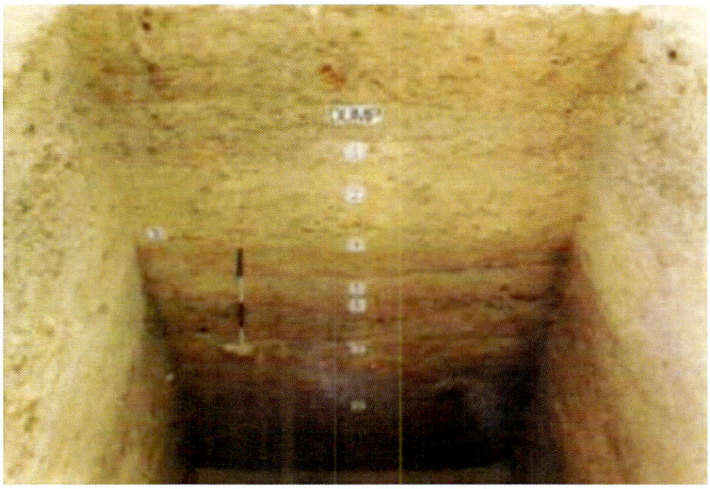

Pl. XXV: Section of trench 14, Mound-1

Pl. XXVI: A partly excavated terracotta Ring well of Period III

Pl. XXVII: Cord-impressed Red Ware, Period-I

Pl. XXVIII: Cord-impressed and Rusticated wares, Period-I

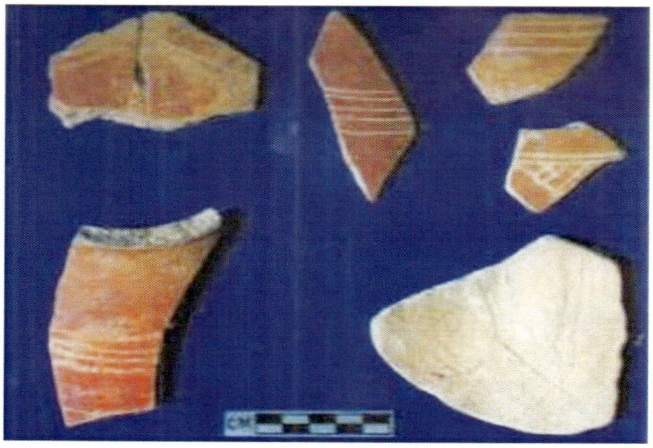

Pl. XXIX: Post-firing scratched pottery, Period-I

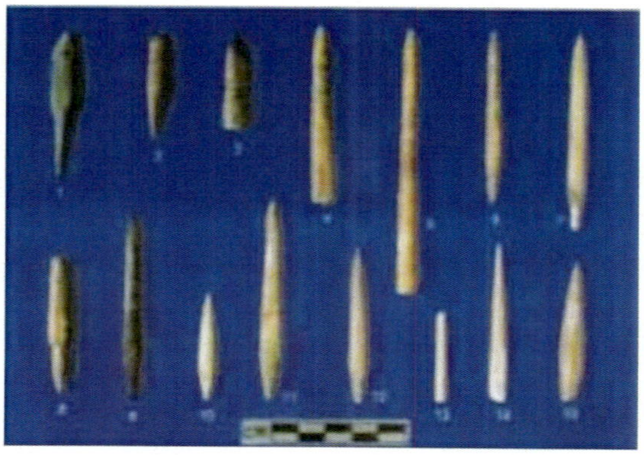

Pl. XXX: Bone-points and Arrowheads, Periods-I, II and III

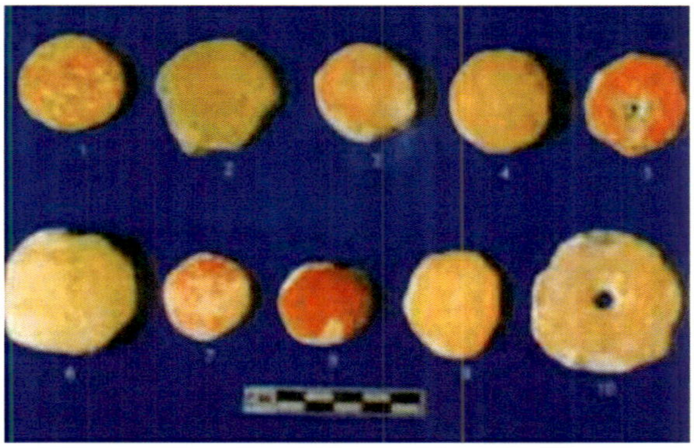

Pl. XXXI: Pottery discs, Period-I

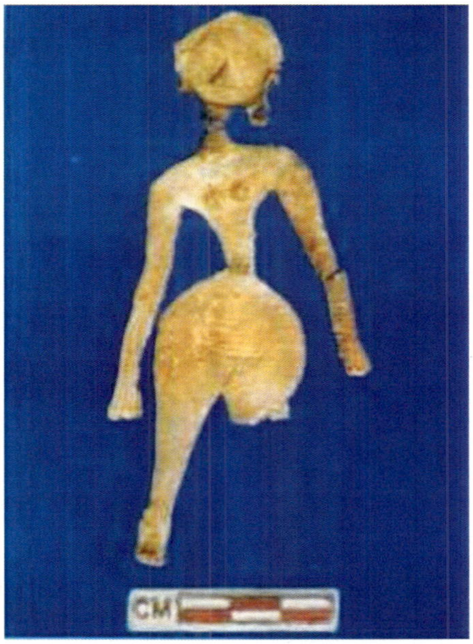

Pl. XXXII: Silver figurine, Period-III

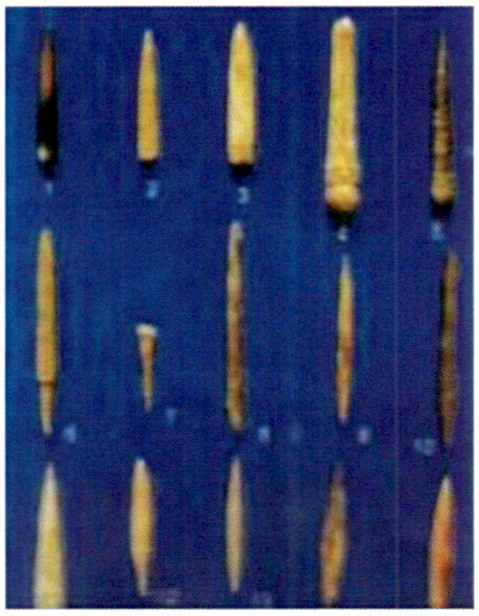

Pl. XXXIII: Bone-points and Arrowheads, Periods-III C

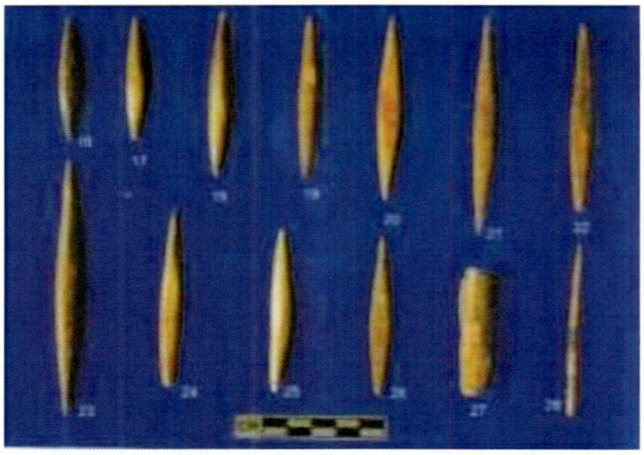

Pl. XXXIV: Bone-points and Arrowheads, Periods-III C

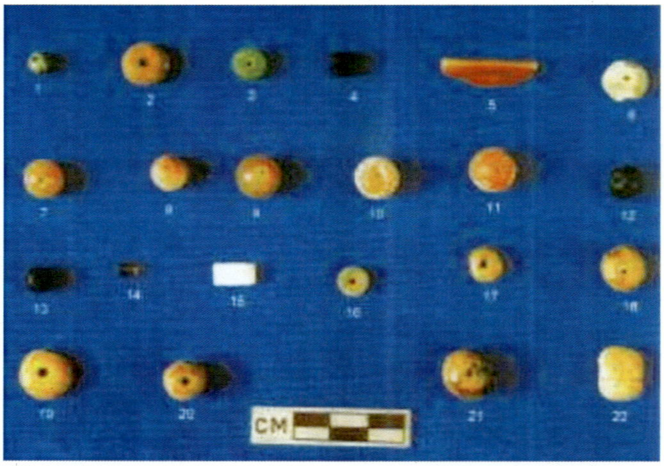

Pl. XXXV: Stone beads, Period-III

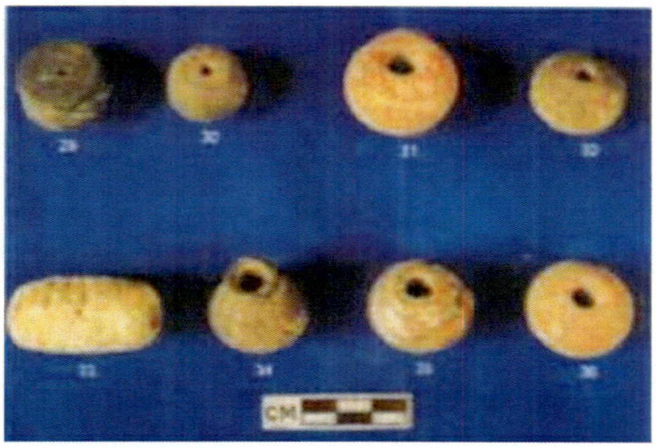

Pl. XXXVI: Terracotta beads, Period-III

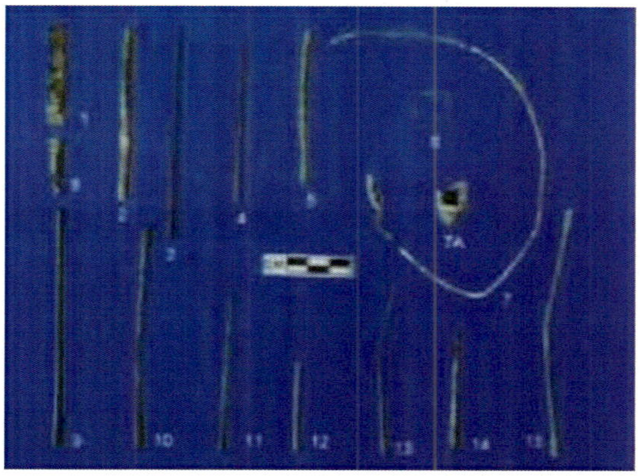

Pl. XXXVII: Copper objects, Period-III, IV and V

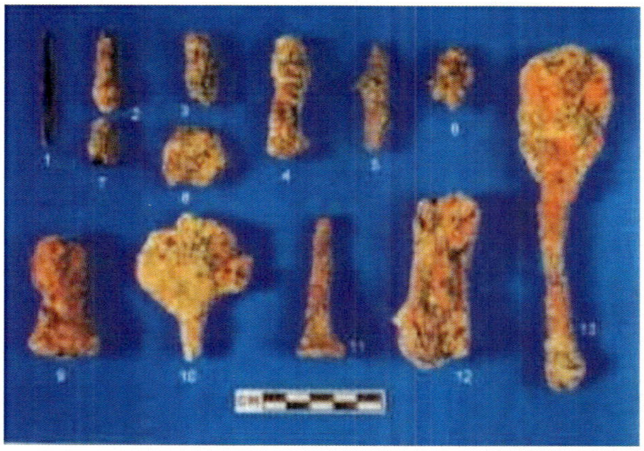

Pl. XXXVIII: Iron objects, Period-III

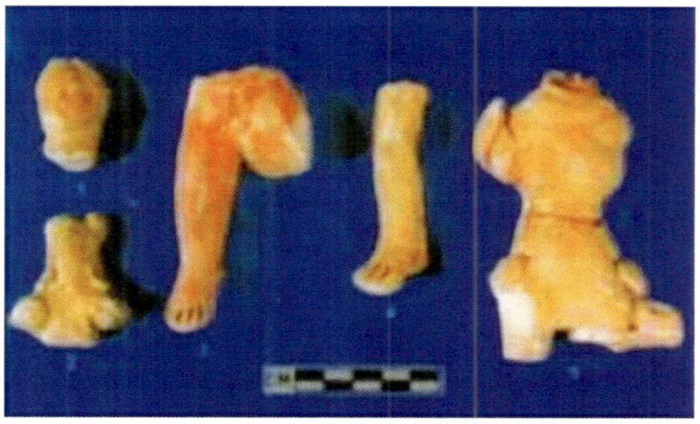

Pl.XXXIX: Terracotta Human figurines, Period-III

Pl.XL: Copper Punch-marked coins, Period-III (Obverse)

Pl.XLI: Copper Punch-marked coins, Period-III (Reverse)

Pl.XLII: Seals of copper and bone, Period-III and IV

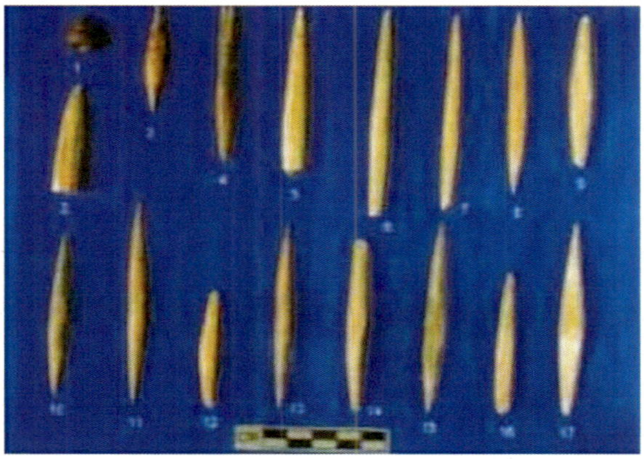

Pl. XLIII: Bone-points, Sharpener and Arrowheads, Periods-IV

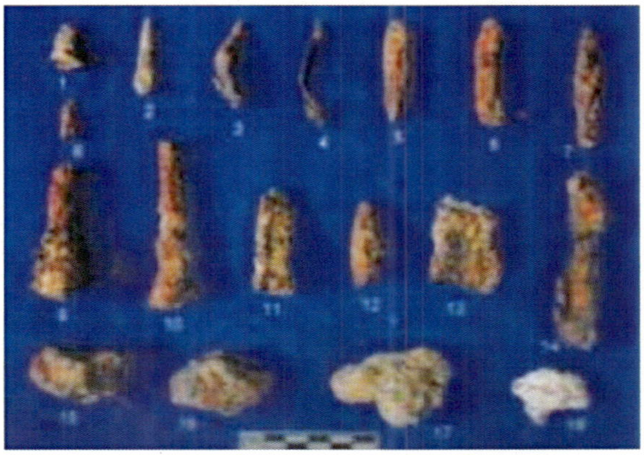

Pl. XLIV: Iron objects, Period-IV

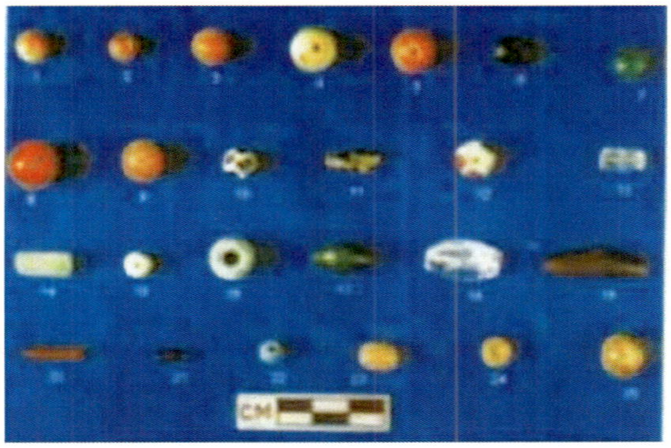

Pl. XLV: Stone beads, Period-IV

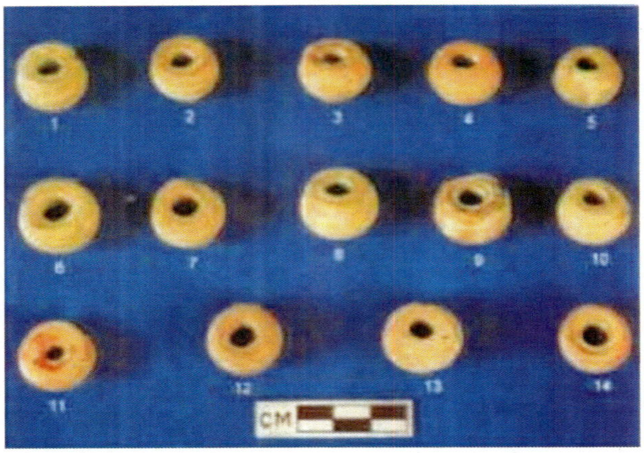

Pl. XLVI: Terracotta beads, Period-IV

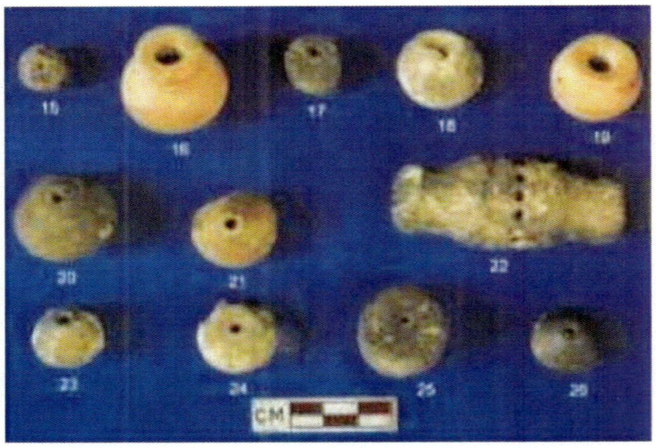

Pl. XLVII: Terracotta beads, Period-IV and V

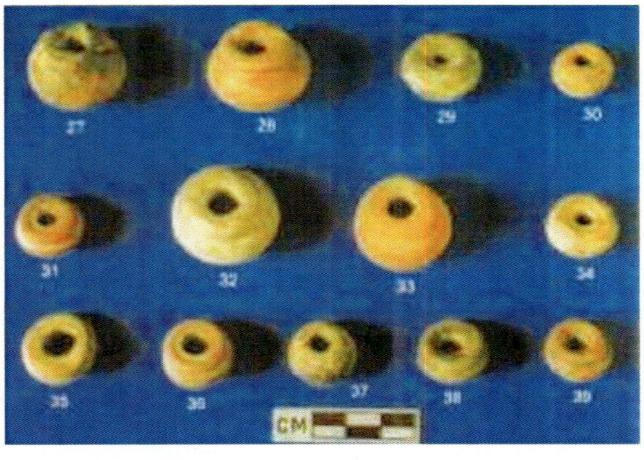

Pl. XLVIII: Terracotta beads, Period-IV

Pl. XLIX: Copper cast coins, Period-IV (Obverse)

Pl. L: Copper cast coins, Period-IV (Reverse)

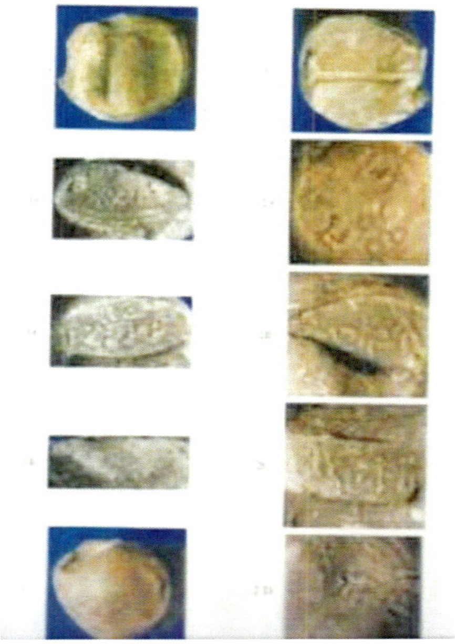

Pl. LI: Sealings of terracotta, Period-IV

Pl. LII: Sealings of terracotta, Period-IV

Pl. LIII: Sealings of terracotta, Period-IV

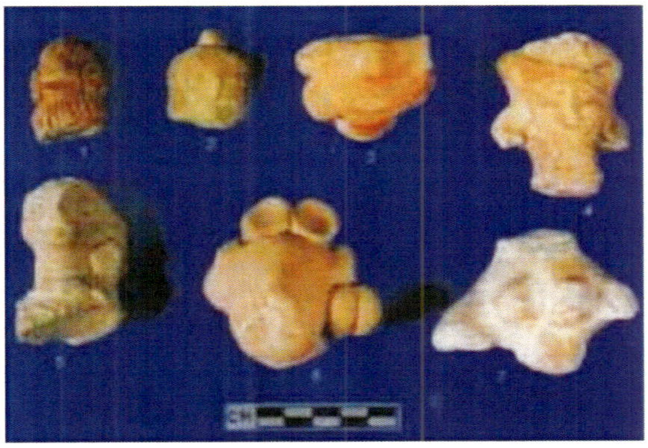

Pl. LIV: Terracotta human figurines, Period-IV

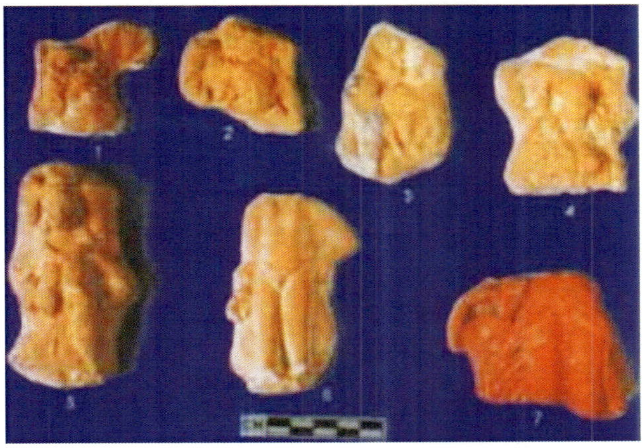

Pl. LV: Terracotta human figurines, Period-IV

Pl. LVI: Terracotta sealings, Period-V

Pl. LVII: Head of Shiva, Period-V

Pl. LVIII: Pendants of stone and terracotta, Period-III, IV and V

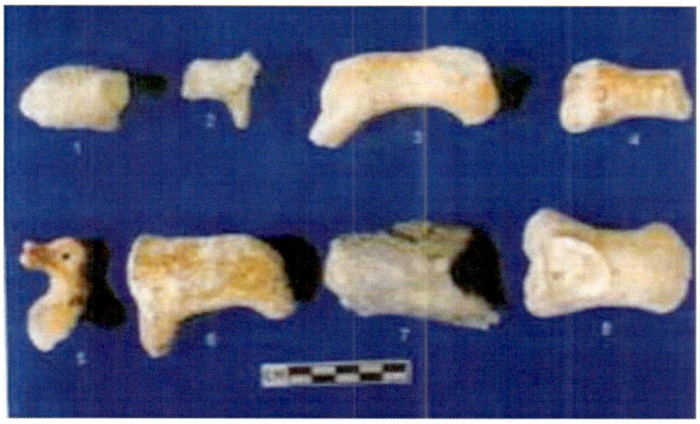

Pl. LIX: Terracotta animal figurines, Period-III C

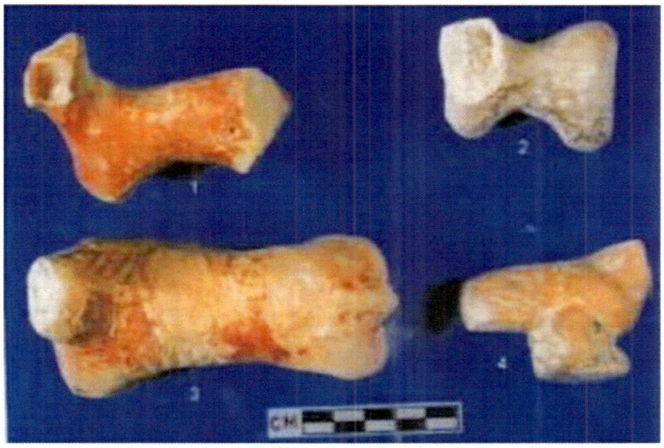

Pl. LX: Terracotta animal figurines, Period-IV

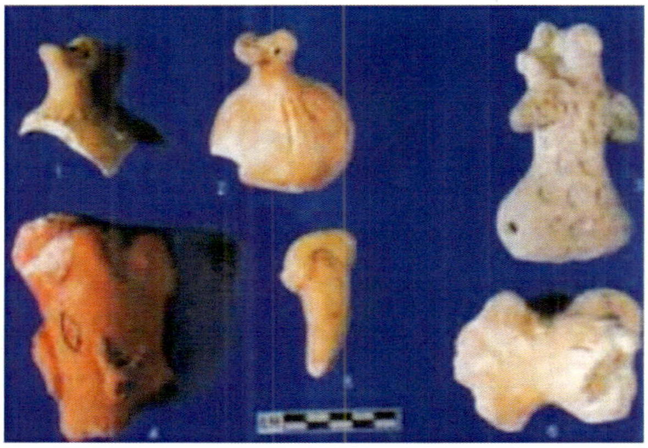

Pl. LXI: Terracotta animal figurines, Period-IV

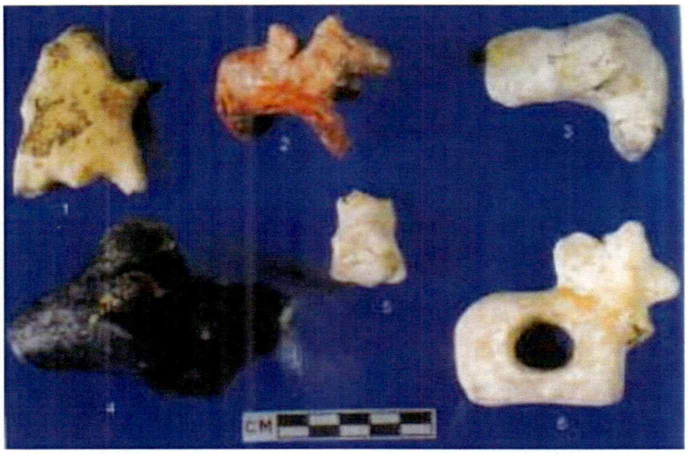

Pl. LXII: Terracotta animal figurines, Period-V

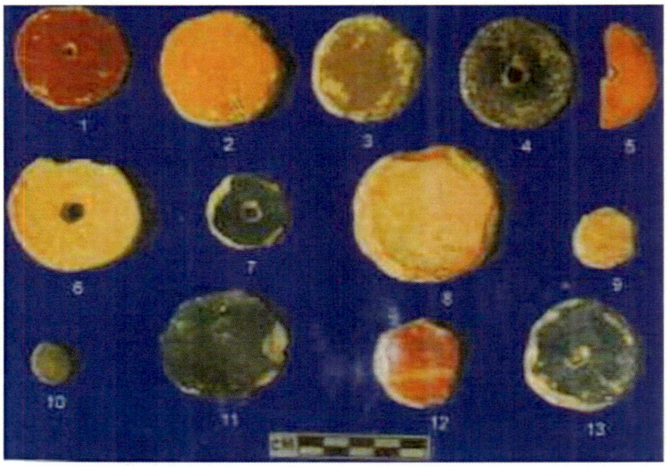

Pl. LXIII: Terracotta and pottery discs, Period-III

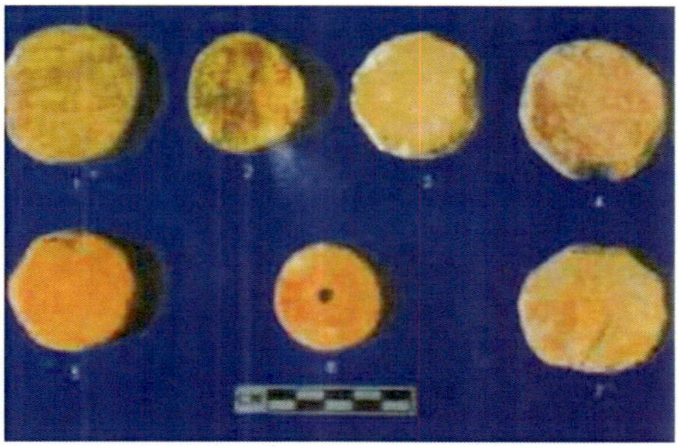

Pl. LXIV: Terracotta and pottery discs, Period-III, IV and V

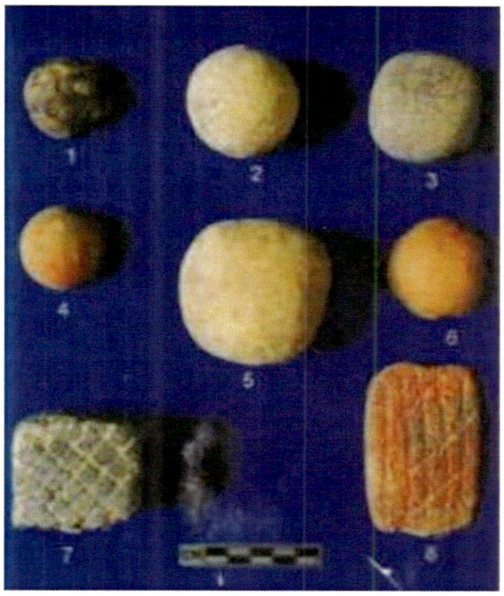

Pl. LXV: Stone balls and terracotta skin rubbers, Period-III, IV and V

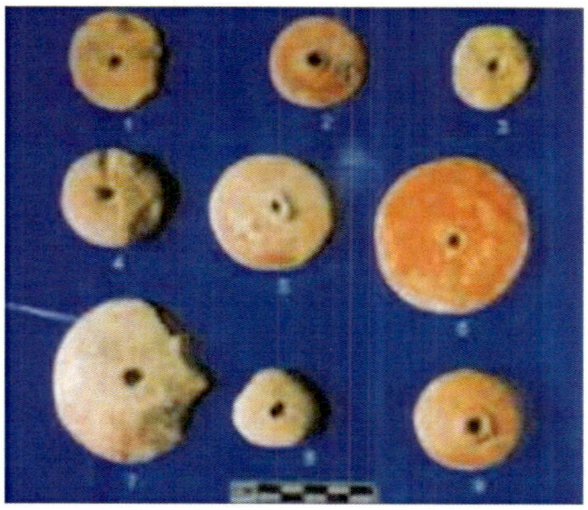

Pl. LXVI: Terracotta wheels, Period-III, IV and V

Pl. LXVII: Terracotta Pestles and Dabbers, Period-III, IV and V

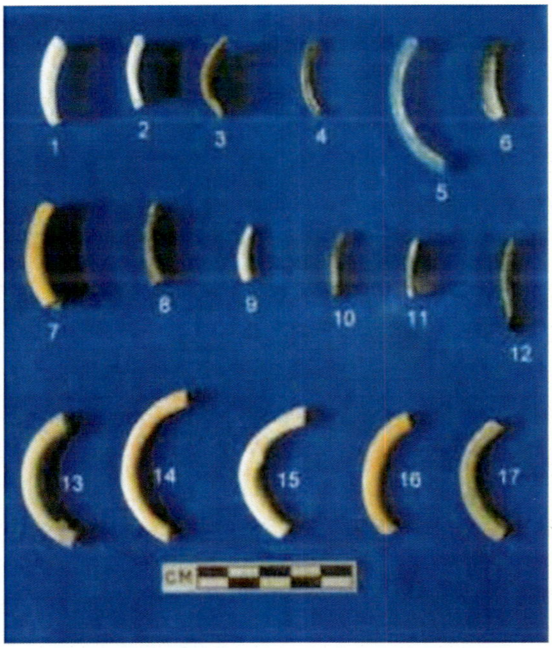

Pl. LXVIII: Stone and terracotta bangles, Period-III, IV and V

Pl. LXIX: Feeding cups and other antiquities, Period-III, IV and V

Pl. LXX: Seeds and other wild taxa, Period-I & II

1. **Triticum aestivum**
2. **Trigonella occulta**
3. **Chenopodium album**
4. **Cypeus sp**
5. **Vigna radiate**
6. **Vigna radiate**
7. **Hordium vulgare**

Pl. LXXI: Seeds and other wild taxa, Period-II

8. **Lens culinaris**
9. **Oriza sativa**
10. **Triticum sphaarococcum**
11. **Dolichus biflorus**
12. **Pisum sp**
13. **Brassica sp**
14. **Nigelia sp**
15. **Trianthema sp**

Pl. LXXII: Bones of Bos indicus, Period-I

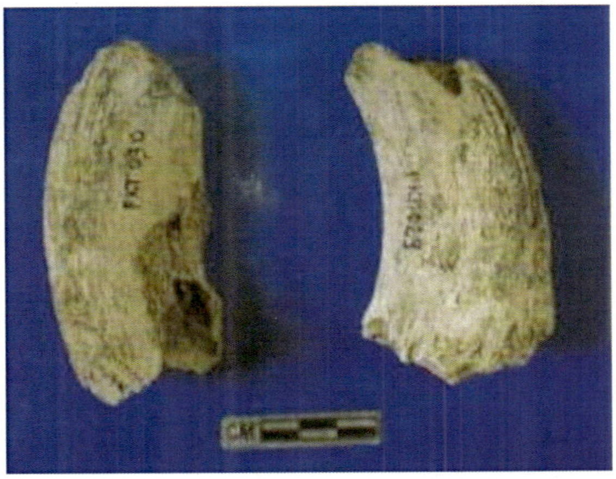

Pl. LXXIII: Horn cores of Bubalus bubalis, Period-I

Pl. LXXIV: Mandible of Sus scrofa, Period-I

Pl. LXXV: Carapace of Kachuga tecta, Period-I

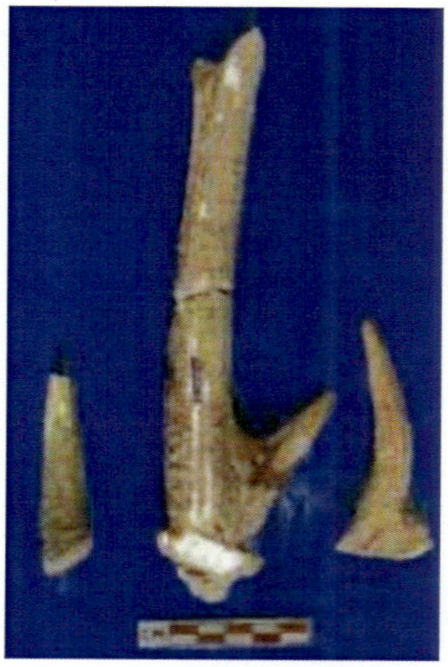

Pl. LXXVI: Antlers of Sambar, Period-II

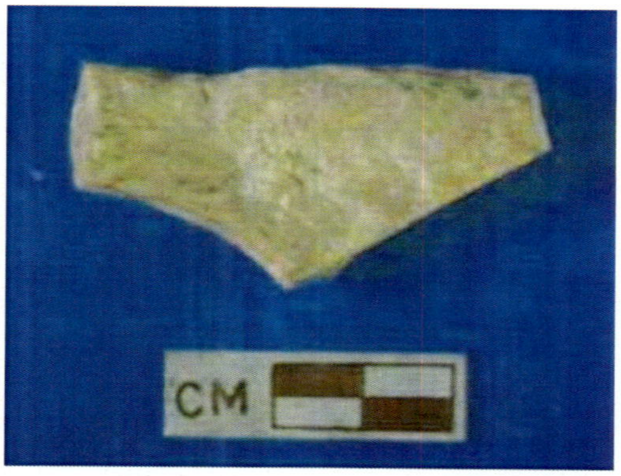

Pl. LXXVII: Antler of Axis axis, Period-III B

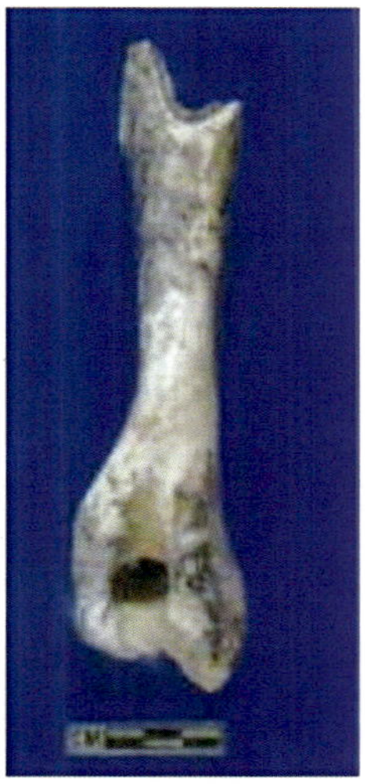

Pl. LXXVIII: Humerus of Sus scrofa, Period-III B

Pl. LXXIX: Rib of Bos/ Bubalus showing butchering mark, Period-III B

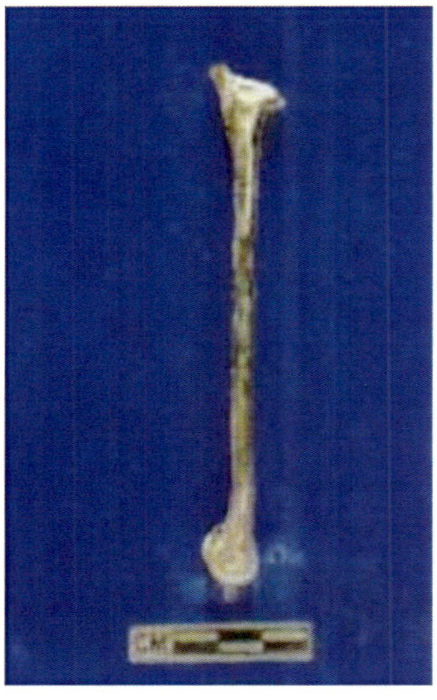

Pl. LXXX: Femur of Saras Crane, Period-III B

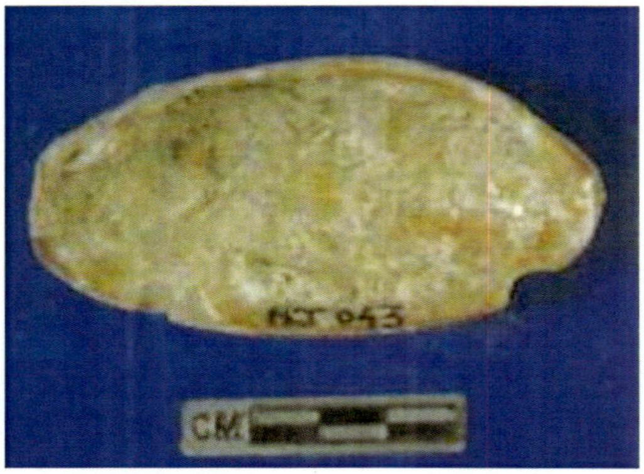

Pl. LXXXI: Lamellidens sp Shell, Period-III C

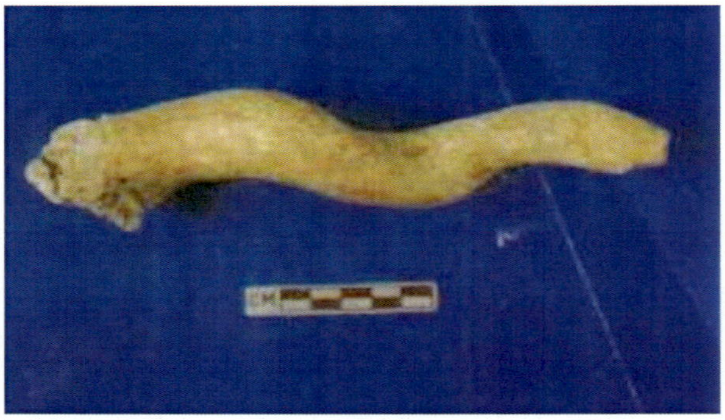

Pl. LXXXII: Horn core of Capra hircus, Period-III C

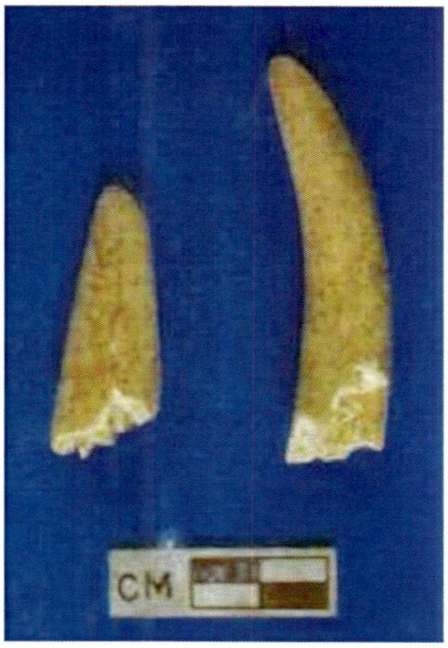

Pl. LXXXIII: Horn cores of Antilope cervicapara, Period-IV

Pl. LXXXIV: Chaturmukhi Linga, Atma

Pl. LXXXV: Nandi, Atma

Pl. LXXXVI: Buddha, Aungari

Pl. LXXXVII: Ashtabhuji Durga, Aungari

Pl. LXXXVIII: Surya, Aungari

Pl. LXXXIX:Buddha in Bhumisparsha mudra, Badagaon

Pl. XC: Marichi, Badagaon

Pl. XCI: Crowned Buddha, Badagaon

Pl. XCII: Mahabhinishkramana plate, Badagaon

Pl. XCIII: Mound of Barah

Pl. XCIV: Four-armed Vishnu, Barah

Pl. XCV: Buddha in Bhumisparsha mudra, Beswak

Pl. XCVI:Uma-Maheshvara, Beswak

Pl. XCVII: Vishnu, Beswak

Pl. XCVIII: Standing Buddha, Chandaura

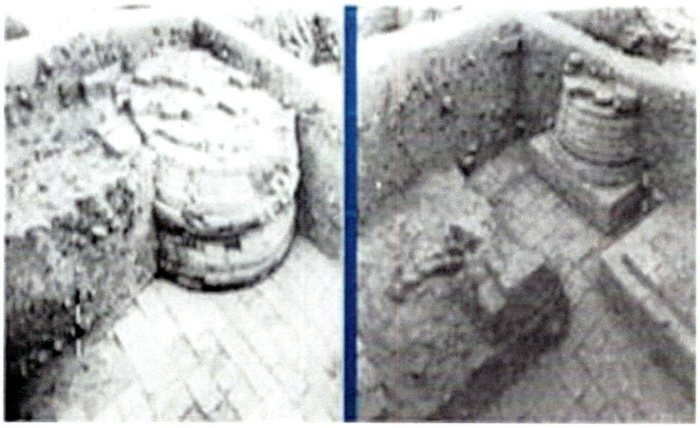

Pl. XCIX: Votive stupas, Chandi Mau

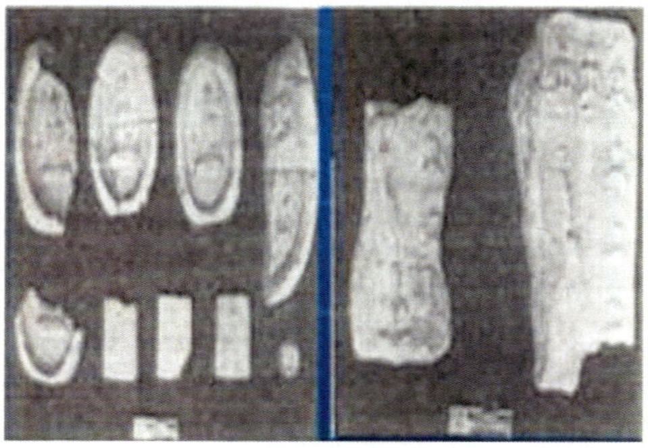

Pl. C: Terracotta objects, Chandi Mau

Pl. CI: Stone sculptures, Chandi Mau

Pl. CII: Saraswati, Chandi Mau

Pl. CIII: Ganesha, Chandi Mau

Pl. CIV: Buddha, Chandi Mau

Pl. CV: Parvati, Dayalpur

Pl. CVI: Potteries of Red Ware, Dhurgaon

Pl. CVII: Four-armed Vishnu, Dhurgaon

Pl. CVIII: Vishnu, Dhurgaon

Pl. CIX: Buddha, Dhurgaon

Pl. CX: Marichi, Eksara

Pl. CXI: Mound of Ghorakatora

Pl. CXII: Indrashila Cave opposite Ghorakatora

Pl. CXIII: Kushan bricks & Ring-well, Ghorakatora

Pl. CXIV: Pottery, Ghorakatora

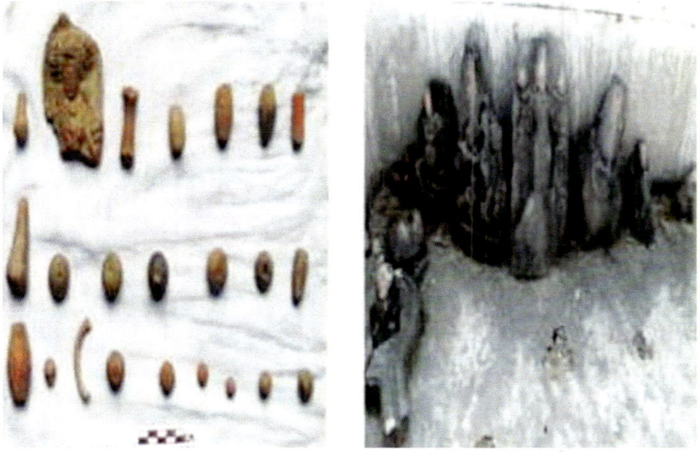

Pl. CXV: Antiquities & Sculptures, Ghorakatora

Pl. CXVI: Bodhisattva with Dhyani Buddhas, Ghosrawan

Pl. CXVII:Buddha in Bhumisparsha mudra, Ghosrawan

Pl. CXVIII: Marichi, Ghosrawan

Pl. CXIX: Buddha in Dharmachakrapravartan mudra, Ghosrawan

Pl. CXX:Ekmukhi Linga, Ghosrawan

Pl. CXXI:Ganesha, Ghosrawan

Pl. CXXII:Ganesha, Ghosrawan

Pl. CXXIII: Vishnu, Ghosrawan

Pl. CXXIV: Durga, Ghosrawan

Pl. CXXV: Durga, Ghosrawan

Pl. CXXVI: Revanta, Ghosrawan

Pl. CXXVII: Excavated mud stupa, Juafartdih

Pl. CXXVIII: Pot-sherds of BW, BSW & NBPW, Juafardih

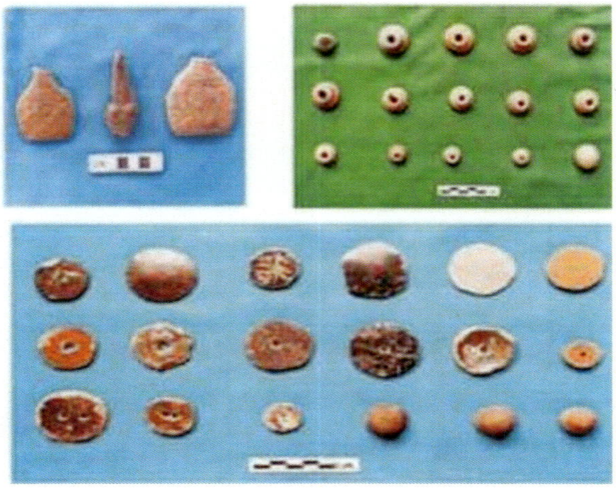

Pl. CXXIX: Terracotta Objects, Juafardih

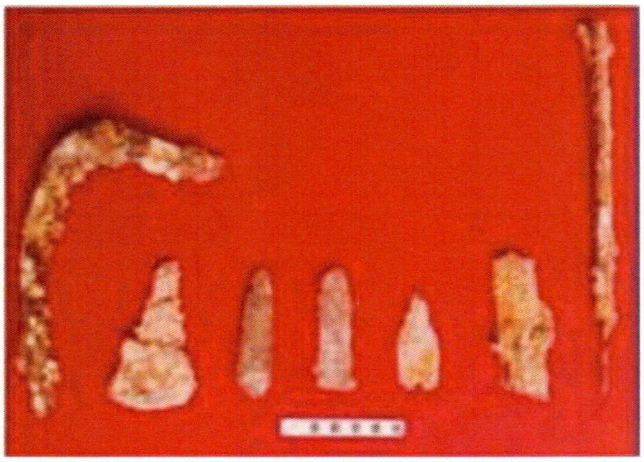

Pl. CXXX: Iron Objects, Juafardih

Pl. CXXXI: Silver & Copper coins and Iron objects, Juafardih

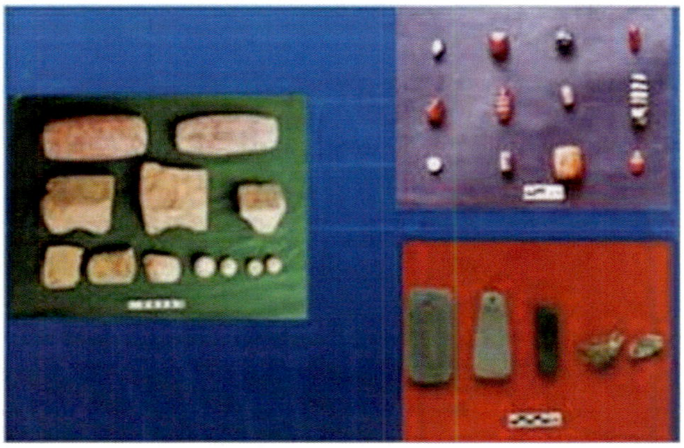

Pl. CXXXII: Stone objects, Juafardih

Pl. CXXXIII: Vishnu, Khaira

Pl. CXXXIV: Uma-Maheshwar, Kolawan

Pl. CXXXV: Buddha in Bhumisparsha mudra, Kondi

Pl. CXXXVI: Buddha in Bhumisparsha mudra, Kul

Pl. CXXXVII: Buddha in Bhumisparsha mudra, Kul

Pl. CXXXVIII: Uma-Maheshwara, Kul

Pl. CXXXIX: General view of the Kundawapar mound

Pl. CXL: Pot-sherds of Black & Black Slipped Ware, Kundawapar

Pl. CXLI: Buddha, Makhdumpur

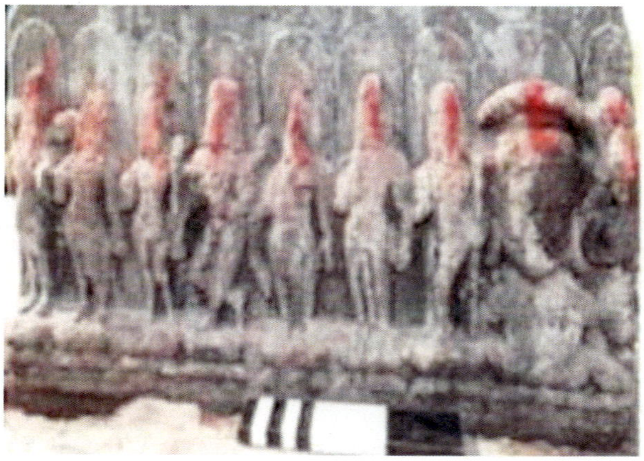

Pl. CXLII: Navagraha, Maniyawan

Pl. CXLIII: Surya riding on 7 horses, Maniyawan

Pl. CXLIV: Parvati, Maniyawan

Pl. CXLV: Stone plaque showing images of Buddhas, Nona

Pl. CXLVI: Inscribed Buddha head, Nona

Pl. CXLVII: Surya image, Nona

Pl. CXLVIII: Saraswati, Nona

Pl. CXLIX: General view of Rukhaegarh mound

Pl. CL: Pot-sherds of Red Ware, Rukhaegarh

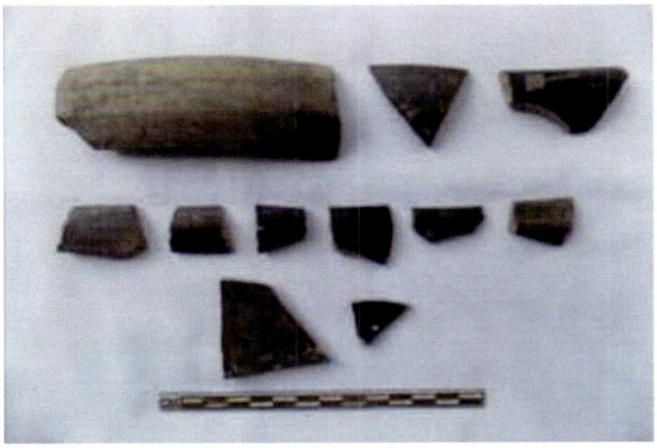

Pl. CLI: Pot-sherds of Black & Black Slipped Ware, Rukhaegarh

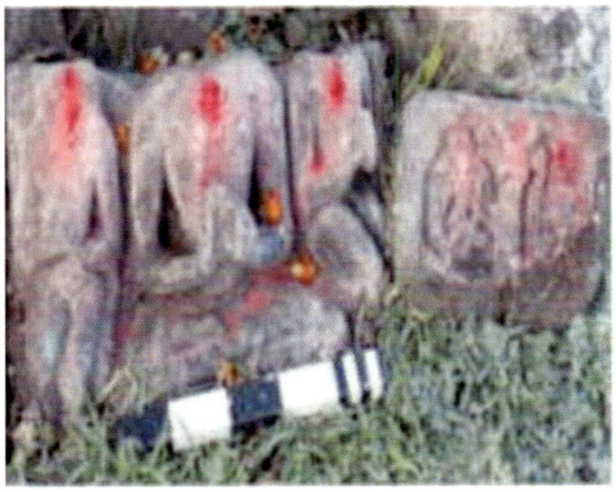

Pl. CLII: Fragments of Buddhist sculptures, Rukhaegarh

Pl. CLIII: Buddha in Bhumisparsha mudra, Rukministhan

Pl. CLIV: Image of Buddha, Sakraudha

Pl. CLV: Inscribed broken image of Mahakashyap, Silao

Pl. CLVI: Buddha in Bhumisparsha mudra, Sonchari

Pl. CLVII: Buddha, Tazu Bigha

Pl. CLVIII: Standing Buddha, Tetrawan, Pala period

Pl. CLIX: Buddha in Bhumisparsha mudra, Tetrawan, Pala period

Pl. CLX: Surya, Tulsigarh

Pl. CLXI: Broken image of Mahishasuramardini, Tulsigarh

Pl. CLXII: Uma-Maheshwara, Tulsigarh

Pl. CLXIII: Vishnu, Tulsigarh

Pl. CLXIV: Broken Buddha image, Tulsigarh

Pl. CLXV: Buddha in Bhumisparsha mudra, Tungi

Pl. CLXVI: Bronze Buddha, Akota, 6th century CE

Pl. CLXVII: Avalokiteshvara, Kurkihara, 11th century

Pl. CLXVIII: Buddha, Kurkihara, 11th century

Pl. CLXIX: Buddha, Kurkihara, 11th century

Pl. CLXX: Buddha, Sirpur

Pl. CLXXI: Buddha in Bhumisparsha mudra, Telhara

Pl. CLXXII: Vajrasattva, 9-10th century, Bangladesh

Pl. CLXXIII: Buddha, China, 6th century

Pl. CLXXIV: Buddha, China, 8th century

Pl. CLXXV: Prjñāpārmitā , Indonesia

Pl. CLXXVI: Buddha, Indonesia, 9th century

Pl. CLXXVII: Buddha, Borobudur, Indonesia

Pl. CLXXVIII: Siddhartha cutting his hairs, Myanmar

Pl. CLXXIX: Buddha, Pagan, Myanmar

Pl. CLXXX: Buddha in Bhumisparsha mudra, Nepal

Pl. CLXXXI: Buddha in Dhyana mudra, Nepal

Pl. CLXXXII: Buddha, Anuradhapur, Sri Lanka

Pl. CLXXXIII: Buddha, Mihintale, Sri Lanka

Pl. CLXXXIV: Samye monastery, Tibet

Pl. CLXXXV: Cultural relics in Samye monastery, Tibet

Pl. CLXXXVI: Unexcavated mound of Telhara

Pl. CLXXXVII: Excavated Telhara mound revealing Tiladhak Monastery

Pl. CLXXXVIII: Remains of Medieval period, Bari Pahari

Pl. CLXXXIX:Mound-I, Garh Par

Pl. CXC:Mound-II, Garh Par

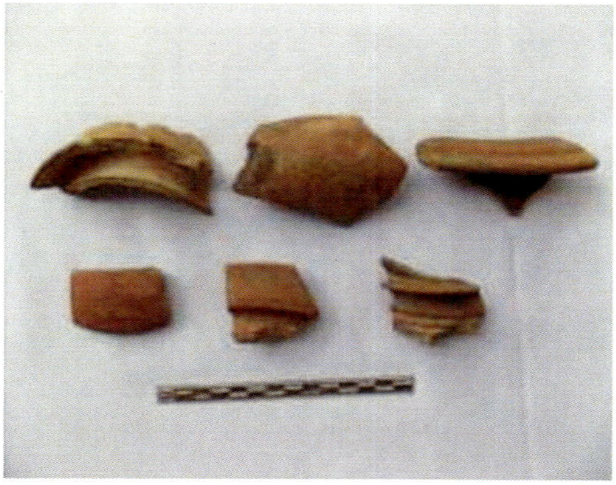

Pl. CXCI:Pot sherds of Red Ware, Garh Par

Pl. CXCII: Kushanan brick wall seen in the section of the mound

Pl. CXCIII:Stone-wall in the section,Nalanda college

Pl. CXCIV: Pot sherds of Red Ware, Nalanda College

Pl. CXCV: Pot sherds of Black Ware, Nalanda College

Pl. CXCVI: Lotus pettled pedestal, Nalanda College

Pl. CXCVII: Avalokiteshwara with Dhyani Buddhas, Nalanda College

Pl. CXCVIII: Buddha, Tibet

Pl. CXCIX: Buddha, Tibet

Pl. CC: General view of Afsad mound

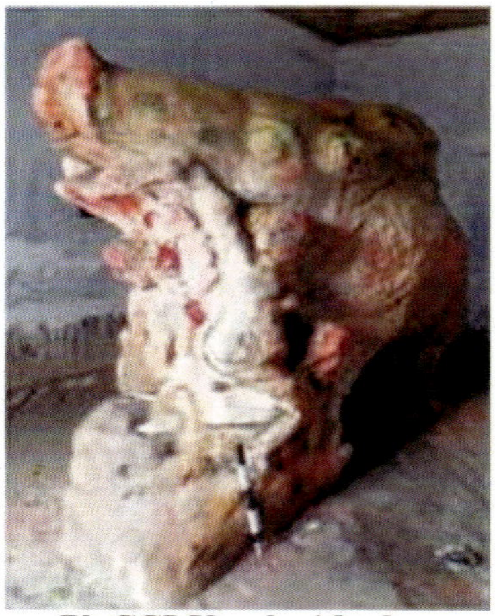

Pl. CCI:Varah, Afsad

Pl. CCII: Ekmukhi Linga, Afsad

Pl. CCIII: Ashtabhuji Durga, Afsad

Pl. CCIV: Mahishamardini Durga, Afsad

Pl. CXV: Stupa-worsahip, Aiyer

Pl. CCVI:Buddha, Parvati

Pl. CCVII:Indrashila Cave, Parvati

Pl. CCVIII: Vishnu, Samas

Pl. CCIX: Mound of Chandelagarh

Pl. CCX: Terrace- shaped stupa, Dam area, Jethian

Pl. CCXI: Buddha in Pralambapada Asana, Jethian

Pl. CCXII: Headless Vishnu, Sarsoo

Pl. CCXIII: Ganesha, Sarsoo

Pl. CCXIV: Crowned Buddha in Bhumisparsha mudra, Sarsoo

Pl. CCXV: General view of Rukhaegarh mound

Pl. CCXVI: Ring-well just west to Trench A1

Pl. CCXVII: Well of Sunga period south of Trench A I

Pl. CCXVIII: Well of Sunga period west to Trench E 5

Pl. CCXIX: Sunga-Kushan brick wall showing plan of five rooms

Pl. CCXX: NBPW and associated ware

Pl. CCXXI: Pot-sherds of Sungan period

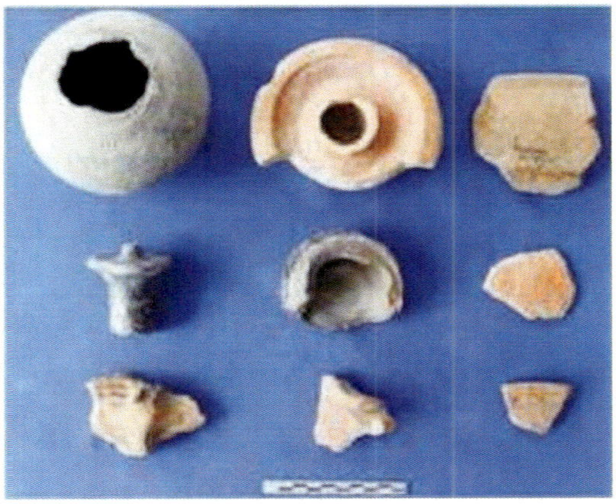

Pl. CCXXII: Pot-sherds of Kushanan period

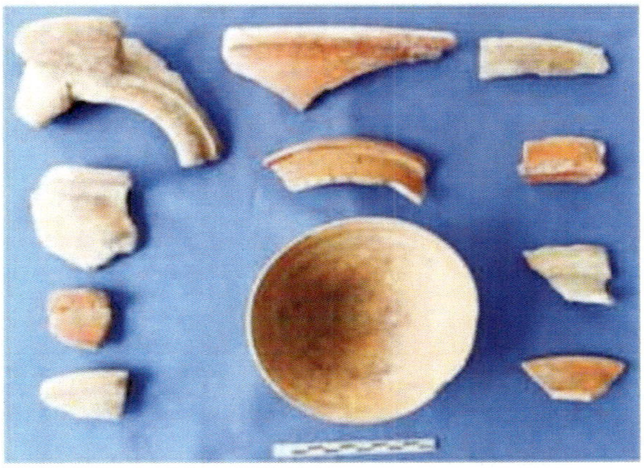

Pl. CCXXIII: Pot-sherds of Gupta period

Pl. CCXXIV: Broken Animal figurines

Pl. CCXXV: Terracotta objects

Pl. CCXXVI: Copper objects

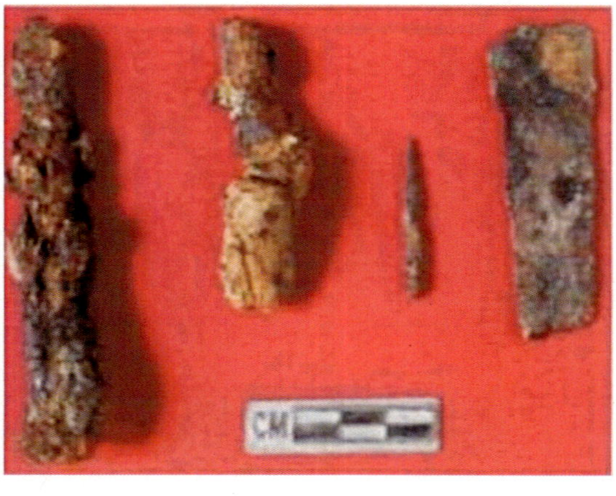

Pl. CCXXVII: Iron objects

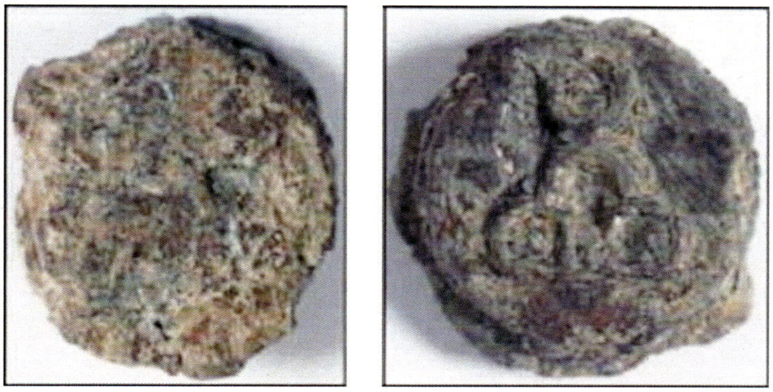

Pl. CCXXVIII: Copper Cast-coin (Obverse & Reverse)

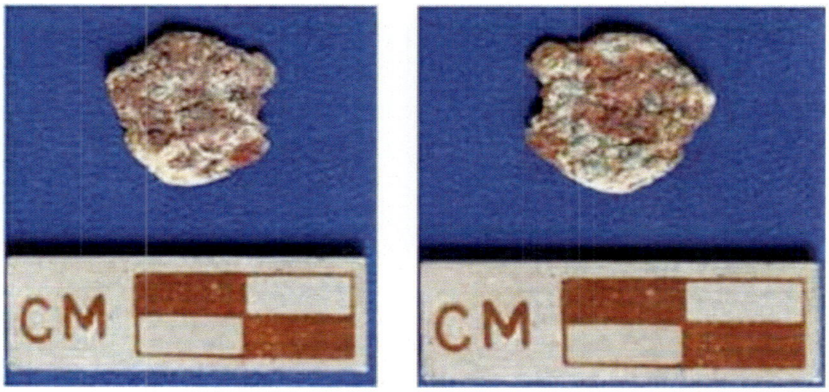

Pl. CCXXIX: Copper Cast-coin (Obverse & Reverse)

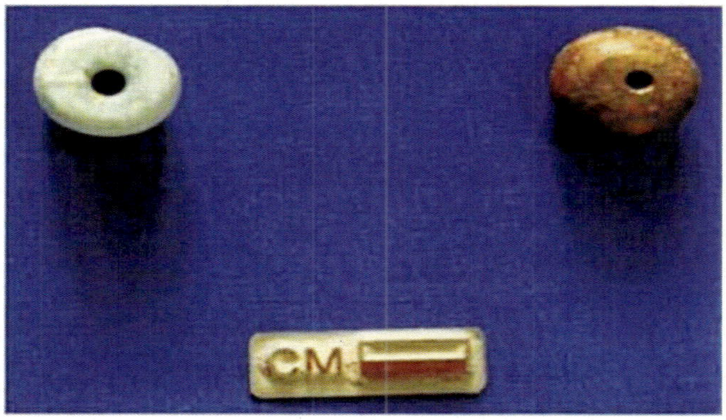

Pl. CCXXX: Stone and bone bead

Pl. CCXXXI: Pot-sherds of Red Ware-Bhadaini Kalan

Pl. CCXXXII: Mound of Barah

Pl. CCXXXIII: Pot-sherds of BSW, NBPW-Barah

Pl. CCXXXIV: Mound of Birbhanpur

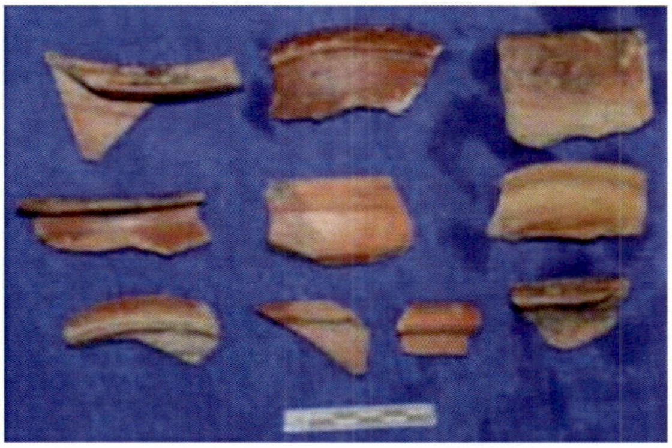

Pl. CCXXXV: Pot-sherds of RW, RSW- Birbhanpur

Pl. CCXXXVI: Mound of Delhana

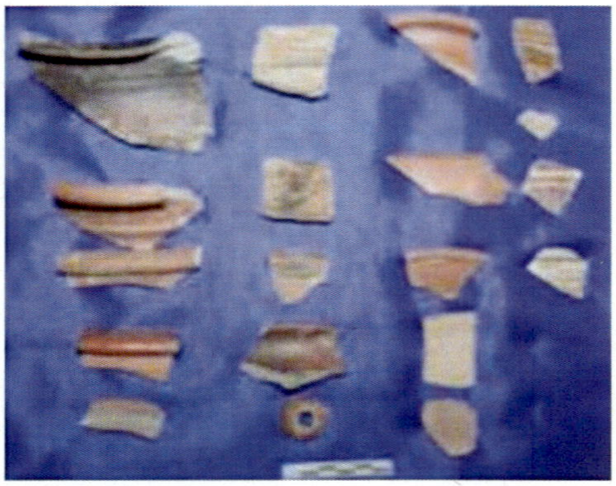

Pl. CCXXXVII: Pot-sherds of Red Ware-Delhana

Pl. CCXXXVIII: Pot-sherds of Red Ware -Harsos

Pl. CCXXXIX: Mound of Kashipur

Pl. CCXL: Pot-sherds of Red Ware & Broken Animal Figurine-Kashipur

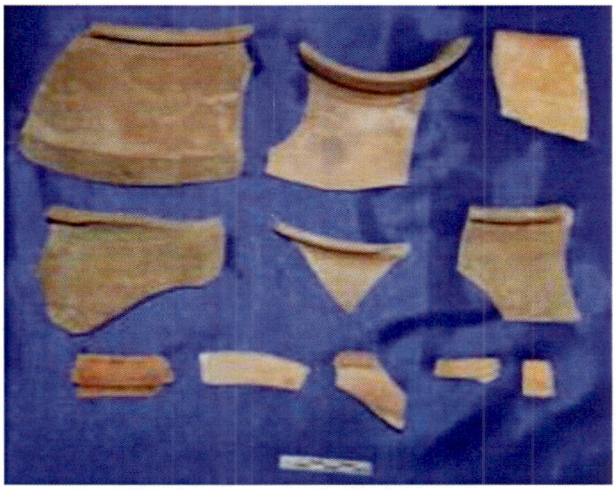

Pl. CCXLI: Pot-sherds of Red Ware -Khusiyari

Pl. CCXLII: Pot-sherds of Red Ware –Khusiyari

Pl. CCXLIII: Pot-sherds of BW, BSW- Khusiyari

Pl. CCXLIV: Hopscotch, Iron slags- Khusiyari

Pl. CCXLV: Mound of Koilo

Pl. CCXLVI: Terracotta Hopscotch-Koilo

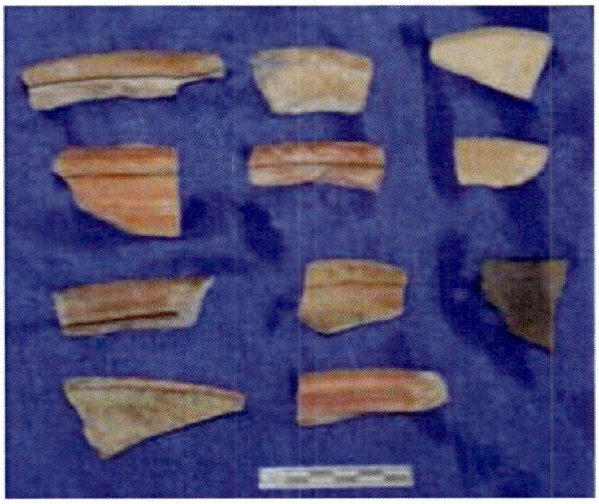

Pl. CCXLVII: Pot-sherds of RW-Koilo

Pl. CCXLVIII: Pot-sherds of BW, BSW, NBPW-Koilo

Pl. CCXLIX: Mound of Mahavan

Pl. CCL: Pot-sherds of Red Ware -Mahavan

Pl. CCLI: Mound of Anjania Baba (Derhgaon)

Pl. CCLII: Mound of Bhagawati Mai Kot (Saiyadraja)

Pl. CCLIII: Mound of Bhagawati Mai Kot (Dharahra)

Pl. CCLIV: Mound of Bhunadih (Onawal)

Pl. CCLV: Mound of Devarapur

Pl. CCLVI: Fragments of sculptures, Devarapur

Pl. CCLVII: Mound of Karjara Kot

Pl. CCLVIII: Mound of Keshavpur

Pl. CCLIX: Mound of Khandwari Kot

Pl. CCLX: Mound of Maheshi

Pl. CCLXI: Fragment of sculpture, Maheshi

Pl. CCLXII: Mound of Mannipatti

Pl. CCLXIII: Mound of Misrapuram

Pl. CCLXIV: Mound of Mundher

Pl. CCLXV: Fragments of Brahmanic deities, Mundher

Pl. CCLXVI: Female figure, Mundher

Pl. CCLXVII: Potsherds of Red Ware, Mundher

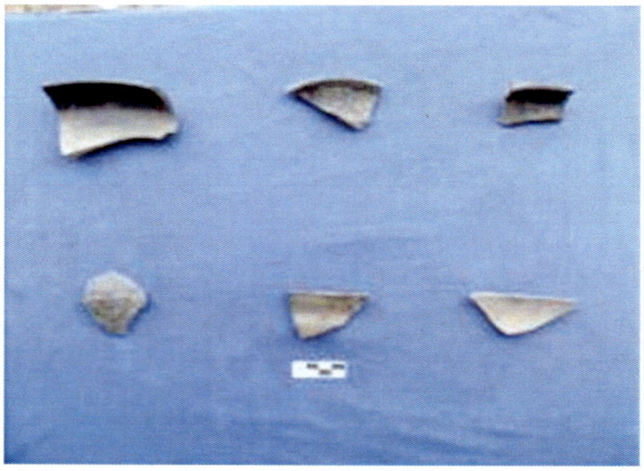

Pl. CCLXVIII: Potsherds of Black Ware, Mundher

Pl. CCLXIX: Potsherds of NBP and associated wares, Mundher

Pl. CCLXX: Terracotta and unidentified copper objects, Mundher

Pl. CCLXXI: Mound of Sakas

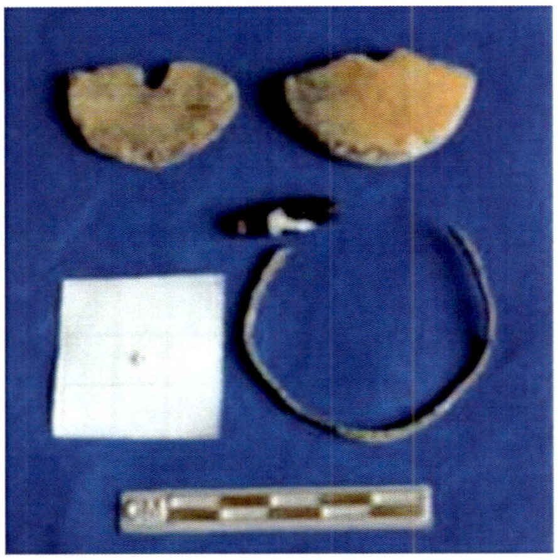

Pl.CCLXXII: TC Wheels Beads of Agate & Steatite, copper bangle

Pl.CCLXXIII: Stone flakes, scraper and blade

Pl.CCLXXIV: Stone flakes

Pl.CCLXXV: Stone flake

Pl.CCLXXVI: Raw material & scraper

Pl.CCLXXVII: Corded BRW & Red Ware

Pl.CCLXXVIII: Vase of Red Ware & BRW

Pl.CCLXXIX: Bowl of BRW, Black Ware & Red Ware

Pl.CCLXXX : Bowl & Basin of Red Slipped Ware

Pl.CCLXXXI:Nosed, grouped & thumb appliqué design on Red Ware & BRW

Pl.CCLXXXII: Bevelled dish, painted bowl (red on white) of Burnished Red Slipped, Red Slipped & NBPW

Pl. CCLXXXIII:Bowl, Vase & Lipped basin of BRW, Burnished Red Slipped, Red Ware, Black Ware and Burnished BRW

Pl. CCLXXXIV: Bowl, basin, lipped basin, vase & beaker of Burnished Red Ware, BRW & Burnished BRW